NONVERBAL COMMUNICATION SYSTEMS

NONVERBAL COMMUNICATION SYSTEMS

DALE G. LEATHERS

The University of Georgia

allyn and bacon, inc. boston london sydney toronto

LIBRARY OF CONGRESS CATALOGING IN PUBLICATION DATA

Leathers, Dale G   1938-
   Nonverbal communication systems.

   Bibliography: p.
   Includes index.
   1. Nonverbal communication. I. Title.
BF637.C45L4   153   75-40251

ISBN 0-205-04894-3

TO HUNDLEY

CONTENTS

PREFACE

Since human beings began interacting, nonverbal communication has had great functional significance. Intuitively, man has grasped this fact for centuries. Empirically, he has not examined the functions of nonverbal communication until the past few decades.

The sudden, dramatic increase in empirical studies of nonverbal communication is hardly a historical accident. An extremely strong and sustained need to know about the true nature of nonverbal communication is now evident at almost all levels of society. Popular treatments of the subject become best-sellers, politicians hire consultants to mould their images by modifying their gestures, postures, and facial expressions, and management consultants in large corporations place increased emphasis on demonstrating to executives how they can communicate the nuances of meaning nonverbally.

The university student and instructor are perhaps most conscious of the great growth of interest in studying nonverbal communication. Courses in nonverbal communication are being added to the curriculum at an accelerating rate. Enrollment in these courses frequently doubles, triples, and quadruples. Courses in interpersonal communication, communication theory, group communication, and related subjects are now emphasizing nonverbal communication. Courses in business, psychology, sociology, anthropology, planning, interior design, and related disciplines are giving more attention to the subject.

Instructors teaching such courses, or those who contemplate developing such a course, report a major frustration, however. They frequently have difficulty finding a comprehensive treatment of nonverbal communication in one book that meets their instructional criteria. The most frequently cited criteria are the following: (1) the book must be designed so that a course can be readily developed to parallel the treatment of subject matter in the book; (2) the book must be designed to promote the students' active involvement in testing and developing their own capacity to communicate nonverbally; (3) the book must clearly delineate and analyze the functional capacity of the different systems that make up nonverbal communication; (4) the book must provide an integrated treatment of the functional relationships between and among the nonverbal communication systems, and of the interaction of these systems with the verbal communication system; and (5) the book should be extensively and creatively illustrated to facilitate the intensive examination of nonverbal communication behaviors.

Nonverbal Communication Systems is designed to meet these specific criteria. The Contents should readily suggest a direct and defensible format for organizing a course in nonverbal communication. Perhaps more importantly, this book provides students with practical and accurate tests of their encoding and decoding capacity, whether they are using facial communication, vocalic communication, tactile communication, or any other of the nonverbal systems presented in this book. Extensive use in the classroom and in consulting suggests that original instruments such as the Facial Meaning Sensitivity Test have many practical advantages. Not only do they promote intense involvement and provide a stimulating learning experience for the user, but also they can be used to increase significantly a communicator's capacity to use a given nonverbal communication system.

Knowing about a given type of nonverbal communication is probably not enough. Most students want to know which nonverbal communication system has the greatest functional potential to exchange specific types of meanings accurately and efficiently. *Nonverbal Communication Systems* is designed to provide an answer to that important question. The chapters on the invisible communication system(s)—tactile, olfactory, and telepathic communication systems—delineate a set of important communication functions that have probably never been treated in the same depth or in the same way in a single volume.

To describe the functions of nonverbal communication systems is one thing. To *rate* their potential to achieve specific communicative objectives is quite another. Such ratings are provided in this book for the first time. Students and colleagues who have read the manuscript feel that this is one of the uniquely useful features of this book. The functional capacity of the nonverbal communication systems should not be treated in isolation, however. The nonverbal communication systems typically interact with the verbal. The nature of this interaction is examined in detail in chapter 10, and the implications of different types of interaction for the communicator are explored.

Finally, it is difficult to capture the true nature of nonverbal media in a verbal medium. For this reason *Nonverbal Communication Systems* is extensively illustrated with photographs and other graphics. Many of the photographs were taken by the author's own photographer to meet the distinctive requirements imposed by the conceptual framework of this book.

From an instructional perspective, *Nonverbal Communication Systems* can be used to satisfy a considerable range of needs. It certainly is intended as the required book for courses in nonverbal communication (some of the more advanced material has been put in two appendixes so that the book may be used at different levels). It is highly suitable as one of the required books in courses in interpersonal communication, small group communication, and communication theory. Moreover, it should prove useful in courses in public communication and public speaking that attempt to give justifiable emphasis to the kinesic, spatial, vocal, and other dimensions of nonverbal communication. Finally, the broad scope of the book should make it very useful as one of the required texts for courses in psychology, sociology, anthropology, business, education, home economics, and related subjects.

Many individuals played an important role in the research and development of *Nonverbal Communication Systems*. I am indebted to Mike Siegel, Pete Sarver, Maureen O'Connell, and Hope Pedrero, who served as research assistants during various stages of the preparation. Gregg Howard deserves special mention for his work as photographic subject in illustrating chapter 9. Warren Busse, photographer, deserves full credit for the set of photographs that make up the Loren Lewis series in chapter 2, the photographs of space utilization in the urban environment in chapter 4, the photographs illustrating the LNFRI in chapter 9, and the stop-action photographs taken from videotape in chapter 10. Finally, Editor Frank Ruggirello of Allyn and Bacon provided timely and shrewd advice.

On a very personal level, my wife Nancy provided expertise as the author of chapter 4, as well as inspiration and love. Cat_2 rendered invaluable service in inspecting the manuscript daily and serving as paperweight on windy days. Finally, I would like to thank my students who reacted and interacted critically and constructively.

NONVERBAL
COMMUNICATION
SYSTEMS

1

THE STUDY
OF NONVERBAL
COMMUNICATION

Human interaction is a quest for meaning. We look anxiously to others to determine whether we have communicated our intended meaning. They look apprehensively at us to judge whether they have accurately perceived our intentions. Interpersonal communication often produces or results in anxiety, apprehension, and uncertainty because it is so complex.

The ways we may exchange meanings are varied. Similarly, the possible sources of error in interpersonal communication are multiple. A single error may make us uncomfortable in an important situation. Multiple errors may be catastrophic.

Consider the following situations. You and your partner are at a fraternity party on your first date. As the evening progresses and the second keg of beer is tapped, you notice that your date's hand is resting lightly on your arm; a strong and rather rapid pulse is detectable. You make your judgments as to what your date is communicating to you. Later you fidget on the doorsteps of the sorority house. Suddenly you lean forward to kiss your date but she turns her face away from you, recoils, and walks briskly into the sorority house. You are left alone to ponder the complexities of the evening's communication situation.

Four years later you are about to be interviewed by the head of a major advertising firm. The job interview is vitally important to you. You realize that you must communicate very effectively if you are to get the job offer. As you enter the interview room, you introduce yourself to the advertising executive and she offers you a seat on the other side of a small table. You feel that it is important to sustain eye contact and attempt to do so. The executive often looks away from you as she speaks, however. She frequently leans far back in her chair. You think you are doing well. As the interview concludes, you cannot help but notice that the advertising executive has her chin tilted up into the air and is looking down at you over her glasses. While looking at you she remarks that she has found your dossier to be most unusual. You are then left alone to ponder the complexities of the afternoon's communication situation.

These two situations may be interpreted in a number of different ways. Your goal is to determine what meanings you communicated and what meanings were communicated to you. To achieve such a goal you must recognize at least two facts at minimum. First, great differences often exist between the meaning you think you communicated and the meaning that was actually perceived. Second, meanings may be exchanged through a great variety of channels.

You may have interpreted your date's hand on your arm as an invitation to more intimate behavior later in the evening; the quickened pulse may have suggested a certain amount of arousal on her part. Her perception of the situation may have been quite different. The hand on your arm could have been a sympathetic response to your nervous mannerisms. The quickened pulse may have been triggered by her apprehension as to what actions you would take on the sorority steps. You need more information and time before attempting a thorough analysis of this situation.

The job situation is also difficult to interpret. You have more facts at your disposal, however. You wisely focused on important factors in this situation. You should not be disturbed by the fact that the interviewer looked away from you as she spoke; this is characteristic eye behavior in an interview situation. You should be concerned about her tendency to lean far back in the chair. Bodily lean is the best indicator of an individual's involvement in this situation. Your biggest problem is the ambiguous message your interviewer conveyed to you (her chin was perceptibly tilted in the air as she said, "I find your dossier to be most unusual"). The verbal and nonverbal cues convey conflicting meanings. Unhappily for you, the nonverbal cue—the upraised chin in this case—is apt to be a much more accurate indicator of your interviewer's true feelings than the verbal cue.

Both situations emphasize what society has been slow to recognize: man does not communicate by words alone. Man has many sensory mechanisms that play a vital role in interpersonal communication. Undeniably, man speaks and he hears, but he also moves and sees and touches and feels. As a communicator he is a man of multidimensional capacity.

Some recent publications have drawn public attention to nonverbal communication. Books such as *Here Comes Everybody* by William Schutz and *Body Language* by Julius Fast have served a useful purpose in this sense. They may have had some undesirable side effects, however. Indeed, they may have helped create the misleading notion that knowledge of nonverbal communication is chiefly useful to investigate and invigorate a communicator's sex life. Schutz notes that "when a group gets advanced and comfortable and trusting with each other, even deeper body concerns can be dealt with. In groups for couples we will often ask them to use a speculum to examine the interior of the vagina."[1] Similarly, Fast talks in some detail about the meaning transmitted nonverbally when a man's "hips are thrust forward slightly, as if they were cantilevered, and his legs are usually apart. There is something in this stance that spells sex."[2]

The functional importance of nonverbal communication is hardly limited to the semantics of sex. While the functions of speech communication are well known, the functions of nonverbal communication may not be apparent to the reader.[3]

Most of us spend a great deal of time attempting to persuade others, attempting to control others, and trying to enhance our own self-image. Whatever our communicative end, the nonverbal channels of communication frequently function most effectively in helping us attain it. To persuade others, for example, you must typically convince them of your honesty, sincerity, and trustworthiness. Think back to the last congressional hearing you observed on television. Did you determine whether the witness was honest, sincere, and trustworthy on the basis of what he said or on the basis of his nonverbal behavior?

Consider also those instances of face-to-face interaction when you have tried to control the communicative behavior of another person. Among the primary means of control at your disposal were your gestures, your posture, and the way you used the small space that separated you.

Consider finally the great amount of time you spend trying to attain or retain a positive self-image. To a very large degree your self-image and social identity are shaped by your personal appearance. This image is controlled to a striking extent by nonverbal factors unrelated to the content of your speech communication.

THE FUNCTIONAL IMPORTANCE OF NONVERBAL COMMUNICATION

When we write of the functional significance of nonverbal communication, the obvious question is what do we mean by function? The answer is complex. Most basically the function of communication is the exchange of meaning. The functional significance of nonverbal communication, therefore, is related to (1) the *purposes* for which meanings are exchanged (information, persuasion, etc.), (2) the *accuracy* with which meanings are exchanged (facial communication has more potential than tactile communication, for example), and (3) the *efficiency* with which meanings are exchanged (the time and effort required for the exchange of meaning).[4]

Viewed from any of the perspectives above, nonverbal communication has great functional significance in our society. In a great variety of situations a communicator can much more easily achieve his communicative purpose by the increased accuracy and efficiency with which nonverbal communication provides him.

More specifically, nonverbal communication has great functional significance for six major reasons.

First, *nonverbal, not verbal, factors are the major determinants of meaning in the interpersonal context.* Birdwhistell asserts that "probably no more than 30 to 35 percent of the social meaning of a conversation or an interaction is carried by the words."[5] Mehrabian goes even further in estimating that 93 percent of the total impact of a message is due to nonverbal factors.[6]

Children, army recruits, and dating couples often find themselves in communication situations that are similar in one respect. They must quickly and accurately determine the meanings of messages being transmitted to them. They typically rely on tone of voice, facial expression, and bodily movement to accomplish this purpose. Children soon learn that the tone and intensity of a parent's voice is their best guide to action. Army recruits do not determine the priority of directives from their drill sergeant by content analyzing the manifest verbal content of those directives. They focus on the sense of physical involvement the sergeant conveys to them nonverbally. Likewise, when your girlfriend says no to your most artful advances, you do not stop and apply the semantic differential to her verbal response to measure her meaning. You rely on her facial and bodily expressions as the primary determinants of her intent.

Second, *feelings and emotions are more accurately exchanged by nonverbal than verbal means.* Davitz has conducted an impressively detailed set of studies on emotional expression. He concludes that "it is the nonverbal, of the formal characteristics of one's environment . . . that primarily determine the emotional meaning of one's world."[7] Expressions like "keep your chin up," "down in the mouth," and "walking on air" are much more than empty figures of speech.[8] They have emotional referents that are rich in meaning and communicative significance.

The rapid development of t-group training, encounter sessions, psychiatric services, and, more recently, sexual therapy clinics is eloquent testimony to society's need to understand what emotions are communicated, how they are communicated, and how they are received. Since intromission and ejaculation are the only emotion-laden behaviors that universally take the same form, our need to understand variability in emotional expression is evident.[9]

Significantly, we now know not only that nonverbal communication is our richest source of knowledge about emotional states but also that nonverbal cues are reliable and stable indicators of the emotion that is being conveyed or received. Laboratory research reveals that "emotional meanings can be communicated accurately in a variety of nonverbal media. . . . In each instance, the accuracy with which emotional meanings were communicated far exceeded chance expectation."[10] In fact, "results demonstrate incontrovertibly that nonverbal, emotional communication is a stable, measurable phenomenon."[11]

Specifically, we now know that nonverbal communication can provide us with the following information about emotions: (1) how sensitive communicators are to emotional expressions, measured in terms of accuracy of identification; (2) the kinds of emotional expressions that can be correctly identified; (3) the specific nature of incorrect identification of emotions; and (4) the degree to which communicators attend to the emotional meaning of a total communication.[12]

Third, *the nonverbal portion of communication conveys meanings and intentions that are relatively free of deception, distortion, and confusion.* Nonverbal cues such as gestures are rarely under the sustained, conscious control of the communicator. For this reason communicators can rarely use nonverbal communication effectively for the purpose of dissembling. In contrast, the verbal dimension of communication seems to conceal or obfuscate the communicator's true intentions much more frequently.

Verbal cues are particularly susceptible to concealment and distortion of intent because they are typically a reflection of careful and, quite often, extended thought. Unlike verbal cues, "bodily expression . . . should be particularly revealing, since so much behavior occurs on this level without the conscious control efforts characteristic of speech."[13]

In an age that places a very high priority on trust, honesty, and candor in interpersonal relationships, nonverbal communication takes on added importance.[14] Such interpersonal relationships are built by using the most effective kinds of communication at our disposal. These are primarily nonverbal. Not only do nonverbal cues typically convey a communicator's real meaning and intent, but they also suggest rather precisely what the communicator thinks of us.[15]

Even such nonverbal cues as gesture, posture, and facial expression may of course be under the conscious control of the communicator. For all but the consummate actor and possibly a few legendary used-car salesmen, however, such conscious control is a temporary phenomenon. In most cases nonverbal cues are not consciously controlled for such extended periods of time as verbal cues, nor do they serve as frequently to transmit deception, distortion, and confusion.

Fourth, *nonverbal cues serve a metacommunicative function that is indispensable in attaining high quality communication.* Often the communicator provides additional cues that serve to clarify the intent and meaning of his message. Verbal expressions such as "now, seriously speaking" and "I'm only kidding" are metacommunicative in nature. A comforting hand on the shoulder or a radiant smile may represent nonverbal means of performing the same function. While both verbal and nonverbal cues can function metacommunicatively, nonverbal cues seem to take precedence in the mind of the receiver of the message.

But what does this mean? How do we know that nonverbal cues are so important metacommunicatively? I designed an experiment to answer those specific questions. One hundred subjects were exposed to a set of messages in which the words conveyed one meaning and the facial expressions of the "planted" communicators conveyed a conflicting meaning.

Imagine yourself in a small group and faced with the following situation. One of the discussants responds to a remark that you have just made. As he responds, he scratches his head vigorously and gets a very confused expression on his face. While looking utterly confused, he says to you, "Yes, I understand. What you just said seems completely clear to me."

You are faced with a clear-cut decision. To resolve the seeming contradiction in meaning, you must rely on either the verbal cues (words) or nonverbal cues (facial expression). In the laboratory situation the subject almost invariably relied on the facial expression as the true indicator of the communicator's meaning.[16]

When the verbal and nonverbal portions of a message reinforce each other and convey the same basic meaning, the metacommunicative value of the two types of cues is relatively unimportant. In contrast, when the verbal and nonverbal cues in a message convey conflicting meanings, the metacommunicative value of these cues becomes of primary importance. At that point the communicator, much like the subjects in the experiment, is faced with a serious problem. He must decide whether he will rely on verbal or nonverbal cues to determine the meaning and intent of the message. In effect he must decide which type of cues has greatest metacommunicative value for him. Typically, people who face such a decision rely on nonverbal rather than verbal cues.

Recent research indicates that individuals employ a systematic and consistent approach in determining the meaning of conflicting cues. One investigator has found that "the impact of facial expression is greatest, then the impact of tone of voice (or vocal expression), and finally that of words."[17] In short, facial expressions have the greatest metacommunicative value. Words have the least value.

We can safely conclude, therefore, that nonverbal cues serve the primary metacommunicative function in interpersonal communication. Since the metacommunicative function is a crucial determinant of high quality communication, the proper decoding of nonverbal cues is one of the most important factors in attaining high quality communication.[18]

Fifth, *nonverbal cues represent a much more efficient means of communicating than verbal cues.* Time is a vital commodity in many communication situations. Corporations willingly pay communication consultants handsome fees to improve the communicative efficiency of their executives. These executives want to know how to communicate more in less time.

This goal is not easily achieved in our highly verbal culture. Verbal discourse is by its very nature a highly inefficient means of communication. Redundancy, repetition, ambiguity, and abstraction have become standard qualities of verbal discourse in America. While sometimes necessary, these qualities help assure that communication will be inefficient.

Do qualities like repetition and ambiguity represent inherent liabilities of verbal discourse or do they simply reflect the ineptitudes of the individual communicator? While that question is probably debatable, there is solid evidence to indicate that verbal communication is intrinsically more inefficient than nonverbal.

Ruesch and Kees write that

> in practice, nonverbal communication must necessarily be dealt with analogically and this without delay. Although verbal communication permits a long interval between statements, certain action sequences and gestures necessitate an immediate reply. Then the reaction must be quick and reflexlike, with no time to ponder or to talk. And whenever such a situation occurs, the slower and exhaustive verbal codifications are out of the question for practical reasons and are clearly more time-consuming and inefficient than nonverbal reactions.[19]

These authors go on to point out that the nature of our language is such that words typically deal with the time dimension in a very inefficient manner.[20] In a limited time frame there are few, if any, sequences of events that cannot be described more quickly and efficiently with gestures than with words. Thus "words or a series of words are emergent phenomena that, because of their step characteristics, lack the property of efficiently representing continua or changes over time."[21]

The old axiom that a picture is worth a thousand words may lack precision, universal applicability, and empirical verification. The axiom suggests an idea of great importance in interpersonal communication, however. Nonverbal channels possess much greater potential for efficient communication than verbal channels.

Sixth, *nonverbal cues represent the most suitable vehicle for suggestion.* The nature of a communication situation often dictates that ideas and emotions can be more effectively expressed indirectly than directly. Suggestion is an important means of indirect expression in our society. When it is employed, either the verbal or nonverbal channels may be used. For tangible reasons, however, suggestion is more closely associated with nonverbal than verbal communication.

In the first place, nonverbal suggestion is much safer. If you solicit the sexual favors of a minor by verbal means you may receive a jail sentence. If you do the same thing nonverbally you are free from legal sanctions. One authority notes that "linguistic messages can be translated, stored, and held up for legal evidence; expressive messages tend to be ones for which the giver cannot be made legally responsible, it being usually possible for him to deny that he meant quite what others claim he meant."[22]

Advertisers of various types of erotic products and services evidently recognize the suitability of using visual communication for purposes of suggestion. Massage parlors have become big business in Los Angeles and their owners rely heavily on visual advertisements to suggest the highly sensual nature of the massages their patrons will receive. One issue of the *Los Angeles Free Press* contains pictorial advertisements for well over twenty different massage parlors. Most of the ads featured nude or nearly nude women in highly suggestive poses. Those few massage parlors that relied entirely on a verbal appeal seemed forced to abandon suggestion for explicit description. Thus one advertisement featured the following caption: "Beautiful Girls—Private Rooms. Our girls have everything it takes to make you come."[23]

The advantages of nonverbal suggestion are not confined to the question of one's legal responsibility for the messages one transmits. In spite of the immense personal satisfaction and control potential that is associated with interpersonal communication, it is a high-risk endeavor. One's ego, self-image, and even psychological equilibrium are intimately bound up in the communicative interaction with other people. Most of us are so acutely sensitive about our own image that we devote a significant proportion of our efforts to preserving or positively modifying that image. Hence the integrative function of communication is becoming increasingly important.[24]

Because many of us are so concerned about our own image, we prefer to use those means of communication that possess maximum potential for enhancing the image and minimum risk of deflating it. Nonverbal suggestion is a particularly suitable vehicle for attaining those ends.

Since one can always deny the seeming intent of nonverbal cues, he has the potential of avoiding many of the negative psychological consequences that may result from his nonverbal suggestions. After all, that man across the room can never be sure that a woman's sustained and seemingly suggestive eye contact is not an idiosyncrasy of hers rather than an open invitation to sexual intimacy. In contrast, as any frustrated lover knows, the most subtle suggestions couched in verbal terms do not provide the same psychological safeguards.

Hence, while nonverbal suggestion does not carry the same legal and psychological risks as verbal suggestion, it may be used for the same instrumental purpose.[25] For this reason nonverbal communication is increasingly associated with suggestion.

In review, the intent of this section has not been to establish that verbal communication and nonverbal communication are separate or completely separable entities. Indeed, the enlightened student of communication would be well advised not to study one to the exclusion of the other. Chapter 10 of this book will be devoted to examining the interrelationships between the verbal and nonverbal channels of communication. The previous section, nonetheless, was designed to emphasize an immediate and compelling need to examine and expand our knowledge of nonverbal communication.

We now have impressive empirical support for the claim that "the nonverbal aspects of any communication, even in the highly verbal culture in which we live, are of prime importance in understanding the message expressed and thus adapting effectively to one's environment."[26]

ILLUSORY BARRIERS TO THE STUDY OF NONVERBAL COMMUNICATION

If the need to study nonverbal communication is so real and compelling, we are faced with an obvious question. Why is the scientific study of nonverbal communication such a recent phenomenon? No simple or single answer will be entirely satisfactory since the question is complex.

Pioneering researchers in the field have had to contend with a formidable array of barriers. While more illusory than real, these barriers have had the unfortunate effect of impeding research on the subject. These barriers take at least three forms. The first type might be labeled conceptual myths. These myths are geared to the errant notion that nonverbal communicative behavior is of secondary importance and not really amenable to scientific study. The second type, historical barriers, can be traced to the elocutionary movement and its unfortunate connotations. The third type of barrier, methodological, took a somewhat different form. Viewed from a great distance, nonverbal research has been seen to require an equipment arsenal rivaling that of the Pentagon.

CONCEPTUAL BARRIERS   Conceptual barriers have taken a number of forms but one misconception has been of overriding importance. Simply put, the skeptics argued that verbal behaviors dwarfed nonverbal in importance. The verbal communication system has been seen as dominant and the nonverbal communication systems as subordinate.

As a respected pioneer in the field of kinesic communication, Ray Birdwhistell has done much to dispel this notion. His carefully considered opinion seems to be gaining wide acceptance among communication scholars. He is "as yet unwilling, from the situations which [he has] examined, to assign . . . priority to any of the infracommunication systems. For the kinecist, silence is just as golden as are those periods in which the linguistic system is positively operative."[27]

As Birdwhistell suggests, evidence is lacking to support the misconception that nonverbal communicative behaviors, such as facial expressions and postures, are of secondary importance. On the contrary, nonverbal cues are clearly primary carriers of meaning in a number of situations. He notes, pertinently, that "it seems proper to study the two systems [verbal and nonverbal] as of comparable weight in the communication process."[28]

Misconceptions about nonverbal communication are not confined to this single type. They take a number of specific forms. Nonverbal communication (1) is the rudimentary, evolutionary predecessor to verbal communication; (2) is idiosyncratic behavior and, as such, comprises a limitless number of unique expressions that do not occur in identifiable and uniform configurations; and (3) is made up of so many gestures and expressions that it cannot be studied.

Such misconceptions, if fact rather than fiction, would limit the value of nonverbal communication. They would mean that we could not communicate important and complex meanings nonverbally. Furthermore, nonverbal communication would be almost impossible since individuals would use different gestures or facial expressions in an attempt to communicate the same meaning (given types of gestures would have no commonly recognized meaning, for example).[29] Worse yet, attempts to communicate by gesture would be highly impractical because an individual would have to choose from an almost limitless number of gestures.

The misconception that nonverbal communication is the rudimentary precursor of verbal communication also suggests that nonverbal cues are instinctual and unlearned. The weight of current evidence contradicts this notion. Not only are meaningful bodily cues repeated and subject to systematization, but they are also learned.[30]

A second misconception has more surface plausibility than the first one. In brief, some scholars still cling to the belief that nonverbal phenomena, such as facial expressions and postures, simply reflect the unique biological and maturational heritage of the individual communicator. If true, such an idea would serve as a major barrier to nonverbal research. Researchers would have to deal with a veritable infinity of unpatterned expressions. Such is not the case. "Although there are many who still believe that nonlexical communicative behaviors—such as postures—are individual, unique expressions which occur in an infinite variety of forms," Scheflen's "research leads [him] to quite another view."[31] Scheflen goes on to attack the misconception that nonverbal communication is basically idiosyncratic in nature. He emphasizes that nonverbal communicative behaviors

> occur in characteristic, standard configurations, whose common recognizability is the basis of their value in communication. That these behaviors are regular, uniform entities within a culture tremendously simplifies both research into human interaction and practical understanding of it. These forms are so familiar that a description of them leads to immediate recognition by most people without elaborate details or measurements.[32]

The final misconception is an understandable one. At first glance, the number of gestures and expressions employed in our culture seems staggering. Superficial observation might support the misconception that we use too many gestures to make practical any systematic study of such behavior.

While nonverbal cues are clearly rich in nuance and while individual repertoires may differ in size, the number of nonverbal cues typically used in our culture is re-markably small. For example, there are only about thirty traditional American ges-tures.[33] In addition, "there is an even smaller number of culturally standard gestural configurations which are of shared communicative significance for Americans. The regularity of the communicative system extends not only to the form of the configura-tions, but to the contexts in which they appear."[34]

HISTORICAL BARRIERS   A number of historical factors have served as barriers to the study of nonverbal communication but one seems of particular importance. That his-torical force is the elocutionary movement. The long-term effects of this movement are both ironic and unfortunate.

Ironically, the movement is now strongly associated with a problem that it was designed to eliminate. Leaders of the elocutionary movement were committed to im-proving the quality of nonverbal communication in public speaking. Because of the excesses of their methods, however, the elocutionists have become personae non gratae to many teachers of speech communication. Classroom training in the proper use of gestures and the voice has become suspect in some quarters. In effect, then, the elocutionary movement has shifted attention away from rather than toward nonverbal communication.

The elocutionary movement was designed to improve the delivery of public speakers in England. In eighteenth-century England in particular "classical rhetorical training was providing sound study of invention and arrangement, but its lack of detail on delivery and corresponding lack of emphasis in training in delivery were opening the door for the Elocutionists."[35]

The general goal of improving delivery still seems praiseworthy, but the methods employed to achieve that goal are now widely condemned. The reasons are under-standable. Elocutionists like James Burgh and Gilbert Austin became so preoccupied with the physical details of delivery as to lose sight of the broader purposes of public speaking. The young orator who studied with the elocutionists was faced with a stag-gering set of instructions. To deliver the brief passage "Romans, countrymen and lov-ers!" the student had to master the following notation: Bshf p------q----------vex sp. This notation translated to both hands supine, horizontal, forwards, pushing—oblique—vertical, elevated, extended, springing; feet retire, to right first.[36]

The response to such training procedures was predictable. The elocutionists be-came susceptible to the charge that their precepts were highly mechanical, artificial, and impractical, and that their training served to impede rather than promote effective delivery.

Teachers of speech have been quick to divorce themselves from the movement and to deny that it was and is part of their intellectual heritage. As Parrish pointed out, "a current fashion among teachers of speech [is] to greet any mention of 'elocution' or 'elocutionists' with a knowing smile of amused superiority."[37] Rejection of the elocutionists remains fashionable today. The reaction against the elocutionary move-ment remains so strong that the systematic study of delivery is rarely an important part of a speech communication curriculum. Hence, while the elocutionary movement was designed to emphasize nonverbal dimensions of speech, it has the effect of reinforcing our cultural preoccupation with verbal communication.

Fortunately, the negative emotional residue of the elocutionary movement seems to be dissipating rapidly in light of the realization that communication does not consist of words alone. The nonverbal systems of communication have begun to be recognized as a vital and integral part of the total communication process.

METHODOLOGICAL BARRIERS   Clearly, the conceptual and historical barriers to the study of nonverbal communication are largely illusory. They are not real but alleged barriers. Until rather recently, however, a methodological barrier existed that was more real than illusory. Simply stated, "the multidetermined nature of a movement requires (ideally) repeated re-viewings and multiple observers before it can be understood and extracted."[38] Such a requirement could easily suggest that the study of nonverbal communication is prohibitively expensive.

Twenty years ago, or even ten, the study of nonverbal communication would have required a very expensive equipment arsenal. Such is no longer the case. One technological advance has revolutionized teaching and research in nonverbal communication—the portable VTR (videotape recorder).

Portable VTR units are now so inexpensive that most communication departments can easily afford them. In fact the VTR unit is only one of a series of monitoring and recording devices that can be used to study nonverbal communication. Still photography, slide projectors, and the movie camera suggest only a few ways for obtaining inexpensive records of nonverbal behavior.

Such equipment works best in a teaching and research laboratory designed for the study of nonverbal communication. Like the equipment, such a laboratory is quite inexpensive; it is well within the reach of even small departments. The detailed treatment of this subject in chapter 9 should convince the reader that equipment need be no barrier to the exciting study of nonverbal communication.

TYPES OF NONVERBAL COMMUNICATION SYSTEMS

Meanings are communicated within systems. This book is designed to illuminate the nature of such communication. The nature of nonverbal communication is examined within the framework of the systems approach to human communication. Systems thinking provides its own rationale. It exhibits the greatest promise for providing a holistic, comprehensive, and realistic picture of the complex set of behaviors that interact to make up human communication.

Ludwig von Bertalanffy is generally credited with being the major pioneering force behind systems thinking. His modern classic, *Modern Theories of Development,* was published in 1928. His subsequent work, *General Systems Theory: Foundations, Development, Applications,* has become the ultimate reference, if not the blueprint, for the rapidly developing systems movement. Indeed, the systems approach now has respected and vigorous advocates in such diverse disciplines as biology, economics, psychology, and communication.

Clearly, the application of systems thinking to communication is very different from the application to chemistry, for example. Human beings are not typically put in bottles. Nor are their interactions with each other controlled by unvarying and thus precisely predictable forces. Indeed, the often highly individualistic and idiosyncratic nature of an individual's behavior makes the study of human communication difficult; it makes the precise predictions of the physical science laboratory impossible.

While systems thinking is currently being used in highly diverse disciplines, the central assumptions that give it wide appeal are the same. Systems thinkers seem to agree that (1) we live in an *orderly and predictable universe,* (2) scientific study of that universe is most fruitfully undertaken from a *holistic perspective,* and (3) *comprehensive models* of that universe are necessary if we are to understand the complex physical and social relationships that give it life.[39]

Such assumptions are very important for the enlightened study of human communication. If communicative behavior exhibited no order, for example, attempts to study it scientifically would be futile. How could we predict the nature of interpersonal communication and increase our control over our environment as a result of such predictions if all communicative behaviors were really idiosyncratic? While communicative interaction is certainly more idiosyncratic than chemical interaction, it is predictable because it exhibits a demonstrable orderliness.

Communicative behavior in its complexity also demonstrates the futility of attempting to reduce it to its smallest isolable components without examining the relationships between those components. To avoid a monadic view of communication we need comprehensive models of communication just as we need comprehensive models of economic resources. The value of comprehensive models is the potential they provide for understanding the nature of the relationships such models are designed to illuminate.

Systems thinking understandably begins with a definition of a system. While the nature of different systems differs drastically, all systems are defined by the relationships of their components. In general a *system* may be defined as a set of objects and their attributes wherein the interaction of the objects is determined by the nature of their relationship with each other. Thus, "the *objects* are the components or parts of the system, *attributes* are the properties of the *objects,* and *relationships* tie the system together."[40]

Concrete illustration makes this definition more meaningful. A home stereo system provides such an illustration. The *objects* or components of such a sound system might be (1) an AM/FM stereo receiver, (2) a set of speakers, (3) a turntable, (4) an 8-track cartridge stereo tape recorder, and (5) a reel-to-reel recorder. The heart of the sound system is typically the AM/FM receiver, since all other components of the system are hooked to it and controlled to one degree or another by it. Each component of the system has a set of attributes that help determine the quality of sound of the system. If you are particularly interested in receiving stereophonic sound from a local FM radio station, the quality of your reception will be determined in part by some or all of the following *attributes* of your stereo receiver: tuning range, signal-to-noise ratio, image rejection, selectivity, total harmonic distortion, channel separation, and antenna input impedance.

The ultimate performance of your sound system will not be determined by how well the individual components operate. How the components work in *relationship* to each other is the vital question.

This simple example suggests only a small portion of the potential of the systems approach for studying human communication. Indeed, the student of human communication is interested in identifying and defining the nature of those factors which materially affect the quality of communicative interaction. Once this objective is accomplished, the larger goals of explaining and predicting the quality of subsequent communicative interaction under given conditions are within reach. Maximum power of explanation and prediction is dependent on our ability to understand *relationships* between communication variables. The most illuminating frame of reference for viewing and analyzing such relationships seems to be general systems theory.

A communication system is a rather special type of system. Much of the terminology and many of the concepts that are endemic to physical and biological systems do not apply to a communication system or are of only peripheral concern.

Thayer perceptively maintains that human communication systems differ from nonhuman communication systems in at least three ways: (1) In the animal kingdom the *necessary* condition for communication is that one animal signal another; in human communication the *sufficient* condition is not only that the human being receive a signal but he is able to assess the consequences of responding to that signal *before* responding. (2) In an information system the data are the message; in human communication systems, "information" is what people do to the data. (3) Communicators are never the same after communicative interaction simply because they have interacted—their identity, however slightly, is changed. "People who talk to each other, particularly when they touch upon vital or fundamental communicational realities, change each other, sometimes peripherally, sometimes centrally, but change nonetheless. The 'information' engineer can assume that a 'bit' can be used over and over again, retaining its initial identity."[41] The communication analyst using the systems approach to interpersonal communication cannot make that same assumption about human beings.

Furthermore, a communication system should not be confused with an information system. Information systems map the flow of data to or from humans or machines from the point at which the data are generated or disseminated to the point of intended destination. The circuitry used to transport information and the energy and time required are the big concerns. Efficiency is the password. Information systems are designed to control not human beings, but data. In contrast, communication systems always affect the communicative abilities of the consumer as well as the producer of the communication. "Communication systems, by definition, always affect the communicate-abilities of the consumer in some way, however minor."[42] Thayer captures the distinction between communication and information systems when he writes:

> All communication systems are control systems. Conventionally, control systems are those rational data systems which are designed to control their own output in some way, or to channel in some way the problem-solving–decisioning behavior of those persons who are linked to it. But data systems do not and cannot control human behavior beyond the *communication* which occurs as a consequence of their outputs.[43]

Since the analysis of human communication as a system is in its infancy, not everyone can agree as to the definition of a communication system. Trying to analyze and illustrate the subsystems that make up the human communication system is an even more venturesome task. What follows in this book may, consequently, be attributed jointly to the idiosyncrasies of the author's creative processes as well as to the insights of systems scholars who have now been working for nearly five decades (the unkind reader might prefer to call it semi-enlightened masochism).

For our purposes the *human communication system* will be defined as *a set of interacting subsystems, each capable of communicating dimensions of meaning that may reinforce each other, conflict with each other, or act in relative isolation; these subsystems, when interacting with each other, produce communicative behaviors that are not simply a sum of the parts and that often cannot be predicted by studying the communication associated with a given subsystem in isolation.*

This definition correctly suggests that human communication is made up of suprasystems, systems, and subsystems. The *suprasystem* is defined by the fact that its components are actually systems. A *subsystem,* on the other hand, is best described in terms of the various activities identified with the subsystem or is identified by the most vital process it performs.[44] In the example of the stereo system the suprasystem was the entire sound system, since it comprised the individual systems of an AM/FM receiver, speakers, record player, etc. The AM/FM receiver, in turn, has at least two subsystems, which are identified by function(s): one subsystem receives signals and reproduces the sounds transmitted by AM stations while the other subsystem performs the same functions with FM radio stations.

This definition of human communication system also raises a very important question. What systems and subsystems make up nonverbal communication? Duncan believes that nonverbal communication is composed of: (1) kinesic behavior or various types of body movement; (2) paralinguistic behavior, such as nonfluencies and vocal variation; (3) proxemic behavior, or the use of social and personal space; (4) olfaction; (5) skin sensitivity; and (6) artifactual factors such as dress and cosmetics.[45] Similarly, Scheflen identifies the "nonlanguage modalities" as kinesic and postural, tactile, odorific, territorial, proxemic, and artifactual.[46]

This author maintains that nonverbal communication is made up of three major interlocking systems, which in turn have their own subsystems. The major nonverbal communication systems identified and described in this book are the visual communication system (in turn comprised of the kinesic, proxemic, and artifactual subsystems), the auditory communication system (which is treated as a single system in this book although it could conceivably be broken down into its subsystems), and the invisible communication system (in turn composed of the tactile, olfactory, and telepathic subsystems).[47] The fourth major communication system, the verbal communication system, will be compared and contrasted with the other three systems in chapter 10 (written and oral communication might legitimately be treated as two subsystems of the larger verbal communication system but will not be treated in detail here).

Each nonverbal communication system, as well as the subsystems, may function with relative independence of the others to communicate meanings. The functional significance and capacity of these systems vary rather dramatically. Facial communication, for example, is particularly impressive. The functional capacity of the face can be measured in terms of the kinds of meaning communicated, the accuracy and efficiency with which such meaning is communicated, and the purposes served by such communication. Facial communication has great functional significance because we can use the face to communicate a great variety of meanings accurately and efficiently.

Separate chapters of this book are devoted to the systems and subsystems that make up nonverbal communication. In each instance the functional capacity of the given nonverbal system is examined in depth. Particular emphasis is placed on the types of meanings that are most effectively communicated by each system and the accuracy and efficiency with which the meanings are communicated.

CONCLUSION

Nonverbal communication functions in vitally important ways in our society. Frequently, a communicator can much more easily achieve his communicative purpose by the increased accuracy and efficiency that nonverbal communication provides.

The functional importance of nonverbal communication is obvious when we realize that: (1) nonverbal communication is typically the dominant force in the exchange of meaning in the interpersonal context; (2) feelings and emotions are more accurately exchanged by nonverbal than verbal means; (3) meanings exchanged nonverbally are relatively free of deception, distortion, and confusion; (4) nonverbal cues serve a metacommunicative function that is indispensable in attaining high quality communication; (5) nonverbal cues represent a much more efficient means of communicating than verbal cues; and (6) nonverbal communication is a particularly suitable vehicle for using suggestion.

The exciting study of nonverbal communication is now a realistic and practical undertaking. Motivation is the primary prerequisite for such study. As the reader will discover, there are currently no significant barriers to such study. Even up to the past few years, the apparent barriers have been more illusory than real. During the current decade, conceptual, historical, and methodological barriers to the study of nonverbal communication have either disappeared or been exposed as merely alleged barriers based on misconception.

This book is designed to help you begin your own systematic study of nonverbal communication. In it nonverbal communication is examined within the framework of the systems approach to human communication. You will study the three major interlocking systems—visual, auditory, and invisible—which make up nonverbal communication. More specifically, you will have an opportunity to test your own capacity to use the nonverbal communication systems and subsystems in attempting to attain your own communicative objectives.

NOTES

[1] W. C. Schutz, *Here Comes Everybody* (New York: Harper & Row, 1971), p. 168.
[2] J. Fast, *Body Language* (New York: M. Evans, 1970), p. 96. For interesting books apparently geared to a general audience see also M. Poiret, *Body Talk: The Sci-*

ence of Kinesics (New York: Award Books, 1970), and G. I. Nierenberg and H. H. Calero, *How to Read a Person Like a Book* (New York: Pocket Books, 1973).

3 A lucid and informative discussion of the functions of nonverbal communication is presented in G. Wiseman and L. Barker, *Speech / Interpersonal Communication* (New York: Chandler, 1974); pp. 223-47.

4 L. Zunin, *Contact: The First Four Minutes* (New York: Ballantine, 1973), pp. 77-101.

5 R. L. Birdwhistell, *Kinesics and Context* (Philadelphia: University of Pennsylvania Press, 1970), p. 158.

6 A. Mehrabian, "Communication without Words," *Psychology Today,* 2 (1968), 51-52.

7 J. R. Davitz, *The Communication of Emotional Meaning* (New York: McGraw-Hill, 1964), p. 201.

8 P. Wachtel, "An Approach to the Study of Body Language in Psychotherapy," *Psychotherapy,* 4 (1967), 97.

9 A. E. Scheflen, "The Significance of Posture in Communication Systems," *Psychiatry,* 27 (1964), 317.

10 Davitz, *The Communication of Emotional Meaning,* p. 178.

11 Ibid.

12 Ibid., pp. 179-80.

13 Wachtel, "Approach to the Study of Body Language," 100. The polygraph, or lie detector, is geared to the same assumption that a change in an individual's emotions will be reflected in telltale changes in bodily cues; changes in breathing, heart rate, and skin resistance are measured by the polygraph. These changes are often not perceptible to the communicator, whereas changes in gestures and posture that may accompany lying, for example, are frequently observable. D. T. Lykken notes that even lie detectors that monitor *internal* changes in bodily cues are far from infallible ["Guilty-Knowledge Test—The Right Way to Use a Lie Detector," *Psychology Today,* 8 (1975), 56-60]. P. Ekman and W. V. Friesen emphasize that we may control *external* bodily cues (which are central to nonverbal communication) to conceal deception or lying although it is difficult to exert such control effectively for any length of time ["Nonverbal Leakage and Clues to Deception," *Psychiatry,* 32 (1969), 88-105].

14 D. G. Leathers, "The Process Effects of Trust-Destroying Behavior in the Small Group," *Speech Monographs,* 37 (1970), 180-87.

15 C. Galloway, "Nonverbal Communication," *The Instructor,* 77 (1968), 38.

16 D. G. Leathers, "The Process Effects of Meta-Incongruent Messages," an experiment in the UCLA series.

17 A. Mehrabian, *Silent Messages* (Belmont, Calif.: Wadsworth, 1971), p. 43.

18 D. G. Leathers, "Quality of Group Communication as a Determinant of Group Product," *Speech Monographs,* 39 (1972), 166-73. See this article for a new method for measuring the quality of communication.

19 J. Ruesch and W. Kees, *Nonverbal Communication* (Berkeley: University of California Press, 1956), p. 14.

20 Ibid., p. 8.

21 Ibid.

22 E. Goffman, *Behavior in Public Places* (London: Collier-Macmillan Ltd., 1963), p. 14.

23 *Los Angeles Free Press,* November 10, 1972, Part 2, pp. 16-19.

[24] L. Thayer, *Communication and Communication Systems* (Homewood, Ill.: Richard D. Irwin, 1968), p. 243.

[25] J. A. Meerloo, *Conversation and Communication* (New York: International Universities Press, 1952), p. 13.

[26] Davitz, *Communication of Emotional Meaning,* p. 201.

[27] Birdwhistell, *Kinesics and Context,* p. 188.

[28] Ibid., p. 189.

[29] A set of commonly used gestures, each of which has single and easily identifiable meanings, is classified in M. Wiener, S. Devoe, S. Rubinow, and J. Geller, "Nonverbal Behavior and Nonverbal Communication," *Psychological Review,* 79 (1972), 210-11.

[30] R. L. Birdwhistell, "Kinesics and Communication," in *Explorations in Communication,* ed. E. Carpenter and M. McLuhan (Boston: Beacon Press, 1960), p. 54. A substantial amount of empirical research will be cited in this book which supports the proposition that much of the behavior that makes up nonverbal communication is learned. A number of authorities, however, maintain that a significant portion of such behavior is spontaneous or unlearned. C. E. Izard, in *The Face of Emotion* (New York: Appleton-Century-Crofts, 1971), pp. 59-62, examines this issue in his superb work on facial expression.

[31] Scheflen, "Significance of Posture," 316.

[32] Ibid.

[33] Ibid., 317.

[34] Ibid.

[35] W. Guthrie, "The Development of Rhetorical Theory in America, 1635–1850: V. The Elocution Movement—England," *Speech Monographs,* 18 (1951), 20-26.

[36] J. Barber, *A Practical Treatise on Gesture* (Cambridge: Hilliard and Brown, 1831, an abstract of G. Austin's *Chironomia*).

[37] W. M. Parrish, "Elocution—A Definition and a Challenge," *Quarterly Journal of Speech,* 43 (1957), 51.

[38] R. Renneker, "Kinesic Research and Therapeutic Processes: Further Discussion," in *Expressions of the Emotions in Man,* ed. P. H. Knapp (New York: International Universities Press, 1963), p. 150.

[39] E. Laszlo, ed., *The Relevance of General Systems Theory* (New York: George Braziller, 1972), pp. 5-6. See also John W. Sutherland, *A General Systems Philosophy for the Social and Behavioral Sciences* (New York: George Braziller, 1973), pp. 89-136, for a more detailed treatment of this subject.

[40] P. W. Watzlawick, J. H. Beavin, and D. D. Jackson, *Pragmatics of Human Communication* (New York: W. W. Norton, 1967), p. 120.

[41] L. Thayer, "Communication Systems," in *Relevance of General Systems Theory,* pp. 108-11.

[42] Thayer, *Communication and Communication Systems,* p. 117.

[43] Ibid., pp. 117-18.

[44] B. D. Ruben, "General System Theory: An Approach to Human Communication," in *Approaches to Human Communication,* ed. R. W. Budd and B. D. Ruben (New York: Spartan, 1972), p. 125.

[45] S. Duncan, Jr., "Nonverbal Communication," *Psychological Bulletin,* 72 (1969), 118.

[46] A. E. Scheflen, "Human Communication: Behavioral Programs and Their Integration in Interaction," *Behavioral Science,* 13 (1968), 44-55.

[47] The reader should note that two types of proxemic subsystems are treated in this book. Chapter 3 focuses on the use of space in the *interpersonal* environment and chapter 4 on the use of space in the *urban* environment. Consequently, the visual communication system is broken down into four subsystems. In a more limited framework, kinesic and proxemic communication may be thought of as systems of nonverbal communication rather than subsystems. To avoid confusing shifts in nomenclature, they will be referred to as communication systems in chapters 2 through 9 of this book.

2

THE KINESIC COMMUNICATION SYSTEM

Movement communicates meaning.[1] This much men have accepted through the ages. While they have accepted the general proposition, they have rarely examined its implications in detail. If movement communicates meaning, it follows that different movements communicate different meanings. It also follows that we must determine the referents of specific movements or combinations of movements.

Certain movements create lasting impressions. Think of the number of friends or acquaintances you remember because of the way they move or use movement to communicate. My own memories are filled with individuals who moved in distinctive ways; two stand out in particular. Old swivel-hips Becker, the local elevator man, is probably still shuffling down the streets of my hometown and moving with the awkward but fluid grace that suggests that his hips are perpetually suspended in a barrel of honey. Similarly, one college professor stands out because his incredibly deliberate gestures drew attention to pauses of remarkable length in his speech. The students were convinced by the gestures and pauses that he either was terribly profound or was taking a nap between pauses.

We know that movement is important in interpersonal communication but our own knowledge about the meaning of movement is probably very limited. Until recently, few systematic efforts had been made to determine how we exchange meaning by movement. We seem to assume that communication by facial expression, or gesture, is a natural physiological function that need not be studied. Much like bodily elimination it is not something we should contemplate at length or practice repeatedly in the company of our peers.

The contrast with written communication is striking. Students in writing classes spend many hours trying to improve their ability to transmit their meanings clearly. Similarly, law students spend hours trying to determine the exact meaning of laws or court decisions on pornography, integration, or pollution. Their aim is to increase their capacity to encode and decode written messages.

This example should help make the point. We have studied communication by oral and written discourse intensively and we assume that we will improve our capacity by practice. In contrast, most of us have not studied communication by movement intensively, and systematic instruction and practice in facial expression, gesture, and posture seem almost to be forbidden thoughts.

The need to know what we communicate by movement and to improve this capacity should be evident. As we shall point out in chapter 10, communication by movement is probably the major source of meaning in interpersonal interaction.

Consequently, this chapter describes how communication by movement has been studied and should be studied. It illustrates how individuals (1) may measure the accuracy with which they communicate by movement, (2) may measure the accuracy with which they perceive meanings communicated by movement, and (3) may improve their capacity to communicate by movement.

The need to know the meaning of movement is resulting in a body of research called kinesics. Kinesics is the study of observable, isolable, and meaningful movement in interpersonal communication. Birdwhistell writes that "kinesics is concerned with abstracting from the continuous muscular shifts which are characteristic of living physiological systems those groupings of movements which are of significance to the communication process and thus to the interactional systems of particular social groups."[2]

Kinesic research begins with the kine, the smallest identifiable unit of motion, and emphasizes the kinemorph, that combination of kines in any part of the body which convey a given meaning. Thus "droopy-lidded" eyelids combined with "bilaterally raised median" brows have an evident differential meaning from "droopy-lidded" combined with a "low unilateral brow lift."[3] The combination of very specific movement of the eyelids and brow into one larger unit, the kinemorph, conveys a meaning that is consistently recognized in our culture.

Movements that convey meaning are hardly limited to the brows. Many parts of the body convey meaning singly and in combination. In the strictest anatomical sense the sources of movement in the human body are almost unlimited. From a more practical perspective, Birdwhistell identifies eight sources of potentially significant body movement: (1) total head, (2) face, (3) neck, (4) trunk, (5) shoulder-arm-wrist, (6) hand,

(7) hip-joint-leg-ankle, and (8) foot.[4] As we shall see, some areas have greater functional significance than others. In addition, some areas are relatively unimportant because they are rarely visible. For example, except for the fetishist, the leg and ankle hardly rival the face in communicative significance.

The major components of the kinesic communication system are facial, gestural, and postural communication. While the components are part of the same system because they communicate meaning by movement, the meanings exchanged may vary in kind as well as in the accuracy and efficiency with which they are exchanged.

FACIAL COMMUNICATION

"The human face—in repose and in movement, at the moment of death as in life, in silence and in speech, when alone and with others, when seen or sensed from within, in actuality or as represented in art or recorded by the camera—is a commanding, complicated, and at times confusing source of information. The face is commanding because of its very visibility and omnipresence."[5]

The face has long been a primary source of information in interpersonal communication. It is an instrument of great importance in the transmission of meaning. Within a matter of seconds facial expressions can move us to the heights of ecstasy or the depths of despair. We study the faces of friends and associates for subtle changes and nuances in meaning and they in turn study our faces.

In a very real sense our quest for meaning in this world begins and ends with facial expression. We study the face of the infant to determine his immediate needs and he reciprocates by communicating many of his needs and emotional states through facial expressions. The elderly hospital patient studies the face of his surgeon to determine his chances of surviving the next operation and the surgeon's facial expression often provides the definitive answer.

While we have relied on the human face as a primary source of meaning for centuries, we have had very little information on how it actually functions as a communicative instrument. Darwin did offer many pioneering insights on facial expression as far back as 1872 in *The Expression of Emotions in Man and Animals* (London: Murray, 1872). It was not until almost sixty years later, however, that the expressive functions of the face were studied in detail.[6] Only in the past two decades did the work of Schlosberg stimulate careful scientific studies designed to determine the true communicative potential of the human face.[7]

It is difficult to treat research on the human face in a systematic manner. The conceptual and methodological assumptions of researchers have differed drastically. Many of the studies are not designed to determine what meanings the face can communicate, but to ascertain what information the face transmits about the emotional states of the individuals using facial expressions. Finally, much research is geared to the investigator's *assumptions about what the face should be able to express* rather than to *verified observations about what the face actually does communicate.*

The following section of this chapter is designed to answer two questions: (1) What meanings can be communicated or exchanged by facial expression? (2) How can the reader measure, and ultimately improve, his capacity to transmit and perceive meanings communicated by facial expression?

THE FACE: DENOTATIVE FUNCTION   Students of the human face do not agree on how it functions communicatively. A number of researchers treat the face as if it served a denotative function. At any given moment the face is seen to transmit only one type of meaning, often associated with such affective states as happiness or anger. The meaning transmitted facially is believed to have a single referent. Thus, at any given point in time, the face does not convey sadness and bewilderment, but sadness *or* bewilderment.

Some of the earliest and most insightful research on the denotative functions of facial expression was conducted by J. Frois-Wittmann. Using himself as the photographic subject, Frois-Wittmann made a series of seventy-two facial photographs. These photographs were designed to represent all the classes and subclasses of facial expression that man is capable of conveying. Subjects were asked to identify the meaning expressed in each photograph by applying their own descriptive labels.

This study strongly suggested that distinct meanings can be communicated by facial expression. Pain, pleasure, superiority, determination, surprise, attention, and bewilderment are among the meanings consistently and accurately perceived by the subjects.[8] At the same time, it became apparent that some of the meanings conveyed by some facial expressions were confused by the subjects. Subjects often had difficulty distinguishing between hate and anger, disappointment and sadness, disgust and contempt, and horror and fear.[9]

The confusion between and among meanings can be attributed either to inadequacies in the posed facial expressions or to subjective errors of perception by the subjects, or both. The reader may make his own judgments by studying the following pictures from the Frois-Wittmann series (reproduced by permission of Trygg Engen). Subjects grouped expressions 28, 29, and 30 together and saw them as conveying the same basic meaning. Do you agree?

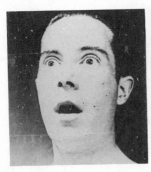  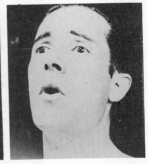

28   29   30

Look at the pictures below and sort out into separate classes those which convey basically the same meaning. How many different classes of meaning do you see? Which pictures fall into each class?

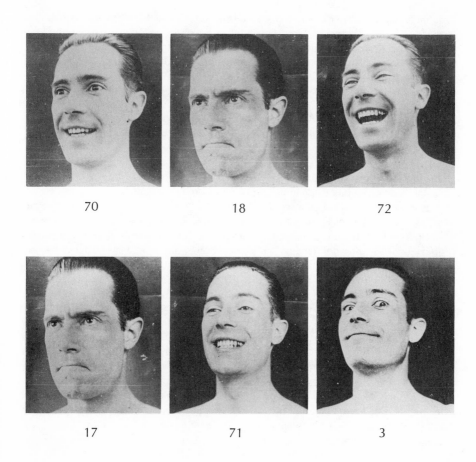

70   18   72

17   71   3

You should have sorted the pictures above into three groups or classes. Picture 3 would be sorted into one class, pictures 17 and 18 into another class, and pictures 70, 71, and 72 into a third class.

Subjects in the Hulin and Katz study were asked to perform a similar discriminatory task using the same photographs although their job was considerably more difficult. In grouping pictures together they had to choose from among seventy-one photographs. Over 63 percent of these subjects agreed that pictures 71 and 72 were conveying the same class of meaning, while over 85 percent agreed that pictures 17 and 18 should be grouped together.[10]

These early studies demonstrated that individuals can distinguish between general types or classes of meaning conveyed by facial expression. They do not, however, demonstrate how many different classes of meaning can be conveyed by facial expression, or how subtle are the differences in meaning that can be communicated by facial means.

Later, research by Woodworth suggested that the six basic classes of meaning communicated facially are happiness, suffering, surprise, determination, disgust, and contempt.[11] Of 390 subjects using six classes of meaning, 366 correctly identified the attempt to communicate happiness by facial means. Accuracy of identification for the other expressions was: suffering (325), determination (310), surprise (304), disgust (294), and contempt (190).[12]

As the figures suggest, some types of meaning were more difficult to communicate than others. You may want to try your perceptual skill on four of the facial expressions that the subjects found hardest to identify (these photographs are from the famous Lightfoot series—see endnote 12). Using only the labels for the six classes of meaning from the Woodworth study—happiness, suffering, determination, surprise, disgust, and contempt—please decide which term most accurately describes the expression in each of the four photographs in Figure 2-1.

One hundred subjects identified picture 3 as contempt, but 102 saw it as disgust, and 69 as happiness. One hundred thirty subjects saw picture 7 as determination, but 114 saw it as contempt, 74 as disgust, and 69 as suffering. One hundred forty-seven subjects identified picture 8 as happiness, but 125 saw it as determination or anger, and 65 saw it as contempt. Finally, 167 subjects saw picture 33 as disgust, but 84 saw it as suffering, 60 as determination or anger, and 58 as contempt.[13]

At this point, the reader will probably agree that the face is capable of conveying distinguishable meanings. However, the question of how many meanings remains unanswered. In *Emotion in the Human Face,* Ekman, Friesen, and Ellsworth make an impressive attempt to answer that specific question. They review, summarize, and analyze many of the major studies that have attempted to determine the number and kinds of meanings that are communicated by facial expressions. They conclude that the face is capable of communicating eight basic types of meaning: (I) happiness; (II) surprise; (III) fear; (IV) anger; (V) sadness; (VI) disgust; (VII) contempt; and (VIII) interest.[14]

Like other researchers they refer to these different classes of meaning as "emotion categories." The term emotion categories correctly implies that each basic type of meaning may include a number of similar facial expressions, but it incorrectly suggests that facial expressions provide information only about emotional or affective states within the communicator. While facial expressions often provide much information about a communicator's emotional state, they also provide us with information about thought processes. "It is possible to decode reliably from facial expressions information other than primary emotion concepts."[15]

Additional research by me and by others suggests that at least ten, rather than eight, basic classes of meaning can be communicated by facial expression.

Class I	Happiness	VI	Disgust
II	Surprise	VII	Contempt
III	Fear	VIII	Interest
IV	Anger	IX	Bewilderment
V	Sadness	X	Determination

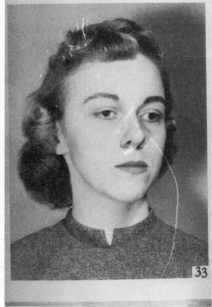

FIGURE 2-1   Facial Communication by Laura Lightfoot.

THE FACIAL MEANING SENSITIVITY TEST   The essential questions in a study of facial expression have been addressed from a variety of perspectives by a number of investigators. Valuable as they may be in the aggregate, the separate studies do not serve to provide the reader of a book like this with any comprehensive answers as to his own ability to encode and decode meanings conveyed by facial expression.[16]

An analogy may serve to emphasize the importance of measuring our ability to use facial expression effectively in interpersonal communication. When Kareem Abdul-Jabbar of the Lakers negotiates a new contract, neither he nor the team's general manager relies on a subjective appraisal of Jabbar's performance on the basketball court. *They rely on precise measurement of performance.* They rely on such exact measures as percentage of field goals and free throws made out of total attempts. In the National Basketball Association two criteria for success are 50 percent accuracy from the field and 80 percent from the free throw line. If Jabbar exceeds these figures, he is in a very strong bargaining position. If he does not, he presumably will try to sharpen his skills.

Similarly, you the reader need a precise measure of your ability to use facial expression in interpersonal communication. If you cannot match or exceed the performance of your peers, you must sharpen your communicative skills.

The facial meaning sensitivity test (hereafter referred to as the FMST) is composed of a set of photographs of forty different facial expressions and is a three-part test. The photographs in the test are all of the same person, Loren Lewis. Loren, an undergraduate at UCLA, was chosen because she was believed to have an expressive and photogenic face. In recognition of her dedication, determination, and sensitivity, this series of photographs is known as the Loren Lewis series.

The facial photographs that make up the FMST were chosen from over 700 photographs from the many sessions held in developing the Loren Lewis series. The extraordinary effort and professional commitment reflected in the series must be attributed in large part to the untiring work of photographer Warren Busse.[17]

Part I of the FMST contains ten photographs representing the ten basic classes of facial meaning. Study the ten photographs and place the numbers in the appropriate blanks of the accompanying chart.

I   II   III

FACIAL MEANING SENSITIVITY TEST, PART I

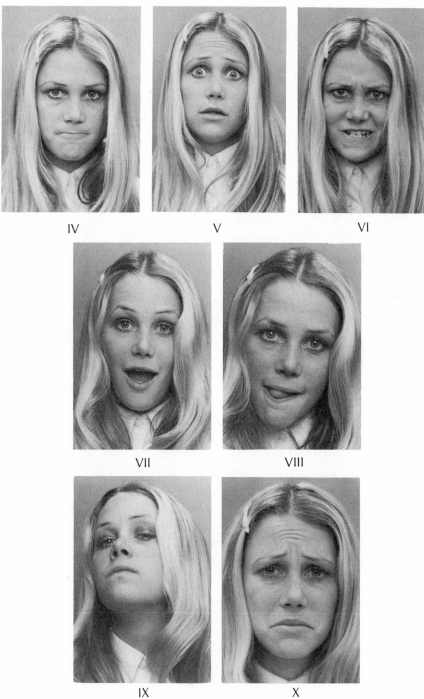

IV   V   VI

VII   VIII

IX   X

FACIAL MEANING SENSITIVITY TEST, PART I (continued)

FACIAL MEANING SENSITIVITY TEST, PART I (continued)

CLASS OF FACIAL MEANING	NUMBER OF EXPRESSION
Disgust	_____
Happiness	_____
Interest	_____
Sadness	_____
Bewilderment	_____
Contempt	_____
Surprise	_____
Anger	_____
Determination	_____
Fear	_____

The correct answers for Part I of the FMST are: disgust = I; happiness = III; interest = VIII; sadness = X; bewilderment = II; contempt = IX; surprise = VII; anger = VI; determination = IV; and fear = V.

On the following pages you will see thirty more photographs of facial expressions. Your task in Part II of the FMST is to group these facial expressions by class of meaning. Three of the photographs, for example, are intended to convey meanings that express some specific kind of disgust and, hence, should be perceived as part of that class of facial meaning. Likewise, among the thirty pictures are three expressions that may be classified as specific kinds of happiness. Your task, then, is to select three photographs which you most closely associate with each of the ten classes of facial meaning. Use each photograph only once.

FACIAL MEANING SENSITIVITY TEST, PART II

CLASS OF FACIAL MEANING	EXPRESSIONS THAT ARE PART OF EACH CLASS (No. of Expression)		
Disgust	_____	_____	_____
Happiness	_____	_____	_____
Interest	_____	_____	_____
Sadness	_____	_____	_____
Bewilderment	_____	_____	_____
Contempt	_____	_____	_____
Surprise	_____	_____	_____
Anger	_____	_____	_____
Determination	_____	_____	_____
Fear	_____	_____	_____

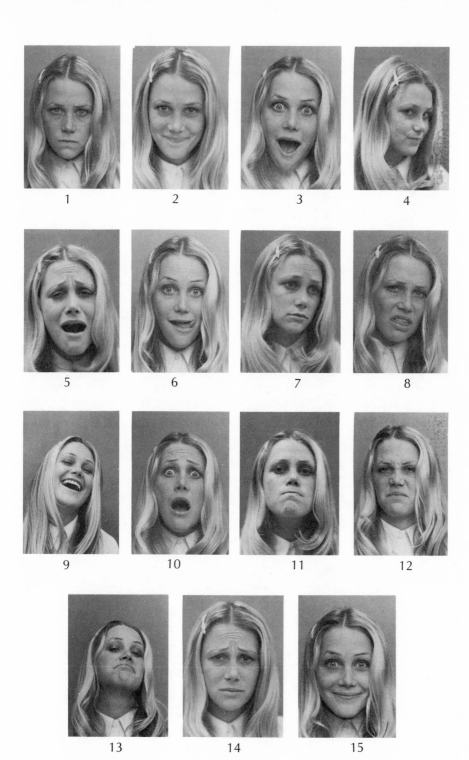

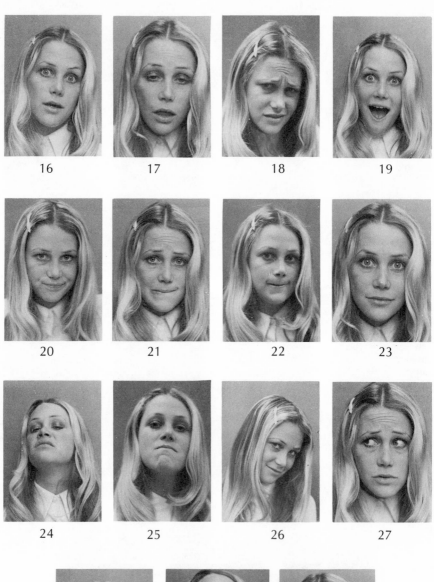

16   17   18   19

20   21   22   23

24   25   26   27

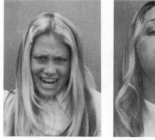

28   29   30

FACIAL MEANING SENSITIVITY TEST, PART II (continued)

The correct choices for Part II of the FMST are: disgust = 8, 12, 30; happiness = 2, 9, 26; interest = 6, 15, 23; sadness = 5, 7, 14; bewilderment = 4, 17,18; contempt = 13, 24, 29; surprise = 3, 16, 19; anger = 1, 20, 28; determination = 11, 22, 25; and fear = 10, 21, 27.

In Part III of the FMST you have a very specific discriminatory task. You must correctly identify very specific kinds of meaning. Consider the preceding thirty photographs three at a time and place the number for the proper photograph in the blank provided. For example, you must decide whether picture 8, 12, or 30 communicates aversion. You must also identify repugnance and distaste in this series of three photographs.

FACIAL MEANING SENSITIVITY TEST, PART III

				PICTURE NO.
SPECIFIC KIND OF FACIAL MEANING				Choose from among the following expressions
Aversion	_____ Repugnance _____	Distaste	_____	8, 12, 30
Amazement	_____ Flabbergasted _____	Astonished	_____	3, 16, 19
Rage	_____ Hate	_____ Annoyance	_____	1, 20, 28
Confusion	_____ Doubt	_____ Stupidity	_____	4, 17, 18
Terror	_____ Anxiety	_____ Apprehension	_____	10, 21, 27
Disdain	_____ Arrogance _____	Superiority	_____	13, 24, 29
Laughter	_____ Love	_____ Amusement	_____	2, 9, 26
Disappointment	_____ Distress	_____ Pensiveness	_____	5, 7, 14
Attention	_____ Anticipation _____	Excitement	_____	6, 15, 23
Stubborn	_____ Resolute	_____ Belligerent	_____	11, 22, 25

The correct choices for Part III of the FMST are: 30, 12, 8; 16, 19, 3; 28, 1, 20; 18, 4, 17; 10, 21, 27; 24, 13, 29; 9, 26, 2; 14, 5, 7; 23, 6, 15; and 11, 22, 25.

Testing of the FMST continues at this point, but sufficient data have already been gathered to suggest that the photographs that represent each of the ten basic classes of meaning come very close to conveying a "pure" meaning. Over three hundred subjects have already taken the FMST and their accuracy of identification for the ten basic photographs exceeds 92 percent. The accuracy-of-identification percentages for Part II (73.5 percent) and Part III (75 percent) are also remarkably high.

The figures provide you with a concrete means to judge your own ability to determine the meaning of facial expression. If your performance exceeded these figures, you can take pride in your sensitivity and acuity of perception. If you did not exceed these figures, finish reading this chapter and wait for a week. Take the FMST again and see if you have improved your decoding capacity by increasing your sensitivity and concentration.[18]

So far you have tested your ability to decode meanings communicated by facial expression. Now you should test your encoding ability. The procedure is simple. Assemble a group of people you know and give them the answer forms for the FMST. Do not give them the Loren Lewis photographs, however. You will assume Loren's role and attempt to communicate each type of meaning to the assembled group via your own facial expression. If their accuracy of identification figures are well below those provided above, you can assume you have a problem. You must practice to improve your capacity to communicate by facial expression.

One obvious question remains. Can you really improve your potential to use facial communication in human interaction? Existing evidence suggests a strong potential for marked improvement. Izard· cites research that suggests that we may improve our ability to communicate facially by as much as 51 percent, although the range is from 5.9 to 51 percent.[19]

My own extensive use of the FMST in the university classroom and in consulting in government and private industry supports this finding. Most individuals markedly improve both their decoding and encoding skills after use of the FMST. A number of executives have emphasized the practical value of using the FMST. One recently reported that the effectiveness of his communication with supervisors in the plant had improved markedly after exposure to the learning experience of using the FMST.

THE FACE: CONNOTATIVE FUNCTION   A substantial number of researchers maintain that the face serves primarily a denotative function in interpersonal communication. They recognize, of·course, that rarely is denotative meaning pure in the sense that the face conveys a single meaning. Ekman and Friesen note pertinently that at any given instant in time the face typically conveys *affect blends* (multiple emotions), rather than a single emotional state.[20] Nonetheless, those who believe that the face functions denotatively operate within a conceptual framework that is easily distinguishable. Central to that framework is the contention that at a given point in time the face communicates one primary type or class of meaning that may be distinguished from all other classes of meaning because of its distinctive referential properties.

This conceptual framework does have some obvious limitations. First, facial communication is treated as basically a unidimensional phenomenon. While "blends" of meanings are conveyed, the objective is to determine the dominant type or class of meaning being conveyed. This suggests a certain perceptual polarity in determining facial meanings. Thus, the dominant meaning of a given expression must be perceived as happiness *or* sadness, not a certain *degree* of sadness. Second, by classifying facial meanings as one type or another we make it difficult to examine the *relationships* between the different meanings.

Few would deny that the face is capable of functioning denotatively in a given context or situation. Many students of facial communication believe, however, that typically the face functions connotatively. That is, at any point in time the face does not convey one dominant meaning but a number of meanings. Those who see the face as functioning connotatively have generally accepted the conceptual model developed by Osgood and associates in their attempt to identify and measure the meanings that are conveyed by verbal means. (See appendix A for a discussion of Osgood's concept of "semantic space" and his dimensional approach to facial communication.)

Until recently the multidimensional framework and the concept of semantic space have not been applied to the study of meanings transmitted by nonverbal means. In the 1950s Schlosberg began research to determine *how* and *how many* meanings are communicated by facial expression. He concluded that facial communication is multidimensional and connotative in nature since the face typically communicates not a single meaning but some combination of meanings. Specifically, Schlosberg found that all meanings communicated by the face are adequately represented by three dimensions:[(1) pleasant/unpleasant; (2) attention/rejection; (3) sleep/tension.[21]]

Since, then, Engen, Levy, and Schlosberg have done follow-up studies that tend to confirm the presence and stability of the same three dimensions in facial communication.[22] The findings of Levy, Orr, and Rosenzweig, and of Abelson and Sermat also support the existence of the same three dimensions of facial expression.[23] While using "pictomorphs" or schematic faces consisting of head shape and eyebrow, eyes, and mouth in various positions rather than photographs as his data base, Harrison also found that facial communication is represented by three dimensions—(1) approval, (2) social potency, and (3) interest.[24] Similarly, in an impressively detailed study Williams and Tolch found that facial expression comprises the dimensions of (1) general evaluation and (2) dynamism, although they did not find the usual third factor.[25]

Recently, Charles Osgood turned his attention from the study of verbal to nonverbal meaning. His objective and conceptual framework were as praiseworthy as in his earlier research on verbal meaning, which led to the development of the semantic differential. He wanted to determine how many dimensions of meaning accurately and adequately characterize facial communication. In pursuit of the objective he treated facial communication as if it took place in "semantic space," which in turn was a multidimensional space composed of some unknown number of dimensions of meaning. Osgood's factor-analytic research suggests that facial communication is composed of the factors of (1) pleasantness, (2) control (represented by such specific expressions as annoyance and disgust versus amazement and excitement), and (3) intensity (rage, scorn, and loathing versus boredom, quiet, and complacency). A fourth, though weaker, factor is labeled interest.

Osgood's research in turn is supported by Mehrabian, who has adopted Osgood's concept of "semantic space" as well as his multidimensional approach to facial communication. Like Osgood, Mehrabian contends that facial communication consists of three dimensions of meaning, which he labels (1) evaluation, (2) potency or status, and (3) responsiveness.[26]

Since so many researchers have found three dimensions of facial meaning, it is easy to come to the conclusion that they have all found the same dimensions. Such a conclusion is not necessarily warranted. Often investigators apply their own, idiosyncratic labels to dimensions of meaning so that direct comparisons are very difficult. In addition, there has probably been a natural tendency to conclude that facial meaning is comprised of the same three dimensions as verbal meaning.

Indeed some of our most impressive and recent research suggests that facial communication comprises not three but at least six dimensions of meaning. In an early study Frijda and Philipszoon found four dimensions of facial meaning, which they identified as (1) pleasant/unpleasant; (2) naturalness/submission; (3) intensity of expression/control of expression; and (4) attention/disinterest. Factor 2 was considered to be a "new" factor not previously found by the "three dimensional" students of facial communication.[27] In a follow-up study Frijda conducted a more detailed study that once again identified four dimensions as well as two additional dimensions. Factor 5 is now labeled understanding/amazed and factor 6 is simple/complicated. Frijda concludes that "the two studies both suggest the importance of not less than five dependent aspects of expression, at least two to three more than in the usual analysis."[28]

There is still dispute as to how many dimensions of meaning can be communicated by facial means. From a review of research to date, we can reach the following conclusions, however: (1) the face communicates *evaluative* judgments through pleasant and unpleasant expressions that suggest whether the communicator sees the current object of his attentions as good or bad; (2) the face communicates *interest* or *disinterest* in other people or in the surrounding environment; (3) the face communicates *intensity* and, hence, degree of involvement in a situation; (4) the face communicates amount of *control* the individual has over his own expressions; and (5) the face probably communicates the intellectual factor of *understanding* or lack of it.

Each of the five dimensions of facial meaning identified above has both positive and negative qualities. For example, while the face may communicate pleasantness in one situation it may communicate unpleasantness in the next. Similarly, the face may communicate interest or disinterest, involvement or uninvolvement, control of emotions or lack of control (which of the qualities for the respective dimensions of facial meaning is considered positive or negative will probably depend on the situation and a number of other factors).

Clearly the face has the potential to produce communication of very high quality where the meanings transmitted and received are virtually identical. The preceding dimensional analysis of meaning in facial expressions establishes that the face is capable of conveying positive reinforcement, interest, involvement, a sense of control over one's self and the immediate environment, and an image of a thoughtful person deliberating on the facts. All of these meanings are of great importance in interpersonal communication and are necessary singly and in various combinations to produce high quality communication.

At the same time, it is now obvious that the face is capable of communicating negative reinforcement, disinterest, withdrawal, lack of control, and a visceral rather than a thoughtful reaction to various messages. The potentially disruptive effects of such meanings are often dependent upon matters such as context.

While facial communication is treated as part of the kinesic system in this chapter, it clearly can be treated as a separate nonverbal communication system. As such a system, it has great potential for the exchange of meaning in interpersonal contexts. First, the face can be used to communicate more emotional meanings more accurately than any other medium in interpersonal communication. Second, because of the visibility of the face and the sensitivity of the complex musculature, facial communication is an efficient and a high-speed medium for communicating meanings—unlike gestures or posture, facial expressions may be changed almost instantly. Finally, facial communication can provide a very useful type of feedback. Without the corrective force of negative feedback, a communicator often continues to transmit confusing, digressive, and irrelevant messages (or messages that exhibit many other undesirable qualities). Facial feedback is a quick and effective way to signal the communicator that such undesirable qualities are present in the communicator's message and that corrective action should be taken.

GESTURAL COMMUNICATION

The face, as we have seen, is a communicative instrument of great importance and flexibility that can accurately convey a great variety of meanings. Except in their wildest dreams, however, people do not communicate by facial expression alone. Clearly we communicate with our body and this fact impels us to ask what do we communicate bodily?

The idea that we talk with our bodies is not farfetched. Goffman has written in detail about our "body idiom." "Body idiom, then, is a conventionalized discourse. We see that it is, in addition, a normative one. That is there is typically an obligation to convey certain information when in the presence of others and an obligation not to convey other impressions, just as there is an expectation that others will present themselves in certain ways."[29]

We may, of course, communicate with our entire body or with some part of it. Such is the basis for distinguishing between posture and gesture. Lamb defines posture as action involving a continuous adjustment of every part of the body with consistency in the process of variation. In contrast, gesture is action confined to a part or parts of the body.[30]

Amount of bodily involvement in communication is not the only basis for distinguishing between gesture and posture. Time used in communicating is also an important factor. Typically, an individual moves quickly from one gesture to another while he maintains a given posture for a much longer period of time. The second or split second is the unit of time with the gesture. In contrast, individuals often assume a given posture for a matter of several seconds and sometimes several minutes.

Scheflen's penetrating research on bodily communication helps clarify the relationship between gesture and posture. He maintains that the three basic units of bodily movement are the *point,* the *position,* and the *presentation*. The point is the nonverbal equivalent of an individual trying to make a point in discussion. While trying to make his point, "an American speaker uses a series of distinctive sentences in a conversation, he changes the position of his head and eyes every few sentences. He may turn his head right or left, tilt it, cock it to one side or the other, or flex or extend his neck so as to look toward the floor or ceiling."[31] Since one part of the body is typically involved for a short time, the point may be seen as a gesture.

In contrast, when several points or gestures are combined we have the *position*. "The position is marked by a gross postural shift involving at least half the body."[32] A typical position is assumed by the discussant who leans toward the person on the opposite side of the conference table.

Finally, the *presentation* "consists of the totality of one person's positions in a given interaction. Presentations have a duration from several minutes to several hours, and the terminals are a complete change in location."[33]

Rather than three units of bodily communication, Ekman and Friesen identify two—body acts and body positions. Body acts are readily observable movements with a definite beginning and end, which could occur in any part of the body or across multiple body parts simultaneously. Body positions are identified by a lack of movement for a discernible period of time—two seconds or more—within any body part.[34] Since Scheflen, and Ekman and Friesen both define the position as a fixed configuration of the parts of the body, the position might be properly identified as postural communication. Gestural communication is more properly associated with the point (Scheflen's term) and the act (Ekman and Friesen's term), since both concepts involve movement of one or more parts of the body with rapid changes to other movements.

Galloway maintains that we can communicate at least seven different types of meaning by gestural means and these types may be defined by seven polar terms: (1) encouraging/restricting, (2) congruity/incongruity, (3) responsive/unresponsive, (4) positive/negative affectivity, (5) attentive/inattentive, (6) facilitating/unreceptive, (7) supportive/disapproving. Gestures are incongruous when they communicate meanings that conflict with the meanings transmitted by vocal qualities and the manifest verbal content of the message. Unresponsive gestures seem to be unrelated to the messages to which they are a response. Negative-affective gestures convey meanings of aloofness, coldness, low regard, indifference, or display of rejection. Unreceptive gestures ignore a request for action and, finally, the meanings conveyed by inattentive and disapproving gestures seem apparent.[35]

As Galloway's research suggests, gestures may function in a disruptive way and serve to lower the quality of communication. Since gestures are much less apt to be under our conscious control than our verbal statements or even our facial expressions, however, they should be a particularly accurate source of information. At minimum they tell us how we are responding and adapting to other individuals and to our environment. Gestural analysis is now being used extensively in psychotherapy as a clue to inappropriate adaptation to one's environment.

Wachtel notes that from the perspective of an individual patient he regards movement, gestures, and postures as "reflecting expressions of drive and defensive processes," as well as conscious and unconscious attempts to communicate with the therapist."[36] Analysis of videotapes of interviews with one patient, a Mrs. L., revealed that "Mrs. L. sat leaning back, with one hand holding the other. Her hands seemed to be acting out a struggle to prevent expression through gesturing, mildly reminiscent of the efforts of Dr. Strangelove to prevent his arm from making a Hitler salute. The hand being held continued to begin movements which were prevented by the holding hand."[37] If gestures tell us so much about maladaptation to one's environment by the mentally ill, it follows that they can tell us much about adaptation to the environment by the average person in interpersonal communication where repression of gestures should be much less frequent.

Mehrabian and Friar have found that gestures, in combination with overall posture, are particularly good indicators of the degree of liking or disliking between communicators and of the perceived status of the communicators.[38]

Bodily cues have also been found to be an accurate indicator of the perceived "genuineness" of the communicators.[39] As the educational and class level of children goes up, so does their ability to accurately interpret gestures.[40] This superiority of middle over lower class children applied to "both the interpretation and transmission of gestures."[41]

THE EYES AS COMMUNICATIVE INSTRUMENTS The head and the eyes must by necessity be treated together, since the position of the head determines both the direction and duration of eye contact (hereinafter referred to as gaze). The type and duration of the gaze probably have a great quantitative impact on interpersonal communication. Without eye contact between the individuals attempting to communicate with each other, facial, gestural, and postural communication becomes impossible.

The question then is how does eye contact, or lack of it, affect the nonverbal component in interpersonal communication. Kendon's strikingly original research suggests that the effects are dramatic. Kendon made detailed sound and film records of two-person conversations. The person attempting to communicate a message was identified as p, while the person to whom the message was directed was identified as q.

The time p spent looking at q varied from 28 percent to 70 percent, depending on the individuals who were communicating. When p began addressing q, over 70 percent of the time he began by looking *away* from q (hereafter referred to as an a-gaze). While p characteristically looked away from q when he *began talking,* he typically looked at q when he *finished talking.* We

> imply here that paying attention to one's interlocutor and planning what to say, are incompatible activities. Analyses of the relationship between sensory input and motor action in serial tasks such as tracking, and studies of selective listening to speech, support the hypothesis that the human being is to be regarded as capable of dealing with only limited amounts of information at once, and this imposes upon him the necessity of distributing his attention among the several facets of the situation where his activity depends upon processing large amounts of information from several sources simultaneously. This is likely to be the case in social interaction.[42]

In addition Kendon found that the time p gazed at q was shorter in duration while p was speaking than when he was listening. Also, p looked at q more when q was conveying positive emotions than when q was conveying negative emotions.[43]

Significantly, the Kendon research demonstrates that the gaze can have a major impact on both the quantity and the quality of interpersonal communication. The sustained use of a-gazes can of course result in an angry disruption or total cessation of communication between individuals. Clearly, the extensive use of the a-gaze by p eliminates the possibility of q providing or p using feedback during those portions of the discussion. Beyond that important fact, the finding that p is much more apt to look at q when q is communicating positive emotions like happiness, pleasure, and agreement than when he is communicating negative emotions such as contempt, disgust, or disappointment is extremely important. Any factor that overemphasizes positive reinforcement in feedback and tends to eliminate negative reinforcement can have disastrous effects on that interaction, particularly if a decision is to result from such a communicative interaction. It is, after all, the critical feedback associated with such negative reactions as disagreement and disappointment that is necessary to eliminate mediocre or inferior ideas from the conversation.

The effects of different types and duration of gaze on interpersonal communication are numerous. Q's look at p's significantly more when the content of the exchange is innocuous and females look at q significantly more (regardless of the sex of q) while exhibiting more affection and a desire to make those with whom they communicate feel included in the conversation.[44] Individuals maintain much more eye contact with those from whom they have reason to expect approval and support.[45] Dominant women exhibit more eye contact than dominant men.[46] The average adult has much more eye contact than the depressed mental patient.[47] As eye contact decreases, so do amount of self-disclosure and degree of intimacy between communicators.[48]

THE HANDS AS COMMUNICATIVE INSTRUMENTS   While the eyes have been a subject of fascination for some time among researchers of nonverbal behavior, the communicative functions of the hands have received limited empirical study. Since even cursory observation suggests that the hands play a central role in gestural communication and that they are used with great frequency and intensity by many communicators, the need for studying manual expression is apparent. Two recent studies do provide some highly illuminating facts about communicative functions of the hands.

Ekman and Friesen have developed a theoretically based classification of hand movements. They contend that there are three major classes of hand movements: emblems, illustrators, and adaptors. Emblems are those nonverbal acts which have a direct verbal translation usually consisting of a word or two, or a phrase for which this precise meaning is known by most or all members of a group, class, or subculture. Examples of emblems are the members of the ground crew bringing the big jet to the airport terminal with hand signals, and duck hunters signaling each other as to where the ducks are.[49]

Illustrators are those hand movements which usually augment the verbal content of a message, but may contradict it. Examples of specific types of illustrators that are frequently used in interpersonal communication are batons (hand movements that accent or emphasize a particular word or phrase) and pictographs (movements that draw a picture in the air of the shape of the referent). By contrast, adaptors are movements first learned as part of an effort to satisfy self needs or body needs or to maintain desired interpersonal contacts. Scratching, squeezing, and covering part of the body for instrumental ends are all examples of adaptors.[50]

This research describes the functions of hand movements in great detail and seems to treat such movements as if they conveyed denotative meaning. Emblems, for example, are hand movements for which a precise meaning is usually known.

While Ekman and Friesen apparently believe that individuals convey denotative meaning by hand movements, Gitin treats hand movements as connotative. Gitin designed an experiment whose main purpose was "to discover the number of factors needed to define the semantic space for manual expression, to name these factors, and to determine their relative importance in describing the semantic space."[51] She found hand movements to comprise four dimensions of meaning, which she labeled *activation, evaluation, dynamism,* and *control.* The first four factors accounted for approximately 50 percent of the variance.[52]

In short, while we currently do not have a consensus as to how hand movements function communicatively or how many meanings are communicated, we do have agreement that the hands are an extremely important communicative instrument.

Clearly gestures communicate a good deal about the communicator and the way he is adapting to his environment, but they are only part of the larger perspective. Unless specially trained in nonverbal communication, most individuals probably find it easier to determine the meanings of postures than gestures.

POSTURAL COMMUNICATION

"Postures . . . speak an eloquent language in social intercourse."[53] Postures do vary among nations and within cultures. Some postures are so highly stylized and formalized that they might be identified as postural codes—good examples are formal military drill, ceremonialized duties, and some forms of religious worship.[54] These types of postures have become almost habitual and, as such, are not of primary interest in this book.

In military drills or religious ritual the postures are predetermined and the communicator is not free to choose the posture which would be prompted by the distinctive characteristics and conditions that define a particular communication situation.

The basic question is relatively simple. What meanings can be communicated by variation in posture when the communicator can choose freely from his postural repertoire? Scheflen maintains that there are three basic types of postures, which in turn convey their distinctive meanings. In the type 1 postural orientation an individual may communicate inclusiveness or noninclusiveness. When your body is placed in such a way as to exclude another person, you are clearly communicating your intent to limit or avoid interaction with that individual. In the type 2 postural orientation the individual may assume the vis-à-vis or parallel bodily orientation. The vis-à-vis orientation is associated with the exchange of rather intimate feelings while the parallel bodily orientation conveys a desire to communicate with the entire group rather than with any individual in it. Finally, with the type 3 postural orientation the individual may assume a congruent or incongruent posture. When you assume a posture similar to that of the person with whom you are communicating, you are probably suggesting that you agree with the individual and that the person is your equal in status. Hence, through postural orientation the individual may communicate involvement or withdrawal, feeling or unresponsiveness, and agreement or disagreement.[55]

Mehrabian maintains that all bodily communication can be adequately described and represented by using the three dimensions of immediacy, power, and responsiveness.[56] Referring to these dimensions as metaphors, Mehrabian maintains that through immediacy, or lack of it, an individual communicates his like or dislike for another individual. He writes:

> Immediacy or closeness in the interaction between two persons includes greater physical proximity and/or more perceptual stimulation of the two by one another. Immediacy between a person and an object involves greater perceptual availability of that object to the person. Approach and immediacy indicate preference, positive evaluation, and liking, whereas avoidance and nonimmediacy indicate lack of preference, dislike, and, in extreme cases, fear.[57]

The power dimension is associated with highly expansive gestures and postures that connote superior status on the part of the communicator. Low power, and hence low status, is associated with rigid and upright posture, extreme bodily tension, and symmetrical stance.[58]

Finally, an individual communicates responsiveness by reacting emotionally to his environment whether in a positive or negative way. A responsive communicator may change his kind of gesture or bodily posture as well as the rate with which he shifts from one gesture or posture to another. Responsiveness is measured by amount of *change* in bodily activity that is communicative. When your body and its moving parts remain in a fixed state you can accurately be described as unresponsive.[59]

In effect, then, Scheflen and Mehrabian agree that we communicate immediacy (or nonimmediacy) and responsiveness (or unresponsiveness) by bodily means. In addition, Scheflen feels that we communicate agreement (or disagreement) and Mehrabian contends that we communicate power or status.

Gestures and postures can be used to communicate a variety of meanings. While they can convey the types of emotion being experienced by a communicator, for example, they tend to be more reliable indicators of the *intensity* rather than the kind of emotion being conveyed. In one fascinating study where subjects were asked to identify the "meaning" of twenty-five stick figures, "those stick figures for which greatest agreement obtained (involved) *intense* inner dynamics, for example, rejecting, welcoming, violent anger."[60]

In summary, bodily communication takes the form of gestures and posture. Communicators use many gestures—identified as points or body acts—in a short period of time and these are capable of communicating a great variety of meanings. By contrast, postures are more limited in number and meaning. We probably communicate at least four types of meaning by different postural orientations: (1) immediacy, (2) responsiveness, (3) agreement, and (4) power or status.

At the conceptual level, the reader should have a much better idea of how movement is used to communicate meaning. The communicative potential of the face, gesture, and posture is no longer a matter of speculation. It has been empirically demonstrated.

At the applied level, the reader may justifiably ask how one uses facial expression, gesture, and posture to improve the quality of his own communication. The reader should certainly be concerned about making optimum use of movement to exchange meanings accurately and efficiently in order to attain his own communicative purposes.

Such a question could, of course, lend itself to an absurd answer. It could suggest that effective communication by movement is simply a matter of finding the proper instruction manual. Furthermore, it could conjure up some fanciful but disturbing images: (1) the reader spending hours in front of the bathroom mirror making faces in an attempt to expand facial expressiveness; (2) the reader huddled over a handbook of gestures in the vain hope that a mind-boggling array of gestures might be used to communicate consensually shared meanings; (3) the reader assuming bizarre postures in social situations in the unreal hope that he will be able to enhance his own status, increase his power over others, or give others a feeling that he is more responsive to their own attempts at communication.

Communication by movement does not lend itself to any easy formula for success or any isometric-type exercises that will quickly transform the communicator from a fumbling recluse into a self-assured extrovert. Indeed, too many factors affect meaning by movement—variation in context, function, personality, and values are among the most important factors—to justify a detailed and unqualified set of prescriptions for communicative success.

On the other hand, some practical suggestions that are grounded in empirical research should definitely help readers improve the quality of their own communication.

Specifically, I would suggest the following:

1. The use of the facial meaning sensitivity test will increase the communicator's sensitivity to the nuances of facial meaning and hence the capacity to decode and encode accurately meanings exchanged by this important medium.

2. Careful study of the dimensions of meaning conveyed by gestures should greatly enhance an individual's ability to define the nature of the relationship to others with whom he or she is communicating. Such study should increase one's capacity to exert some degree of control over a discussion or a conversation and allow a much more accurate assessment of the sincerity and truthfulness of those who are using gestures. (Consistency between gestures, and between gestures and verbal meaning, is generally considered to be the best clue as to whether an individual is engaging in sincere communication.)

3. Sustaining eye contact during critical points of communicative interaction clearly increases an individual's ability to communicate meaning directly and efficiently and, perhaps more importantly, provides the opportunity to use corrective feedback from others. Using such feedback is necessary to adjust messages to assure their high quality.

4. Communicators can take careful note of their own posture and the posture of others as very accurate indicators of the degree of involvement, forcefulness, and activity they are communicating, and the degree to which such important communication qualities are being reciprocated. In fact, calculated use of posture may determine whether one dominates others or is being dominated by them.

Additional ways of improving the quality of communication by movement are limited to a large degree by the individual's creativity and the systematic application of concepts such as those discussed in this chapter.

CONCLUSION

This chapter treats movements that communicate meanings as part of the kinesic communication system. The major components of the kinesic communication system are facial, gestural, and postural communication.

The chapter describes the nature and functions of communication by movement. Specifically it illustrates how individuals (1) may measure the accuracy with which they communicate meaning by movement, (2) may measure the accuracy with which they perceive meanings communicated to them by movement, and (3) may improve their capacity to communicate by movement.

Major emphasis is placed on facial expression because of the vitally important role of the face in interpersonal communication. The chapter examines two competing viewpoints on how the face functions communicatively—the denotative and connotative functions. Those researchers who believe that the face functions denotatively assert that eight to ten distinctive classes of meaning can be conveyed facially. In contrast, those who believe that the face functions connotatively see facial expression composed of three to six different dimensions of meaning that are conveyed through semantic space.

The facial meaning sensitivity test provides the means for testing and improving the quality of one's facial communication, with particular emphasis on the accuracy with which one decodes facial meaning. With diligent use of the facial meaning sensitivity test the reader should be able to increase the capacity to exchange shared meaning with others by facial expression.

Gestural communication conveys different meanings and serves different functions. The gestural functions of the hands and eyes are particularly important. The type and duration of eye contact have a great quantitative, as well as qualitative, impact on interpersonal communication. The hands are associated with three classes of movement—emblems, illustrators, and adaptors—and can be used to convey four dimensions of meaning—activation, evaluation, dynamism, and control.

Postural communication is primarily useful in communicating immediacy (or nonimmediacy), responsiveness (or unresponsiveness), agreement (or disagreement), and power (or status).

There are numerous ways to improve the quality of one's communication by movement.

NOTES

[1] The reader may wonder at this point how communication is defined. Many problems present themselves in any attempt to define communication but two stand out: (1) Can we distinguish communication behavior from other types of behavior? and (2) Does all communication behavior involve the conscious attempt to exchange meaning? For an illuminating but esoteric discussion of such central problems confronting those who attempt to define communication, see M. Wiener, S. Devoe, S. Rubinow, and J. Geller, "Nonverbal Behavior and Nonverbal Communication," *Psychological Review*, 79 (1972), 185-214. Wiener and colleagues argue persuasively that communication behavior may be distinguished from other types of behavior because it involves the exchange of *shared* meaning. Autistic gestures, for example, which do not convey shared meaning for two or more individuals, represent a type of noncommunicative behavior. The question of conscious intent is perhaps more difficult to answer. First, we should recognize that a large part of nonverbal behavior involves the conscious attempt of individuals to exchange one or more meanings. In my view, however, encoding with conscious intent is not a necessary condition for communication to take place. As long as consensually shared meanings are exchanged we have communication behavior. Extending upon the views of Wiener et al., therefore, we define *communication* as the *process of exchanging consensually shared meanings. Nonverbal communication* is the *process of using the nonverbal communication systems for the exchange of consensually shared meanings.* Clearly these definitions exclude the old linear model of communication. While we often write of movement communicating meaning, for example, we are not thinking of a simple stimulus/response relationship. We are thinking of the complex type of processes described in chapters 2 through 9 and the functional *relationships* between the nonverbal communication systems that will be described in detail in chapter 10.

[2] R. L. Birdwhistell, *Kinesics and Context* (Philadelphia: University of Pennsylvania Press, 1970), p. 192.

3 R. L. Birdwhistell, "Kinesics and Communication," in *Explorations in Communication,* ed. E. Carpenter and M. McLuhan (Boston: Beacon Press, 1960), p. 54.

4 R. L. Birdwhistell, *Introduction to Kinesics* (Louisville: University of Kentucky Press, 1952), p. 17.

5 P. Ekman, W. V. Friesen, and P. Ellsworth, *Emotion in the Human Face: Guidelines for Research and an Integration of the Findings* (New York: Pergamon Press, 1972), p. 1.

6 J. Frois-Wittmann, "The Judgment of Facial Expression," *Journal of Experimental Psychology,* 13 (1930), 113-51.

7 H. Schlosberg, "Three Dimensions of Emotion," *Psychological Review,* 61 (1954), 81-88.

8 Frois-Wittmann, "Judgment of Facial Expression," 122.

9 Ibid., 126.

10 W. S. Hulin and D. Katz, "The Frois-Wittmann Pictures of Facial Expressions," *Journal of Experimental Psychology,* 18 (1935), 482-89.

11 R. S. Woodworth, *Experimental Psychology* (New York: Henry Holt, 1938).

12 N. Levy and H. Schlosberg, "Woodworth Scale Values of the Lightfoot Pictures of Facial Expression," *Journal of Experimental Psychology,* 60 (1960), 122.

13 Ibid.

14 Ekman, Friesen, and Ellsworth, *Emotion in the Human Face,* pp. 57-65.

15 C. E. Izard, *The Face of Emotion* (New York: Appleton-Century-Crofts, 1971), p. 216.

16 Ibid., pp. 427-29. Izard does provide what he calls an emotion labeling experiment and an emotion recognition experiment in his stimulating book, but both differ significantly in form and function from the facial meaning sensitivity test.

17 Busse was an undergraduate at UCLA at the time that he took and meticulously processed and catalogued all the prints. The level of his professionalism is attested to by the fact that he interrupted work on the photographs for this book several times to fly to Europe to cover Grand Prix races as a free-lance photographer.

18 For practical reasons we used only one subject to pose the photographs that make up the Loren Lewis series. For this reason some minorities in our society may find it somewhat more difficult to judge Loren's expressions than expressions posed by a member of their own minority group. Existing evidence does not suggest that this is a serious problem.

19 Izard, *The Face of Emotion,* p. 218.

20 P. Ekman and W. V. Friesen, "The Repertoire of Nonverbal Behavior: Categories, Origins, Usage, and Coding," *Semiotica,* 1 (1969), 75.

21 Schlosberg, "Three Dimensions of Emotion," 81-88.

22 T. Engen, N. Levy, and H. Schlosberg, "A New Series of Facial Expressions," *American Psychologist,* 12 (1957), 264-66.

23 L. H. Levy, T. B. Orr, and S. Rosenzweig, "Judgments of Emotion from Facial Expression by College Students, Mental Retardates, and Mental Hospital Patients," *Journal of Personality,* 28 (1960), 341-49; R. P. Abelson and V. Sermat, "Multidimensional Scaling of Facial Expressions," *Journal of Experimental Psychology,* 63 (1962), 546-54.

24 R. P. Harrison, "Picture Analysis: Toward a Vocabulary and Syntax for the Pictoral Code: with Research on Facial Communication," unpublished dissertation, 1967.

25 F. Williams and J. Tolch, "Communication by Facial Expression," *Journal of Communication,* 15 (1965), 20.

[26] Mehrabian, "A Semantic Space for Nonverbal Behavior," *Journal of Consulting and Clinical Psychology*, 35 (1970), 248-49.

[27] N. H. Frijda and E. Philipszoon, "Dimensions of Recognition of Expression," *Journal of Abnormal and Social Psychology*, 66 (1963), 46.

[28] N. H. Frijda, "Recognition of Emotions," in *Advances in Experimental and Social Psychology*, ed. L. Berkowitz (New York: Academic Press, 1969), 178-79.

[29] E. Goffman, *Behavior in Public Places* (London: Collier-Macmillan, 1963), p. 35.

[30] W. Lamb, *Posture and Gesture* (London: Gerald Duckworth, 1965), p. 16.

[31] A. E. Scheflen, "The Significance of Posture in Communication Systems," *Psychiatry*, 27 (1964), 320. See also A. E. Scheflen, *Body Language and the Social Order* (Englewood Cliffs, N. J.: Prentice-Hall, 1972), pp. 61-103, for an interesting, illustrated discussion of movement as a means of controlling the behavior of other persons.

[32] Scheflen, "Significance of Posture," 321.

[33] Ibid., 323.

[34] P. Ekman and W. V. Friesen, "Head and Body Cues in the Judgment of Emotion: A Reformulation," *Perceptual and Motor Skills*, 24 (1967), 713-16.

[35] C. Galloway, "Nonverbal Communication," *Theory and Practice*, 7 (1968), 172-75.

[36] P. Wachtel, "An Approach to the Study of Body Language in Psychotherapy," *Psychotherapy*, 4 (1967), 97-100.

[37] Ibid.

[38] A. Mehrabian and J. T. Friar, "Encoding of Attitude by a Seated Communicator via Posture and Position Cues," *Journal of Consulting and Clinical Psychology*, 33 (1969), 330-36.

[39] J. G. Shapiro, C. P. Foster, and T. Powell, "Facial and Bodily Cues of Genuineness, Empathy, and Warmth," *Journal of Clinical Psychology*, 24 (1968), 233-36.

[40] G. Michael and N. Willis, Jr., "The Development of Gestures as a Function of Social Class, Education, and Sex," *Psychological Record*, 18 (1968), 515.

[41] Ibid., 518. For a review and critique of recent publications that treat communication by movement, see J. H. Koivumaki, "Body Language Taught Here," *Journal of Communication*, 25 (1975), 26-30.

[42] A. Kendon, "Some Functions of Gaze Direction in Social Interaction," *Acta Psychologica*, 26 (1967), 34-35.

[43] Ibid., 46.

[44] R. Exline, D. Gray, and D. Schuette, "Visual Behavior in a Dyad as Affected by Interview Content and Sex of Respondent," *Journal of Personality and Social Psychology*, 1 (1965), 202, 208.

[45] J. S. Efran and A. Broughton, "Effect of Expectancies for Social Approval on Visual Behavior," *Journal of Personality and Social Psychology*, 4 (1966), 103-7. Also J. S. Efran, "Looking for Approval: Effects on Visual Behavior of Approbation from Persons Differing in Importance," *Journal of Personality and Social Psychology*, 10 (1968), 21-25.

[46] S. L. Gray, "Eye Contact as a Function of Sex, Race, and Interpersonal Needs," unpublished dissertation, Case Western Reserve University, 1971.

[47] M. K. Hinchliffe, M. Lancashire, and F. J. Roberts, "A Study of Eye Contact Changes in Depressed and Recovered Psychiatric Patients," *British Journal of Psychiatry*, 119 (1971), 213-15.

[48] G. R. Breed, "Nonverbal Communication and Interpersonal Attraction in Dyads," unpublished dissertation, 1969.

[49] P. Ekman and W. V. Friesen, "Hand Movements," *Journal of Communication,* 22 (1972), 353-58.

[50] Ibid., 358–62.

[51] S. R. Gitin, "A Dimensional Analysis of Manual Expression," *Journal of Personality and Social Psychology,* 15 (1970), 272.

[52] Ibid., 275.

[53] G. W. Hewes, "The Anthropology of Posture," *Scientific American,* 196 (1957), 123.

[54] Ibid., 130.

[55] A. E. Scheflen, "Significance of Posture," 326-29.

[56] A. Mehrabian, *Silent Messages* (Belmont, Calif.: Wadsworth, 1971), pp. 113-18.

[57] Ibid., p. 114.

[58] Ibid., pp. 115-16.

[59] Ibid., pp. 116-18.

[60] B. G. Rosenberg and J. Langer, "A Study of Postural-Gestural Communication," *Journal of Personality and Social Psychology,* 2 (1965), 593-97. Ekman and Friesen note that "the face usually is an affect display system, while the body shows adaptive efforts of the organism to cope with the affect state" ("Head and Body Cues in the Judgment of Emotion," 718).

3

THE PROXEMIC COMMUNICATION SYSTEM: PROXIMATE ENVIRONMENT

Spatial relationships communicate meaning. Different meanings are communicated in many different ways and places throughout our universe. The beliefs, values, and, ultimately, the meaning of a culture are communicated by the way people handle space. The German culture has long emphasized orderliness and clearly defined lines of authority. Hence, Germans object to individuals who literally "get out of line" or those who disregard signs such as "keep out" and "authorized personnel only," which are intended to stipulate the approved use of space.[1]

Americans are inclined to think of space and react to it as "empty." In contrast, in Japan it is space—and not objects—that communicates meanings. The Japanese customarily assign specific meanings to specific types of spaces. For this reason, intersections are given names in Japan, but not streets. The particular space with its functional characteristics is the thing. Particular places with their identifying spaces supersede other factors in importance.[2]

Whereas Americans covet privacy by demanding their own offices and maintain their distance from others through the use of large and elevated desks, the Arabs know no such thing as "privacy" in public and are offended by anything less than intimacy of contact while carrying on a conversation. Such conversations characteristically feature "the piercing look of the eyes, the touch of the hands, and the mutual bathing in the warm moist breath during conversation [which] represent stepped-up sensory inputs to a level which many Europeans find unbearably intense."[3] In effect, the Arab's use of space and olfactory stimuli communicates two meanings. It invites and demands intense involvement in interpersonal communication, and it assures the withdrawal of those who reject this method of relating.

Meanings communicated by the use of space are not confined to the sometimes gross differences between cultures. Differences within cultures are probably of more practical importance and they abound. Spatial needs seem to vary dramatically among citizens of a nation, residents of a city, and even members of a family. To satisfy those needs some people appear to define and protect a set of spatial boundaries with a persistence and vigor that would put the family dog or cat to shame. The fact that one man's spatial boundaries may enclose another man's territory makes for the distinctive type of communication problem that is associated with spatial needs and their frustrations. What is intimate distance to one person may be impersonal distance to the next; what seems proper communicating distance to one person may seem personally insulting to another. What seem like spacious living accommodations to one family may seem like an oppressively claustrophobic dungeon to another.

In our use of space there is often a great disparity between the meanings we intend to communicate and the meanings we actually do communicate. At a recent cocktail party, another professor engaged my wife in conversation. While so doing, he was standing so close to my wife that she became extremely uncomfortable and, unconsciously, began backing away. Later she noted that she was eventually backed up against a wall on the other side of the room and in her continuing attempts to maintain a comfortable distance ran one of her nylons. By his use of space the professor probably intended to communicate a sense of involvement, pleasure, and vigor. By his inadvertent violation of my wife's invisible spatial boundaries he had communicated a drastically different set of meanings—most noticeably an unseemly aggressiveness.

As the need to understand the meaning of movement resulted in the specialized type of research known as kinesics, the need to understand how man communicates through his use of space produced a search for knowledge known as proxemics. The innovator of proxemic research is Edward T. Hall. He coined the term *proxemics* because it suggests that proximity, or lack of it, is a vitally important factor in human interaction.

In broadest perspective Hall defines proxemics as the study of how man unconsciously structures microspace—the distance between men in the conduct of daily transactions, the organization of space in his houses and buildings, and ultimately the layout of his towns.[4] He views proxemics as "the study of man's perception and use of space,"[5] which focuses on the "interrelated observations and theories of man's use of space as a specialized elaboration of culture."[6]

For our purposes *proxemics* is defined as the *study of how man uses space to communicate*. There can be little doubt that man does communicate through his use of space. Hall emphasizes that "spatial changes give a tone to a communication, accent it, and at times even override the spoken word. The flow and shift of distance between people as they interact with each other is part and parcel of the communication process."[7]

The discussion above suggests that man may communicate meaning by his use of both microspace and macrospace. The use of either microspace or macrospace involves what may be properly called proxemic behavior although the terminology sometimes changes as we cross disciplinary lines. Thus some researchers see the use of microspace as part of small group ecology, while others view the use of macrospace as part of municipal or regional planning. While the concepts of microspace and macrospace may be profitably treated together, they will be examined in separate chapters in this book so that each can be covered in depth. This chapter emphasizes how man uses his microspace to communicate; that is, it stresses how human beings use small amounts of space to communicate in face-to-face encounters with other individuals. Chapter 4 focuses on the communicative impact of the manner in which men structure their macrospace with particular emphasis on how men use space within the boundaries of the city in which they live.

The most obvious way we communicate through our use of microspace is by the distance we maintain, or attempt to maintain, between ourselves and those with whom we are communicating. Except for the rare eccentric who carries a tape measure around with him, people rarely measure interpersonal distance by highly objective means. Even as meaning is perception, so is meaning defined by spatial criteria.

"Interpersonal distance is a constellation of sensory inputs that is coded in a particular way" and, as such, is apt to be influenced by both physiological and psychological factors.[8] The eight types of sensory inputs that affect our perception of interpersonal distance are seen by one authority as "subsystems [that] are operable within a system of proxemic behavior. Eye contact and directness of facing (SF-SP axis), for instance, seem to make up one such subsystem, one which might serve to classify a certain group along a direct / indirect dimension. Closeness and touching perhaps make up another such subsystem, one which might serve as an indicator of what groups were contact and non-contact."[9]

Hall identifies eight types of sensory inputs which he believes individuals use in determining how much interpersonal distance they have between themselves and the persons with whom they are communicating. They are: (1) postural-sex identifiers; (2) sociofugal-sociopetal orientation (SFP axis); (3) kinesthetic factors; (4) touch code; (5) retinal combinations; (6) thermal code; (7) olfaction code; (8) voice loudness scale.

Postural-sex identifiers simply suggest whether a man *or* woman is communicating while standing, sitting, or prone. The sociofugal-sociopetal orientation is a measure of how directly two individuals are facing each other. The sociopetal orientation has people facing each other with maximum contact while the sociofugal orientation has people back to back with minimum contact. The touch code is a measure of the amount of touching that occurs between individuals and ranges from mutual caressing to a point where there is no contact. Obviously, mutual caressing requires minimum interpersonal distance between people.[10]

The five other types of sensory inputs are illustrated in Figure 3-1. As Figure 3-1 indicates, a given individual determines interpersonal distance by the way he perceives basic types of stimuli that are available to him. In effect "the ways in which humans perceive and structure microspace is a function of all the senses."[11]

Looking from left to right across Figure 3-1 the reader will notice that interper-

CHART SHOWING INTERPLAY OF THE DISTANT & IMMEDIATE RECEPTORS IN PROXEMIC PERCEPTION

FEET: 0 1 2 3 4 5 6 7 8 10 12 14 16 18 20 22 30

INFORMAL DISTANCE CLASSIFICATION

- **INTIMATE** — CLOSE | NOT CLOSE
- **PERSONAL** — CLOSE | NOT CLOSE
- **SOCIAL-CONSULTIVE** — CLOSE | NOT CLOSE
- **PUBLIC**

KINESTHESIA

- HEAD, PELVIS, THIGHS, TRUNK CAN BE BROUGHT INTO CONTACT OR MEMBERS CAN ACCIDENTLY TOUCH.
- HANDS CAN REACH AND MANIPULATE ANY PART OF TRUNK EASILY.
- HANDS CAN REACH AND HOLD EXTREMITIES EASILY BUT WITH MUCH LESS FACILITY THAN ABOVE. SEATED CAN REACH AROUND & TOUCH OTHER SIDE OF TRUNK. NOT SO CLOSE AS TO RESULT IN ACCIDENTAL TOUCHING.
- ONE PERSON HAS ELBOW ROOM.
- 2 PEOPLE BARELY HAVE ELBOW ROOM. ONE CAN REACH OUT AND GRASP AN EXTREMITY.
- JUST OUTSIDE TOUCHING DISTANCE.
- OUT OF INTERFERENCE DISTANCE. BY REACHING ONE CAN JUST TOUCH THE OTHER.
- 2 PEOPLE WHO'S HEADS ARE 8' – 9' APART CAN PASS AN OBJECT BACK & FORTH BY BOTH STRETCHING.
- MANDATORY RECOGNITION DISTANCE BEGINS HERE.
- NOT CLOSE BEGINS AT 30'–40'.

THERMAL RECEPTORS

- **CONDUCTION (CONTACT)**
- **RADIATION** — NORMALLY OUT OF AWARENESS. ANIMAL HEAT AND MOISTURE DISSIPATE (THOREAU)
- CULTURAL ATTITUDE

OLFACTION

- **WASHED SKIN & HAIR** — OK --- TABOO ---
- **SHAVING LOTION–PERFUME** — VARIABLE | OK --- TABOO ---
- **SEXUAL ODORS** — ANTISEPTIC OK OTHERWISE TABOO
- **BREATH** — TABOO
- **B O** — TABOO
- **SMELLY FEET** — TABOO

VISION

DETAIL VISION (VIS.–OF FOVEA 1°)
- VISION BLURRED FACE PHYSICALLY DISTORTED
- ENLARGED DETAILS OF IRIS EYEBALL, PORES OF FACE. FINEST HAIRS
- DETAIL OF FACE SEEN. FINE BLOOD VESSELS IN CORNEA, NOSE SKIN TEETH CONDITION EYE LASHES HAIR ON BACK OF NECK
- SMALLEST BLOOD VESSELS IN EYE LOST. HEAD HAIR SEEN CLEARLY
- FINE LINES OF FACE FADE, SEE OUT OF RIGHT EYE WINK LIP MOVEMENT SEEN CLEARLY
- SHARP FEATURE DISSOLVE. EYE COLOR NOT DISCERNIBLE. WINK SEEN, VERBAL HEAD BOBBING MORE PRONOUNCED
- SNELLEN'S STANDARD FOR DISTANT VISION EMPLOYING ANGLE OF MINIMUM SEPARABLE CHART. A PERSON WITH 20–40 VISION HAS TROUBLE SEEING EYES & EXPRESSION AROUND EYES THOUGH EYE BLINK IS VISIBLE

CLEAR VISION (VIS.–AT MACULA 12° HOR., 3° VERT)
- 25" × 3" ON EYE, NOSTRIL OR MOUTH
- 1.3 OF FACE EYE EAR OR MOUTH AREA (FACE DISTORTED)
- 6.25" × 3.66" UPPER OR LOWER FACE
- NOSE PROJECTS WHOLE FACE SEEN FACE UNDISTORTED
- 10" × 2.5" LOWER UPPER OR LOWER FACE
- 20" × 5" 1 OR 2 FACES
- 3½' × 7.5 FACES OF TWO PEOPLE
- ENTIRE CENTRAL FACE INCLUDED
- 4.7' × 1'6" TORSOS OF TWO PEOPLE
- 6'3" × 17' TORSOS OF 4 OR 6 PEOPLE

60° SCANNING
- HEAD
- HEAD AND SHOULDERS
- HEAD & SHOULDERS
- UPPER BODY CAN'T COUNT FINGERS
- UPPER BODY & GESTURES
- WHOLE BODY
- WHOLE SEATED BODY VISIBLE. PEOPLE OFTEN KEEP FEET WITHIN OTHER PERSON'S 90° ANGLE OF VIEW
- WHOLE BODY HAS SPACE AROUND IT. POSTURAL COMMUNICATION BEGINS TO ASSUME IMPORTANCE

PERIPHERAL VISION
- HEAD AGAINST BACKGROUND FIELD VISUAL FIELD FAR OVER LIFE SIZE
- WHOLE BODY MOVEMENT IN HANDS, FINGERS VISIBLE
- OTHER PEOPLE SEEN IF PRESENT
- OTHER PEOPLE BECOME IMPORTANT IN PERIPHERAL VISION

HEAD SIZE
- SENSATION OF BEING CROSSED EYED
- OVER NORMAL
- NORMAL SIZE
- NORMAL TO BEGINNING TO SHRINK
- VERY SMALL

ADDITIONAL NOTES
- 6% OF TASKS IN THIS RANGE
- 22% FALL IN THIS RANGE
- DIMMICH FL. & FARNSWORTH D VISUAL ACUITY TASKS IN A SUBMARINE NEW LONDON 1951
- PEOPLE & OBJECTS SEEN AS ROUND UP TO 12–15 FEET
- ACCOMODATIVE CONVERGENCE ENDS AFTER 15' PEOPLE & OBJECTS BEGIN TO FLATTEN OUT

TASKS IN SUBMARINES

ARTISTS OBSERVATIONS OF GROSSER
- VERY PERSONAL DISTANCE
- A PICTURE PAINTED AT 4–8 OF A PERSON WHO IS NOT PAID TO "SIT" IS A PORTRAIT. AT 13–16 THE MODEL HAS TO DOMINATE.
- BODY IS 1/3 SIZE
- 4.7' × 1'6" FULL LENGTH STATE PORTRAITS HUMAN BODY SEEN AS A WHOLE. COMPREHENDED AT A GLANCE WARMTH AND IDENTIFICATION CEASE

ORAL AURAL

- GRUNT / GRUNG
- WHISPER — SOFT VOICE INTIMATE STYLE
- CONVENTIONAL MODIFIED VOICE CASUAL OR CONSULTIVE STYLE
- FULL VOICE CONVERSATION
- TOO FAR FOR CONVERSATION
- LOUD VOICE WHEN TALKING TO A GROUP MUST RAISE VOICE TO GET ATTENTION FORMAL STYLE
- FULL PUBLIC SPEAKING VOICE FROZEN STYLE

NOTE: THE BOUNDARIES ASSOCIATED WITH THE TRANSITION FROM ONE VOICE LEVEL TO THE NEXT HAVE NOT BEEN PRECISELY DETERMINED.

sonal distance is measured in feet with intimate distance judged to be 0 to 1½ feet and public distance ranging from 10 to around 25 feet. To perceive and interpret these various types of stimuli, we must of course use our different senses; Hall refers to the senses we use in determining interpersonal distance as distant and immediate receptors. For example, we perceive kinesthetic stimuli (bodily movements) with our eyes while we perceive thermal stimuli (degrees of bodily heat) with our sense of touch, and we perceive olfactory stimuli (different bodily odors) with our sense of smell.

The communicator, therefore, relies on these types of stimuli, singly and in combination, as a measure of interpersonal distance and, then, as his guide in determining whether he is using them to maintain appropriate interpersonal distance between himself and the individual with whom he is communicating. For example, when you get close enough to another person to smell his breath you can be confident that you are at least as close as the personal distance and maybe as close as the intimate distance—within 4 feet of the individual or closer. If the person has a bad breath, the condition is acceptable if it can be detected no more than a foot and a half away— after all, Americans seem to have a compulsion for detoxifying their breath with mouthwash and hardly consider the breath a legitimate means of communicating as the Arabs do. Since the breath is considered such a personal thing in the American culture, it is acceptable to have bad breath at the intimate distance but taboo to have halitosis at the personal level. Similarly body odor is acceptable at the intimate distance but taboo at the personal distance.

The same principle applies to sexual odors and smelly feet. We use them as measures of interpersonal distance, but when they are detectable beyond a certain culturally prescribed distance they become the object of disapproval or even censure. The reader can probably think of a number of instances where this principle was in operation. For example, if an attractive girl stands right next to you in an elevator and exudes both the natural odors of her femaleness and the artificial scents of her perfume cabinet, you may very well be turned on. On the other hand, if the same girl reeks with the redolence of a musk oxen when she is still 10 feet from the elevator, you will probably be turned off and begin speculating about her personal hygiene.

Figure 3-1 demonstrates that our sense of hearing (see Oral Aural) works much the same way as the olfactory sensory receptors which determine interpersonal distance. If you can hear someone grunting and groaning or whispering you can be fairly confident that the individual is at intimate distance or no more than 1½ feet from you. Likewise, when you hear someone using a very loud voice you can use this as an indicator that the individual is at public distance, that is, at least 10 but not more than 25 feet from you. If he is talking in a very loud voice and is only a foot from you, you will disapprove even as you would disapprove if you were 15 feet away and the individual was whispering to you.

By studying Figure 3-1 very carefully you may come to accept Hall's thesis that the way man perceives and determines interpersonal distance, and ultimately uses microspace, is a function of all his senses. While our various senses may help us determine and define spatial relationships, it is important to note that each sense has such distinctive qualities that it can function as a separate communication system. This

FIGURE 3-1 Proxemic Perception in Interpersonal Communication. From E. T. Hall, ''Proxemics,'' *Current Anthropology*, 9 (1968), 92. (c) 1968 by The University of Chicago Press.

is a concept that will be explored in detail in a later chapter where we compare and contrast the various systems that are part of nonverbal communication.

MAN'S PROXIMATE ENVIRONMENT

Man uses space to communicate. When he uses that space which can be perceived directly and unaided by his senses, he is working within his proximate environment. The proximate environment "includes everything that is physically present to the individual at a given moment. The proximate environment of a student in a classroom includes his desk, the other students, the teacher, the blackboard, the windows, the doorway. His proximate environment does *not* include the football team practicing outside or his friend in another classroom."[12] The space that man attempts to control in his proximate environment is microspace, while the space that exists beyond the immediate reach of his senses is macrospace.

SPACE   The concepts of space, distance, and territory are extremely important in understanding the nature of communication within the proximate environment. Since we have already established that all of our senses may be applied in our perception and use of space, space is multidimensional from a perceptual standpoint. For example, there is both visual space and auditory space and they are of an entirely different character.

Visual information tends to be less ambiguous and more focused than auditory information.[13] "Since the optic nerve contains roughly eighteen times as many neurons as the cochlear nerve, we assume it transmits at least that much more information. Actually, in normally alert subjects, it is probable that the eyes may be as much as a thousand times as effective as the ears in sweeping up information."[14] In addition "at temperatures of 0° C (32° F) at sea level, sound waves travel 1,100 feet a second and can be heard at frequencies of 50 to 15,000 cycles per second. Light rays travel 186,000 miles a second and are visible at frequencies of 10,000,000,000,000,000 cycles per second."[15]

In spite of the fact that we may use either visual or auditory sense receptors to perceive space, most proxemic research focuses on what we might call visual space.[16] The concept of visual space in nonverbal communication is somewhat analogous to the concept of silence in verbal communication. Though both are devoid of content in a sense, the ways we use them may be rich in communicative significance. Edward Hall, for example, contends that our culture places severe constraints on the ways in which we may use space. In fact he maintains that there are basically three types of space: fixed-feature, semifixed-feature, and informal space.[17]

Fixed-feature space refers to the characteristic arrangement of rooms by function within the home. Thus, formal meals are rarely served in the bedroom and bookcases rarely line the walls of the bathroom. Ironically, the fixed-features that define how space is to be used in the home are often quite dysfunctional. For example, "the lack of congruence between the design elements, female stature and body build (women are not usually tall enough to reach things), and the activities to be performed while not obvious at first, is often beyond belief."[18] Floor plans for some of our newest houses make such ineffective and inefficient use of space as to suggest that the architect was either demented or a sadist, or both. How many times have you visited a home where one had to walk through the living room to get from the kitchen to the dining room?

Semifixed-feature space refers to the placement of objects in the home. These objects may be moved but are typically left in one place for a substantial period of time. While the functional value of furniture arrangement should serve as an important criterion in determining how effectively semifixed-feature space is being utilized, the communicative value may be even more important (this assumes the arrangement of objects in the home often serves a number of functions that are not primarily communicative). As we shall soon demonstrate, perhaps the most important communicative function of semifixed-feature space is the degree to which it promotes involvement or withdrawal among those who are using the space.

Informal space is the third type of space and is a concept with which we should all be rather familiar. Unlike fixed-feature or semifixed-feature space, there are no physical factors in informal space to identify its unstated boundaries. While objects do not make assumptions about the proper spatial relationships people should assume vis-à-vis one another, human beings do make such assumptions. Sommer writes perceptively that "the best way to learn the location of invisible boundaries is to keep walking until somebody complains. Personal space refers to an area with invisible boundaries surrounding a person's body into which intruders may not come. . . . Personal space is not necessarily spherical in shape, nor does it extend equally in all directions. (People are able to tolerate closer presence of a stranger at their sides than directly in front.) It has been likened to a snail shell, a soap bubble, an aura, and 'breathing room.' "[19] The implications of violating personal and societal expectations about the use of personal space will be examined later in this chapter.

Semifixed-feature space and informal space are of primary importance in interpersonal communication because of the great variety of ways in which they can be used to transmit meaning. While the uses vary widely, they are generally seen as serving one of two communicative functions. Either they bring people together and stimulate involvement (in which case they are serving a sociopetal function) or they serve to keep people apart and promote withdrawal (in which case they are serving a sociofugal function). Sommer, who has been a leader in research on the sociopetal and sociofugal functions, maintains that we transmit very different connotative meanings by the way we use space. He refers to the sociofugal function as "sociofugal space" and finds that sociofugal spatial arrangements or conditions suggest the following meanings: large, cold, impersonal, institutional, not owned by an individual, overconcentrated, without opportunity for shielded conversation, providing barriers without shelter, isolation without privacy, and concentration without cohesion.[20] Predictably, sociopetal spatial arrangements connote an opposite and generally much more positive set of meanings.

To date, the attempts to create sociopetal or sociofugal space has focused largely on the arrangement of furniture, often in mental hospitals. Craik et al. emphasize that "clearly, one goal of environmental psychological research on psychiatric wards is to identify and achieve sociopetal conditions."[21] Sommer illustrates how to create sociofugal or sociopetal space in Figure 3-2.

As Figure 3-2 indicates, spatial relationships are most sociopetal, and most conducive to the involvement of the communicators, when individuals are seated side by side. Conversely, sociofugal conditions prevail when individuals are seated diagonally across from one another at the ends of tables.

The creation of sociopetal or sociofugal spatial relationships is not limited to the *placement* of furniture. Many large companies, particularly the franchise restaurants, are interested in how such furniture as tables can be *designed* to affect not only atmosphere but customers. Both factors are thought to bear a significant relationship to the number of people a restaurant can handle and, hence, to its profits.

One major restaurant was sufficiently interested in the effects of creating sociopetal or sociofugal conditions as to partially subsidize a research project on the effects of table barriers. Figure 3-3 shows the "no barrier" condition, Figure 3-4 the "with barrier" condition, and Figure 3-5 shows via videotape four discussants interacting in the "with barrier" condition.

While researcher Ted Kaye has not completed his Ph. D. research on this particular project, his pilot study suggests that a table barrier may have significant effects on the flow, direction, and quality of communication as well as on the postural orienta-

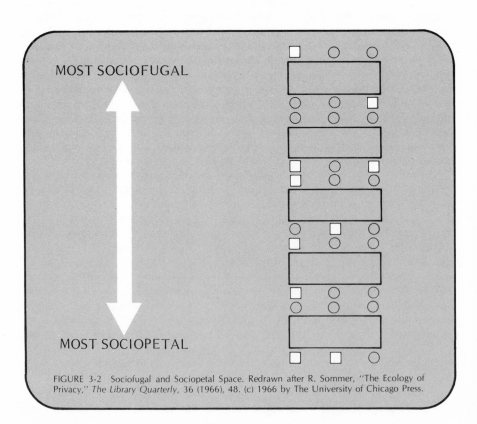

FIGURE 3-2 Sociofugal and Sociopetal Space. Redrawn after R. Sommer, "The Ecology of Privacy," *The Library Quarterly*, 36 (1966), 48. (c) 1966 by The University of Chicago Press.

tion of the communications. In addition there may be some relationship between the "with barrier" condition, the perceived ability of the discussants to communicate effectively with one another, and their success in maximizing interpersonal contact. Kaye's exciting research on "sociofugal screens," or more specifically table barriers in the present case, helps to demonstrate some of the practical applications of knowledge about the Proxemic Communication System.[22]

DISTANCE   At least in theory, space has no finite barriers and becomes a tangible concept only when people or objects occupy space and individuals attempt to define its boundaries. In contrast, distance is a relational concept and is typically measured in terms of how far one individual is from another.

Once again, Hall has done pioneering work in attempting to identify and classify the distances people use to separate themselves from others in order to satisfy their various needs. If you glance back at Figure 3-1 you will note that Hall identifies four types of informal distance: intimate, personal, social-consultative, and public.

Type 1, or intimate distance, is easily distinguishable because of the number and intensity of sensory inputs of which the communicators are intensely aware. Intimate distance has both a close and a far phase. In the close phase we engage in intimate activities such as lovemaking, which requires extensive contact of head and the erogenous zones of the body. By contrast the distance that separates people in the far phase (6 to 18 inches) means that it is difficult to make contact between intimate parts of your own and your partner's body. Intimate distance of either type is considered inappropriate in public by the typical middle-class American.[23] The fact that people have rather well defined proxemic expectations about appropriate distance for different types of communication implies that violation of those expectations can have a very disruptive effect on subsequent communication. If you have ever been in a packed elevator you should be able to appreciate the disruptive effect of a situation where possibly all of the people in the elevator are violating each other's proxemic expectations.

Type 2, or personal distance, is "the distance that an individual customarily places between himself and other organisms."[24] The more prosaic among writers have taken to associating personal distance with an imaginary "body bubble" which surrounds an individual and into which only the foolhardy or uninformed will intrude. However, the notion of a body bubble hardly seems consistent with Hall's contention that personal distance has both a close and far phase.

At the close phase of personal distance (1½ to 2½ feet) the three-dimensional quality of objects becomes readily apparent. American proxemic expectations dictate that husband and wife can, and often should, communicate at this distance. For a husband or wife to consistently communicate at this distance with some other member of the opposite sex is to invite gossip, rumors, and certainly the ire of the involved spouse. In contrast the far phase of personal distance (2½ to 4 feet) precludes truly intimate interaction no matter what the identity of the interactants.[25]

Type 3, or social distance, separates interactants far enough so that communication reflects an impersonal quality. The close phase of social distance (4 to 7 feet) is the characteristic communicating distance of people who work together or are attending a casual gathering. On the other hand, people are far enough away from each other at the far phase of social distance that sustained eye contact between subordinates and superordinates is often avoided and people can give the impression of *not*

FIGURE 3-3

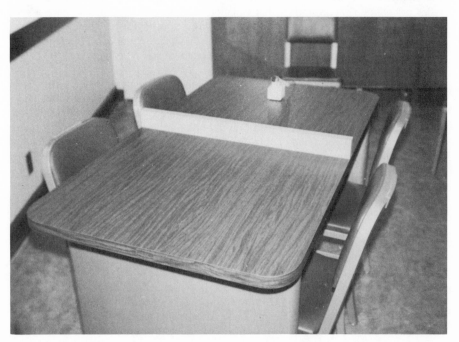

FIGURE 3-4

FIGURE 3-5

seeing someone else without appearing to be rude. At this "distance the finest details of the face, such as the capillaries in the eyes, are lost" and "desks in the offices of important people are large enough to hold visitors at the far phase of social distance."[26]

Finally, the shift from social to public distance has tangible and important implications for interpersonal communication. At the public distance of 12 to 25 or more feet the types of nonverbal meanings that one attempts to transmit and the meanings that can be perceived vary rather dramatically. At the close phase of public distance (12 to 25 feet) an alert communicator can give the appearance that he has received no message or he can remove himself physically from the situation. If he does communicate at this distance, he will find that the interaction is of a very formal nature.

The communicative features of the far phase of public distance (25 feet or more) can be even more disruptive than the distinctive features of the close phase of public distance. Beyond 25 feet the voice loses much of its potential to transmit meanings accurately and facial expressions and movements must become rather expansive to be recognized. As Hall emphasizes, "much of the nonverbal part of communication shifts to gestures and body stance."[27]

The four basic types of informal distance are illustrated in Figure 3-6.

TERRITORY   The concept of territory has vast implications for interpersonal communication and many of these implications remain unexplored. Much of our knowledge of the concept comes from studies which illustrate how animals identify and defend clearly delineated territories by means of instinct. Territoriality in this sense is a

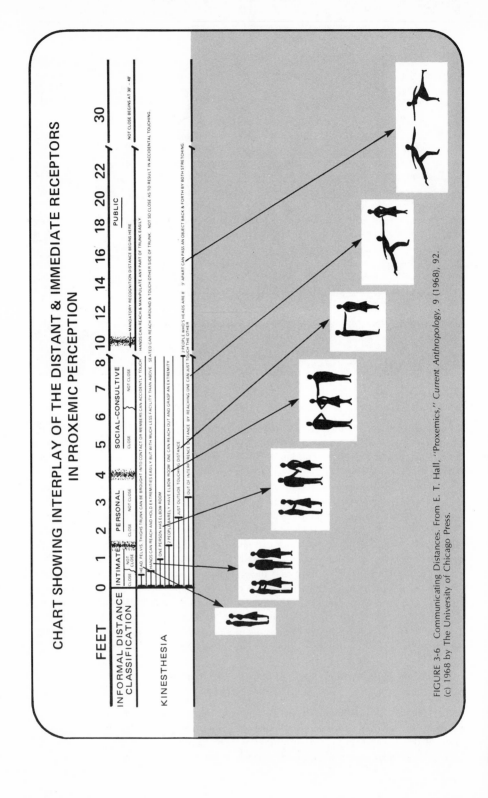

CHART SHOWING INTERPLAY OF THE DISTANT & IMMEDIATE RECEPTORS IN PROXEMIC PERCEPTION

FEET   0   1   2   3   4   5   6   7   8   10   12   14   16   18   20   22   30

INFORMAL DISTANCE CLASSIFICATION

INTIMATE   PERSONAL   SOCIAL-CONSULTIVE   PUBLIC

CLOSE / NOT CLOSE   CLOSE   NOT CLOSE   CLOSE   NOT CLOSE   NOT CLOSE BEGINS AT 30' - 40'

MANDATORY RECOGNITION DISTANCE BEGINS HERE

HANDS CAN REACH & MANIPULATE ANY PART OF TRUNK EASILY   NOT SO CLOSE AS TO RESULT IN ACCIDENTAL TOUCHING

KINESTHESIA

HEAD, PELVIS, THIGHS, TRUNK CAN BE BROUGHT INTO CONTACT OR MEMBERS CAN ACCIDENTLY TOUCH

HANDS CAN REACH AND HOLD EXTREMITIES EASILY BUT WITH MUCH LESS FACILITY THAN ABOVE   SEATED CAN REACH AROUND & TOUCH OTHER SIDE OF TRUNK

ONE PERSON HAS ELBOW ROOM

PEOPLE BARELY HAVE ELBOW ROOM. ONE CAN REACH OUT AND GRASP AN EXTREMITY

JUST OUTSIDE TOUCHING DISTANCE

OUT OF INTERFERENCE DISTANCE BY REACHING ONE CAN JUST TOUCH THE OTHER

2 PEOPLE WHO'S HEADS ARE 8'   9' APART CAN PASS AN OBJECT BACK & FORTH BY BOTH STRETCHING

FIGURE 3-6 Communicating Distances. From E. T. Hall, "Proxemics," *Current Anthropology*, 9 (1968), 92. (c) 1968 by The University of Chicago Press.

basic concept in the study of animal behavior; it is defined as behavior by which an organism characteristically lays claim to an area and defends it against members of its own species, and in so doing assures the propagation of the species by regulating density.[28]

In the animal world, and to an amazing extent among humans, territoriality serves the following functions: (1) protection from predators; (2) maintenance of status; (3) determination of flight and fight distance; (4) determination of "critical distance or the narrow zone separating flight distance from attack distance"; (5) maintenance of personal distance, the spacing that noncontact animals maintain between themselves and their fellows; (6) establishment of social distance, a psychological distance at which an animal apparently begins to feel anxious when it exceeds its limits.[29]

Sommer recognizes that the concept of territoriality now has great relevance for the study of human behavior even if humans do not define their territories exclusively or even primarily by instinctual means. He sees territory as an area controlled by an individual, family, or other face-to-face collectivity with the emphasis on physical possession, actual or potential, as well as defense.[30] The essential nature of territoriality is captured by Sommer's delightfully homespun ruminations on the concept:

> Since human communication is based largely on symbols, territorial defense relies more on symbols such as name plates, fences, and personal possessions than on physical combat, or aggressive displays. . . . Salesmen have, and actively defend, individual territories. One criterion of territoriality is . . . the home team always wins . . . [and] an animal on its own territory will fight with more vigor. . . . [Hence] a male on its own territory is almost undefeatable against males of the species.[31]

If the concept of territoriality is so important in explaining aggressive involvement and withdrawal in interpersonal communication, the obvious question is: what types of territories are typically defined and defended? Writing from a broad perspective, Lyman and Scott observe that there are four kinds of territories: public, home, interactional, and body.[32]

Public territories are those areas where individuals may enter freely. Great constraints are placed on human interaction within public territories, however, because of explicit laws and social traditions. The struggles to desegregate buses, restaurants, and beaches suggest that the term *public territory* can have a very restricted connotation for those who choose to enter and atempt to interact within the territory.

By contrast, home territories feature freedom of interaction by individuals who claim the territory.[33] Fraternities, private clubs, and even gay bars all constitute home territories. "Home territories sometimes enjoy a proactive status beyond the presence of their inhabitants in the form of reserved chairs, drinking mugs, signs or memorabilia that serve to indicate special and reserved distinctions."[34]

Interactional territories are areas where individuals congregate informally. A party, a local pool hall, and an informal meeting on campus may all serve as interactional territories. While every territory makes a claim of boundary maintenance, interactional territories are unique in that they have boundaries that may move.[35]

Finally, body territories consist of the space that is occupied and used by our bodies. A very explicit set of rules and norms governs the way we may use our own or someone else's body. It is interesting to note that one type of territory is potentially convertible to another type and this principle applies with particular force to the conversion from body territory to home territory. As more than one frustrated lover learned as they cautiously invaded their dates' body territory, the risks of territorial violation sometimes exceed the possible pleasures of consummation. Marriage or mutual consent can convert body territory into home territory for both parties "to handle and use as [they] desire."[36]

While Lyman and Scott write from a broad perspective and view individuals as operating primarily within physical territories, Goffman suggests the provocative thesis that "eight territories of the self" exist and their changeable boundaries are a function of both variability in individual behavior and environmental conditions. These eight territories of the self he sees as (1) personal space, (2) stalls, (3) use space, (4) turns, (5) sheath, (6) possessional territory, (7) information preserves and (8) conversational preserves.[37]

Of the eight territories of the self identified by Goffman, six seem particularly relevant and important for interpersonal communication. First, the stall is space with clear-cut boundaries that individuals claim exclusively for their own use. Telephone booths and parking places are obvious examples of stalls. Unlike personal space, stalls have highly visible and fixed boundaries that can easily be protected from intruders.

While stalls identify themselves by their structure, use space identifies itself by its function. Use space is that space immediately surrounding us which we must have to perform personal functions such as lighting our cigarette or swinging at a golf ball. Our claim to use space is typically respected by others in close proximity to us because they realize that they would require similar space to perform similar functions.

The turn represents a territorial claim based on both structure and function. Expressions such as "take your turn" and "get in line, Bud" suggest the nature of this type of territorial behavior. We have been socially conditioned to expect that such territorial claims will be honored.

The sheath, which consists of both the skin covering and clothes, functions "as a preserve in its own right, the purest kind of egocentric territoriality."[38]

Much like the sheath, possession territory is closely identified with the human body. Rather than skin or clothes as coverings for the body, possessional territory is made up of "any set of objects that can be identified with the self and arrayed around the body wherever it is."[39] Objects such as gloves and handbags often function as markers to delineate the boundaries of possessional territory.

THE DISRUPTIVE EFFECTS OF VIOLATING PROXEMIC NORMS AND EXPECTATIONS

The violation of individual distance is the violation of society's expectations; the invasion of personal space is an intrusion into a person's self-boundaries. Individual distance may be outside the area of personal space—conversation between two chairs across the room exceeds the boundaries of personal space, or individual distance may be less than the boundaries of personal space—sitting next to someone on a piano bench is within the expected distance but also within the bounds of personal space and may cause discomfort to the player. If there is only one individual present, there is infinite individual distance, which is why it is useful to maintain a concept of personal space, which has also been described as a *portable* territory, since the individual carries it with him wherever he goes although it disappears under certain conditions, such as crowding.[40]

Whether we are talking about the concept of space, distance, or territory individuals have very definite expectations which specify what is acceptable proxemic behavior. Many of these expectations are sufficiently stable and enduring, and are shared by enough people, that they might be called proxemic norms. While it is difficult to generalize about proxemic behavior, one generalization seems to warrant a good deal of support. Simply put, the violation of proxemic expectations, or norms, results in consistently disruptive effects on the communication between two or more people.

Unfortunately, few studies of the communicative impact of the violation of spatial expectations, in particular, have been undertaken. Existing studies have been undertaken in the somewhat antiseptic and unreal environment of classrooms, libraries, and mental hospitals. In the classroom and library studies typically a "plant" is used and one or more unsuspecting subjects is approached. The plant approaches the seated subject and violates his spatial expectations in different ways under different experimental conditions. For example, in one library study a plant decreased immediacy between himself and the subject by successively (1) sitting adjacent to the subject, (2) across from the subject, (3) two seats adjacent to the subject, and (4) three seats adjacent to the subject. Only eighteen of eighty subjects actually left during the ten-minute period when they were intruded upon and during which, presumably, some of their proxemic expectations were being violated.

While few subjects withdrew completely their behavior was affected. As immediacy increased so did leaning and sliding away from the intruder and blocking with elbows. In short, a number of defensive measures were employed to avoid the effects of spatial intrusion and the experimenters concluded that "a variety of nonverbal behaviors may be reciprocally altered to maintain a relatively constant degree of interpersonal involvement."[41] Similarly, Sommer found in his library studies that "no matter how great the pressure on the study facilities, room density was limited to one person per station at the eighteen tables."[42]

Studies using a similar methodology in mental hospitals revealed similar results although total physical withdrawal (87 percent of the experimental subjects) was the characteristic response to the violation of proxemic expectations. Moreover, "the intensity of [the subject's] reaction [flight or withdrawal] is influenced by many factors including territoriality, the dominance-submission relationship between invader and victim, the locus of the invasion, the victim's attribution of sexual motives to the intruder, etc."[43]

Assessing the effects of the violation of proxemic norms and expectations is very difficult, however, because we have a limited amount of data to suggest how individuals relate to each other spatially outside of the laboratory. In one of the few highly realistic studies on the subject, Baxter observed dyads at the Houston zoo in order to determine preferred interaction distances of subcultural groups in this country. He found that Mexican-Americans of all age and sex groupings interacted "most proximally"—were consistently closest together; Anglos were intermediate and blacks stood most distant; children interact more proximally than adults; male-female groups interacted most proximally, female-female groups were intermediate, and male groups were most distant.[44] The interaction of two-person groups in the zoo seemed to support the notion that groups communicating in "differing spatial conditions may be relying to varying degrees on different channels of information and may be employing different communication mechanisms."[45]

The communicative impact of violating (or conforming) to spatial expectations has been measured largely in quantitative terms. The questions asked are straightforward. How many people will physically withdraw from a social situation if their spatial boundaries have been violated? How many people in rather close physical proximity to him will an individual tolerate? How much space do people require to separate themselves from others? When we turn from space to the second of the important concepts discussed in this chapter, distance, we find investigators concerned with the relationships between distance and both quantity and quality of communication.

In fairness we must observe that a number of studies have found that much proxemic behavior, involving the distances that separate individuals, is highly facilitative in that the proper use of distance can stimulate involvement, elicit much positive reinforcement, and help build stable and trusting interpersonal relationships. Since this section deals with the disruptive impact of the violation of proxemic norms and expectations, however, only passing attention will be given to the facilitative effects of appropriate and desirable proxemic behavior.

Distance between communicators seems to have a particularly important impact on amount of eye contact and, as we already know, insufficient eye contact can have highly undesirable effects on interpersonal communication. The affiliative-conflict theory of eye-contact supports the conclusion that as distance between communicators increases recorded eye contact also increases. Ironically, this relationship is the reverse of what we might expect and desire in interpersonal communication. In separate interviews with thirty-seven Yale College men an interviewer found subjects sitting 6 feet from him were spending 60 percent of the interview gazing at him (the interviewer) while subjects 2½ feet away were spending 40 percent of their time gazing at him.[46] This finding should be qualified, however, in view of Stephenson and Rutter's conclusion that with increasing distance, gaze directed at the ear and shoulder is increasingly recorded as eye contact, and that increasing eye contact with increasing distance is a function of observer performance, not subject performance.[47] Perhaps the more limited amount of eye contact when distances between people are minimal may be attributed to an avoidance reaction associated with physical discomfort. At the very least it is interesting to note that the galvanic skin response (GSR) of subjects was significantly less intense when the distance separating them from others was 9 feet rather than 1 foot. Furthermore, the GSR was greatest when an individual was approached frontally.[48]

Distance between individuals seems to have its greatest impact on interpersonal relationships. The research literature is quite consistent in supporting the conclusion that increasing the distance between yourself and the person(s) with whom you are communicating will help create a negative impression of yourself and may help destroy interpersonal trust. One interesting study directly examined impression formation as a function of interpersonal physical distance. As distances between individuals increased, their personal impressions of each other became much more negative. Individuals not only viewed each other as less socially active, as distance between them increased, but as less friendly, aggressive, extroverted, and dominant.[49]

Conversely, it now seems clear that one of the quickest means of gaining the approval of those persons with whom you communicate[50] and of being liked is to minimize the distance between yourself and those persons.[51] Indeed, even with children, the closer they are to one another when interacting the more likely their interactions are to be friendly.[52] More specifically, attitude change has been found to be greatest for the friendly speaker when he minimizes distance between himself and his audience.[53]

While some of the research findings may not fit neatly into one conceptual framework, the available evidence does strongly suggest that the type of relationships and nature of communication between two people is strongly affected by the distance they maintain between each other. One researcher went so far as to suggest that distance might be employed as an operational definition of interpersonal relationships.[54]

If the violations of individual expectations about space and distance typically produce identifiably disruptive effects on interpersonal communication, the effects of violating territorial expectations are often more extreme and dramatic. "Territory-like preserves are the central claim in the study of co-mingling. . . . The central offense is an incursion, intrusion, encroachment, presumption, transgression, defilement, besmearing, contamination—in short a violation."[55]

Goffman identifies at least five types of territorial violation that seem particularly important in the conceptual framework of this chapter: (1) closer placement of your body to another individual than your status allows; (2) use of your body, and hands, to "touch" and "defile the sheath or possessions of another"; (3) the use of the penetrating gaze to transgress or circumvent societal expectations; (4) use of the voice or other sounds, to intrude upon someone's auditory preserve; (5) bodily excreta which violate social expectations by virtue of spatial proximity to the communicator.[56]

The disruptive effect of each of the five types of territorial invasion on interpersonal communication can be rather clearly illustrated. First, the physical distance that should separate you and the person with whom you are communicating is a function of social distance. In a high proportion of instances, when superordinates and subordinates communicate the subordinate approaches the superordinate. The status of the subordinate determines how closely he may approach the superordinate. The offices of major business executives are typically arranged to provide cues to subordinates as to proper approaching distance and, consequently, warn the subordinate of that point at which the executive's personal territory has been violated. Second, the body and hands can be used to violate the territorial preserve of another. Rape is the most extreme example while unsatisfactory conformance to your host's conception of rules of etiquette is perhaps one of the least significant types.

Third, territories can be violated through the penetration of the eyes. "Although in our society the offense that can be committed by intrusive looks tends to be slighter than other kinds of offensive incursions, the distance over which the intrusion can occur is considerable, the directions multiple, the occasions of possible intrusion very numerous and the adjustments required in eye discipline constant and delicate."[57] Not only is the penetrating glance often perceived as a type of behavior which is demeaning, but also a type of behavior which can be used to establish dominance at the expense of the individual to whom it is directed.

Fourth, violation of personal territories by high volume, or otherwise objectionable sounds, is becoming an increasingly pervasive and insidious form of disruption. Such violations may occur in an intimate encounter when the sound level is considered inappropriate or when sounds are simply insinuative because they have sexual or other connotations. As any city planner knows, this type of territorial invasion may occur in a much larger setting. Citizens groups in virtually every major city are attempting to tighten restrictions against noise from commercial jet airliners, noise from motorbikes, or just plain vehicular traffic. Many cities have become the defendants in large lawsuits as the result of their alleged violations of the plaintiff's auditory territory or preserves.

Finally, bodily excreta can function as a particularly disruptive type of territorial violation. It is important to note that odor, a direct by-product of bodily excreta "operates over a distance, and in all directions; unlike looking, it cannot be cut off once it violates and may linger in a continued place after the agency has gone."[58] More directly while spittle, snot, perspiration, food particles, blood, semen, vomit, urine, and fecal matter are perhaps not disruptive in themselves when confined to the original source of excretion, they can become extremely odious when present while individuals are attempting to communicate at the intimate or even personal distance.

In short, space and spatial relationships quite clearly communicate meanings. When the meanings communicated violate personal or social expectations, we are dealing with a source of communicative disruption of almost unlimited implications.

CONCLUSION

Spatial relationships communicate a great variety of meanings. The need to understand how and what man communicates through his use of space is producing a search for knowledge known as proxemics. Proxemic research has, to a large extent, been based on Hall's finding that humans use eight types of sensory inputs in determining how much interpersonal distance they have and should have between themselves and the person(s) with whom they are communicating: (1) postural-sex identifiers, (2) sociofugal-sociopetal orientation, (3) kinesthetic factors, (4) touch, (5) vision, (6) heat, (7) smell, and (8) vocal qualities.

This chapter concentrates on the factors that affect interpersonal communication within man's proximate environment, or microspace, while the next chapter emphasizes those broader variables that affect communication in macrospace. To understand the full importance and significance of our proxemic behavior the meaning and functions of the three related concepts of space, distance, and territory must be clear.

The three types of space—fixed-feature, semifixed-feature, and informal—differ drastically in their functional value in communication. Semifixed and informal space are particularly important since they can be used to create either sociopetal or sociofugal conditions. Sociopetal conditions are associated with those spatial relationships which are most conducive to the involvement of the communicators, while sociofugal conditions often feature barriers or "screens" which tend to result in withdrawal of the communicators.

The major types of distance—informal, intimate, personal, social-consultative, and public—each dictate the type of communication that is socially acceptable.

Particular emphasis should be placed on the concept of territory as it applies to human communication. Territory is defined as an area controlled by an individual, family, or other face-to-face collectivity with emphasis on physical possession, actual or potential, as well as defense. The four major types of territories are public, home, interactional, and body. Significantly, the provocative notion of "eight territories of the self" can be used to explore the notion of territoriality in greater specificity.

Finally, the chapter explores the communicative impact of the violation of individual and societal expectations with regard to space, distance, and territory. Studies of the violation of spatial expectations have focused largely on the degree to which such violations will result in the withdrawal of those involved, although the effects are hardly limited to that variable.

The violation of distance norms or expectations has perhaps its greatest impact in negatively affecting interpersonal relationships. As distance is increased between yourself and another individual his impression of you will become less positive. Specifically, you will be viewed as less socially active, less friendly, less aggressive, less extroverted, and less dominant. While the violation of distance expectations can be highly disruptive, the potentially facilitative impact of maintaining proper distances may be even greater.

Finally, the disruptive effects of territorial violation on communication are very important. Violation of body territory affects the quality of interpersonal communication in strikingly negative ways.

There can be little doubt that man communicates many things in many ways through his use of space or that such communication constitutes a system which may be properly identified as the Proxemic Communication System. The importance of what we already know about that system should stimulate us to press for answers to the many important questions about proxemic communication which remain unanswered.

NOTES

[1] E. T. Hall, *The Hidden Dimension* (New York: Doubleday, 1969), pp. 136-37. See H. Morseach, "Aspects of Nonverbal Communication in Japan," *Journal of Nervous and Mental Disease*, 157 (1973), 262-77.

[2] Ibid., 150-53.

[3] Ibid., 158.

[4] E. T. Hall, "A System for the Notation of Proxemic Behavior," *American Anthropologist*, 65 (1963), 1003.

[5] E. T. Hall, "Proxemics," *Current Anthropology*, 9 (1968), 83.

[6] Hall, *The Hidden Dimension*, p. 1.

[7] E. T. Hall, *The Silent Language* (New York: Doubleday, 1959), p. 204. See also O. M. Watson, "Proxemics and Proxetics," paper presented at the 67th annual meeting of the American Anthropological Association, Seattle, Washington, November 21, 1968, for an interesting argument that Hall is actually studying proxetics (approaching spatial behavior as a system of behavior with the approach from the outside, using criteria that are external to the system) rather than proxemics (which studies behavior from within a single, culturally specific system).

[8] Hall, "Proxemics," 94.

[9] O. M. Watson, "On Proxemic Research," *Current Anthropology*, 10 (1969), 223.

[10] Hall, "System for Notation of Proxemic Behavior," 1006-11.

[11] Watson, "Proxemics and Proxetics," 2.

[12] R. Sommer, "Man's Proximate Environment," *Journal of Social Issues*, 22 (1966), 60.

[13] Hall, *The Hidden Dimension*, p. 43.

[14] Ibid., p. 42.

[15] Ibid., p. 43.

[16] Sommer, "Man's Proximate Environment," 60. Sommer cites research done by the Office of Civil and Defense Mobilization that focused on minimal space requirements for human beings: (1) 12 square feet per person in a well-ventilated shelter, (2) 10 square feet if triple-tiered bunks are provided along with 2 square feet additional for storage, (3) 8 square feet per person is adequate in a well-designed shelter.

[17] Hall, *The Hidden Dimension*, pp. 103-12.

[18] Ibid., p. 105. R. Sommer, *Tight Spaces: Hard Architecture and How to Humanize It* (Englewood Cliffs, N.J.: Prentice-Hall, 1974), pp. 81-101, deals graphically with the forces that lead to the dysfunctional use of space in institutions such as the school.

[19] R. Sommer, *Personal Space: The Behavioral Basis of Design* (Englewood Cliffs, N.J.: Prentice-Hall, 1969), p. 26.

[20] R. Sommer, "Sociofugal Space," *American Journal of Sociology*, 72 (1967), 655.

[21] K. H. Craik, "Environmental Psychology," in *New Directions in Psychology*, ed. T. M. Newcomb (New York: Holt, Rinehart and Winston, 1970), p. 37.

[22] T. Kaye, "A Proposal for a Pilot Study of the Communication Effects of Sociofugality within the Small Decision-Making Group," unpublished paper, UCLA, December 11, 1972. (Figures 3-3, 3-4, and 3-5 are reprinted with T. Kaye's permission.)

[23] Hall, *The Hidden Dimension*, pp. 117-18.

[24] R. Sommer, "Studies in Personal Space," *Sociometry*, 22 (1959), 247.

[25] Hall, *The Hidden Dimension*, pp. 119-20.

[26] Ibid., p. 122.

[27] Ibid., p. 125.

[28] Ibid., pp. 7-8.

[29] Ibid., pp. 1-15.

[30] Sommer, "Man's Proximate Environment," 61.

[31] Ibid.

[32] S. M. Lyman and M. B. Scott, "Territoriality: A Neglected Sociological Dimension," *Social Problems*, 15 (1967), 237-41.

[33] Ibid., 238.

[34] Ibid., 239.

[35] Ibid., 240-41.

[36] Ibid., 241.

[37] E. Goffman, *Relations in Public* (New York: Harper & Row, 1971), p. 40.

[38] Ibid., pp. 32-38. The examples that Goffman uses to illustrate the stall, use space, the turn, and the sheath are illuminating.

[39] Ibid., p. 38.

[40] Sommer, *Personal Space,* p. 27. In my course in communication theory—Speech Communication 520-720, fall 1974, and spring 1975—students recently went into Athens, Georgia, and violated individual's proxemic expectations, and then wrote papers on their experiences. One student in particular wrote incisively about the defensive behavior and withdrawal which resulted from his violation of spatial barriers. His favorite tactic was to enter a nearly empty bus, disregard all the empty seats, and sit down in the same seat with an isolated bus rider.

[41] M. L. Patterson, S. Mullens, and J. Romano, "Compensatory Reactions to Spatial Intrusion," *Sociometry,* 34 (1971), 116-20.

[42] R. Sommer, *Personal Space,* p. 46.

[43] N. J. Felipe and R. Sommer, "Invasions of Personal Space," *Social Problems,* 14 (1966), 211-13.

[44] J. C. Baxter, "Interpersonal Spacing in Natural Settings," *Sociometry,* 33 (1970), 449-50.

[45] Ibid., 454.

[46] G. Goldberg, C. Kiesler, and B. E. Collins, "Visual Behavior and Face-to-Face Distance During Interaction," *Sociometry,* 32 (1969), 48.

[47] G. M. Stephenson and D. R. Rutter, "Eye Contact, Distance, and Affiliation: A Re-Evaluation," *British Journal of Psychology,* 61 (1970), 391-92.

[48] G. McBride, M. G. King, and J. W. James, "Social Proximity Effects on GSR in Adult Humans," *Journal of Psychology,* 61 (1965), 154-56.

[49] M. L. Patterson and L. B. Sechrest, "Interpersonal Distance and Impression Formation," *Journal of Personality,* 38 (1970), 166.

[50] H. Rosenfeld, "Effect of Approval-Seeking Induction on Interpersonal Proximity," *Psychological Reports,* 17 (1965), 120.

[51] M. Meisels and C. Guardo, "Development of Personal Space Schemata," *Child Development,* 40 (1969), 1171.

[52] M. J. King, "Interpersonal Relations in Preschool Children and Average Approach Distance," *Journal of Genetic Psychology,* 109 (1966), 113.

[53] S. Albert and J. M. Dabbs, Jr., "Physical Distance and Persuasion," *Journal of Personality and Social Psychology,* 15 (1970), 266.

[54] F. N. Willis, "Initial Speaking Distance as a Function of the Speaker's Relationship," *Psychonomic Science,* 5 (1966), 221-22.

[55] Goffman, *Relations in Public,* p. 44.

[56] Ibid., pp. 44-48.

[57] Ibid., p. 45.

[58] Ibid., p. 47. For a comprehensive review and critique of research that examines the implications of proxemic behavior as a system, see D. M. Pedersen and L. M. Shears, "A Review of Personal Space Research in the Framework of General System Theory," *Psychological Bulletin,* 80 (1973), 367-88.

4

THE PROXEMIC COMMUNICATION SYSTEM: URBAN ENVIRONMENT

Environment is a term with many facets. Webster defines environment as the aggregate of all external conditions and influences affecting the life and development of an organism. Environment is a broad and sweeping term. This chapter will not deal with environment in all its aspects. Rather, it will examine communication in the man-made environment, and, more particularly, as viewed in the urban scene. It will review some work done in design and policy-making professions, which have been active in studying and creating the urban environment.

Chapter 3 discussed space and distance in the micro-environment. Its emphasis was on the communication of meaning through spatial relationships. At the level of the urban environment too, space and distance, both actual and per-

FIGURE 4-1

ceived, serve to communicate meaning, images, and ideas. The facilitation of human communication has been pointed out by Meier as a significant reason for the evolution of cities, and he has gone on to state that "an intensification of communications, knowledge, and controls seemed to be highly correlated with the growth of cities."[1]

At this larger level, institutional controls, like zoning and subdivision regulations, set a framework for and have a significant effect on the design of the man-made environment. They set standards for such items as lot sizes for residences, yard dimensions, building heights, density (number of dwelling units per lot), amount of parking space provided, and whether sidewalks are required. Figures 4-1 through 4-4 show differences in lot sizes in single-family areas and differences in density in multi-family residential areas regulated by zoning ordinance.

FIGURE 4-2

FIGURE 4-3

These regulations in the United States are local and may vary substantially from community to community. The general authority to establish such regulations comes from the states. In effect, zoning and subdivision regulations are exercises of the police power, the basic power of the state to enact legislation to protect the public health, safety, and welfare of its citizens. The states, through enabling legislation, have authorized local governments to utilize these tools, if they wish. With the exception of

FIGURE 4-4

Houston, all major cities in the United States have both zoning and subdivision regulations in effect.

Other public actions and regulations also influence the urban scene. Examples of public actions are the design and location of public buildings and urban renewal projects. Design controls for private buildings and projects are examples of additional regulations. They are usually applied to limited areas. The impact of these public actions and regulations has not been substantial, except in limited geographic areas. Much more significant in setting the large-scale pattern of urban development are public policy decisions on the provision (or nonprovision) of various services, such as water and sewer. Without these services, only limited development can occur, no matter what zoning regulations are in effect. Zoning may, for example, permit 5,000 square foot residential lots in an area. If there is no sewer service, however, public health considerations will preclude such dense development.

This background information is intended to briefly acquaint the reader with the kind of institutional regulations and public policy actions and decisions against which this examination of communication in the larger urban milieu must take place. Two qualifying statements need to be emphasized when evaluating the effect of such controls. One is that land regulation and many other public policies affecting land use are locally established and tend to reflect local tastes, needs, and concerns. The second is that these regulations and policy decisions set a general framework, but normally permit considerable individual flexibility in design at the project level.

SPACE AND DISTANCE

The effect of distance on communication has been examined in the professional literature both as an absolute measurement and as it may be perceived in a context of existing physical development and social relationships. Although common physical or objective distance (the total distance between two points, as described by some standard measure) is an easily defined dimension, how people perceive it may show only a weak relationship to the actual distance. In particular, two concepts involving distance give some insight into how people view space. They are accessibility and perceptual distance.[2]

Accessibility describes distance in terms of the ease (minimization of time and cost) with which a particular distance can be traversed.[3] For the commuter, physical distance is often of relatively minor importance. More significant in his decision of how he will get to work are the time and cost of his various alternative routes and transportation modes.

Perceptual distance refers to whether the distance between two places is symbolically conducive to being traversed.[4] A residential area may be close to where you live in terms of physical distance. However, if a visual barrier, such as an elevated freeway constructed on fill, is located in between, even if some of the local streets connect under the freeway, the nearby neighborhood may not be close in perceptual distance.

FIGURE 4-5

Another barrier might be a wide street with heavy traffic, such as in Figure 4-5. By comparison, the lack of streets and the small scale common pedestrian areas shown in Figure 4-6 would probably not appear to be a separation to residents of that residential complex.

The distance between houses in two neighborhoods may be the same, but if one neighborhood has sidewalks and the other does not, the perceived distances between houses in the two neighborhoods will probably be different. In addition, "the various

FIGURE 4-6

...ius of urban perspectives held by the residents of a city are constructed from spatial representations resulting from membership in particular social worlds."[5] Appleyard, in his work in the new Venezuelan city of Ciudad Guayana, found that "perceptual distance from a similar social area is apparently less than actual distance, while perceptual distance from a lower social group is greater than actual distance."[6]

Michelson talks of the urban environment as the separation of people from others and from objects in perceptual, accessible, and physical space. He goes on to describe some dimensions of this separation: housing type, private or semi-private outdoor space, perceptual distance to objects (perceptually separated refers to a person's being unable to see, hear, or smell an object), and differential accessibility of objects.[7]

Accessibility and perception have been shown to modify actual physical distance for the individual. Distances between individuals, whether they be physical or perceived, reduce the opportunities for communication. Gans has pointed out, however, that the effects of proximity on informal relationships are somewhat contingent on life style. Distances are controlled, to an extent, by the various planning tools and architecture. However, Gans' research would seem to indicate that the same architectural design, for example, may not have the same effect on individuals of different social groups.[8] Spatial meaning is derived from individual styles of perception. That is, meaning and perception are inseparable.[9]

STRUCTURING THE CITY

The urban environment provides meaning for people, and they make decisions which transform it. Whether passively observing or actively transforming, man makes decisions based on his *perception* of the environment, rather than on the environment as it is. Downs has developed a useful abstraction to describe man's interaction with the environment, in which man is viewed as part of a complex information-processing system.

> The basic process in interaction in the schema is as follows. The *real world* is taken as the starting point, and it is represented as a source of *information*. The information content enters the individual through a system of *perceptual receptors,* and the precise meaning of the information is determined by an interaction between the individual's *value system* and their [sic] *image of the real world*. The meaning of the information is then incorporated into the image. On the basis of the information, the individual may require to adjust himself with respect to the real world. This requirement is expressed as a *decision* which can, of course, be one that involves no overt reaction. The links from the concept of a decision are two-fold (although these could be amalgamated). The first link is a recycling process, called *search,* whereby the individual searches the real world for more information. This process can continue until the individual decides that sufficient information has been acquired, or some time/cost

limitation acts as a constraint to further search. A decision is then made which may be expressed as a pattern of *behaviour* which will in turn affect the *real world*. Since the real world undergoes a change, fresh information may result, and the whole process can continue. The schema therefore allows the space perception process to occur in a temporal as well as a spatial context.[10]

Although man's perception of his physical environment is influenced by who he is, there has been evidence that many individuals living within the same urban environment do hold in common a mental "base map" of their city.[11]

The question of how a person mentally structures the city has been examined in a number of articles and publications, beginning with Lynch's *The Image of the City* in 1960.[12] He concentrated on the apparent "legibility" of the cityscape—"the ease with which its parts can be recognized and can be organized into a coherent pattern"[13]— and observed that "a distinctive and legible environment not only offers security, but also heightens the potential depth and intensity of human experience."[14] *Imageability* is the term that he used to describe the "quality in a physical object which gives it a high probability of evoking a strong image in any given observer."[15]

Lynch's study involved lengthy interviews with a small sample of residents in three large cities. Each interview included requests for descriptions, locations, and sketches and the performance of imaginary trips. Lynch concluded that there seemed to be a "public image of any given city which is the overlap of many individual images,"[16] and that its contents could be classified into five types of elements: paths, edges, districts, nodes, and landmarks.

Paths are the channels along which the observer customarily, occasionally, or potentially moves. For most people interviewed, paths were the basic structural element of their mental map.

Edges are linear elements not used as or considered to be paths by the observer. They usually serve as boundaries between different areas and can be important organizing features in that they hold together generalized areas.

Districts are medium to large portions of the city that the observer mentally enters "inside of" and that are recognized because of some common or identifying characteristic.

Nodes refer to points in the city that the observer can enter and that also serve as a focus, usually visual. A city square would be an example of this element.

Landmarks are also point references, but the observer does not enter within them.[17]

RESIDENTIAL AREAS

Although people maintain a general mental image of the city, their basic perspective is of the place where they live, the areas with which they are most familiar. Home usually involves more of a person's time than any other single place in the city. It is the center from which a person's activities emanate. The significance of residential areas to the planning and design professions is underscored by the fact that residences cover more of the area of cities than any other land use.

Two seemingly opposite characteristics of residential areas will be examined in this section: the *separation* in space of people from other people and from objects, and the elements of *cohesiveness* that make residential areas identifiable neighborhoods.

Michelson discussed four dimensions of separation that affect the physical form of residential areas. Perceptual and accessible distances are affected by *type of housing unit* (single-family residence as in Figure 4-7, garden apartment shown in Figure 4-8, high-rise apartment as seen in Figure 4-9) and the design and nature of the building itself. *Private or semi-private outdoor space* creates the separation between buildings, as seen in Figures 4-10, 4-11, and 4-12. The other two dimensions that create separation have been discussed earlier, the *perceptual distance to objects* and the *differential accessibility of objects*. Accessibility is a continuum, but perceptual space may well not be continuous in all cases.[18] These distinctions can play an important role in the design of residential areas and on a larger scale in the planning of the city. People's choices of perceptual and accessible distance are reflected in the distance of their residences from other functional areas in the city, lot sizes, and a number of other variables related to urban form.

While separation is a characteristic of urban residential areas, so too is cohesiveness. Michelson indicates that his data "provides a measure of proof to the assertion of others that the crucial intermediate residential unit between self and the whole metropolis is indeed salient to ordinary people."[19] Lee concurs when he states that "except for the few upper-middle class professional people who turn up in a random sample, neighborhood was a really salient experience; not a vague shifting one, but something that could be quickly and easily acknowledged and fairly easily described."[20]

Buttimer expands Lee's distinction and says that the design of residential areas can be evaluated on the basis of the individual's expectations. She contrasts hypothetical polar types of residents. The *localite* tends to develop a strong sense of territoriality and prefers an environment providing for neighborly relations, community activities, and convenient services and institutions. The *urbanite* is one who does not identify strongly with place, wants privacy, prefers high quality and status of services, and places high priority on the amenities and visual qualities of an area and on accessibility to other areas of the city.[21] Interaction with neighbors is a minor consideration. This polar distinction expands on earlier work by the Webbers, who speculated that the intellectual class comes to maintain a behavioral and value system which is not "place-based" in a community or neighborhood, as contrasted with the working class who maintain most close ties within a single community.[22]

Yancey, in his case study of the Pruitt-Igoe Housing Project in St. Louis, points out that "informal networks among neighbors are an important means by which the urban lower and working classes cope with poverty and deprivation and that these networks are at least in part dependent on the semi-public space and facilities that are present in many working- and lower-class neighborhoods."[23] He then goes on to state that the new project he is studying does not meet these particular needs of its residents, even though the apartment units themselves are a substantial improvement over the units from which the residents had moved.

Lee, in evaluating residential areas as neighborhoods, describes three types. The

FIGURE 4-7

FIGURE 4-8

FIGURE 4-9

FIGURE 4-10   FIGURE 4-11

FIGURE 4-12

social acquaintance neighborhood is a small physical area, the boundaries of which are determined by social interaction. The *homogenous neighborhood* has boundaries set by the size, price, or condition of houses in an area and the kind of people who live in them. The *unit neighborhood* is a larger area with a range of services and amenities, such as shopping and churches, as well as residences. It is the traditional neighborhood for which the planners plan.[24]

All of this would indicate that neighborhood as a concept is more complicated and varied in its manifestations than the concept used by planners and designers. The idea of neighborhood involves how people perceive their surroundings. Their perception is a product of their backgrounds and general circumstances in life and of the design and content of the environment.

SOME IMPLICATIONS FOR PLANNING AND DESIGN

"If we could predict how well buildings and structures were known, planners and architects would be in possession of a powerful design tool, for we could begin to gain some control over that elusive communication medium, the urban environment."[25] Control is a strong term and one that seems excessive to many people. Lynch, for example, discussed the variety of regulatory devices used at the city level and the positive design actions taken by public agencies in their public works, and then went on to point out that "there is much to be done before far-reaching controls are justified."[26] A variety of studies have been undertaken which give some insight into communication implications of some of the current regulations, policies, and actions.

Appleyard[27] investigated the esthetics of urban highways because he felt that new expressways might be designed to meet objectives in addition to the movement of people from place to place at the least cost and inconvenience. He was concerned with building predictive tools for understanding the importance of various urban attributes. He pointed out that such predictability could permit the planner or designer to achieve several objectives:

1. to coordinate urban form and visibility with the experience of coherent urban form;
2. to relate form and visibility to community significance in order to create a more meaningful city;[28]
3. to encourage a sense of community, to preserve privacy, or to stimulate change by proposing elements either increasing or decreasing ambiguity of the urban form.

In his work in Ciudad Guayana, Appleyard took a similar approach to another component of the urban environment, buildings. He was concerned with whether the traditional graphic vocabularies of land use and site planning corresponded with the inhabitants' experience or perception of the city. Appleyard used lengthy interviews and mapping to obtain his basic data and independent raters to scale the characteristics of buildings mentioned on the maps or in interviews. He then intercorrelated the building attributes and recall frequencies. A wide array of attributes, which can be grouped into three general categories, appeared to affect the individual's recall of buildings in the city*:

1. *Physical Form Attributes*
   a. *Movement* associated with buildings in this study refers to people doing their various activities around and near buildings. Both actual and potential movement (such as parked cars) excited interest by the subjects.
   b. *Contour* or boundary defines a building from its ground. A building is more noticeable if it is singular, that is, if the building and background are clearly differentiated.
   c. *Size* is a relative term since a tall building in Manhattan may not be as noticeable as a four-story building in a single-family residential area.
   d. *Shape* was shown in the study to be an imageable characteristic at both extremes of the simplicity-complexity scale.
   e. *Surface* (brightness, texture) can contribute to imageability according to Appleyard, but was not significant in Ciudad Guayana because almost all buildings were constructed of the same material and were of the same color.
   f. *Quality* in the study was a combination category for the juxtaposition of expensive materials, careful landscaping, cleanliness, and good condition. Buildings of a particular quality level tended to be grouped together so quality was significant only at the boundary between areas.
   g. *Signs* were either small and similar or nonexistent in Ciudad Guayana and so were not significant elements of recall.

2. *Visibility Attributes*
   a. *Viewpoint intensity* was measured by the number of people likely to pass the most prominent viewpoint of the building in a day.
   b. *Viewpoint significance* occurred at decision points, locations where people needed to identify a distinctive feature for orientation purposes.
   c. *Immediacy* is the closeness or centrality of a building to the core of vision.

3. *Use and Significance Attributes*
   a. *Use intensity* is the number of people using a building in a day.
   b. *Use singularity* refers to the uniqueness of a structure's use in the city and the fact that it is clearly defined, single use.
   c. *Symbolism* is a term used primarily to describe structures not heavily used, but which have significance for political, economic, or other reasons.[29]

In his work on spatial meaning and the environment, Beck found it clear that different professions, age groups, and sexes use spatial variables in significantly different ways. Our concepts of spatial meaning come from individual modes and styles of perception. We build up assumptions or expectations which lead to meaning systems.[30] These assumptions were also observed by Appleyard in Ciudad Guayana, Venezuela. In reviewing people's subjective city maps, he found it difficult to disen-

---

* This excerpt from "Why Buildings Are Known: A Predictive Tool for Architects and Planners," by Donald Appleyard is reprinted from *Environment and Behavior*, Vol. I, No. 2 (Dec. 1969), pp. 141–47, by permission of the Publisher, Sage Publications, Inc.

tangle inferential structuring from direct experience. People sometimes included things on their maps that they expected to be there. For example, one man thought a railroad line should go to an industrial plant. Even though he had never seen such a railroad, he showed it on his map. There was no such rail line.[31]

The effect of design on human interaction can occur in variety of ways. For example, Appleyard and Lintell did field interviews and observation on three San Francisco streets with different levels of traffic in order to evaluate the effect of traffic conditions on livability (as measured by variables representing stress, noise, pollution, social interaction, territory, and environmental awareness). They found that on the light traffic street, people had significantly more friends and acquaintances than on the heavy traffic street, and that contact across the street was much less frequent on the heavy traffic street. Another interesting result related to the residents' ideas of personal territory. Although a householder's responsibilities legally include maintenance of the front sidewalk, residents on the moderate and light traffic streets considered part or all of the street as their territory. On the heavy traffic street, this extension of personal territory into the street did not occur and, in some cases, mostly for renters, it was confined to their own apartments.[32]

Other investigations into the meaning conveyed by man's urban environment have dealt with the concept of "neighborhood." Lee, for example, created the neighborhood quotient, the area an individual specified as his neighborhood expressed as a ratio of an area of one-half mile radius surrounding his home. He reported a fairly clear direct relationship between his neighborhood quotient and variables measuring social class, length of residence, and the subject's age.[33]

Yancey, in his case study of a St. Louis public housing project, observed that without the semi-official public spaces around which friendships develop, people in a public housing project withdraw into the internal structures of their apartments and do not have the social support, protection, or informal social control found in other lower-class or working-class neighborhoods. He pointed out the absence of what is often called wasted space. The equivalent of the alleys and back yards of the tenements were missing in the housing project.[34]

Probably the most far-ranging effort to relate the meaning of the man-made environment to positive design and control policies has been put forth by Alexander.[35] He began with the question "what physical organization must an urban area have to function as a mechanism for sustaining deeper contacts?" To answer this question, he proceeded first to develop evidence to suggest that "social pathologies associated with urban areas . . . follow inevitably from the lack of intimate contact," and that the lack of intimate contact is brought about by design aspects of the urban environment, such as distance, and by such personally or socially motivated factors as stress and autonomy. His conclusion was that "in order to overcome this autonomy-withdrawal syndrome, a city's housing must have 12 specific geometric characteristics" which taken together define a housing pattern different from any existing subdivision or site designs.

Alexander's geometrics have not taken hold in the planning and design professions, but his concern for conveying meaning in the urban environment which is supportive of people's wants and needs is a common one in the profession. Lynch stated this most aptly when he said,

> In a democracy, we deplore isolation, extol individual development, hope
> for ever-widening communication between groups. If an environment has
> a strong visible framework and highly characteristic parts, then explora-

tion of new sectors is both easier and more inviting. If strategic links in communication (such as museums or libraries or meeting places) are clearly set forth, then those who might otherwise neglect them may be tempted to enter.[36]

CONCLUSION

Space and distance, both actual and perceived, communicate meaning, images, and ideas. In this chapter, space and distance relationships in the urban environment are seen to reflect not only individual decisions, but also a framework of institutional regulations and policies.

The design and policy professions in the United States by both action and inaction have played a substantial role in the form and shape of the urban environment. Institutional land regulations, public works of various sorts, and policies on the provision of public services and utilities lay a general framework for urban development. Within this framework, individual projects and buildings are designed and executed.

Distance, defined in standard measurements, is modified by individuals' perceptions of it and by the ease with which it can be traversed (accessibility). Perceptual distance refers to whether a distance is symbolically conducive to being traversed. Visual and social barriers can modify a person's perception of distance.

Although urban space and environment are perceived through individual perspectives, there have been some common elements found in studies of how people structure the city. Legibility and imageability were examined in classifying paths, edges, districts, nodes, and landmarks.

Both separation and cohesiveness play a role in the design of residential areas. Whether such areas are neighborhoods and what constitutes a neighborhood are questions which can be answered only by evaluating backgrounds and general circumstances of residents, as well as the physical form of the environment.

The real thrust of this chapter has been to shed some light on existing work which might begin to lay a base for a more sophisticated use of tools modifying the urban environment.

NOTES

Note: Nancy J. Leathers assumed the primary responsibility for researching and writing this chapter. She received her A.M. in urban geography from the University of Chicago. She currently works as an Urban Planner with Eric Hill Associates of Atlanta, Georgia.

[1] R. L. Meier, *A Communications Theory of Urban Growth* (Cambridge: Massachusetts Institute of Technology Press, 1972), p. 43.

[2] W. Michelson, "An Empirical Analysis of Urban Environmental Preferences," *Journal of the American Institute of Planners,* 32 (1966), 356.

[3] Ibid.

[4] Ibid.

[5] A. L. Strauss, *Images of the American City* (New York: Free Press of Glencoe, 1961), p. 67.

[6] D. Appleyard, "Style and Methods of Structuring a City," *Environment and Behavior,* 2 (1960), 117.

[7] Michelson, "Empirical Analysis of Urban Environmental Preferences," 356-57.

[8] H. Gans, "Effect of the Move from City to Suburb," pp. 184-98 in *The Urban Villagers,* ed. J. L. Duhl (New York: Free Press, 1963).

[9] R. Beck, "Spatial Meaning and Properties of the Environment," p. 21 in *Environmental Perception and Behavior,* ed. D. Lowenthal (Chicago: University of Chicago, Department of Geography, Research Paper No. 109, 1967).

[10] R. M. Downs, "Geographic Space Perception: Past Approaches and Future Prospects," *Progress in Geography,* 2 (1970), 84-85.

[11] H. Harrison and W. A. Howard, "Role of Meaning in Urban Images," *Environment and Behavior,* 4 (1972), 391.

[12] K. Lynch, *The Image of the City* (Cambridge: Massachusetts Institute of Technology Press, 1960).

[13] Ibid., pp. 2-3.

[14] Ibid., p. 5.

[15] Ibid., p. 9.

[16] Ibid., p. 46.

[17] Ibid., p. 47-83.

[18] Michelson, "Empirical Analysis of Urban Environmental Preferences," 356-57.

[19] Ibid., 358.

[20] T. Lee, "Psychology and Living Space," *Transactions of the Bartlett Society,* 2 (1963-64), 16.

[21] A. Buttimer, "Social Space and Planning of Residential Areas," *Environment and Behavior,* 4 (1972), 279-318.

[22] M. Webber and C. Webber, "Culture, Territoriality, and the Elastic Mile," pp. 35-46 in *Taming Megalopolis I,* ed. H. W. Eldredge (New York: Doubleday, 1967).

[23] W. L. Yancey, "Architecture, Interaction, and Social Control: The Case of a Large-Scale Public Housing Project," *Environment and Behavior,* 43 (1971), 4. Although Yancey does not refer to the concept of "defensible space," this is a related matter discussed at length in *Defensible Space* by Oscar Newman (New York: Macmillan, 1972). Defensible space refers to a "residential environment which can be employed by inhabitants for the enhancement of their lives, while providing security for their families, neighbors, and friends."

[24] Lee, "Psychology and Living Space," 16.

[25] D. Appleyard, "Why Buildings Are Known: A Predictive Tool for Architects and Planners," *Environment and Behavior,* 1 (1969), 131-56.

[26] Lynch, *Image of the City,* pp. 116-17.

[27] D. Appleyard, K. Lynch, and J. R. Myer, "The View from the Road," pp. 75-88 in *Environmental Perception and Behavior,* ed. D. Lowenthal (Chicago: University of Chicago Department of Geography, Research Paper No. 109, 1967).

[28] C. Steinitz, "Meaning and the Congruence of Urban Form and Activity," *Journal of the American Institute of Planners,* 34 (1968).

[29] Appleyard, "Why Buildings Are Known."

[30] Beck, "Spatial Meaning and Perception of the Environment,"29.

[31] Appleyard, "Style and Methods of Structuring a City," 116.

[32] D. Appleyard and M. Lintell, "The Environmental Quality of City Streets: The Residents' Viewpoint," *Journal of the American Institute of Planners,* 38 (1972), 84-101.

[33] Lee, "Psychology and Living Space," 19.

[34] Yancey, "Architecture, Interaction, and Social Control," 3.

[35] C. Alexander, *The City as a Mechanism for Sustaining Human Contact* (Berkeley: University of California, Center for Planning and Development Research, October, 1966).

[36] Lynch, *Image of the City,* p. 110.

5

THE ARTIFACTUAL COMMUNICATION SYSTEM

Appearance communicates meaning. In an age that gives lip service to the cliché that beauty is only skin deep one might surmise that physical appearance represents a secondary and superficial value, and that few people devote any attention or time to their physical appearance. Exactly the reverse is true. Our physical appearance has a pervasive impact on our self-image. As such, it is a major factor in shaping our behavior and the behavior of those with whom we interact.

In *Orpheus Descending* Tennessee Williams wrote that "we're all of us sentenced to solitary confinement inside our own skins for life." For many Americans that can be a severe sentence. Our skin and overall appearance in many cases dictate that we cannot date or marry a person more attractive than we are, that our social and sexual success is heavily dependent on our attractiveness, and that our vocational success can often be predicted by how attractive others perceive us to be.

A billion-dollar cosmetics industry testifies to the fact that millions of Americans realize that their self-image may depend to a large extent upon the quality of their skin. "We can cold-cream it, suntan it, bleach it, lift it, and paint it—but we cannot shed it. And, unless we are willing to adopt the tactics of the Oregon State student who enclosed himself in a large black bag, our physical appearance is our most obvious personal characteristic."[1] Plastic surgeon Kurt Wagner writes

> it used to be the great truism that it was the inner qualities that counted and the outer ones were superficial—as in the old saying that beauty is only skin deep. But we know now that there is no such thing as separating the mind from the body. The organism, like the Lord our God, is one. When you look in the mirror and what you see doesn't match what you think you are—when the reflection is alienated from yourself then the inner and outer selves are bound to have an effect on each other. The physical image becomes the mental reality.[2]

When we realize that plastic surgery on the eyelids (blepharoplasty) costs up to $1000, a face lift (rhytidectomy) up to $1500, and hair implants up to $2500, the high priority that Americans attach to appearance becomes strikingly clear.[3] The obvious affluence of well-known plastic surgeons such as Kurt Wagner is no mystery since he and many other top practitioners have long waiting lists of patients who gladly pay the prices quoted above. Of course plastic surgery represents perhaps both the most expensive and drastic means of modifying our bodily appearance. Plastic surgery does represent a more dramatic means of modifying image than the use of clothing or cosmetics for example. However, people use all three to attain the same general purpose—to modify their appearance positively in order to enhance their self-image.

As we noted in chapter 1, many individuals feel that we communicate solely to persuade, to inform, or to give ourselves absolute control over others by giving them orders or commands. The integrative function of communication is often overlooked entirely and may be the most important.[4] The integrative function of communication involves our attempt to modify our own self-image in at least two ways: (1) we attempt to modify our physical or reflective image (the image that we actually "reflect" to others) so that it is consistent with the image we have of ourselves; (2) we try to enhance our physical or reflective image so others will perceive us as more attractive and so that change in the perception of others will in turn enhance our own self-image. Much of our communicative efforts are designed to make consistent, or integrate, our own image of ourself with those others have of us. The ultimate objective in integrative communication is to convey an extremely flattering image that is perceived by intimate associates exactly as you perceive it and want it to be perceived.

This chapter deals with communication by appearance. While very different in kind from kinesic or proxemic communication, artifactual communication (communication by appearance) has great functional significance. There is no more intimate form of communication. *Our visible self functions to communicate a constellation of meanings which define who we are and what we are apt to become in the eyes of others. In interpersonal communication the appearance of the participants establishes their social identity.*

Once established, our social identity—as perceived by others and by us—places identifiable limits on how, when, and where we are expected to engage in interpersonal communication. Our social identity carries with it the implicit responsibility to communicate in such a way as to meet the expectations of those for whom that identity has meaning. When we violate those expectations, our communicative interaction with others is apt to become ineffective and inefficient.

Recently I walked into one of my classes dressed in a bathrobe and tennis shoes. My hair, which had just received a wild treatment from a dryer, was sticking out in all directions; much of it was combed down to obscure most of my face. I was wearing sunglasses and smoking a long black cigar. Placing my bare legs and tennis shoes ostentatiously on a desk I began my remarks to the students by asserting that "appearance communicates meaning."

Because the meanings communicated by my altered appearance conflicted so strikingly with the meanings associated with my social identity, the students became rather disoriented. They did not know whether to laugh, to squirm uncertainly, or even to refuse to acknowledge the incongruous sight in front of them. A few laughed, many squirmed, and the rest tried to be cool. Later, when they realized that they were being put on, my appearance triggered an intense and fascinating discussion of the functions of artifactual communication.

The content of this chapter certainly can stimulate just such a discussion in your classroom. Specifically, the chapter is designed (1) to examine the most important factors which affect appearance, (2) to examine the types of meanings communicated by appearance, (3) to illustrate how changes in appearance affect the types of meaning communicated, and (4) to suggest how we may use modification of appearance to achieve a more positive social identity.

Appearance begins with the human body. Recently, over 62,000 Americans were surveyed for their own views of their bodies. They reported that their body image was strongly related to self-esteem. Only 11 percent of those with a below-average body image, compared to 50 percent of those with an above-average body image, had an above-average level of self-esteem. Furthermore, the most important part of the body for building self-esteem is one's face.[5]

Since our body image is so important in building our self-esteem and since so many individuals are exhibiting increasing concern with improving their body image, the obvious question is how can one's body image be improved? Through the ages, a wide variety of methods has been used to enhance body image ranging from body paint to jewelry to various forms of clothing. Items of dress and ornamentation which have been used since the beginning of recorded history are referred to as artifacts. While a great many of the artifacts from an earlier age have been destroyed or have deteriorated badly, we still have some original artifacts and copies or descriptions of others. Few preserved garments date earlier than the seventeenth century, although hard body equipment such as armor and some items of body ornament, such as beads made of nonreactive minerals, have lasted for thousands of years and are identified as possessions of prehistoric men.[6]

Because of a favorable combination of burial arrangement and soil conditions many artifacts have been found in Scandinavian graves of the Bronze Age (1500–1100 B.C.) in good condition. In these oak coffin burial sites some of the oldest artifacts of Western Europe have been discovered, including complete garments, pins, earrings, armrings, and combs.[7] Our American artifacts trace back directly to the Indians and often functioned as ornaments as well as protection from the elements. Shoshones wore woven rabbit-skin robes while the Plains Indians used the buffalo-hide robe as a form of cape which was later replaced by the trader's blanket. In the southeastern states the natives went naked except for loin cloths.[8]

The terms *artifact* and *artifactual* may be said to have connotations much broader than the use of dress, body paint, and the many other items utilized to modify appearance. Indeed you may associate artifacts with the relatively esoteric findings of an archaeological expedition; such findings often date back centuries. Primitive tools used to build the pyramids are a prime example. While the varied meanings of the term *artifactual* are certainly broad enough to cover a variety of examples, two things should be kept in mind. First, one of the most central and commonly used meanings of artifact refers to things used to serve an ornamental function and thereby modify body appearance. Second, while some might argue that items must be properly aged before being identified as artifacts, one should remember that today's most elegant and fashionable attire will be tomorrow's artifacts. Consequently, the *artifactual communication system* is defined as including *all things that humans wear on their body or do to their body in order to modify appearance.*

BODILY APPEARANCE

Bodies are certainly different. Both the common and uncommon man have recognized this fact for centuries. Shakespeare, a man of uncommon insight, expressed in *Julius Caesar* what the common man has long recognized.

> *Caesar:*   Let me have men about me that are fat;
>   Sleek-headed men, and such as sleep o' nights:
>   Yond Cassius has a lean and hungry look;
>   He thinks too much: such men are dangerous.
> *Antony:*   Fear him not, Caesar; he is not dangerous.
>   He is a noble Roman and well given.
> *Caesar:*   Would he were fatter! . . .

People have known for centuries that their bodies differ in appearance but they made few systematic efforts to measure the differences. Ernst Kretschmer, a professor of psychiatry and neurology, probably made the first comprehensive effort to record differences in bodily appearance. In 1925 Kretschmer published the first edition of *Physique and Character: An Investigation of the Nature of Constitution and of the Theory of Temperament.* Kretschmer concluded that individuals who share morphological similarities may be classified into three major groups—*asthenic* (skinny, bony, and narrow body), *athletic* (muscular body), and *pyknic* (fat body).[9]

Sheldon's follow-up research has established the empirical practice of somatyping or classifying people as to body type. Sheldon's classification is now widely used; the student must study these three body types to understand the material in the next section. According to Sheldon your body will be classified into one of three body types—*endomorphic* (soft, fat, etc.), *mesomorphic* (bony, athletic, etc.), or *ectomorphic* (thin, fragile, etc.).[10]

BODY TYPE AND EFFECTS ON BEHAVIOR At first glance, some people might compare somatyping (classification of people by body type) with goldfish swallowing. It is interesting but not socially useful. In fact somatyping is not merely an academic exercise. We now know that a person's body type may have a significant impact on his behavior.

In this section we are assuming that the body type to which a communicator has been assigned by his peers is accurate. *Whether the somatyping by one's associates is actually accurate or not is not as important as the fact that you, the communicator, are aware of how your body has been typed.* Experts disagree as to the exact effects of somatyping and as to how precisely we can predict behavior from body type. Most experts agree, on the other hand, that somatyping of an individual by others has a significant impact on his behavior.

Wells and Siegel found that *endomorphs* were more old-fashioned, lazier, weaker, more talkative, more warm-hearted and sympathetic, more good-natured and agreeable, more dependent on others, and more trusting of others. *Mesomorphs* were perceived to be stronger, more adventurous, more mature, and self-reliant. *Ectomorphs* were seen as more ambitious, suspicious, tense and nervous, inclined to be difficult, more pessimistic, and quieter.[11]

Walker did a much more detailed examination of the relationship between body build and behavior in young children. The school children were classified into the three categories of body type at a reliability or agreement level close to .90. Once classified, the child's parents were asked to apply the adjectives that they thought best described their child's behavior. The author was able to confirm two-thirds of the predictions he made about the children's behavior based solely on their body type. The behavior of boys was much more difficult to predict from body types than girls' and only a chance number of the predictions of boys' behavior were confirmed at statistically significant levels. In contrast, substantial numbers of predictions about girls' behavior for those with an *endomorphic* or *ectomorphic* body build were confirmed.[12] *Endomorphic* girls were eager to please, even-tempered, friendly, relaxed and were *not* uncooperative, moody, bashful, suspicious of others, or impudent. In contrast *ectomorphic* girls were tense, jealous, unpredictable, moody, suspicious, worried and afraid of failure, but were *not* eager to please, well-mannered, orderly and did not love physical comfort. In short, Walker found a definite and positive relationship between body build and behavior, but the relationship was not nearly as strong as that reported by Sheldon.[13]

Recently, investigators have found that *mesomorphs* have a strong achievement need while *ectomorphs* are well below average in need for achievement.[14] Tests performed on nondelinquent boys confirmed the finding that boys with athletic, muscular bodies had a strong need to achieve while the tall, thin, fragile boys exhibited a below average need to achieve.[15]

The general physical appeal of the body, as well as body type, has a significant impact on an individual's interaction with others. For example, individuals will feel stronger interpersonal attraction to a physically appealing stranger than one with low physical appeal.[16] Physical attractiveness among couples paired at a "computer dance" was by far the most important factor in determining whether individuals liked each other and also in determining the probability that the male would ask his female partner for another date.[17] Similarly, the female communicator who is very attractive and openly states a desire to influence the views of the audience will be much more effective than her less attractive peer.[18]

Clearly, some of the results showing body build to affect behavior may be biased by what may be called a "self-fulfilling prophecy." It is not clear for example whether the lethargic but friendly behavior of the obese is a function of their body build or whether they behave as they do because they are simply meeting societal expectations. The latter view is supported by recent research. Children who have been treated as if they were anti-social soon began to exhibit anti-social behavior. Similarly, students who were told that they had high IQs were actually found to have higher IQs when tested a year later.[19]

In summary, it seems safe to conclude that the body type of a communicator will significantly affect his behavior and the effectiveness with which he communicates with others. Nonetheless, some of the results involving the three body types of *endomorph, mesomorph,* and *ectomorph* are obvious and a bit circular. Thus, it is predictable that an *endomorphic* person will be a bit short of energy and overly eager to please as a way of compensating for the negative connotations associated with his body typing. On the other hand there seems to be a relatively consistent pattern of specific behaviors associated with given body types that is neither obvious nor trivial. Whether or not the somatyping is accurate, it surely can have a dramatic effect on how one relates to others and how they relate to him.

One's own body image seems to be much more important than actual body type, however. While one's own body image is obviously affected by the perception of others, it is a complex phenomenon affected by many factors.

BODY IMAGE

Human beings tend to have detailed images of their own bodies. Sometimes these images are accurate. Often they are not. (See Figure 5-1.) Whether accurate or not, the important point to emphasize is that body image has a great impact on behavior. Since body image is such a highly personal concept, it is not surprising that people react to their own bodies in judgmental terms. They do not typically describe themselves as an ectomorph, and endomorph, or a mesomorph and leave it at that. They typically see their own bodies in negative or positive terms and, on that basis, determine how *satisfied* or *dissatisfied* they are with their own body. This is their body image.

To be satisfied or dissatisfied with your body suggests that somehow your body deviates from the *American ideal* for bodies. While a number of individuals still cling to the notion that beauty is highly subjective and that few can agree as to the exact nature of beauty, recent evidence suggests a high degree of consensus among Americans as to what is beautiful and ugly.

People who come to plastic surgeons because they are dissatisfied with their appearance or body concept are remarkably consistent in their agreement as to what constitutes beauty. The *ideal body* can be described in rather objective terms. This is particularly true when talking of the ideal face. Noted plastic surgeon Kurt Wagner writes that the sculptor Schadow geometrically laid out his ideal of facial beauty in the

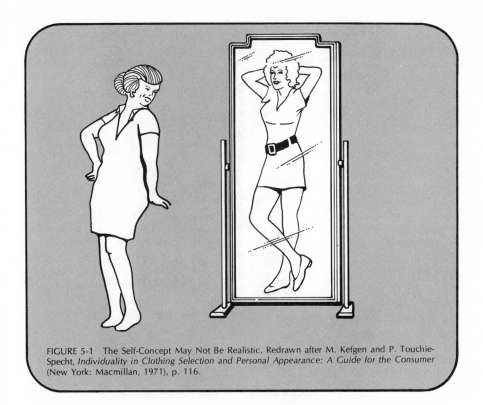

FIGURE 5-1 The Self-Concept May Not Be Realistic. Redrawn after M. Kefgen and P. Touchie-Specht, *Individuality in Clothing Selection and Personal Appearance: A Guide for the Consumer* (New York: Macmillan, 1971), p. 116.

nineteenth century. In so doing Schadow "formulated the facial proportions for a prevailing standard of symmetry which the occidental world accepts as the ideal. . . . Our own eyes automatically accept the standard of what is aesthetically pleasing. Take any super example—from Greta Garbo to Rock Hudson—to even *any* example of the good-looking individual, and you know they pass the Schadow test before you apply the calipers."[20]

Schadow's model of perfect facial proportions has been adopted by plastic surgeons, and their clients begin their treatment by undergoing profile analysis. The term *profile analysis* correctly suggests that plastic surgeons generally agree on a very specific ideal for facial beauty. The profile analysis "indicates the necessity for a definite proportion between the forehead, nose, lips, and chin. To correct a nose alone, without considering the related features, is going on a fool's journey."[21]

As Figure 5-2 indicates, plastic surgeons use a profilometer to determine exactly how far a patient's facial features deviate from the perfect profile or ideal face. The profilometer, a special instrument that resembles and functions like the protractor, is used to measure the length and angles of the nose from tip through bridge to top in centimeters. "The ideal nose for a man . . . is straight with a bridge angle of 30 to 35 degrees and an 8- to 12-degree tip angle. As to length, the nose should roughly correspond to the man's height measured in feet. Thus, a 6-foot man would ideally have a nose of about six centimeters (2.35 inches) in length."[22]

In an interview with this author Wagner emphasized the conviction of his fellow

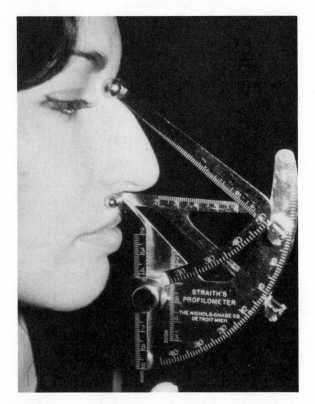

FIGURE 5-2 Use of the Profilometer. Photo courtesy of Dr. John Lewis.

plastic surgeons that Americans have a rather well-developed and consistent notion of beauty or ideal appearance. He stressed that

> the reason that you know [what the ideal model or profile is for beauty] is that people still have a good idea of what is beautiful. Ok. Now you might not like Elizabeth Taylor, or her life style, or what she stands for but nobody is going to deny that Elizabeth Taylor is beautiful. Ok. By the same token, no one will deny that Rita Hayworth is beautiful. . . . Then you take the males and push them in the profile. . . . We tend to go for real anti-heroes now. Right now it is just a rebellion against male beauty where you have Charles Bronson or Richard Boone. Yet, they have strong, square faces, except their nose is a little weird, but even their nose isn't too weird. Redford, very popular. James Coburn, very popular. Ok. Ah, Rock Hudson, perfect. All right, perfect. John Wayne, almost perfect, although older. . . . *There never has been* a successful leading man who has no chin [author's italics].[23]

Clearly, there is an ideal for bodily appearance. Americans agree on what serves as their standard for developing their own body image and also on what serves as a model by which others form their body concept of a given individual. When the individual develops a negative body concept, because he feels his own appearance deviates significantly from the ideal or he feels that friends and associates see his body as deviating from the ideal, the negative body concept can have marked affects on his communication.

Recent research suggests that most Americans have a reasonably positive body concept when that body is taken as a whole. They are very *concerned that certain parts of their body deviate from the ideal,* however. For example, 25 percent of women in a recent survey *expressed dissatisfaction* with their hair; 28 percent with their nose; 36 percent with their complexion; 41 percent with their teeth; 59 percent with size of abdomen; 60 percent with buttocks; 71 percent with hips. Similarly, 18 percent of the males expressed dissatisfaction with their nose; 29 percent with their complexion; 38 percent with their teeth; 47 percent with size of abdomen. Almost 70 percent of the women were dissatisfied with their weight while 45 percent of the males were not satisfied.[24]

Jourard and his associates have done a great deal of research on their concept of body-cathexis—the degree of feeling of satisfaction or dissatisfaction with the various parts or processes of the body. Early research on the concept confirmed the hypothesis *that body-cathexis or image is integrally related to the self-concept.* Furthermore body image was found to have significant behavioral implications. People with low body-cathexis, or a negative body image, were anxious, concerned with pain, disease, or bodily injury, and people with a negative body image were insecure.[25] In addition individuals with a positive body concept (those who saw themselves as mesomorphs) had a much more sophisticated concept of their own body than those with a negative image of their body.[26] From this finding we might infer that individuals with negative body concepts attempt to avoid the negative connotations of such a concept by deliberately maintaining a fuzzy or incomplete concept of their own body.

We do know that some people have understandable reasons for maintaining unrealistic body concepts. Many obese individuals probably recognize, for example, that "once the endomorphic phenotype is firmly established, stigmatization sets in and blocks the exit to normal acceptance in interpersonal relationships."[27] Similarly, of ninety-three female students who were asked to report their own measurements as well as those for the ideal female figure, most of the female subjects distorted their self-estimates toward the ideal.[28] Individuals also tend to associate a more positive body image with those to whom they ascribe superior status. Thus, five separate groups were asked to estimate to the nearest half-inch the height of a man who was represented to the different groups as possessing different degrees of status. Results indicated that as the ascribed status of the man increased his perceived height increased and so did the amount of perceptual distortion.[29]

Such studies demonstrate that an individual's *actual* (or *reflected*) body image is often very different from what the individual or others perceive it to be. In fact the communicator may have to cope with three different body images which may be consistent, but are often drastically different—(1) his own body image as he perceives it; (2) his body image as others perceive it; (3) his *reflected* body image which is an accurate picture of his body as it currently appears.

If it is true that an individual's own body image (and the image that friends and associates have of his body) is often highly distorted, such distortion is very apt to lead to surrealistic communication that features fantasy rather than objectivity. To avoid such self-deception and the deterioration in the quality of interpersonal communication typically associated with it, the reader obviously needs some objective means of measuring his own body image as well as the image his friends have of his body. By comparing your own body image with the image friends have of your body you can engage in a very useful form of reality testing.

To make such a comparison, the reader must take the body image test, have one or more associates apply the same test to his body, and compare results.

THE BODY IMAGE TEST

Below you will find a number of parts of the body broken down by section. Please take the following scales and rate the body of D. Gordon Lather. The scales are seven-point scales so if you think that the individual's face is extremely beautiful you would put a 1 in the blank next to the face. In contrast if you feel that the individual's face is extremely ugly you would put a 7 in the appropriate blank. If you feel the face is average you rate it a 4 on this scale. Choose the number between 1 and 7 for each scale which comes closest to representing how you would rate a given part of the body on a given scale. The scales by number are[30]:

	1	2	3	4	5	6	7
SCALE #1 BEAUTIFUL							UGLY
SCALE #2 HARD							SOFT
SCALE #3 STRONG							WEAK
SCALE #4 PLEASANT							UNPLEASANT
SCALE #5 ANGULAR							ROUNDED
SCALE #6 ROUGH							SMOOTH
SCALE #7 GOOD							BAD
SCALE #8 APPEALING							UNAPPEALING

PART OF BODY	NUMBER OF EVALUATIVE SCALE							
	1	2	3	4	5	6	7	8
A Face (overall)								
A(1) Hair								
A(2) Eyes								
A(3) Ears								
A(4) Nose								
A(5) Mouth								
A(6) Teeth								
A(7) Chin								
A(8) Complexion								
B Extremities								
B(1) Shoulders								
B(2) Arms								
B(3) Hands								
B(4) Feet								
C Mid Torso								
C(1) Abdomen								
C(2) Buttocks								
C(3) Hips								
C(4) Thighs								
C(5) Legs								
C(6) Ankles								

Once the body image test has been completed, the person whose body has been rated (D. Gordon Lather in this instance) can determine whether he is satisfied with his overall body image and with specific parts of that image. If he is not satisfied, he may choose to use one of the major artifactual means to enhance his body image and improve his scores on the body image test. One of the most effective means of modifying that body image is by the intelligent use of clothing.

MODIFICATION OF APPEARANCE BY THE USE OF ARTIFACTS

CLOTHING AS A MEDIUM OF COMMUNICATION   Clothing represents a vitally important medium of communication. "Clothing transmits a message. It is seen before the voice is heard. Sensitivity to the message depends on a number of variables such as setting, task acquaintanceship, cultural background, experience, and awareness. Certain types of clothing are always related to specific behavior. The perceiver automatically associates the action with the dress."[31] While clothing serves a number of functions, its primary use today is to help the wearer project the most positive and appealing image possible.[32]

Certainly appearance is a factor in determining the first impression you communicate to others. *You communicate your own identity by means of your visible self.* Thus, Stone in his brilliant essay, "Appearance and the Self," writes that "*appearance* . . . is that phase of the social transaction which establishes identification of the participants. As such, it may be distinguished from *discourse*, which we conceptualize as the text of the transaction—*what* the parties are discussing. Appearance and discourse are two distinct dimensions of the social transaction. The former seems more basic. It sets the stage for, permits, sustains, and delimits the possibilities of discourse by underwriting the possibilities of meaningful discussion."[33]

We can be sure that one's name and *identity* are established by appearance if we imagine singer Johnny Cash dressed in white or rock star Alice Cooper without his body paint. Cash and Cooper help make a point which remains as valid for them as it was for Teddy Roosevelt with the pince-nez and F. D. R. with his cigarette holder. Our social identity and image is defined, sustained, and positively or negatively modified by communication through appearance. For most individuals the major medium of communication by appearance is clothing.[34]

As a communicative medium clothes serve many functions. Kefgen and Touchie-Specht maintain that clothing communicates three dimensions of meaning or information about individuals: (1) emotion; (2) behavior; (3) differentiation. First, clothing symbolizes and communicates a great amount of information about the emotions the communicator may be experiencing. For example, the fact that clothes express specific emotions and feelings is illustrated by the common use of such terms as "glad rags," "Sunday clothes," and "Widow's weeds." When viewed from a broader perspective "clothing has been used to arouse mass emotions such as patriotism and nationalism. . . . Examples are the images conjured by the 'brown shirts' of the Nazis, the peasant garb of Red China, and the Green Beret."[35]

Second, as we shall soon demonstrate, clothing has a great impact on the behavior of the wearer as well as on the behavior of those who perceive it. The young girl who wears a "training bra" and sheer nylons for the first time is transformed into the *femme fatale* and her behavior as well as that of her male admirers changes accordingly. Indeed, some groups such as the Hell's Angels probably would find it difficult to behave in as stereotyped a manner without their distinctive garb; and Mardi Gras celebrants have at times engaged in anti-social behavior which may have been strongly related to attire that concealed their identity and removed inhibitions and obligations associated with that identity. Certainly the *femme fatale*, the Hell's Angel, and the Mardi Gras celebrant would lose their unique identification without their clothes, and their behavior as well as responses to that behavior would be altered dramatically.[36] A policeman in street clothes loses his means of social identification and, consequently, he loses his authority. We must recognize that "*by wearing the uniform of a particular group, a man shows by his clothing that he has given up his right to act freely as an individual but must act in accordance with and under the limitations of the rules of his group.*"[37]

People in highly visible jobs such as policemen are expected to wear uniforms and to behave in a way consistent with the meanings that the uniform communicates. That the typical police uniform communicates a sense of arrogant superiority and brute force to some minority Americans has been recognized by some enlightened police chiefs and many police officers are now dressing in more casual and less visible attire. While the results from such experimentation are still being gathered, such attempts to communicate by clothing are apt to have a humanizing and moderating impact on relationships between minority group members and police officers.

People who wear uniforms can assume that the public will expect them to behave in very specific ways. The man in clerical garb is not expected to frequent pornographic movies or host pot parties in his home. Similarly, the man cloaked in judicial robes is not expected to own a nightclub on the side or to fraternize with known criminals.

A study by Hamilton and Warden strongly suggests that the use of clothing that is perceived as inappropriate by one's peers can have very negative effects on the behavior of the wearer. These authors found that boys who wore unacceptable clothing—even though their achievement scores were 22 percentile points *higher* than the median score of boys with acceptable clothing—had a lower grade-point average. In addition students who wore acceptable clothing participated in more extracurricular activities and held more offices than did students with nonacceptable clothing. *Boys who wore unacceptable clothing were more consistently in conflict with their peers and society.*[38]

Third, as implied above, clothes function to differentiate one individual from another and one group from another. The so-called hippie movement is a good example of a large and vaguely defined group of individuals who were able to differentiate themselves from others whose values they rejected by wearing clothes that outsiders probably thought were Salvation Army rejects. Of course, clothing was only one means used to differentiate their group from the establishment. Long hair was probably the single most prominent symbol of rebellion. Other examples of differentiation through the medium of clothing are not lacking.

Zweig notes that the different age groups differentiate themselves from one another by clothing standards and the habits they reflect. Thus, a young single man of 20 to 25 will spend nearly twice as much on clothes as a middle-aged man of 45 to 50 and three times as much as a man of 65 to 70. A young man's clothes "will be varied and sometimes extravagant, while those of an older man will be more drab and uniform. . . . Young men often wear raincoats, and older men woollen [sic] overcoats. Most young men wear nothing on their heads; older men caps, and some middle-aged men trilbies. Young men do not like to show they are workmen in their dress, and try to conform to the standards of the middle classes, while older men are content to be taken for what they are."[39]

Many blacks make a successful attempt to differentiate themselves from the average American by the use of "dress as a communication medium." Schwartz contends that when the Negro community, or any other minority community, is denied access to many status symbols, it is forced to use compensatory devices to raise self-esteem, aid status symbolization, and cushion the traumatic effects of a subordinate position. Clothing is one of the available devices."[40] A study done on the styles and items of clothing which were emphasized in *Ebony* and *Life* suggests that blacks who hold non-professional jobs may use different fabrics and clothing styles to communicate a dissociation from the traditional working classes. Thus, blacks preferred reptile, unborn calf, pony, polka-dotted and suede-reptile shoes which were sharply pointed, and delicate fabrics which are not generally identified with manual labor.[41]

Such research suggests that the *primary function of clothing is decorative and the decorative functions of the clothing tend to provide the fastidious dresser with a unique identification.* A factor analysis done by Ailen confirms this conclusion. The most important function of clothing was decoration, followed by comfort, interest, conformity, and economy.[42] Gibbins did a much more specific study in which he tried to determine the different classes of meaning individuals attempt to communicate by the clothing they wear. He asked fifty English grammar school girls aged 15 to 16 to judge pictures of clothing cut out of popular fashion magazines such as *Harper's Bazaar, Honey,* and *Petticoat.* He then had the girls apply semantic differential scales to the pictures and factor analyzed the ratings. His results clearly indicated that (1) *people do make judgments about each other on the basis of their clothes and there is considerable agreement as to the meaning conveyed by a costume,* and (2) *liking for particular clothes is positively related to the degree of similarity between the impression conveyed by the clothes and the judge's self-image.*[43]

Gibbins's research convinced him that "clothes act as a medium of communication." Most important—he found that three classes of meaning can be communicated by clothing: (1) *fashionability*—the degree to which others perceive one's clothing as contemporary, fresh, and beautiful; (2) *socialization*—the degree to which the clothes clarified the girl's social role and made her appear feminine; (3) *formality*—the degree to which the clothes suggested whether the wearer wanted to be perceived as formal or casual.[44] Since fashionability was by far the most important class of communication, it seems safe to conclude that young people choose clothes primarily on the basis of how well they feel others will like them, not on the basis of such pedestrian considerations as comfort or durability.

COSMETICS AS A MEDIUM OF COMMUNICATION Short of an actual change in bodily contours or frame, cosmetics probably follow clothing as the most important medium of communication by appearance. The cosmetics industry is a multi-million dollar business and men as well as women are making increasing use of cosmetics to enhance their appearance. For decades *many Americans have considered cosmetics one of the basic requirements of life rather than a luxury.* Thus, even when they did not have enough money for food, people have purchased cosmetics. "Cosmetics still sold well during the depression. It's [cosmetics are] so important to them that they will put themselves in hock for maybe $3000."[45]

The quote above is from Mike and Marvin Westmore, who own and operate the noted M. S. Westmore Cosmetic Studio in Encino, California. They are heirs to a proud family tradition of makeup artists that includes one of the most famous makeup men that Hollywood has ever produced, Percy Westmore. He is their uncle. The Westmores spent a good part of one afternoon in their cosmetic studio with the author talking about the need for and the behavioral effects of the use of cosmetics.

While the Westmores still do work on movie stars, their main specialty is therapeutic as opposed to aesthetic cosmetics. Therapeutic cosmetics are typically applied to the client after he has undergone plastic surgery for a cleft palate, facial cancer(s), or for the removal of scars due to burns. The Westmores work closely with plastic surgeons, therefore. They do devote some of their time to aesthetic cosmetics.

Unlike therapeutic cosmetics, however, aesthetic makeup is not preceded by medical treatment and/or surgery.

The Westmores emphasized that virtually all of their clients had a deficient self-image. "The major need these people come in with is an enhanced self-image."[46] Unlike many cosmeticians the Westmores are actively involved in studying the behavioral impact on their clients due to the use of cosmetics. The first thing the Westmores attempt to determine is the nature of the individual's "reflective image." This is the physical image that their client reflects or conveys to others and it may deviate significantly from the client's own image of himself. They emphasize that they "are interested in the impact of the reflective image on the self-image. And the self-image relationship with social intercourse. Because this is what we are dealing with. We are working on a reflective image but the impact is on the self-image. And the self-image determines our place in society."[47]

The most dramatic illustration of the effects of cosmetics on the communicator's reflective image comes in the form of *before* and *after* pictures of the Westmore's clients.

In Figure 5-3 you see a client before she has had what the Westmores call aesthetic makeup. At that point, she suffered from the following deficiencies in reflective image: (1) face is void of makeup which reveals an uneven skin tone; (2) eyes appear weak partially because of unexpressive brows that lack definition; (3) skin has a washed out and unhealthy appearance; (4) lips appear weak and bland. Figure 5-4 shows the result after the Westmores did the following things to modify the client's image and produce the visual effect which you can observe: (1) applied base makeup to even out skin tone to create healthier look; (2) healthy blush to skin restored in proper places where needed; (3) eyebrows defined and shaped to aid client in being more expressive facially; (4) eyes defined to make them appear to be more communicative; (5) mouth defined in warm, pleasing colors. The reader can draw his own conclusions about the changes in the client's reflective image.

While Figures 5-3 and 5-4 illustrate how the image of a nondeformed individual can be modified by cosmetics, the following pictures feature a young woman who suffered from serious physical defects of the face. These defects in turn had an extremely negative impact on her behavior and a very inhibiting effect on her interaction with others. The young lady in Figure 5-5 is Rebecca Richardson and the Westmores described her case history to me in detail.

When Rebecca Richardson came to the Westmores, she had been through a series of traumatic operations, her self-confidence was very low, and she was withdrawn and difficult to communicate with. "Rebecca Richardson came from a family of congenital cleft palates. Hers was extremely bad. She had had seventeen operations and they had all been through clinics. . . . She was twenty-two years old and obviously was not getting her share of the social intercourse with male members of society."[48] Even Figure 5-5 does not fully illustrate the extent of Becky Richardson's problems because she is wearing makeup in that picture which—while inadequate in the trained eyes of the Westmores—covered skin blemishes and part of the cleft palate operations. In Figure 5-5 the Westmores feel that Becky has an unbecoming silhouette because of her hair style, pallid and uneven skin tone, poorly shaped eyebrows which give her a frowning appearance, and an unnatural outline to the upper lip due to surgery to correct cleft lip, which resulted in the mouth appearing bland and undefined.

Figure 5-6 shows Becky Richardson after she received the full therapeutic makeup

FIGURE 5-3

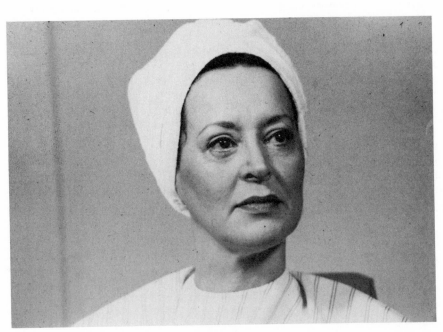

FIGURE 5-4

FIGURE 5-5   FIGURE 5-6

at the Westmore Cosmetic Studio. The Westmores feel that now (1) her silhouette is improved with a new hairstyle, (2) skin tone is evened out which disguises scars from cleft lip repair, (3) healthy blush is restored to skin, (4) eyebrows are reshaped for definition, pleasing appearance, and to make her appear more expressive, (5) eyes are defined which enhances them and draws attention away from the lip defect, (6) the mouth is defined with shape normalized so that cleft lip repair is not obvious and the definite lip line created by lipstick draws attention away from unnatural lip line. In broadest perspective, the application of cosmetics was designed to draw attention to the facial features which give Becky Richardson the greatest expressive and communicative potential—the eyebrows and the eyes—and to divert attention from the lip defect.[49]

Most importantly, the scientific use of cosmetics in Becky Richardson's case has resulted in a dramatic metamorphosis in her behavior. Where she was once withdrawn and uncommunicative, she is now a confident and sought-after young lady who is actively involved in many social activities and has developed to the point where she is actually becoming socially aggressive. In this instance, the change in her reflective image produced a significant and highly beneficial change in her self-image and, consequently, in her behavior. Not only has she become a much more effective communicator, she has become a much more effective and satisfied human being.

By the systematic alteration of her appearance Becky Richardson has positively modified her social identity in a most functional way. By the consensus of her peers her appearance now communicates meanings which expand rather than contract her potential for satisfying social interaction. By making her reflective and desired image more nearly compatible she has greatly expanded her communicative potential. She need no longer dissipate her energies in the frustrating task of continuous self-appraisal. She may now concentrate on interpersonal rather than intrapersonal communication with expanded opportunities to exert control in the communicative environments in which she finds herself.

HAIRSTYLE AND GLASSES AS SECONDARY MEANS OF COMMUNICATION
Given man's imagination and ingenuity, there are obviously countless means that can be used to modify appearance. This chapter does not attempt to deal with all of them but only the most important.[50] While clothing and cosmetics represent major means of modifying appearance, hairstyle and glasses also have had a significant impact on personal appearance for centuries.

Hairstyle has long been an important determinant of the image you convey to others. Except in those times when the state imposed standards to which the citizenry had to conform, the chief criterion in judging the value of a given hairstyle has been its fashionability. Thus, "whatever the century, the so-called leaders of fashion have been those who were first to follow the latest styles, not necessarily those who created them. Whether this is done to curry favor with royalty, to express one's own individuality, or to outdo one's friends, it becomes a sort of status symbol."[51]

In any era, hairstyles tend to range from nonconforming to conforming. Of the four major hairstyles—eccentric, fashionable, conservative, and individual—eccentric is the most nonconforming.[52]

Eyeglasses must conform to many of the same social expectations and standards as clothes and hair if they are to enhance the image of the communicator. While glasses have been an invaluable tool in the fight against illiteracy, many Americans are more concerned with the question of what they will do to their image than what they will do to their eyesight. Figure 5-7 illustrates the styles of eyeglasses worn from 1800 to 1850 and identifies the specific individual or class of people who wore a specific style. It is interesting to note that the eyeglasses of the peasants were probably fairly functional although crude. John Jay and William Whittingham, in contrast, wore eyeglasses that reflected a concern with their fashionability.[53] In modern times contact lenses seem to suggest the ultimate preoccupation with fashionability.

MODIFICATION OF APPEARANCE BY PLASTIC SURGERY

The most drastic means of changing your body image and, consequently, your self-image is probably plastic surgery. Until fairly recently, many individuals dismissed plastic surgery as a luxury of the rich or the desperate effort of aging women to recapture their beauty. Such is no longer the case. Plastic surgery is no longer confined to

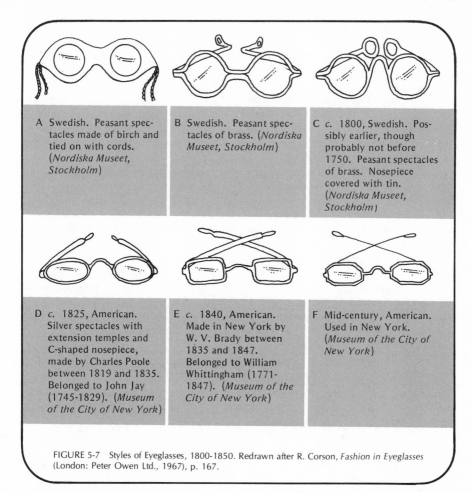

A Swedish. Peasant spec-
tacles made of birch and
tied on with cords.
(*Nordiska Museet,
Stockholm*)

B Swedish. Peasant spec-
tacles of brass. (*Nordiska
Museet, Stockholm*)

C *c.* 1800, Swedish. Possibly earlier, though
probably not before
1750. Peasant spectacles
of brass. Nosepiece
covered with tin.
(*Nordiska Museet,
Stockholm*)

D *c.* 1825, American.
Silver spectacles with
extension temples and
C-shaped nosepiece,
made by Charles Poole
between 1819 and 1835.
Belonged to John Jay
(1745-1829). (*Museum
of the City of New York*)

E *c.* 1840, American.
Made in New York by
W. V. Brady between
1835 and 1847.
Belonged to William
Whittingham (1771-
1847). (*Museum of the
City of New York*)

F Mid-century, American.
Used in New York.
(*Museum of the City of
New York*)

FIGURE 5-7   Styles of Eyeglasses, 1800-1850. Redrawn after R. Corson, *Fashion in Eyeglasses*
(London: Peter Owen Ltd., 1967), p. 167.

the rich or the neurotic although these groups certainly are not excluded from the beneficial effects of plastic surgery. Increasingly, men as well as women, black as well as white, and people from all economic levels are making use of the great potential of plastic surgery to alter their appearance and make their lives more satisfying. Over one million Americans had elective plastic surgery in 1973 and fully 30 percent were men.[54]

To get a highly authoritative perspective on the motivational patterns of those who seek plastic surgery, to determine how plastic surgery actually changes images, and to assess the changes in communicative behavior which result from plastic surgery, the author and a research assistant interviewed two of the most famous plastic surgeons in America—Dr. Kurt Wagner of Beverly Hills, California, and Dr. Milton Edgerton of the University of Virginia Hospital, Charlottesville, Virginia. In life style and temperament the two surgeons seem to be opposites. Wagner talks and lives the affluent life style of the Hollywood stars on whom he operates, although he has patients with a wide variety of jobs and incomes. Both he and his wife have undergone plastic surgery a number of times and they seem eager to describe their experiences whether it is in Wagner's new book—*How to Win in the Youth Game*—or while being interviewed on a national television NBC special program entitled "The Pursuit of Youth."[55]

Dr. Edgerton, in contrast, seems much more conservative in life style and expression, and less preoccupied with his own physical appearance (when at work Dr. Edgerton wears the doctor's highly traditional white coat while Wagner makes a point of working on patients in attire which would suggest that he just came in from a round of golf at the Bel Air Country Club). In spite of apparent differences in value systems both men have well-deserved national reputations which they have worked very hard to earn. Both men share an impressive commitment to extremely high performance standards as plastic surgeons, and a belief—grounded in years of experience—that plastic surgery is an extremely valuable means of modifying body image, self-image, and, ultimately, the way the patient communicates with others and they with him.

Almost without exception individuals who seek plastic surgery have a negative image of their own body. Their own sense of identification is fuzzy at best and extremely self-deprecating at worst. Many of them appear to be masochistic in that they start with a negative sense of identification and seem to make a conscious effort to make others aware of their feelings of inferiority. Thus, Dr. Wagner, who served part of his residency performing plastic surgery on inmates in a prison in Oklahoma, observes that "many inmates feel ugly, or they don't feel accepted or they have been made fools of. . . . With tatoos they go out of their way to mark themselves and further isolate themselves" from society.[56]

While the patient's own self-image may be very inaccurate, the way he perceives himself is the important thing. Thus, Dr. Edgerton notes that

> the patient's deformity is not as important in considering surgery as the patient's sense of the deformity—of the way that he or she feels that he appears to the rest of the world. We use the term in plastic surgery of body imagery to describe the way the patient conceives of himself or herself physically. . . . To a very real degree our entire society has a subconscious set of guidelines which gives them either a good value or a poor value about their own self-image.[57]

MOTIVATION OF THOSE WHO SEEK PLASTIC SURGERY   A number of individuals have what we might term an insatiable and abnormal need for plastic surgery and they go from one plastic surgeon to another seeking additional operations. Typically, such individuals have low self-esteem; grandiose ambitions too difficult to achieve; extreme obsessionalism concerning their appearance, to the point of preventing them from engaging in constructive endeavors; passivity and obsequiousness in their dealings with the surgeon; and vagueness concerning what they hope to finally achieve by means of the surgery—among other things.[58] Reputable surgeons like Edgerton and Wagner typically refer such patients to psychiatrists.

Another group of individuals seeks probably the most drastic of all changes in appearance—a change in sex.

Many people with desperate concerns about their true gender are seeking the help of plastic surgeons, gynecologists, and urologists. The number of such patients increases each year. Surgeons now have the technical capability of performing the operations so urgently requested by people seeking sex conversion surgery. Before recommending or undertaking such treatment, a physician must acquaint himself with the nature and prognosis of this condition, with the limitations of, and indications for such surgery, and with the probable consequences of this profound change in the self-image of the patient.[59]

The motivation and personality of the "insatiable" patient and those seeking a sex change is atypical, however. Most patients seeking cosmetic surgery do have fairly serious personality problems but are not obsessed with them. The aim of the average patient is "to get rid of self-conscious preoccupations and body-concerns as a way of freeing [oneself] of emotional barriers and blocks to the end of better managing the fundamental problems of living. *A change in physical appearance is a change in the basic foundation of personality function, i.e., the physical or body-image*" (italics supplied by the author).[60]

The motivation of the average patient seeking plastic surgery may be classified according to whether the pressure the patient feels is *external* or *internal*. External pressures include (1) the need to please others, (2) paranoid ideation (he *thinks* he would please others), (3) personal career or social ambitions which seem obstructed because of a flaw in physical appearance. As we already know, the need to please others is strong and can be illustrated by the young woman who seeks augmentation mammaplasty in the unreal hope that she can save her marriage with bigger breasts. Patients with paranoid ideation often feel that a change in physical appearance will make their environment less threatening. A good example is the young man who seeks changes in his small chin or thin lips because these physical features convey a homosexual connotation to others. Finally, career and social ambitions often motivate those who have been unsuccessful in acting, or jobs where appearance is particularly important, to seek surgical modification of appearance. In a high percentage of cases, plastic surgery to relieve external pressures is disappointing to the patient.[61] The plastic surgery is disappointing because the real cause of the patient's problem is *not* a defect in personal appearance.

The person who experiences inner motivation or pressure to have plastic surgery is much more likely to be satisfied with the subsequent change in body image and, ultimately, self-image. The most commonly experienced inner motivation for plastic surgery comes from depression and a sense of inadequacy. "If I had to pick out one or two feelings that a patient seeks coming to surgery designed primarily to change appearance, I would say the idea of the patient is being able to feel lovable," says Dr. Edgerton.[62]

CHANGES IN IMAGE THROUGH PLASTIC SURGERY   People who seek changes in image through plastic surgery obviously differ in attractiveness. For example, please apply part A of the body image test on pp. 94-95 to the young ladies shown, respectively, in Figures 5-8 and 5-9. The young woman in Figure 5-9 probably received much more positive ratings than the young woman in Figure 5-8. Since body image has such a significant impact on self-image you can surmise that the subject in Figure 5-9 has a much more positive body image than the subject in 5-8. By this time, you may also have surmised that the identity of the young women in the two pictures is the same. The difference, and a very important difference it is, is that Figure 5-8 shows a young woman *before* plastic surgery by Dr. Kurt Wagner (nose and chin augmenta-

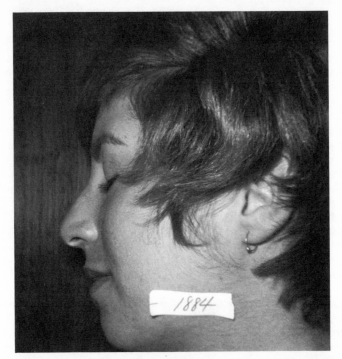

FIGURE 5-8

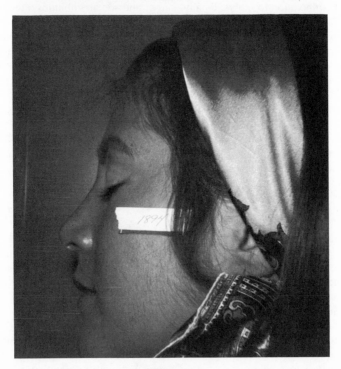

FIGURE 5-9

tion) and Figure 5-9 shows that same person *after* plastic surgery. Certainly, the difference in appearance, and hence probably self-image, is very striking.

The foregoing photographs represent the changes due to cosmetic or aesthetic plastic surgery as opposed to reconstructive plastic surgery, which often involves the attempts to repair an entire face because of the mutilation of a fire or auto accident. For a detailed discussion of how specific types of plastic surgery are performed, the reader is directed to several articles in two of the scientific journals in this field.[63]

It is important to remember that people are identified by their appearance and when that appearance is changed by plastic surgery they may temporarily lose their own self-identity. When patients come to the plastic surgeon, they are warned that they may experience the trauma of losing their self-identity. In fact, Dr. Edgerton notes perceptively that patients "may not expect the change in self-imagery that will follow and their sense of identification may be lost temporarily. We must guard against this. . . . The patient must be warned that it will take several weeks or months to become comfortable with the new identity. Some people fear plastic surgery even though they want a change."[64]

CHANGES IN COMMUNICATION BEHAVIOR DUE TO PLASTIC SURGERY In spite of the psychological risks, patients come because they have a strong need to change their appearance. As our pictures illustrate, a skillful plastic surgeon can make dramatic improvements in the appearance of a patient. While the change in appearance is highly visible and often striking, the more striking change is in the patient's communicative behavior.

Obviously, plastic surgery may affect the general behavior of patients in many ways but few experts would disagree that the primary effects are on self-image, what the patient is able to communicate with that new self-image, and in the ways the patient actually does communicate. Certainly, the typical patient communicates a much more positive self-image and an eagerness to interact vigorously with those people he typically encounters. Thus, one plastic surgeon notes that "I like to call plastic surgery, psychiatry of the skin. There is no doubt about it, if you are satisfied with your outer self-image, you can function better—with much more confidence as a human being. I've seen people come in who were morose and sullen . . . who after surgery, if they are realistic in their approach, come in always smiling, happy, bubbling, effervescent. . . . You can see the change in their personality."[65]

Typically, the change in communicative behavior after plastic surgery seems to manifest itself in a drastic reduction in inhibitions and in an openness, candor, and trusting type of behavior which is the ideal sought by so many authorities in interpersonal communication. For example, before plastic surgery some women with small breasts (those who later resort to plastic surgery) seem to "have a behavioral disorder. Now, it is not noticeable perhaps, but they will never dress or undress in front of another group of women. They are very bashful in front of men. They will avoid contact because they feel inadequate."[66] After surgery for breast augmentation however, a stunning change in behavior takes place. "Now she'll undress at the drop of a hat in front of everybody. . . . It gets to the point where you can bring in eight people from the street and . . . these women will just knock it off."[67]

The Westmore brothers typically apply cosmetics to their clients after surgery and referral by men like Wagner. They note that the change in behavior is sometimes dramatic.[68]

While most patients typically adjust to their new self-identity after a short period and prove to be much more effective communicators, some patients are unable to cope with their change in identity. Dr. Edgerton, who takes great pains to determine the pre-operative motivations of his patients, recalls one such case with seeming regret:

> I remember one such patient years ago. A young man who came in with a fractured nose as the result of an injury from a rifle butt in military service. His nose was badly deflected and it had a rather large, bony hump on it. He asked for a correction and in my rather hasty review of his very obvi-ous problem I asked him if he wished the bony hump removed as we were straightening and he replied he did. It was only three or four days after surgery when I found him reading a psychiatric textbook on Jung that I began to wonder if I had made as careful study of his problem as I should. And, sure enough, when the bandages were removed, he had a straight bridge which by any normal standard would have been judged quite at-tractive on a normal male face, but he was very distressed and anxiety-ridden because his bony hump had really been the feature with which he had *identified* [author's italics] with his father, the only member of his family whom he respected deeply; and he refused to go home until some-thing could be done to correct this feature.[69]

A loss of identification which results in an adverse impact on self-image and on one's communicative interaction with others is rare. Much more frequently individuals attempt to lose or hide their self-identity *before* plastic surgery because they have a negative self-image which has a stultifying effect on their interaction with others. Thus, one of Wagner's female employees worked for him before he "did her nose. She was a very intelligent girl and because she sensed that she was ugly, her whole be-havior changed to accommodate for this. She became very competitive. Ok. She did things like skydive, she was a roller-skating champion when she was young. She com-peted on every level to lose her identity as a girl."[70] After plastic surgery she was perceived as very attractive and, consequently, no longer had any reason to hide her self-identity. Indeed she asserted her new self-identity so vigorously that she had trou-ble in her relationship with her husband and other intimates. In the long run she adjusted, however, and plastic surgery has had a very beneficial impact on her be-havior. Like so many others she became less defensive, more confident, more in-volved, and more trusting. In short she became a more effective communicator and in so doing seems to be leading a much more satisfying life.

There can be little doubt that a physical defect, or generally unattractive features, can communicate some very negative meaning to others. In composite such meanings constitute a reflective image which an individual very much wants to change. Thus, "a male with a strong, jutting chin, short of being prognathic, ok, is . . . [perceived] as strong, forceful, iron-willed, able to make decisions, virile. A person with no chin is like Andy Gump—weak, ineffectual, dominated by his mother, insignificant."[71] Any individual who realizes that he is perceived in this latter way might justifiably spend much of his time on the integrative function of communication. That is, his com-municative efforts would be directed toward changing the image he projected and/or trying to prepare himself for the discomfort of consistently getting negative reactions to his reflective image. Not surprisingly, such a communicator is not apt to be effective or efficient in his efforts to persuade, inform, or direct others because so much of his energy is diverted from these important types of communication.

Plastic surgery provides a quick and reliable means of modifying an individual's reflective image and in so doing may remove the communicator's preoccupation with that image. With his image modified the individual typically becomes both a more effective and efficient communicator.

In retrospect, the artifactual communcation system is rather different from the other nonverbal systems. Certainly we cannot alter our appearance as easily or quickly as we can change facial expressions or vary the pitch of our voice. In this sense artifactual communication is inflexible and inefficient. On the other hand, by our appearance we do communicate consensually shared meanings which can and often do have a pervasive impact on the other communication systems.

The obvious question which remains is how do we make optimum use of the artifactual communication system? A careful reading of this chapter should provide a good part of the answer. We must know initially what type of social identity we wish to communicate to others. Since body image is such an important part of our perceived social identity, we must have some objective measure of our bodily image. The body image test has been devised to provide such a measure. The most practical procedure is to let your associates apply the body image test to you and see if you are satisfied with the results. If you are not, you may want to use clothing, cosmetics, plastic surgery or other available means to modify your appearance. Then have the body image test applied again to determine whether your perceived body image is helping you to shape the social identity which is compatible with your communicative objectives.

CONCLUSION

Appearance communicates meaning. Americans recognize this fact and are spending large amounts of time and energy to modify their physical image in such a way that it will enhance their self-image. Since the physical image has been found to be a major determinant of self-image, the communicator typically begins by trying to improve the attractiveness of his body.

In an attempt to improve our appearance we may use clothing, cosmetics, hairstyle, fashionable glasses, and contact lenses in addition to many other things. Individually and collectively these items are defined as artifacts and this chapter is designed to examine the nature of artifactual communication and its effects. The artifactual communication system is defined as including all things that humans wear on their body or do to their body in order to modify appearance.

We start with the realization that human bodies are very different in form and appeal. Early morphological research by Kretschmer suggested that there are three principal types of physique which human beings exhibit. The *asthenic, athletic,* and *pyknic* body types of Kretschmer were very similar to the *ectomorphic* (tall, thin), *mesomorphic* (muscular, athletic), *endomorphic* (soft, fat) body types developed later by Sheldon.

A person's body type (or somatype) has a significant impact on his behavior. *Endomorphic* individuals have generally been found to be lazier, more good-natured and agreeable, and more trusting. *Mesomorphs* appear to be stronger, more mature, and self-reliant, and have a strong achievement need. *Ectomorphs* are often tense, suspicious, moody, quiet, and pessimistic. Some of these behaviors may be part of a self-fulfilling prophecy in that individuals with a given body type are simply behaving as society expects them to behave. On the other hand, there seems to be a relatively consistent pattern of specific behaviors associated with given body types which has little if anything to do with social expectations or stereotyping.

While an individual's body type is important, his own body image is much more important. Body image is a highly personal concept and individuals react to their own bodies in judgmental terms. Their ability to judge their own bodies is greatly enhanced by the fact that there is a rather well-developed *American ideal* as to what an attractive body should look like. Authorities such as doctors Wagner and Edgerton agree on this point and have developed a very specific profile of the ideal human face, for example. All of their patients undergo profile analysis before plastic surgery and the goal is that after plastic surgery the patients facial features fit the profile.

In practice the individual communicator often has to cope with three body images which may be consistent, but are often disturbingly different: (1) his own body image as he perceives it; (2) his body image as others perceive it; (3) his *reflected body image* which is an accurate picture of his body as it currently appears. Often a person's own body image is highly distorted and this can lead to surrealistic and ineffective communication. In order to provide you with a test of the accuracy of your own body image, the body image test has been developed and is included in this chapter.

Clothing probably represents the most important artifactual means of modifying appearance and, hence, body image. Certainly clothing is a major medium of communication and, as such, is the major means by which we establish our self-identity in interpersonal communication. More specifically clothing transmits three types of information or meaning. First, it symbolizes and conveys a great deal of information about the emotions the communicator may be experiencing. Second, clothing has a great impact on the behavior of the wearer. Third, clothing serves to differentiate one group or class of people from another. Taken collectively, clothing has been found to communicate accurately the degree(s) of fashionability, socialization, and formality characteristic of the wearer.

Cosmetics also function as a major means of communication. The use of cosmetics can be particularly effective in modifying the communicator's reflective image so that is comes much closer to the desired image. The work of the Westmore brothers demonstrates the great communicative potential of cosmetics when applied by professionals. Whether aesthetic or therapeutic makeup is used, the results are striking as the photographs in this chapter illustrate. Finally, the case of Becky Richardson demonstrates what a beneficial impact therapeutic cosmetics can have on reflective image, self-image, and, ultimately, on communication.

Hairstyle and eyeglasses are treated as secondary means of communication. Similarly, the fashionability and functionality of eyeglasses is discussed in the context of their impact on interpersonal communication.

Finally, plastic surgery, the most drastic means of modifying body image, is examined from the personal perspective of two of the most prominent plastic surgeons in the country. The relevance and importance of plastic surgery is demonstrated by the fact that over one million Americans had elective plastic surgery last year. The reasons for the dramatic growth in plastic surgery seem rather clear. Leading authorities now agree that plastic surgery is an extremely valuable means of modifying body image, self-image, and, ultimately, the way the patient communicates with others and they with him.

Those who seek plastic surgery are motivated by both external and internal pressures. The three external pressures are (1) the need to please others, (2) paranoid ideation, and (3) personal career or social ambitions that seem obstructed because of a flaw in physical appearance. When externally motivated, plastic surgery patients are usually disappointed in the results because the real cause of their personal problem is not a physical defect. In contrast the internally motivated, those who seek plastic surgery simply to modify their appearance and please themselves, are usually very happy with the results.

Plastic surgery typically results in a significant change in the reflective image, the self-image, and, finally, the communication behavior of the patient. This metamorphosis is illustrated through the research of Dr. Wagner and Dr. Edgerton, and the pictures of Dr. Wagner's patient. After plastic surgery, the communication of the patient is usually characterized by much more involvement, confidence, vigor, aggressiveness, and an eagerness to build trusting relationships with others.

NOTES

[1] E. Berscheid and E. Walster, "Beauty and the Best," *Psychology Today*, 6 (1972), 43.

[2] K. Wagner and H. Gould, *How to Win in the Youth Game: The Magic of Plastic Surgery* (Englewood Cliffs, N. J.: Prentice-Hall, 1972), p. 22.

[3] Ibid., pp. 214–15.

[4] L. Thayer, *Communication and Communication Systems* (Homewood, Ill.: Richard D. Irwin, 1968), p. 243.

[5] E. Berscheid, W. Walster, and G. Bohrnstedt, "The Happy American Body, a Survey Report," *Psychology Today*, 7 (1973), 123. R. K. Gable, A. J. LaSalle, and K. E. Cook ["Dimensionality of Self-Perception: Tennessee Self-Concept Scale," *Perceptual and Motor Skills*, 36 (1973), 551] emphasize that the Tennessee Self-Concept Scale used eight measures to define self-concept: identity (awareness), self-satisfaction (acceptance), behavior (acts), physical self, moral-ethical self, personal self, family self, and social self. This chapter emphasizes the vitally important role of the body image in shaping the total self-image or self-concept, however.

[6] M. E. Roach and J. B. Eicher, *The Visible Self: Perspectives on Dress* (Englewood Cliffs, N. J.: Prentice-Hall, 1973), pp. 4-5.

[7] Ibid., pp. 5-6.

[8] E. Adamson Hoebel, "Clothing and Ornament," in *Dress, Adornment and the Social Order*, ed. M. E. Roach and J. B. Eicher (New York: Wiley, 1965), pp. 16-18.

[9] E. Kretschmer, *Physique and Character*, 2nd ed. (New York: Cooper Square, 1970), pp. 18-35.

[10] W. H. Sheldon, *Atlas of Man: A Guide for Somatyping the Adult Male at All Ages* (New York: Harper & Row, 1954).

[11] W. E. Wells and B. Siegel, "Stereotypes Somatypes," *Psychological Review*, 8 (1961), 78.

[12] R. N. Walker, "Body Build and Bahavior in Young Children: II Body Build and Parents' Ratings," *Child Development*, 34 (1963), 20-23.

[13] Ibid., 8-10.

[14] J. B. Cortes and F. M. Gatti, "Physique and Motivation," *Journal of Consulting Psychology*, 30 (1966), 408-14.

[15] J. B. Cortes and F. M. Gatti, "Physique and Propensity," *Psychology Today*, 4 (1970) 42.

[16] D. Byrne, O. London, and K. Reeves, "The Effects of Physical Attractiveness, Sex, and Attitude Similarity on Interpersonal Atttraction," *Journal of Personality*, 36 (1968), 264.

[17] E. Walster, V. Aronson, and L. Rohmann, "Importance of Physical Attractiveness in Dating Behavior," *Journal of Personality and Social Psychology*, 4 (1966), 508-14.

[18] J. Mills and E. Aronson, "Opinion Change as a Function of the Communicator's Attractiveness and Desire to Influence," *Journal of Personality and Social Psychology*, 1 (1965), 176.

[19] Berscheid and Walster, "Beauty and the Best," 45-46.

[20] Wagner and Gould, *How to Win in the Youth Game*, p. 45. S. M. Jourard and P. F. Secord ["Body-Cathexis and the Ideal Female Figure," *Journal of Abnormal and Social Psychology*, 50 (1955), 245-46] found "the existence of a shared ideal for certain dimensions of the female figure" in their sample of college women. "With the exception of bust measurement, these dimensions are smaller than the actual body measurements found in our sample. It appears likely that the restrictive nature of these ideal dimensions is, in some cases, a source of anxiety and insecurity."

[21] Wagner and Gould, *How to Win in the Youth Game*, p. 47.

[22] J. R. Routh, "Cosmetic Surgery Is for Men, Too," *The Atlanta Journal and Constitution Magazine*, April 7, 1974, p. 39.

[23] Interview with Dr. Kurt Wagner at his home in Sherman Oaks, California, May 10, 1973.

[24] Berscheid, Walster, and Bohrnstedt, "The Happy American Body," 121.

[25] P. F. Secord and S. M. Jourard, "The Appraisal of Body-Cathexis: Body-Cathexis and Self," *Journal of Consulting Psychology*, 17 (1953), 347. See also S. M. Jourard and J. J. Landsman, "Cognition, Cathexis, and the 'Dyadic Effect' in Men's Self-Disclosing Behavior," *Merrill-Palmer Quarterly of Behavioral Development*, 6 (1960), 178-86, and S. M. Jourard, *Disclosing Man to Himself* (Princeton, N.J.: Van Nostrand Reinhold, 1968).

[26] A. A. Sugerman and F. Haronian, "Body Type and Sophistication of Body Concept," *Journal of Personality*, 32 (1964), 393.

[27] W. J. Cahnman, "The Stigma of Obesity," *Sociological Quarterly*, 9 (1968), 297.

[28] J. E. Singer and P. F. Lamb, "Social Concern, Body Size, and Birth Order," *Journal of Social Psychology*, 68 (1966), 144-47.

[29] P. R. Wilson, "Perceptual Distortion of Height as a Function of Ascribed Academic Status," *Journal of Social Psychology*, 74 (1968), 97-100.

[30] While this test is different in form and function, many of the terms for the body parts come from the body survey reported in Berscheid, Walster, and Bohrnstedt, "The Happy American Body," 121.

[31] M. Kefgen and P. Touchie-Specht, *Individuality in Clothing Selection and Personal Appearance: A Guide for the Consumer* (New York: Macmillan, 1971), pp. 10-11.

[32] M. E. Roach and J. B. Eicher, *The Visible Self: Perspectives on Dress*, p. 112. "Dress has meaning as well as form. The total visual effect or total form of dress can be analyzed by breaking it down into elemental aesthetic forms (colors, lines, shapes, textures, values) and describing *how* these elements are organized into particular relationships. Analyses of *meaning* are concerned with emotional responses to the form of dress and reasons *why* certain arrangements of dress may be thought more beautiful than others."

[33] G. P. Stone, "Appearance and the Self," in *Dress, Adornment and the Social Order*, p. 220.

[34] Ibid., p. 234.

[35] Kefgen and Touchie-Specht, *Individuality in Clothing Selection and Personal Appearance*, pp. 12-14.

[36] *Ibid.*, p. 16.

[37] L. Langner, "Clothes and Government," in *Dress, Adornment and the Social Order*, p. 127. It is interesting to note [H. Freed, "Nudity and Nakedness," *Sexual Behavior*, 3(1973), 3-5] that there is a cultural bias in America against removing all clothing and being immodest. There is greater acceptance of nudity at upper socioeconomic levels and a greater restraint at lower socioeconomic levels. About 90 percent of persons surveyed in the upper socioeconomic levels had coitus in the nude. In contrast, nude coitus was the mode in only 66 percent of those who never went beyond high school, and only 43 percent of those with grade school educations were nude during intercourse. This surprising finding suggests that Americans distinguish between the naked and the nude. To be naked is to be deprived of clothes and to feel embarrassed, uncomfortable, and immodest. To be nude suggests the image of a confident individual who feels the body is aesthetically pleasing. Women who feel no uneasiness at being naked have been found to be lacking in sexual attractiveness to the normal male.

[38] J. Hamilton and J. Warden, "Student's Role in a High School Community and His Clothing Behavior," *Journal of Home Economics*, 58 (1966), 789-91.

[39] F. Zweig, "Clothing Standards and Habits," in *Dress, Adornment and the Social Order*, pp. 111-12.

[40] J. Schwartz, "Men's Clothing and the Negro," in *Dress, Adornment and the Social Order*, p. 164.

[41] Ibid., p. 172. Laura V. Rouzan [Clothing as a Communication Medium Among Afro-Americans," Unpublished Paper, University of Georgia, spring 1975] has done some fascinating research on the major meanings communicated by such black clothing styles as the Superfly and the Dude look.

[42] L. Ailen, "Relationships of Dress to Selected Measures of Personality in Undergraduate Women," *Journal of Social Psychology*, 59 (1963), 121.

[43] K. Gibbins, "Communication Aspects of Women's Clothes and Their Relation to Fashionability," *British Journal of Social and Clinical Psychology*, 8 (1969), 306-7.

[44] Ibid., 309-10.

[45] Interview with Mike and Marvin Westmore at the M. G. Westmore Cosmetic Studio, 15910 Ventura Blvd, Suite 1027, Encino, California, May 29, 1973. Since both brothers were present throughout the interview, both will be identified in future references to this interview. The author owes the Westmore brothers a special note of thanks for their cordiality, intense interest in the subject matter of this

book, and their willingness to release the remarkable photographs of Becky Richardson.

[46] Ibid.

[47] Ibid. The purpose of this section is not to deal with the basic materials of cosmetics such as the foundation treatment, eyeshadow, powder, eyebrow pencil, eyeliner, mascara, lipstick. This subject is covered in professional detail by Mike Westmore in his new book, *The Art of Theatrical Makeup for Stage and Screen* (New York: McGraw-Hill, 1973; in Kefgen and Touchie-Specht, "Skin Care and Cosmetics," *Individuality in Clothing Selection and Personal Apperance* pp. 143-57; and by other authorities.

[48] Ibid.

[49] Ibid. In view of President Nixon's much publicized trouble with inadequate makeup in first televised debate with John Kennedy, the Westmores were asked what kind of makeup would enhance Nixon's communicative potential. They responded that "he has a hard appearance. Rough with that dark beard that shows through. There is nothing you can do to control that. You can shave twenty times a day and that color is still there. And his features, the way he scowls with his eyebrows, you know. . . . One of the problems is that they over made him up in the beginning. What I would do with him colorwise would be to give him a healthy look. He is very light. And not totally block out his beard but let just enough of it to come through to denote that I am virile enough to have a beard. . . . There is not too much you can do with the eyebrows. He shows very much the intensity of what he is saying with his eyebrows—very obvious. I think this is one of the things, that and his beard and his angular, square jaw, sort of set—this has got him into a lot of visual trouble as opposed to one of the Kennedy boys who are Tom Sawyer grown up."

[50] C. T. Kenny and D. Fletcher, "Effects of Beardedness on Person Perception," *Perceptual and Motor Skills,* 37 (1973), 413-14, found that bearded man were perceived more favorably than nonbearded men on seven of eight adjective checklists where there were differences. Certainly there are many secondary means of modifying appearance—such as the straightening of teeth, contact lenses, and hair-straightening and tinting—which cannot be covered in a single chapter.

[51] R. Corson, *Fashions in Hair: The First Five Thousand Years* (New York: Hillary House Publishers, 1969), p. 19.

[52] Ibid., p. 20.

[53] R. Corson, *Fashions in Eyeglasses* (London: Peter Owen Ltd., 1967), p. 18. At present, we tend to take eyeglasses for granted and emphasize their fashionability while downplaying their functionality. Such an attitude is one more measure of the speed of technological change in our society, for "people with poor eyesight in the Dark Ages were given very crude remedies: 'And they shall use little and careful . . . meats, and comb their heads and drink wormwood before they take food. Then shall a salve be wrought for unsharp-sighted eyes; take pepper and beat it, and bettle nut and a somewhat of salt and wine; that will be a good salve.' "

[54] Routh, "Cosmetic Surgery Is for Men, Too," p. 34.

[55] "The Pursuit of Youth," NBC News Special on Americans' expensive attempts to regain their youth, WSB-TV, Atlanta, Georgia, May 31, 1974. Dr. Wagner was interviewed on the program and emphasized that he had rebuilt his wife with plastic surgery on her eyes, silicone in her chin, and a breast lift operation. Wagner's wife referred to him, admiringly, as "her own Ponce de Leon." The program emphasized that many individuals will seek almost any means to regain their youthful appearance. For example, Winston Churchill, Emperor H. Selassie, and actress Lillian Gish all allegedly had injections from "unborn sheep fetuses" in an effort to rejuvenate themselves and retain or regain a youthful appearance.

56 Interview with Dr. Kurt Wagner at his home in Sherman Oaks, California, May 10, 1973. Dr. Wagner was most gracious in his lengthy interview with me and I wish to express appreciation for his cooperation and the release of photographs of his patient which appear in this chapter. Dr. Wagner seemed to be delighted that a professor in speech communication had the interest and motivation to explore the communicative potential of plastic surgery.

57 Interview with Dr. Milton Edgerton at his office, University of Virginia Hospital, Charlottesville, Virginia, April 10, 1974, conducted by John Bloodworth, research assistant to the author.

58 N. J. Knorr, M. T. Edgerton, and J. E. Hoopes, "The 'Insatiable' Cosmetic Surgery Patient," Plastic and Reconstructive Surgery, 40 (1967), 285.

59 M. T. Edgerton, N. J. Knorr, and J. R. Callison, "The Surgical Treatment of Transsexual Patients," Plastic and Reconstructive Surgery, 45 (1970), 38.

60 M. T. Edgerton, W. E. Jacobson, and E. Meyer, "Surgical-Psychiatric Study of Patients Seeking Plastic (Cosmetic) Surgery: Ninety-Eight Consecutive Patients with Minimal Deformity," British Journal of Plastic Surgery, 13 (1960), 144.

61 M. T. Edgerton, and N. J. Knorr, "Motivational Patterns of Patients Seeking Cosmetic (Esthetic) Surgery," Plastic and Reconstructive Surgery, 48 (1971), 553-54.

62 Interview with Dr. Milton Edgerton.

63 M. T. Edgerton and M. D. Wolfort, "The Dermal-Flap Canthal Life for Lower Eyelid Support," Plastic and Reconstructive Surgery, 42 (1969), 42-52; E. Falces, D. Wesser, and M. Gormey, "Cosmetic Surgery of the Non-Caucasian Nose," Plastic and Reconstructive Surgery, 45 (1970), 317-25; K. L. Stephenson, "The 'Mini Life' an Old Wrinkle in Face Lifting," Plastic and Reconstructive Surgery, 46 (1970), 226-35; M. T. Edgerton, "Surgical Correction of Facial Paralysis: a Plea for Better Reconstructions," Annals of Surgery, 165 (1967), 985-98; M. T. Edgerton, L. O. McKnelly, and F. G. Wolfort, "Operating Room Photography for the Plastic Surgeon," Plastic and Reconstructive Surgery, 46 (1970), 93-95.

64 Interview with Dr. Milton Edgerton.

65 Interview with Dr. Kurt Wagner.

66 Ibid.

67 Ibid.

68 Interview with Mike and Marvin Westmore. Obviously impressed with Wagner's professionalism, the Westmores noted that "Wagner did a film. Did he tell you about it? He did surgery on a gal. He took a grandmother who had a face like a prune. And kind of not really heavy, but the type of body where she wears dresses down to the wrists. . . . She lost weight, went to a gym, had her surgery done, and when it was all over with, this gal was walking down the street with uplifted boobs and a miniskirt on and she looked like a million bucks and she was like sixty-three years old. Before that [cosmetic surgery] she would have resigned herself to being a wrinkled old grandmother."

69 Interview with Dr. Milton Edgerton.

70 Interview with Dr. Kurt Wagner.

71 Ibid.

6

THE VOCALIC COMMUNICATION SYSTEM

Sounds communicate meaning. The meanings exchanged by sound are vitally important in communicating the emotional state and the perceived personality of the communicator. If you doubt the truth of this assertion, listen to the audiotapes of Franklin Roosevelt's Fireside Chats during World War II.

The expressed purpose of Roosevelt's extemporaneous speeches was to allay the fears of the nation. Roosevelt's consummate use of sound as a communication medium was highly instrumental in helping him achieve his purpose. Imagine for a moment the following situation. Roosevelt comes on the radio talking in a high-pitched, quavering voice at an extremely rapid rate. He stutters repeatedly and fills his frequent pauses with perceptible sighs. The nation might have experienced a real panic. Americans would probably have been even more fearful of an emotionally distraught president than of the Nazis.

In fact Roosevelt recognized what many subsequent studies have verified. The voice can be a powerful instrument for transmitting the emotional state of the communicator. Perhaps more important in the long term, the voice can be used as a major force in shaping the perceived personality characteristics of the communicator. Roosevelt put this knowledge to good use during the war. He used his voice to communicate the image of a vigorous, confident, and decisive leader who was completely in control of his emotions. Not so incidentally, he used his voice to mold a political personality which successfully withstood the critical scrutiny of four presidential campaigns.

At least intuitively most students recognize the role of the voice in shaping their perceived personality. The point was demonstrated graphically in the author's class on communication and conflict. Former Secretary of State Dean Rusk appeared in this class recently. The students asked him many questions. They obviously were concerned with putting their best personality forward. Significantly, their vocal pattern was very different when addressing Rusk than it had been previously in the class. Almost invariably the students paused before addressing Rusk. Typically the pitch of their voice became much lower, the rate was much slower, the cadence more measured, and the nonfluencies less frequent. Clearly, the students wanted to be perceived as serious and thoughtful observers of the international scene who were in control of their emotions. They knew that Rusk's perception of them would be affected materially by their use of their voice.

This chapter is designed to examine how the voice can be used to exchange meanings accurately and efficiently. Particular emphasis is placed on those communicative functions that can be more appropriately identified with the vocalic communication system than any of the other systems. Specifically, this chapter illustrates how individuals (1) may more effectively use vocal cues to communicate specific emotions and to modify their perceived personality characteristics, (2) may measure the accuracy with which they communicate by sound, (3) may measure the accuracy with which they perceive meanings communicated by sound, and (4) may improve their capacity to communicate by sound.

The semantics of sound is not a simple matter; the physiology of sound production and the methods for studying this physiology are complex—see Appendix B. We can safely conclude, however, that vocalic communication uses vocal cues. *Vocal cues consist of all attributes of sound that can convey meanings and have some measurable function in interpersonal communication.* The *sound attributes that give any given vocal cue its unique characteristics are: (1) loudness, (2) pitch, (3) rate, (4) duration, (5) quality, (6) regularity, (7) articulation, (8) pronunciation, and (9) silence.*

Loudness or power of the human voice is perhaps the most basic attribute because if a voice cannot be heard none of its other attributes can be used to convey meaning. Loudness is defined in terms of decibels, a measure of the acoustic energy reaching the receiver in interpersonal communication at a given second. Table 6-1 should give the reader a good grasp of the decibel level customarily encountered in varying types of locations and conditions.

The quiet whisper at 10 decibels can be just as disruptive to interpersonal communication as the construction worker's hammer blows on steel plate at 114 decibels. Very often as individuals experience anxiety while they are delivering a speech or engaging in interpersonal communication, the power of their voice drops quickly and they are talking in a whisper which is unintelligible to the individual(s) with whom they are trying to communicate. On one occasion the author had a student who might literally have been called whispering Smith. A prominent and affluent businessman, the man whom we will call Smith experienced great anxiety when giving a public speech. As his anxiety increased Smith's volume dropped until he was whispering and his audience was left in silent exasperation.

TABLE 6-1   Noise Levels for Various Sources and Locations. From Ostwald, P. F., *Soundmaking: The Acoustic Communication of Emotion,* 1963. Courtesy of Charles C Thomas, Publisher, Springfield, Illinois.

SOURCE OR DESCRIPTION OF NOISE	NOISE LEVEL IN DECIBELS
Hammer Blows on Steel Plate at 2 ft.	114
Riveter at 35 ft.	97
Factory	78
Busy Street Traffic	68
Large Office	65
Ordinary Conversation at 3 ft.	65
Large Store	63
Factory Office	63
Medium Store	62
Restaurant	60
Residential Street	58
Medium Office	58
Garage	55
Small Store	52
Theatre	42
Hotel	42
Apartment	42
House, Large City	40
House, Country	30
Average Whisper at 4 ft.	20
Quiet Whisper at 5 ft.	10
Rustle of Leaves in Gentle Breeze	10

In spite of the fact that studies have been conducted on a great variety of conditions in big companies using the assembly-line technique, few have focused on the damaging effects of excessive noise. Please note that the noise level in an average factory is 10 decibels above the noise level of a big city street. This fact was dramatically emphasized for me recently when I toured an assembly plant of one of the world's largest auto manufacturers with a group of my students. In response to my question the personnel director indicated that he had no idea what the noise level on the assembly line was, but that he knew for certain that his assembly line was really rather quiet and that his company had never been sued for job-related hearing disability. Interestingly, communication with the personnel director, who was 3 to 6 feet away as we toured the assembly line, was often impossible because of the noise level.

Anyone who has played a musical instrument is familiar with the concept of pitch. Pitch is the musical note which the voice produces. When you strike middle C on the piano, the C string is vibrating at the rate of 256 times per second. Likewise a human voice which produces the middle C note is conveying the same pitch. Each communicator has a *modal pitch* or one that occurs more frequently than any other pitch in his extemporaneous speech. You can easily identifiy your *modal pitch by recording a brief sample of your speech and matching the pitch of the sound which most frequently occurs with the appropriate note on your piano keyboard.*

The communicator should note that a number of factors affect modal pitch. Most importantly, "emotion affects modal pitch. A person who is sad or stunned is likely to use a lower modal pitch. Excitement and gaiety are normally shown by higher modal pitch. The quietly angry individual may use a low pitch, while the volatile type of anger may be high-pitched. We tend to associate low pitch with affection between sexes, but higher pitch with talking to babies."[1]

Your speaking or communicating "pitch range" is a measure of the musical interval, the number of notes, between the high and low pitch which you use in speaking.[2] Fisher notes that the "range" we employ in speaking depends on our intent, and on the content of what we are attempting to communicate. Figure 6-1 shows that factual communication has a much more limited pitch range than emotional communication and that emotional communication is apt to be high-pitched since most of it falls above your modal speaking range. Notice also that apathetic and apparent monotone speech both have a very narrow range.

Rate is the third sound attribute of vocal cues which may facilitate or disrupt

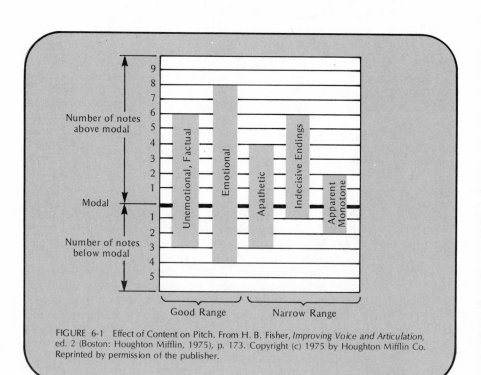

FIGURE 6-1 Effect of Content on Pitch. From H. B. Fisher, *Improving Voice and Articulation,* ed. 2 (Boston: Houghton Mifflin, 1975), p. 173. Copyright (c) 1975 by Houghton Mifflin Co. Reprinted by permission of the publisher.

the transfer of meaning. As previously identified, rate refers to the number of sounds emitted during a given unit of time—usually one second. Of course when the communicator uses sounds to produce speech, speaking rate can have a vitally important impact on the quality of communication. Irregular rate may result in the communicator combining words into units that are unconnected phrases rather than thought units.

Intelligibility and/or comprehension decline when rate of utterance exceeds 275 to 300 words per minute although individuals can learn to comprehend material presented at faster rates through training in simple listening routines.[3] While we recognize that the average individual's thought rate is considerably faster than his speech rate, accelerated rate of utterance is not always the answer. People differ substantially as to the optimum rate of utterance which they prefer as listeners. If the rate is too slow or the pauses too long, the communicator will lose the attention of the person(s) with whom he is trying to communicate.

Finally, rate is a variable of primary interest to the paralinguists since it helps determine how fluent or dysfluent the communicator is and, hence, how effective a speaker he is.

The attributes of rate and duration are integrally related since the length of time a communicator emits a given sound or sounds is a major factor in determining the short-term and often long-term rate at which he delivers sounds. While duration is sometimes treated as a component of rate, it is treated separately here because duration is an identifiable attribute of sound and, as such, may either hinder or help the communicator in his attempt to transmit distortion-free meanings.

Quality, the fifth attribute of sound, has a variety of connotations and is difficult to define precisely. However, there is general agreement among students of vocalic communication that voice quality refers to those vocal characteristics that allow you to differentiate one person's voice from another.

More than one authority now maintains that an individual's vocal qualities are so distinctive that an expert can pick a given individual's voice from tape containing the voices of many other individuals. In the past few years "voiceprints" have been used increasingly in criminal trials in an attempt to provide positive identification of the suspect.

One of the foremost students and proponents of the voiceprint technique is Lawrence G. Kersta of New York, a retired technical specialist for Bell Laboratories and president of Voiceprint Laboratories, Inc., of New York. Kersta has appeared frequently as an expert witness for the prosecution and has attempted to identify the accused. Probably his most famous appearance involved the trial of a defendant who admitted to a network newsman—in an interview put on audiotape—that he had committed arson during the Watts riots in Los Angeles. The newsman would not reveal the identity of the arsonist on the grounds that the confidentiality of his sources of news had to be protected. Kersta was brought in to the trial and asked to identify the arsonist by matching the voice in the taped interview with known samples of the alleged arsonist's voice included among samples of a number of other voices. Although the identification of the defendant by voiceprints was not used by the jury as a piece of evidence to convict him, voiceprints have been used as admissible and persuasive evidence in subsequent trials.[4]

Crystal maintains that voice quality is "a single impression of a voice existing throughout the whole of a normal utterance. . . . The formal analysis of voice-quality would thus seem to be most satisfactorily carried out using a componential approach, establishing as small a number of independently varying parameters as possible."[5] There is not complete agreement on the components which make up voice quality, however. Ogilvie and Rees identify nasality, denasality, breathiness, hoarseness, huskiness, harshness, and stridency.[6] Whether a voice has glottal fry or glottal shock, or is thin or muffled, such components help make up overall voice quality.

The sound attribute of regularity refers to whether your production of sound has a rhythmical and possibly even predictable nature. If you have ever listened to Walter Cronkite you know what regularity of sound and sound pattern is. In contrast Dick Smothers has made a lot of money by emphasizing the arrhythmic or irregular nature of his sound production. Depending on the communicative situation, the sound attribute of regularity can be highly desirable or undesirable.

Articulation involves the use of movable parts at the top of the vocal tract such as tongue, jaw, and lips to shape sounds and, in speech communication, to make transitions between individual sounds and words. While primarily physiological, articulation represents an attribute of sound, much like loudness, which must be present in acceptable form or communication virtually ceases to exist. If you remember saying "Peter Piper picked a peck of pickled peppers" in your grade school days, you know that very careful articulation was necessary or the listener would never be able to determine the exact nature of Peter's task.

Pronunciation "involves the choice of particular vowel or consonant sounds to be used in a specific word, and the syllable to be accented."[7] If you pronounce a word in a way which is inconsistent with general usage or usage among the social groups with which you associate it almost surely will result in confusion at minimum. Perhaps more importantly in terms of its long-range effect on the communicator, consistent mispronunciation of words may impair a speaker's credibility and communicative effectiveness. For example, irrelevant is probably one of the most commonly mispronounced words in our society. Often irrelevant is pronounced "irrevelant." Such mispronunciations, if persistent, markedly lower the quality of an individual's communication.

In the strictest technical sense, silence is not an attribute of vocal cues because silence assures that none of the other eight defining attributes of vocal cues can be present. On the other hand, any sensitive observer of interpersonal communication recognizes that silence is a variable that is closely related to the other eight attributes of vocalic communication, and that silence may have a greater impact in conveying meanings than attributes such as loudness, pitch, rate, or any of the others. For some, silence is a means of clarifying and emphasizing meanings. For others, taciturnity or extended silences may be symptomatic of a personal fear of vocalic communication. Ostwald writes poignantly of a virginal piano player whose great fear was of communicating vocally:

> Her soundmaking pathology involves silence. Words she finds useless vehicles for communication; they seem like empty forms devoid of feeling. Anyway, to use the mouth is a terrible threat, because it reminds this patient that as a baby she was not well fed and weaned too early. A compromise solution is musical soundmaking. . . . [Her desire for physical contact] is partly gratified at each music lesson; teacher and pupil sit closely together and symbolically hold hands while interdigitating the

keyboard with octave passages. Also there is the vicarious experience of a family, for the teacher has a charming wife who serves French pastry and coffee after each lesson, making the miserable girl feel accepted and at home. Nonverbal communication suffuses the atmosphere, from oversize diaper-like napkins offered by the hostess, to the authoritative emotive storytelling of the host.[8]

The nine sound attributes which make up vocal cues, and hence vocalic communication, can obviously be used singly and in combination to clarify meanings which the communicator is attempting to convey by visual and verbal means. Moreover, these attributes when present in appropriate combinations and in the right degree can create a very favorable impression of the communicator. On the other hand these sound attributes can have the opposite effect. For example, Diehl and McDonald found that breathy and nasal vocal qualities interfered with a speaker's ability to communicate information.[9] Moreover, "a low pitch which is less than three notes below modal sounds indecisive. For most speakers an increase in the upper range interval (from modal pitch to high pitch) will increase effectiveness of speech more surely than any other one device."[10]

The communicator who uses improper pronunciation, poor articulation, excessive loudness, etc., will find that the doors to many prestigious business firms are closed to him as are the upper strata of society in many cities. Admittance to a narrowly defined and exclusive social circle may not depend exclusively on the dominant attributes of one's vocalic communication. However, where acceptable "speech" is required, proper articulation and pronunciation are an essential part of one's personal credentials.

VOCALIC COMMUNICATION OF EMOTIONS

Vocal cues represent an important medium of emotional communication. Moreover, individuals differ significantly in their capacity to exchange emotional meaning by sound. Some can use vocal cues to communicate emotional meanings at high levels of accuracy but their decoding ability is limited. With others their abilities are reversed. Most significant of all, however, is the fact that our encoding and decoding capacity to use sound to communicate can be improved rather dramatically. To exploit this important finding this section presents the vocalic meaning sensitivity test and demonstrates how it can be used to expand communicative capacity.

Since we have already studied what man can communicate by movement (kinesic behavior), by space (proxemic behavior), and by artifact (appearance) as separate systems of communication, it is obvious that we must have some means of studying *only* the effects of vocalic communication. To do so we must have some method of separating the effects of vocalic communication from the effects of kinesic, proxemic, and artifactual communication as well as from verbal communication. Students of vocalic communication have been particularly interested in how effectively vocal cues, as opposed to verbal cues, can convey the emotions of the communicator. To study this question with any degree of precision, however, researchers were forced to make the assumption that the effects of verbal and vocal communication could be separated. Indeed "the assumption lying behind most experimental work in this sphere is that before one can assess the nature and extent of the latter [vocal cues] one must first find some way of eradicating the influence of the former [verbal cues]."[11]

At least five different methods have been used to attempt to separate vocal cues and their effects from the influence of all other types of communication. The first method attempts to limit the effects of verbal content by using texts which are so ambiguous as to have no readily indentifiable meanings. Subjects are then asked to read these texts in such a way as to convey specific emotions to listeners by means of the distinctive sound attributes which make up the vocal cues of the reader.

A second method requires that communicators articulate nonsense words and syllables in order to eliminate or severely restrict the influence of the verbal channel. Such nonsense words and syllables are uttered in the form of vocal cues which, ideally, are easily identifiable because of their distinctive sound attributes—very loud, low pitch, fast rate, and extended duration, for example. This has been a particularly popular technique for studying the effects of vocal cues.

A third technique used by Mahl and others is simply to try to ignore the verbal content completely while attempting to identify the meanings conveyed by such sound attributes as silence, laughs, and sighs and nonfluencies such as "ah," "uh," and others. While this technique has yielded many insights as to the impact of vocal cues, it places great strain on the integrity and intuitive skills of the investigator.

The fourth technique employs electronic "filters." Speech samples are passed through filters which eliminate sounds of higher frequencies, making "speech" unintelligible and, in the process, eliminating verbal content. While this technique probably is most successful in eliminating verbal content, it has other disadvantages which will be discussed in a later section of this book.

Finally, a fifth technique has been devised which has much promise for the experimenter who is bilingual. The experimenter, or his confederate(s), attempts to convey certain emotions to a group of judges, but in a language other than English. Japanese was probably the first language used. Since English subjects obviously cannot understand the verbal meanings being conveyed in Japanese they are free to concentrate solely on vocalic communication and the sound attributes which comprise the individual cues.[12]

Fairbanks and Pronovost were among the earliest experimenters in speech communication who attempted to determine whether individuals could communicate significant emotions solely by vocal cues and, if so, how accurately the different emotions could be communicated. They used the first technique, an ambiguous text, in an attempt to assure that meanings communicated were solely the result of the sound attributes of the vocal cues used in reading the passage.

Six competent actors were asked to read the following passage repeatedly:

> You've got to believe it in time to keep them from hanging me. Every night you ask me how it happened. But I don't know! I don't know! I can't

remember. *There is no other answer. You've asked me that question a thousand times, and my reply has always been the same.* It always will be the same. You can't figure out things like that. They just happen, and afterwards you're sorry. Oh, God, stop them . . . quick . . . before it's too late.[13]

As the actors repeated the passage to a group of 64 student judges they were to vary the nature of the vocal cues in such a way that they believed they were accurately conveying the emotions of contempt, anger, fear, grief, and indifference.

The experiment demonstrated not only that all *emotions could be conveyed accurately by vocalic communication* at a level which greatly exceeds chance, but that the *vocal cues which conveyed the different emotions had readily identifiable and distinctive sound attributes.* Average accuracy of identification for the five emotions was 88 percent for indifference, 84 percent for contempt, 78 percent for anger and grief, and 66 percent for fear.[14]

Contempt was communicated by extreme variations in inflections at the ends of phrases, a low median pitch level, and a wide total pitch range. Anger was associated with the greatest variability in all sound attributes, the widest mean extent of all pitch shifts, and the most downward pitch shifts. Fear was associated with the highest median pitch level, the widest total pitch range, and the fewest pauses within phrases at which shifts of pitch were not made. Grief exhibited the least variability among the attributes of sound, the presence of vibrato, the shortest duration of sound, and the slowest rate of pitch change. Finally indifference was communicated by the lowest pitch, the narrowest total pitch range, and shortest duration of sound when downward or upward inflections occurred.[15]

Fairbanks followed this pioneering effort with a study with Hoaglin using the same data but a somewhat different focus. In this study the emphasis was on comparing and contrasting the sound attributes used to communicate each of the five emotions rather than on trying to determine whether the five emotions could be communicated accurately by vocal means. The experimenters found that anger, fear, and indifference were communicated by vocal cues that were comprised of very similar sound attributes. All three of these basic emotions were effectively communicated by rapid rate, short duration of phonations and silence (pauses). Contempt and grief, on the other hand, were communicated by vocal cues that were different from each other and different from the vocal cues that communicated anger, fear, and indifference. While slow rate was a sound attribute associated with both contempt and grief, contempt was identified by the slowest rate of sound production with both long phonations and silences (pauses). Contempt was communicated with phonations and silences of approximately equal length. In contrast, the slow rate of grief was caused almost entirely by prolongation of periods of silence, particularly between phrases. This phenomenon was so marked in the communication of grief that total pause time was almost equal to phonation time.[16] While contempt and grief seem to be expressing rather different affective states of the human being, the reader will recognize that they are communicated by vocal cues with very similar sound attributes.

The second technique for testing the accuracy with which emotions can be communicated vocally was employed in an early study by Dusenbury and Knower. These experimenters and their students made a number of phonograph recordings on which they tried to communicate a detailed list of emotions by reciting letters of the alphabet through the letter K. Two hundred and ninety-four student judges listened to the recordings and were asked to place each separate recitation of part of the alphabet into one of eleven classes of emotions.

Accuracy of identification for contempt ranged from 97 to 81 percent, for grief 93 to 75 percent, for anger 89 to 74 percent, and for fear 89 to 70 percent. No attempt was made to communicate the emotion of indifference, but the reader will note that the pattern is the same as in the earlier study by Fairbanks and Pronovost. Contempt was communicated most accurately followed by grief and anger with fear the most difficult emotion to communicate by vocal means.[17]

Seven other classes of emotion were included in the same experiment. The experimenters note that determination, doubt, and sneering were all communicated vocally at very high levels of accuracy while amazement, pity, and fear were much more difficult to communicate vocally. Torture stood by itself as an emotion that was communicated by voice much less accurately than the other ten types of emotion.

This experiment was particularly important because it provided compelling evidence to support the authors' conclusions that different emotions can be communicated with "a high degree of accuracy" by vocal means. Less central to the study but of substantial relevance for this chapter were the findings that *there are marked differences in the ability of individuals to communicate emotions by vocal means, that the accuracy of such communication depends upon the emotion one attempts to communicate, and that women appear to be more accurate decoders of messages, or more specifically emotions in this case, transmitted vocally than men.*[18]

As instructive as this key experiment was, it suffers from at least two methodological problems. First, emotions were grouped by categories of three. Thus, horror, terror, and fear were listed together as though they were synonyms and represented exactly the same emotion. Similarly, anger, hate, and rage were grouped together as a single class of emotion. Thus definition and differentiation of emotions lacked specificity. Second, the communicators may not have had realistic conceptions of the emotions they attempted to communicate. As Kramer points out in his critical review of research on vocal communication, "these studies [using the technique of reciting the alphabet] unfortunately cannot confirm whether these speakers, or any others, would use these same 'tonal codes' when experiencing the emotions in real situations."[19]

Probably the most detailed and enlightening contemporary research on vocal communication, using the second technique, has been done by Davitz and Davitz. Rather than using eleven groupings of emotions as Dusenbury and Knower had done, they used ten specific emotions and asked eight subjects, four male and four female, to attempt to communicate these ten feelings or emotions by reciting the alphabet. Thirty graduate students at Columbia University were given a list of the ten emotions and made eight recordings. On each of the eight recordings one of the students recited the alphabet eleven times. The first recitation was to establish conversational level and the other ten in random order were intended to communicate each of the ten separate emotions.

Unfortunately, we cannot make detailed comparisons between the recent work of the Davitzes and the earlier work of Fairbanks, Pronovost, Hoaglin, Knower, and Dusenbury. Unlike Fairbanks and his collaborators, the Davitzes did not attempt to have their subjects express contempt, grief, or indifference. Anger was communicated at 65 percent accuracy of identification as compared with 78 percent in the earlier studies by Fairbanks. In contrast, fear was communicated at only 26 percent accuracy in the Davitz study while it was communicated at 66 percent accuracy in the Fairbanks research—it is only fair to point out, however, that of the five emotions that

Fairbanks tried to communicate vocally, fear was the most difficult to express accurately as it was in subsequent studies.

For the Davitz study the judges were asked to make 240 total judgments of the eight speakers. Chance expectancy for the correct identification of each emotion is one in ten. Thus, if the emotions were judged merely on the basis of chance, 24 correct identifications would occur for each emotion. The number of correct identifications for each *emotion expressed* was: (1) anger, 156; (2) nervousness, 130; (3) sadness, 118; (4) happiness, 104; (5) sympathy, 93; (6) satisfaction, 74; (7) and (8) fear and love, 60; (9) jealousy, 59; (10) pride, 50.[20]

While most of the major studies of vocalic communication support the notion that emotions can be communicated at levels of accuracy that far exceed chance expectation, it is obvious that some emotions are more difficult to communicate than others. Consequently, some emotions are more readily confused with each other than other emotions. For example "although fear was correctly identified 60 times, it was mistakenly identified as nervousness 41 times and as sadness 48 times. Similarly, love was correctly identified 60 times, but mistakenly identified as sadness 54 times and as sympathy 47 times. Pride was correctly identified 50 times, but mistakenly identified as satisfaction 48 times and as happiness 37 times."[21]

Davitz also did a followup study to the earlier work by Fairbanks and Pronovost in which he had four female and three male speakers attempt to communicate 14 feelings or emotions vocally by using the technique of the ambiguous text. In this case the same two sentences were used in an attempt to convey each of the 14 emotions: "There is no other answer. You've asked me that question a thousand times and my reply has always been the same."[22] The *percentages of correct identifications for each emotion conveyed vocally* by the most effective male speakers were: (1) despair and impatience, 100 percent; (2) amusement and fear, 90 percent; (3) anger, 80 percent; (4) boredom, 75 percent; (5) affection, disgust, and surprise, 60 percent; (6) joy, 55 percent; (7) dislike, 50 percent; (8) cheerfulness, 45 percent; (9) satisfaction, 35 percent; (10) admiration, 30 percent. For the most effective female speakers the percentages of correct identifications for each emotion were: (1) despair and fear, 100 percent; (2) amusement and boredom, 95 percent; (3) anger, 90 percent; (4) impatience and affection, 75 percent; (5) joy, 60 percent; (6) disgust and surprise, 55 percent; (7) satisfaction, 50 percent; (8) cheerfulness and dislike, 45 percent; (9) admiration, 30 percent.[23]

Along with Davitz, Kramer is one of the few experimenters who have contrasted the relative effectiveness of a number of the major methods or techniques for communicating emotions solely by vocal cues. In one of his most imaginative experiments he used each of the following three methods: (1) subjects using constant, ambiguous sets of words; (2) electronically filtered speech wherein the higher frequencies of speech—upon which word recognition seems to depend—are attenuated by means of an electronic filter; (3) the subject attempting to communicate emotions by vocal cues speaks in a language unknown to the judges—Japanese in this case.

Accuracy of identification for the first method (ambiguous words) was: (1) contempt, 85 percent; (2) indifference, 76 percent; (3) anger, 74 percent; (4) grief, 58 percent; (5) love, 56 percent. Accuracy of identification for the second method (electronically filtered speech) was: (1) anger, 76 percent; (2) grief, 71 percent; (3) indifference, 63 percent; (4) and (5) contempt and love, 48 percent. Accuracy of identification for the third method (Japanese) was: (1) grief, 90 percent; (2) indifference, 73 percent; (3) anger, 67 percent; (4) love, 38 percent; (5) contempt, 20 percent.[24]

While there are obvious differences between the three methods, there is also *an impressive degree of accuracy or fidelity with which the five types of emotions are expressed by vocalic communication.*

In broadest perspective, we should now ask which meanings can be communicated accurately by vocal cues, whether there are individual differences in vocalic communication ability and, if so, whether an individual can improve the quality of his vocalic communication of emotions by practice. Certainly the discussion of relevant research to this point demonstrates clearly that a significant number of emotions can be communicated with such accuracy that there is only 1 chance in a 1,000 with the stronger emotions that their identification could be due to chance. Even one of the most skeptical critics of the potential of vocalic communication, Starkweather, agrees that judges "agree substantially when asked to identify emotions being expressed and the strength of feeling."[25] While the accuracy of identification of a particular emotion depends on the decoding skill of the listener, it seems safe to conclude that contempt, indifference, grief, anger, anxiety, sadness and happiness, as well as a number of other meanings or emotions, can be communicated with rather high degrees of accuracy. The accuracy with which given emotions are identified from one experiment to another has varied somewhat, but considering the variety of experimental techniques and procedures employed the results are amazingly consistent. Generally speaking emotions such as contempt and indifference are communicated at very high levels of accuracy. Emotions like sympathy and satisfaction are moderately difficult to identify and fear and love are extremely difficult to identify by relying solely on vocal cues.

The results reported in this chapter document the fact that significant differences exist between individuals in their ability to communicate a variety of emotions accurately by vocal cues. Indeed, in a cleverly designed study addressed to this very point Levy found significant differences (1) in ability of judges to recognize feelings expressed vocally by others, (2) in ability of individuals to express feelings vocally to others, and (3) in individuals' ability to identify their own feelings which had previously been recorded in their own voice on tape.[26]

The vocalic meaning sensitivity test (VMST) has been developed to test the accuracy with which individuals can communicate and perceive meanings conveyed solely by vocal cues. Extensive use in the author's own classes suggests that it is an extremely useful instrument. All students are given the test and almost without exception they become very involved in the learning experience it provides. Many students have emphasized that the VMST gives them a much better appreciation of the functions of vocalic communication, and with repeated use it significantly improves both their encoding and decoding abilities.

To use the vocalic meaning sensitivity test in its simplest form you must do two things. First have a friend or acquaintance attempt to communicate disgust, happiness, interest, sadness, bewilderment, contempt, surprise, anger, determination, and fear solely by the vocal cues he uses in reading the following two sentences: "There is no other answer. You've asked me that question a thousand times, and my answer is always the same." Your friend should repeat the two sentences above ten times; each time he is trying to communicate a different meaning by varying such sound attributes as pitch, loudness, and rate. He should randomize the order in which he attempts to communicate each class of vocalic meaning (thus sadness may be the first type of meaning he attempts to communicate and determination the second). To separate one reading from another, your friend should begin each reading by saying "this is vocal message number 1" or "this is vocal message number 2." If your friend is particularly interested in communication of the highest possible quality, he may want to practice and put his best efforts on audiotape—then, rather than listening to your friend directly you will listen to him on tape. When attempting to communicate vocally before a live audience the communicator at minimum should sit with his chair turned away from the audience. Ideally, the communicator will sit behind a screen to eliminate the possibility of kinesic of other nonverbal cues.

Second, you should take the vocalic meaning sensitivity test by following the directions below:

THE VOCALIC MEANING SENSITIVITY TEST*

The communicator you are listening to—either live or on tape recording—is attempting to communicate ten different classes or kinds of meaning to you. Each attempt to communicate a class of meaning will begin with the words "this is vocal message number__." You are to listen very carefully and place the number of the vocal message in the blank across from a word, such as disgust or happiness, which comes closest to representing the meaning which has just been communicated to you vocally. Follow the same procedure for each of the ten vocal messages.

CLASS OF VOCALIC MEANING	NUMBER OF VOCAL MESSAGE
Disgust	____
Happiness	____
Interest	____
Sadness	____
Bewilderment	____
Contempt	____
Surprise	____
Anger	____
Determination	____
Fear	____

The asterisk at the top of the VMST is meant to suggest that you may use an expanded form of the test if you desire. The ten terms used here were used for two reasons. They have previously been used in tests of vocalic communication and they are the same terms used in Part I of the facial meaning sensitivity test. Therefore, the reader can make direct comparisons between his ability to perceive and communicate meanings by facial and vocal means. He should simply compare his accuracy of identification scores for Part I of the facial meaning sensitivity test with his scores on the vocalic meaning sensitivity test. If the reader wants to make a more extended test of his ability to perceive and transmit meanings communicated vocally, however, he should add ten terms to the test. These terms, also frequently used in tests of vocalic communication, are the following: indifference, grief, anxiety, sympathy, pride, despair, impatience, amusement, satisfaction, and dislike. By adding these ten terms to the vocalic sensitivity meaning test, the reader has a more comprehensive and demanding test of his vocalic skills.

To test your ability to communicate meanings accurately as opposed to testing your ability to perceive meanings transmitted by vocal cues, you should attempt to communicate the ten emotions which comprise the vocalic meaning sensitivity test by making a tape recording and then giving the VMST to a group of people of your own choice.

Students' ability to communicate the ten meanings which comprise the VMST vary dramatically (6 correct choices out of 10 would be an accuracy of identification of 60 percent). The scores of the "vocal communicators" in my classses have ranged from 85 percent to 30 percent; the scores of the "vocal perceivers" have fallen in about the same range. As a rule of thumb you can assume that a score of 70 percent or above is excellent, 69 to 50 percent is average, and below 50 percent is poor.

Repeated use of the VMST usually leads to marked improvement in both the ability to encode and decode messages conveyed by sound. While the instrument is still being tested, it is safe to conclude that you have the potential to improve your scores on the test by at least 20 percent. If you set realistic goals for yourself, the VMST can be a great help to you in attaining them.

VOCALIC COMMUNICATION OF PERSONALITY CHARACTERISTICS

Clearly, vocal cues represent an effective medium for the exchange of emotional meanings. It is clear also that we can greatly improve our capacity to exchange meanings vocally. The functions of vocalic communication are hardly limited to the exchange of emotional meanings, however. Another function may be even more important to some readers. *A communicator can make marked changes in his personality, as it is perceived by others, by his use of vocal cues.* The implications of this finding are striking for a communicator who wishes to change the perceived characteristics of his personality.

Such a finding could, of course, be misinterpreted. A course or two in voice training is not apt to result in a startling transformation of personality. Indeed the calculated use of your voice is not apt to change your basic personality, but it may result in perceptible differences in the *ways others perceive your personality.*

Interest in the possible relationships between vocal cues and personality characteristics can be traced to the early days of radio when massive national audiences were first attracted. Not surprisingly, many radio listeners became convinced that they could formulate an accurate personality profile of a radio performer simply by listening to his voice. A more limited group was convinced that they could also accurately predict what an announcer looked like by listening to him.

Stimulated by the intense curiosity of radio listeners, Pear analyzed the reaction of over 4,000 radio listeners to nine trained radio voices and concluded that listeners consistently identified certain patterns of vocal cues with certain occupations like clergyman and judge. Pear also found, however, that listeners consistently agreed that certain "vocal stereotypes" identified certain professions, although they made a number of errors in the application of such stereotypes.[27]

In 1934 Allport and Cantril conducted the first major study specifically designed to examine the question of *whether, and to what extent, the natural voice is a valid indicator of personality.* Their results strongly affirmed a positive relationship. The authors wrote that the voice definitely conveys "correct information concerning inner and outer characteristics."[28] Specifically, they found that the sound attributes which comprise vocal cues are accurate indicators of the important personality dimensions of introversion/extroversion and ascendance/submission. Moreover, vocal cues were found to be much more consistent indicators of personality characteristics than indicators of features of physical appearance."[29]

While the pioneering study by Allport and Cantril did suggest a strong relationship between the nature of vocal cues and dimensions of the speaker's personality, the authors were bothered by the apparent fact that a limited number of vocal cues seemed to create a stereotype of the speaker in the mind of the listener.[30] Initially, the tendency of listeners to deal in stereotypes suggested that the listeners took a limited number of vocal cues and erroneously concluded that a large group of people, who conveyed vocal cues with the same sound attributes, had the same personality characteristics.

The concern that "vocal stereotypes" might invalidate research which attempts to predict personality characteristics from vocal cues has persisted up to the present. Such concern seems unwarranted for a number of reasons: (1) Stereotypes, while sometimes inaccurate, are often accurate; (2) When the vocal stereotypes are inaccurate the judges typically make the same error. Thus, as Crystal writes, "such consistency in error may well be indicative of the existence of unformulated but none the less systematic voice-quality/trait correlations, or *vocal stereotypes* as they are usually called in this literature, and is an important piece of evidence justifying the psychologists' optimism that a systematic basis for personality in vocal cues does exist."[31] (3) The accuracy of an audience's or individual's inferences about a speaker's *real* personality characteristics is not as important as an audience's agreement about a speaker's *perceived* personality characteristics. As Pearce and Conklin write, "it should be noted that the accuracy of audience inferences about a speaker is not particularly important in this context. Experienced public speakers develop characteristic manners of presentation that lead audiences to draw desired or undesired inferences about them which, *whether accurate or not* [author's italics], affect the continuation and effectiveness of the communication situation. If a speaker is perceived as effeminate, arrogant, unscrupulous, or incompetent because of vocal cues . . . his actual personality and credibility may be superfluous."[32]

In spite of the great promise of the Allport and Cantril research, World War II, and perhaps the cyclical rhythms of researchers, resulted in a period of almost twenty-five years when little effort was made to examine the relationship between vocal cues and perceived personality characteristics.

Addington has conducted perhaps the most exhaustive, recent research on the question of *which specific attributes of sound are indicators or predictors of certain, specific personality characteristics.* In work for his doctoral dissertation he attempted to simulate a number of vocal qualities (breathy, thin, flat, nasal, tense, throaty, and orotund), to manipulate rate, and introduce variety in pitch. Judges consistently agreed on the personality attributes associated with the different sound attributes in the vocal cues. Judges' agreement was highest on the feminine/masculine ratings of personality (.94) and lowest for the extroverted/introverted ratings (.81). The most uniformly perceived personality dimensions were feminine/masculine, young/old, enthusiastic/apathetic, energetic/lazy, good looking/ugly, co-operative/uncooperative, unemotional/emotional, talkative/quiet, intelligent/stupid, interesting/uninteresting, and mature/immature.[33]

Male communicators were seen as varying along four relatively unique personality dimensions: (1) lanky/dumpy, (2) hearty/glum, (3) potent/impotent, and (4) softhearted/hard-hearted. In contrast, female communicators were seen as varying along five personality dimensions: (1) social/anti-social, (2) agressive/unresisting, (3) urbane/coarse, (4) passionate/dispassionate, and (5) wise/foolish. Thus, personalities of males were perceived from vocal cues in terms of physical characteristics while females were evaluated in more social terms.[34]

The specific findings are particularly enlightening in view of the conceptual framework of this chapter. For both male and female speakers, those who used greater variety in *pitch* were thought to be *dynamic* and *extroverted.* Male and female speakers who used variety in *rate* were both thought to be extroverted but the males were also seen as animated while the females were seen as *high-strung, inartistic,* and *uncooperative.*

The specific sound attributes seemed to be associated with very specific personality characteristics in the minds of the listeners. For example, *both* males and females with flat voices were evaluated as *sluggish, cold,* and *withdrawn,* and *both* males and females with *nasal* voices were evaluated as *unattractive, lethargic,* and *foolish.* Other vocal qualities were associated with very different personality characteristics for males and females. For example, males with breathy voices were perceived as youthful and artistic while females with breathy voices were viewed as feminine, but callow and high-strung. Males with tense voices were perceived as cantankerous, but females with tense voices as high-strung and pliable. Even more strikingly, the male with a throaty voice was evaluated as suave but the female with a throaty voice was evaluated as oafish or a "clod"; males with orotund voices were perceived as vigorous and aesthetic while the female with an orotund voice was perceived as a "clubwoman."[35]

Certainly, "this study has made it quite evident that it is possible for a speaker, through a variety of vocal changes, to make gross or subtle alterations in his personality as it is perceived by listeners cued only by a sample of the speaker's speech. . . . For those speakers interested in creating a perceived personality they would be pleased to claim as their own, and for those interested in character interpretation, vocal dexterity is a mandatory skill."[36]

Research in the last decade following Addington's comprehensive efforts has consistently confirmed the idea that the nature of vocalic communication materially affects the personality characteristics which listeners identify with the communicator. In addition, specific sound attributes—such as high pitch or nasality—are consistently associated with the same, specific personality traits by the listener.

Markel, Meisels, and Houck studied a group of schizophrenics and a group of non-schizophrenics. They found that specific impressions of a speaker's personality, as well as his physical characteristics, are determined by the speaker's voice qualities.[37] Lambert, Frankel, and Tucker found that 33 French-Canadian girls could accurately identify the "ethic personality" of speakers by listening to their vocal cues.[38] In further interpreting and refining his earlier research Addington concluded that "judgments of listeners ascribing personality from samples of speakers' voices tended to be uniform" and that this relationship was "well supported in the present findings."[39] The results of current research make clear that vocal manipulations do markedly affect the nature of personality perceptions and are effective in altering the listeners' image of the communicator. Interestingly enough females were substantially more effective than males in altering personality ascriptions by manipulating the sound attributes of their vocal cues.[40]

As already suggested, vocal cues are not only good predictors of personality traits but such closely related personal characteristics as credibility and image. Recent research indicates that a communicator's credibility drops with (1) decreases in vocal variety, (2) the presence of nasality, tenseness, and throatiness, and (3) faulty articulation. The simulation of faulty articulation may not have been too realistic in one experiment, however, as the author admits that it featured speakers with pencils lodged horizontally in their mouths.[41] While faulty articulation had the most damaging effect on the speaker's credibility, normal vocal quality was clearly superior to all the rest in eliciting impressions of high credibility.[42] Additional research supports the view that a speaker's credibility or image can be greatly enhanced or damaged depending on the nature of the vocal cues used by the communicator.[43]

The reader with a rather negative self-image may have found this section of the chapter to be rather illuminating. Certainly, you have the potential to enhance your perceived personality by the calculated use of vocal cues. Variation in pitch is strongly associated with the personality characteristics of dynamism and extroversion, for example. If you want to be perceived as dynamic and extroverted, you may want to practice recording your voice on audiotape until pitch variation becomes a dominant feature of your vocalic communication. The same principle applies to the relationship between many other perceived personality characteristics and sound attributes.

There are many public figures such as Franklin Roosevelt and Billy Graham who have used the voice to project a winning personality. Whether you can and should take practical advantage of the knowledge contained in this chapter probably depends to a large degree on the soundness of your own judgment.

PARAVOCAL COMMUNICATION

So far we have been examining the effects of vocalic communication while excluding the effects of verbal communication. A significant portion of our communication can neither be clearly defined as vocal nor verbal in nature, however. Speech habits like "you know" and "sort of" appear to be clearly verbal or linguistic in form but they are not recognized as units of language. Consequently, they are listed as paralinguistic or extralinguistic phenomena. In the same manner belching, coughing, and laughing are essentially different sounds but they too have been identified as extralinguistic phenomena.

Since most of the researchers dealing with such phenomena are linguists or psycholinguists it is not surprising that they would try to place all identifiable behavior within a linguistic framework, and that those phenomena that do not conform to the rules or definitions of language would be placed in the all-inclusive category labeled paralinguistic or extralinguistic. Mahl and Schulze have made perhaps the most thorough and precise attempt to distinguish between linguistic and what they term extralinguistic factors in communication. Linguistic variations include the choice of the language (French or English, for example), variation in dialect, the use of simple or complex sentences, active of passive voice, present or past tense, and extensive or restricted vocabulary. Extralinguistic factors include variation in rate of speech, general loudness, general pitch level, throat clearing, belching, and a wide variety of body movements.[44] In their detailed classification of extralinguistic phenomena the vast majority of the variables they classify would be perceived by this author as vocal and not linguistic. Voice quality, rhythm, continuity of sound, and speech rate are just a few examples of phenomena that are vocal and not linguistic in nature.

Since virtually all of the variables we will discuss in this section are strictly vocal in nature, or closely related in nature to one of the nine attributes of sound previously identified in this chapter, these variables will be referred to as paravocal, rather than paralinguistic or extralinguistic variables.

While there are a large number of factors that might be fairly classified as part of paravocal communication, four of the most significant factors will be examined in this section: (1) rate of utterance, (2) rhythm, (3) hesitations, and (4) nonfluencies. Ideally, *we should be able to assess the effect of these four paravocal factors on communication. Unfortunately, we can do so only by inference since most studies attempt to determine what variables affect rate of utterance, rhythm, hesitations and nonfluencies rather than studying the effects of these factors on interpersonal communication.* As two authorities aptly note, one of the most striking revelations of an exhaustive survey of studies covering paravocal communication *"is the absence of systematic study of how the extralinguistic phenomena affect the listener's spontaneous, communicative behavior or his underlying psychological states and processes."*[45]

From a paravocal perspective, rate of utterance as perceived by listeners is not defined primarily in terms of how fast an individual is talking or uttering sounds. Rate of articulation is determined by the number of halts and pauses which interrupt the flow of utterance. A high rate of utterance has been found to be disruptive in interpersonal communication. High rates of utterance indicate an increase in the use of prepared and well-learned sequences or words, of cut and dried phrases and clichés, of trite and vernacular speech, and of commonplace utterance or professional jargon. As Goldman-Eisler so perceptively concludes, high rate of utterance

> indicates that there is less creative activity and that time serves no function other than that of sound transmission. While the mood which goes with speech that is being organized while being uttered seems to tend towards an arrest of time, that which accompanies speech requiring no further activity beyond the vocalization of learned connections travels through time at a pace dictated, at the best, only by external requirements

such as intelligibility. Such speech will more easily become subject to corruption in the form of slurring, gabbling, etc., and the reason why we find these characteristics in pathological speech or speech produced under abnormal conditions may be due to the fact that such speech consists mainly of established speech habits.[46]

The most consistent finding is that rate of utterance is a valid and accurate indicator of a speaker's psychological state. While this finding applies to both normal and abnormal speakers, emotional disturbance must still be regarded as directly related to variations in speech rate. By inference we can certainly conclude that a communicator using excessive rate is losing or apt to lose self-control, may become highly defensive, and, as cited above, is less capable of modifying his message to meet the demands of the situation.

The rhythm which characterizes a communicator's utterances is of great potential importance and its nature and effects are just beginning to be examined.[47] Dittmann notes that "the aspect of speech we have been working on is its rhythmical characteristic, its prosodic nature." To date, he has found a significant but not very close relationship between speech rhythm and body movements.[48] Goldman-Eisler has offered the provocative hypothesis that rhythmical utterances are directly related to cognitive rhythm in the communicator's thought processes. To paraphrase her findings: cognitive rhythm may result in periods of fluency characterized by rhythmicity in utterance. The only necessary, though not sufficient, condition for the appearance of temporal rhythm is that at least 30 percent of utterance be pausing time.[49]

Pauses or hesitations have a great impact in disrupting or facilitating the transmission of meaning in interpersonal communication. Pauses are defined as nonphonations of 200 milliseconds or more, measured on an oscillographic record of the speech.[50] Pauses or hesitation correspond to the highest point of uncertainty for the communicator which is typically the beginning of a unit of encoding or the beginning of the attempt to communicate a new idea.[51] This finding held up whether the pauses were filled or unfilled.[52] The duration of hesitation pauses was shown to be a highly variable phenomenon, symptomatic of individual differences, sensitive to the pressures of social interaction, and to the requirements of verbal tasks. What is experienced as an increase of speed in talking proved to be variation in amount of pausing. *If you eliminate pauses, the perceived rate of articulation for a given communicator remains virtually constant.*[53]

Finally, perhaps the most studied factors which comprise paravocal communication are the eight types of nonfluencies identified by Mahl. Mahl identifies the eight types of nonfluencies as: (1) *"ah"* (Well . . . ah when I first came home.); (2) *sentence change* (Well she's . . . already she's lonesome.); (3) *repetition* (Cause they . . . they get along pretty well together.); (4) *stutter* (It sort of well I . . . I . . . leaves a memory); (5) *omission* (She mour . . . was in mourning for two years before.); (6) *sentence incompletion* (Well I'm sorry I couldn't get here last week so I could . . . ah . . . I was getting a child ready for camp and finishing up swimming lessons.); (7) *tongue slips* (includes neologisms and the substitution of an unintended for an intended word); (8) *intruding incoherent sound* (If I see a girl I'd like to take out I just . . . dh . . . ask her.)[54] While Mahl designed his speech disturbance categories as a measure of anxiety, they have two more important uses for the purposes of this chapter. In the first place they represent one definition of *disruptive paravocal communication* since each of the eight types of speech disturbance will tend to distort or prevent the exchange of meaning by vocal means. Second, and perhaps more importantly, they can serve to record the impact of such variables as interpersonal trust, confidence, and sincerity on the quality of paravocal communication. For example, one would expect the paravocal communication of an individual whose trust was being destroyed to be characterized by many more nonfluencies than an individual whose trust was being built. In fact this is precisely what Prentice found in a detailed study which examined the impact of trust destruction on a communicator's fluency.[55]

In brief, paravocal communication can reveal much about the emotions a communicator is experiencing. More importantly, paravocal communication can be a major factor in determining the accuracy and efficiency with which meanings may be exchanged. It may serve as a reliable indicator that the vocalic communication system is not functioning as desired.

CONCLUSION

The vocalic communication system operates at the phonological level and is used by the communicator to exchange emotional meaning and shape perceived personality characteristics. It also functions as a metacommunicational vehicle in the form of paravocal communication. Vocalic communication is made up of vocal cues which in turn are comprised of nine different types of sound attributes that give vocal cues their unique characteristics: (1) loudness, (2) pitch, (3) rate, (4) duration, (5) quality, (6) regularity, (7) articulation, (8) pronunciation, (9) silence.

Vocalic communication is a particularly effective medium for the exchange of specific emotions. Research begun in the 1930s and continued to the present date strongly supports the conclusion that emotions can be communicated and perceived accurately by vocal cues, and that individuals differ significantly both in their ability to communicate emotions by vocal means and in their ability to accurately identify them.

Perhaps most importantly, individuals can substantially increase their capacity to exchange meanings accurately by sound. The vocalic meaning sensitivity test provides the reader with the opportunity both to test and to increase this capacity.

The voice has also proved to be a valid indicator of the personality characteristics of the communicator. While there has been some dispute over whether the personality characteristics *ascribed* to a communicator because of his dominant vocal qualities correspond closely with the communicator's *actual* personality characteristics, such an issue is of secondary importance in interpersonal communication. As long as a communicator is perceived as arrogant and incompetent because of the nature of his vocal cues, his personality may be irrelevant. Indeed, the communicator need not suffer endlessly from the effects of a negatively perceived personality. He has the potential for positively modifying his perceived personality by modifying the nature of his vocalic communication.

Finally, we know that some of our utterances are neither clearly verbal nor vocal in nature. Nonetheless many of the variables that have been classified as paralinguistic or extralinguistic—such as belching or throat clearing—are defined primarily by the nature of the sounds they represent. For that reason these variables are collectively identified as paravocal communication. The four paravocal factors of rate of utterance, rhythm, hesitations, and nonfluencies are discussed and their importance in interpersonal communication assessed.

In short, man communicates many meanings by sound. While vocalic communication can be a source of great disruption and confusion in interpersonal interaction, negative effects of the ineffectual use of the voice should not be emphasized. As this chapter demonstrates, vocalic communication is a medium of almost unlimited potential when the medium is used by a highly motivated and skilled person.

NOTES

[1] H. B. Fisher, *Improving Voice and Articulation*, ed. 2 (Boston: Houghton Mifflin, 1975), p. 155.

[2] Ibid., pp. 172-73.

[3] D. B. Orr, "Time Compressed Speech—A Perspective," *Journal of Communication*, 18 (1968), 288-91.

[4] "Criminal Investigation Seminar Ends Here," *The Clarion-Ledger*, Jackson, Mississippi, October 18, 1973. For further information on voiceprints and voice quality profiles see N. N. Markel, "The Reliability of Coding Paralanguage: Pitch, Loudness, and Tempo," *Journal of Verbal Learning and Verbal Behavior*, 4 (1965), 306-308; F. S. Costanzo, N. N. Markel, and P. R. Costanzo, "Voice Quality Profile and Perceived Emotion," *Journal of Counseling Psychology*, 16 (1969), 267-70; N. N. Markel, "Relationship Between Voice-Quality Profiles and MMPI Profiles in Psychiatric Patients," *Journal of Abnormal Psychology*, 74 (1969), 61-66.

[5] D. Crystal, *Prosodic Systems and Intonation in English* (Cambridge: Cambridge University Press, 1969), p. 123.

[6] M. Ogilvie and N. S. Rees, *Communication Skills: Voice and Pronunciation* (New York: McGraw-Hill, 1969), pp. 69-87.

[7] Fisher, *Improving Voice and Articulation*, p. 9.

[8] P. F. Ostwald, *Soundmaking: The Acoustic Communication of Emotion* (Springfield, Ill.: Charles C Thomas, 1963), p. 151.

[9] C. F. Diehl and E. R. McDonald, "Effect of Voice Quality on Communication," *Journal of Speech and Hearing Disorders*, 21 (1956), 236-37.

[10] Fisher, *Improving Voice and Articulation*, p. 174.

[11] Crystal, *Prosodic Systems and Intonation in English*, p. 70.

[12] Ibid., pp. 70-75.

[13] G. Fairbanks and W. Pronovost, "An Experimental Study of the Durational Characteristics of the Voice During the Expression of Emotion," *Speech Monographs*, 6 (1939), 88.

[14] Ibid., 91.

[15] Ibid., 103-104.

[16] G. Fairbanks and S. W. Hoaglin, "An Experimental Study of the Durational Characteristics of the Voice During the Expression of Emotion," *Speech Monographs,* 8 (1941), 90.

[17] D. Dusenbury and F. H. Knower, "Experimental Studies of the Symbolism of Action and Voice—II," *Quarterly Journal of Speech,* 25 (1939), 67-71.

[18] Ibid., p. 75.

[19] E. Kramer, "Judgment of Personal Characteristics and Emotions from Nonverbal Properties of Speech," *Psychological Bulletin,* 60 (1963), 409.

[20] J. R. Davitz and L. J. Davitz, "The Communication of Feelings by Content-Free Speech," *Journal of Communication,* 9 (1959), 9.

[21] Ibid., 104.

[22] J. R. Davitz, ed., *The Communication of Emotional Meaning* (New York: McGraw-Hill, 1964), p. 102.

[23] Ibid., p. 104.

[24] E. Kramer, "Elimination of Verbal Cues in Judgment of Emotion from Voice," *Journal of Abnormal and Social Psychology,* 68 (1964), 390-92.

[25] J. A. Starkweather, "Vocal Communication of Personality and Human Feelings," *Journal of Communication,* 11 (1961), 69.

[26] P. K. Levy, "The Ability to Express and Perceive Vocal Communications of Feeling," in *The Communication of Emotional Meaning,* pp. 44-45. Predictably H. Nash ["Perception of Vocal Expression of Emotion by Hospital Staff and Patients," *Genetic Psychology Monographs,* 89 (1974), 25-87] found that members of a hospital staff were much more sensitive to emotions conveyed by voice than were patients.

[27] T. H. Pear, *Voice and Personality* (London: Chapman and Hall, 1931).

[28] G. W. Allport and H. Cantril, "Judging Personality from Voice," *Journal of Social Psychology,* 5 (1934), 49.

[29] Ibid., 40-45.

[30] Ibid., 51.

[31] Crystal, *Prosodic Systems and Intonation in English,* p. 70.

[32] W. B. Pearce and F. Conklin, "Nonverbal Vocalic Communication and Perception of a Speaker," *Speech Monographs,* 38 (1971), 237.

[33] D. W. Addington, "The Relationship of Certain Vocal Characteristics with Perceived Speaker Characteristics," Ph.D. dissertation, University of Iowa, 1963, p. 151.

[34] Ibid., pp. 153-54.

[35] Ibid., pp. 157-58.

[36] Ibid., p. 163. The reader interested in making positive changes in his perceived personality by modifying the nature of his vocalic communication should see B. L. Brown, W. J. Srong, and A. C. Rencher, "The Effects of Simultaneous Manipulations of Rate, Mean Fundamental Frequency, and Variance of Fundamental Frequency on Ratings of Personality from Speech," *Journal of the Acoustical Society of America,* 55 (1974), 313-18. These researchers found that as a communicator's speaking rate increased his *benevolence* ratings decreased and as speaking rate decreased *competence* ratings decreased. Furthermore, an increase in mean fundamental frequency decreased the ratings on both competence and benevolence.

[37] N. N. Markel, M. Meisels, and J. E. Houck, "Judging Personality from Voice Quality," *Journal of Abnormal and Social Psychology,* 69 (1964), 461.

[38] W. E. Lambert, H. Frankel, and G. R. Tucker, "Judging Personality through Speech: A French-Canadian Example," *Journal of Communication,* 16 (1966), 312-13.

[39] D. W. Addington, "The Relationship of Selected Vocal Characteristics to Personality Perception," *Speech Monographs,* 35 (1968), 498.

[40] Ibid., 499. See also W. J. Weaver and R. J. Anderson, "Voice and Personality Interrelationships," *Southern Speech Communication Journal* 38 (1973), 275-78. In this study the authors assert that the personality characteristics inferred from the vocal cues actually represent an accurate description of the speaker's personality. This claim goes substantially beyond the typical claim that *sound attributes are related to ascribed personality characteristics,* which may or may not be reflected in the communicator's actual personality.

[41] D. W. Addington, "The Effect of Vocal Variations on Ratings of Source Credibility," *Speech Monographs,* 38 (1971), 245-47.

[42] Ibid.

[43] L. S. Harms, "Listener Judgments of Status Cues in Speech," *Quarterly Journal of Speech,* 47 (1961), 164-68; Pearce and Conklin, "Nonverbal Vocal Communication," 237; F. S. Dubner, "Nonverbal Aspects of Black English," *Southern Speech Communication Journal,* 37 (1972), 368.

[44] G. F. Mahl and G. Schulze, "Psychological Research in the Extralinguistic Area," in *Approaches to Semiotics,* ed. T. A. Sebeok, A. S. Hayes, and M. C. Bateson (The Hague: Mouton, 1964), p. 59.

[45] Ibid., p. 78.

[46] F. Goldman-Eisler, "The Significance of Changes in the Rate of Articulation," *Language and Speech,* 4 (1961), 174.

[47] A. Henderson, F. Goldman-Eisler, and F. A. Starbek, "Temporal Patterns of Cognitive Activity and Breath-Control in Speech," *Language and Speech,* 9 (1966), 216.

[48] A. T. Dittmann, "The Body Movement–Speech Rhythm Relationship as a Cue to Speech Encoding," in *Studies in Dyadic Communication,* ed. A. W. Siegman and B. Pope (New York: Pergamon Press, 1972), pp. 136-41.

[49] F. Goldman-Eisler, "Sequential Temporal Patterns and Cognitive Processes in Speech," *Language and Speech,* 10 (1967), 123-26.

[50] Dittmann, "The Body Movement–Speech Rhythm Relationship," p. 138.

[51] F. G. Lounsbury, "Pausal, Juncture, and Hesitation Phenomena," *Journal of Abnormal Social Psychology,* 49 (1954), 99.

[52] D. S. Boomer, "Hesitation and Grammatical Encoding," *Language and Speech,* 8 (1965), 152-62. In F. Goldman-Eisler, "A Comparative Study of Two Hesitation Phenomena," *Language and Speech,* 4 (1961), 18-26, the author makes the point that "filled pauses" are comprised of sounds such as ɑ, ɛ, æ, r, ə, m while silent hesitations are "unfilled pauses."

[53] F. Goldman-Eisler, *Psycholinguistics: Experiments in Spontaneous Speech* (New York: Academic Press, 1968).

[54] G. F. Mahl, "The Lexical and Linguistic Levels in the Expression of the Emotions," in *Expression of the Emotions in Man,* ed. P. Knapp (New York: International Universities Press, 1963), p. 81.

[55] D. S. Prentice, "The Process Effects of Trust-Destroying Behavior on the Quality of Communication in the Small Group," Ph.D. dissertation, University of California at Los Angeles, 1972.

7

THE TACTILE AND OLFACTORY COMMUNICATION SYSTEMS

Touch and smell communicate meanings. Both types of nonverbal communication have substantial communicative potential. Unfortunately, the exact nature of that potential has been little explored. Our lack of knowledge about touch and smell as communication systems can be attributed to a number of factors. First, many individuals have accepted the misconception that touch and smell are such primitive senses that they have very limited value in the transmission and reception of meanings in interpersonal communication. Second, ironic as it may seem in an age that highlights the rise of the Esalen Institute with nude encounter sessions and scented lingerie, ours is a society with strong inhibitions and taboos about touching or smelling others. Third, little empirical research has been done on touch and smell. Consequently, we lack a sufficiently precise terminology to describe adequately the many ways we may touch others or the countless odors we may perceive.

Touch and smell share the dubious distinction of being the forgotten senses. They also share an important defining attribute. Neither requires the light of day to function communicatively. Thus, they may both be accurately referred to as the invisible communication systems (telepathic communication is also an invisible means of communication, but will be treated in a separate chapter). Obviously, sight plays no part in the reception of smells, odors, aromas, fragrances, or related olfactory messages. Similarly, the primary stimulus property of one person touching another comes from the nature of the touch. The fact that the *part* of the body which is touched may be observed in some cases simply means that both touch and sight are active.

Touch and smell are being treated in the same chapter, then, because they can both be properly identified as invisible communication systems and because they are the forgotten senses. As previously stated, the amount of research done on each of these communication systems is very limited. Most major studies can be treated in one chapter. The quantity of research has not resulted in research of poor quality, however. On the contrary, the exciting communication potential of both touch and smell has been explored in highly creative ways in the last few years.

TACTILE COMMUNICATION

We are just beginning to realize that the skin is a sense organ of great value in interpersonal communication. In fact Scott maintains that: "the skin is the greatest sense of all. There are those physiologists, in fact, who consider touch the only sense. Hearing begins with sound waves touching the inner ear; taste with a substance touching the taste buds; and sight with light striking the cornea. All the other senses are therefore really derivations of touch as an expression of stimulation to the skin, muscles, and blood vessels."[1] The great applied communication value of touch can be illustrated by the experience of Helen Keller. More than one authority has argued that if Helen Keller had lost her sense of touch, even while regaining hearing and sight, it is doubtful whether her spirit and talent would have left such a mark.[2]

Until recently we knew little about what could be communicated by touch. For some time, however, serious students of the skin have known that the amount and kind of touching received by both animals and humans as they matured have a great impact on their behavior. The effect of touching on behavior is strongly associated with the fact that "the sense of touch, 'the mother of the senses,' is the earliest to develop in the human embryo. When the embryo is less than an inch long from crown to rump, and less than eight weeks old, light stroking of the upper lip or wings of the nose will cause bending of the neck and trunk away from the source of stimulation."[3]

The skin is such a sensitive organ because its surface area has a tremendous number of sensory receptors that receive stimuli of heat, cold, pressure, and pain. Montagu estimates that there are 50 receptors per 100 square millimeters, that tactile points vary from 7 to 135 per square centimenter, and that the number of sensory fibers from the skin entering the spinal cord by the posterior roots is well over half a million.[4] Thus, "what a man experiences through his skin is more important than most of us realize. As proof, there's the surprising size of the tactile areas of the brain, both the sensory and motor regions. The lips, the index finger, and the thumb, especially, take up a disproportionate amount of cerebral space."[5]

We have known for some time that baby monkeys do not develop properly without physical intimacy and that lack of caressing is positively associated with a high death rate among nursery babies.[6] Harlow in his famous experiments exposed baby monkeys to two types of surrogate mothers. One mother was made out of wire and provided milk and protection to the infant monkeys; the other mother was made of rubber and terry cloth but provided no milk or protection. Since the infant monkeys consistently chose the terry cloth mother, it seems obvious that the need to be touched was overriding. Harlow concluded, therefore, that a monkey's access to physical contact was a crucial variable in the development of normal behavior when the monkeys became adults, and in assuring normal affectional responsivity and normal sexual behavior.[7] Subsequent studies on other monkeys, rats, lambs, and other animals have supported the same central conclusion. Touching is a requirement for the healthy development of animals.

Many of the animal experiments seemed to be designed to support the same analogy and inference—suitable maturation of human beings also requires an extensive amount of touching whether in the form of fondling, stroking, caressing, or even licking. Hence, when we speak of "skin (cutaneous tactile) stimulation, we are quite evidently speaking of a fundamental and essential ingredient of affection, and equally clearly of an essential element in the healthy development of every organism."[8]

Adult behavior is markedly affected by one's tactile history. For example, Hollender found that the need for some women to be held is so compelling that it resembles addiction. Those deprived of tactile stimulation earlier in their lives used both direct and indirect means (i.e., sexual enticement and seduction) to obtain the holding or cuddling desired. Not suprisingly, half of Hollender's sample was composed of female psychiatric patients. Their behavior supported his conclusion that the need or wish to be held is a revelant consideration in the treatment of several psychiatric disorders.[9] Similarly, Hollender, Luborsky, and Scaramella studied the correlation between the intensity of the need to be held or cuddled and the frequency with which sexual intercourse is bartered for this satisfaction. They found that every high scorer on the body contact scale (those with a great need to be touched) used sex to be held whereas not a single low scorer did so.[10]

The behavioral effects of quantitative and qualitative insufficiency of touch in childhood are numerous and generally accepted. The communicative potential of the skin has remained a mystery until recently, however. Slowly, we have begun to recognize that the skin is not only our most sensitive organ, but also our first means of communication.

As a reader, you may remain skeptical. You may say it is fine to talk of touch as a communication system, but can anything of any importance really be communicated solely through the medium of touch? Using electrodes attached to the fingers to monitor the electrical messages which the skin transmits to the brain, Brown has demonstrated the remarkable capacity of the skin as a communication sender. In contrast, Geldhard has documented the skin's great value as a communication receiver. In so doing he has established that the skin is capable of decoding a set of electrical impulses into specific symbols, words, and thoughts. He has developed a language of the skin. Finally, Smith has done some highly creative research which suggests that the skin will function as a high fidelity medium for *both* the sending and reception of tactile messages. In effect she has shown that the skin can function as a complete and separate communication system.

THE SKIN AS A COMMUNICATION SENDER   Can the skin send or transmit meaning? Barbara B. Brown in her exciting new book, *New Mind, New Body,* answers yes, emphatically. The mind boggles at the possibility that the skin is capable of sending messages which convey rather specific information and meanings. Such is the case, however. "All that is necessary to listen to the skin's emotional talk is several small electrodes taped to the skin, and a proper recording instrument. Then you listen. The skin will tell you when there is emotion, how strong the emotion is, and even just how emotional a person you are. It also will very likely tell you when you are lying."[11]

The skin can send messages because the strength of the electrical currents it gives off vary significantly. Moreover, such variation in the strength of the skin's electrical currents seems to be directly related to the emotional state of the person whose skin is being monitored. A simple device much like an EEG (electroencephalograph) will produce a written record of electrical changes taking place in the skin. If a writing pen is positioned midway between the jaws of a magnet, the pen will deflect back and forth between the jaws as the magnet responds to changes in the electrical current of the skin. The readout looks the same as if you were having your heart monitored.

A series of experiments have been conducted which suggest that the skin will much more accurately signal the brain as to what events are being perceived in the environment than the eye, for example. Since the skin operates at the subconscious level it is not biased by group conformity pressures and other external stimuli which might affect the accuracy with which our various senses perceive events and stimuli in our external environment.

The skin's communicative capacity has perhaps best been demonstrated in the area of subliminal perception. In one experiment "naughty" and "emotion arousing" words were flashed on a screen so briefly that the subjects could not report what they had seen. Neutral words were mixed in with the arousing words. "Although it was impossible for the subjects to see the words and consciously to recognize them, something in their brains did recognize every word, and this recognition was voiced by the skin. For *every* naughty word there was an orienting response by the skin, but no response to the neutral or bland words."[12]

Such research and the results seem astounding. Nonetheless, a reputable scholar reports that simple electrodes attached to an individual's fingers will pick up the electricity of the skin and separate the slow from the fast activity. Slow activity is converted into a signal that represents the *level* of emotional response; fast activity reflects the *type* of emotional response.[13] Obviously, this newly discovered communicative capacity of the skin has many practical applications. The foremost application, currently employed during psychotherapy, is to use the messages sent by the skin to pinpoint emotional difficulties.[14] Obviously, many other applications are possible, including the determination of whether the communicator is lying and *whether the emotion the skin indicates an individual is really experiencing is consistent with the emotion he attempts to convey by some other means such as facial expressions.*

THE SKIN AS A COMMUNICATION RECEIVER   Few people would argue that the skin has no communicative value. Is there anyone who does not receive a message from the bite of an insect, from an angry jab in the ribs, or from a light touch on the thigh? We can and do recognize that the skin functions as a crude form of communication. Furthermore, as the examples suggest, most of us tend to think of the skin as a communication receiver. It is doubtful, however, whether very many of us have thought of the skin as a sophisticated receiving instrument capable of deciphering complex ideas and emotions transmitted by an outside source.

Thanks to the research of Frank A. Geldhard at Princeton's Cutaneous Communication Laboratory we now know that the skin does have amazing communicative capabilities. While the visual and auditory channels are our greatest informers about the external world, "the skin combines the best abilities of the eye and the ear."[15] It does not perform quite as well as the eye or ear as a communication receiver. The eye is the greatest sense organ where messages involve spatial orientation and guidance, while the ear possesses the greatest capacity to make temporal distinctions. The skin, however, is the body's only communication receiver that can handle both spatial and temporal distinctions fairly effectively. The skin

> can make both temporal and spatial discriminations, albeit not superlatively good ones in either case. It is a good "break-in" sense; cutaneous sensations, especially if aroused in unusual patterns are highly attention-demanding. It is possible, therefore, that the simplest and most straightforward of all messages—warnings and alerts—should be delivered cutaneously. . . . If we add the clear superiority of touch (when vision and hearing are lacking or impaired) to the remaining modalities, the chemical senses, smell and taste, we have a formidable set of properties to utilize in cutaneous message processing—a list that ought to challenge us to find ways to capitalize on it.[16]

In order to make reasonably effective use of the skin's communicative potential it soon became obvious to Geldhard and his associates that a means for sending electrical impulses to different parts of the body would be necessary. In effect these electrical impulses would symbolize thoughts and emotions which the skin would have to decode by assigning meanings to groups of symbols. Given this means of message transmission, the central question was how many different ways could the electrical impulses be used to transmit messages. In a very real sense the problem was analogous to that faced by Morse as he contemplated telegraphic communication. Morse's deductions were simple but important. Variation in the length of time the telegraph key was held down, and variation in the periods of time between the striking of the key could be used to send messages by a code which was understandable to a communication receiver on the other end of the telegraph line.

To develop a comparable code or language to be understood by the skin, Geldhard had to determine how many different stimulus dimensions or message properties could be *transmitted* by electrical impulses; these impulses are actually perceived as vibrations. He and his colleagues discovered that four stimulus properties can be transmitted to the skin by vibration: (1) location, (2) intensity, (3) duration, and (4) frequency.[17]

Unlike static pressure, mechanical vibration to the skin does not stay within bounds unless special steps are taken to prevent the spread. In effect if too many vibrators are placed on the body, an individual will not be able to distinguish the location of one vibrator from another. Research indicates that seven vibrators can be spaced on the ventral rib cage with 100 percent identifiability of location by individuals receiving vibrations to the skin. "This is perhaps the limit for a practical cutaneous communication system. The chest accommodates five conveniently, and it is tempting—until one finds that it won't work—to consider the combinations of vibrators (31 signals for five contractors) that might be coded. The difficulty is that two or more simultaneously acting vibrators feel no different from one."[18]

Intensity is defined by the power of the vibrations. In the chest region a useful range of stimulus power is that limited by the values 50 and 400 microns. The former value is safely above the 100 percent absolute threshold, the latter falls well below the threshold of discomfort. Between these limits the average human receiver in the laboratory can detect about 15 steps of intensity. In contrast to intensity, duration refers to the amount of time a vibration continues. Geldhard and associates do not deal with vibrations which last under 0.1 second on the ground that an impulse much shorter than this is likely to be mistaken for a nudge or a poke. The longest vibrations do not exceed 2.0 seconds since a communication system which employs units lasting more than 2.0 seconds is apt to be very inefficient. Between the duration range of 0.1 second and 2.0 seconds there is a durational continuum within which the average observer can make about 25 distinctions.[19]

Finally, frequency is the fourth stimulus property that can be varied in transmitting messages to the skin. This variable has not proved as useful as one might think. First, unless very careful controls are put on the intensity of vibrations, the receiver may confuse intensity and frequency. Second, changing the frequency of vibrations also affects the perceived pitch of the vibration thereby creating the potential for great confusion for the receiver. Both the ear (sound from vibrating vocal cords) and skin (vibrations of the skin induced by electrical impulses) depend on pitch, or the frequency of vibrations, to determine the meanings of messages. If the frequency of the vibrations being perceived by the ear and skin, respectively, should differ, the receiver can become very disoriented.[20] Furthermore, as the reader will recognize, some vibrations—such as base sounds coming from stereophonic speakers—may be intended for the ears but they can also be felt by the skin.

In spite of the problems associated with transmitting messages to the skin by means of vibration, a workable system has now been developed. We now have a carefully tested instrument for transmitting such messages and a code or alphabet that is used to actually communicate specific words and even sentences to the skin. The instrument is known as the Optohapt (see Figure 7-1). Using the Optohapt alphabet (see Figure 7-2) and the typewriter keyboard of the Optohapt, any letter in the alphabet can be transmuted into sequences and combinations of vibratory bursts which are distributed to nine locations on the body (Figure 7-1).

Using the Optohapt alphabet and the Optohapt we now have a language of the skin that is spoken by machine and received by human beings. The language, called Vibratese, has 45 separate signals. Three intensities (weak, medium, strong), and three durations (short, medium, long) can be delivered to five different spots on the chest. All steps could be combined with all others, $3 \times 3 \times 5$, giving 45 steps or signals. Letters of the alphabet are

> each assigned a signal representing a unique combination of duration, intensity, and location. The times were kept short—0.1, 0.3, 0.5 second

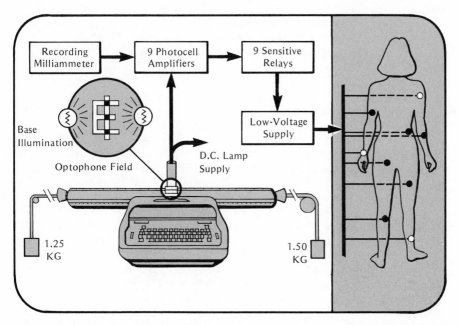

FIGURE 7-1   Optohapt. Reprinted from *Psychology Today* Magazine, December 1968. Copyright (c) 1968. Ziff-Davis Publishing Company. All rights reserved.

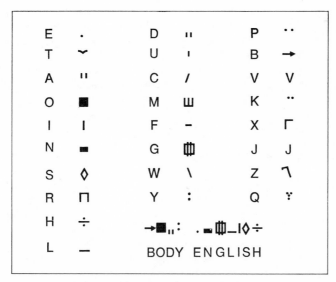

FIGURE 7-2   Optohapt Alphabet. Reprinted from *Psychology Today* Magazine, December 1968. Copyright (c) 1968. Ziff-Davis Publishing Company. All rights reserved.

for short, medium, and long, respectively. The most frequently occurring language elements were assigned shorter durations, enabling the system to "fly" at a rapid pace. This proved quite efficient, since the all-important vowels were assigned each to its own vibrator, and since letters followed each other promptly, with none of the wasteful silences that are built into International Morse.[21]

Most readers will probably marvel at the ingenuity and attention to detail which is reflected in the research of Geldhard and his associates. Nonetheless, the reader may be bothered by two unanswered questions. First, does Vibratese as transmitted by the Optohapt have much practical, communicative value? Second, can the process of transmitting messages to the skin be modified in such a way that human beings can transmit as well as receive messages by Vibratese?

The first question can probably be more readily answered than the second. Certainly Vibratese can have great value in accurately communicating to individuals whose major senses such as sight and hearing are temporarily impaired. The most obvious example is the airplane pilot. Several years ago a commercial jet plunged into the Pacific Ocean upon takeoff from Los Angeles International Airport killing all aboard. The main and auxiliary generators both ceased to function and all lights in the airplane went out, including those in the cockpit. Suddenly bereft of his primary means of determining distance, the pilot apparently became highly disoriented and flew the plane straight into the ocean. There is good reason to believe that he could have averted the disaster had his body been equipped with the nine vibrators illustrated in Figure 7-1. The vibrators would have enabled the air traffic controller at Los Angeles to use his radar screen to give the pilot specific flight directions via electrical impulses sent by remote control; a pilot trained in Vibratese could easily have understood such tactile messages and could have maintained level flight while in a darkened cockpit. This is hardly a far-fetched idea since way back during World War II research was conducted to determine if warning signals could be built into seat cushions so that pilots could literally hear and fly by the seat of their pants.

Clearly, Vibratese can be used as a warning system, as a means of supplementary information about one's environment, as a sophisticated language for the blind or deaf, as a command system for pilots, auto drivers, and others. Of course, the possible applications in the area of surveillance and spying are enough to make 007's mouth water. All of the applications above are based on the assumption that a wireless means of activating the vibrators on the body will be developed. Such an invention should hardly tax the creativity of the modern engineer.

The greatest deficiency of Vibratese, as a language of the skin, is that an individual must be wired up and impulses transmitted to a human receiver in order for communication to take place. Obviously, such a requirement places great restrictions on the receiver's mobility and the wires and vibrators may be so distracting as to alter the nature of messages perceived. In addition, it is obvious that Vibratese gives an individual only a receiving capacity; he has no independent capacity to transmit messages to the skin. While solutions to these problems are not available at this moment, they should not be long in coming. Anyone who has seen policemen communicating by walkie-talkie or radio will realize that the same principles can be applied to tactile communication. There is no reason why messages in the form of electrical impulses can not be sent by remote control and received by another individual who is not hampered by wires. Once this goal is achieved, tactile communication by electrical impulse will have almost the same flexibility as kinesic communication. Certainly the potential for practical application will be greatly expanded.

THE SKIN AS A COMPLETE COMMUNICATION SYSTEM

Researchers at Princeton's Cutaneous Communication Laboratory have treated the skin strictly as a communication receiver and have used only mechanical means of transmitting messages. A new and highly creative set of studies by Alma I. Smith goes one giant step further, however. She has examined both the sending and receiving capacities of the human skin. With this conceptual breakthrough the skin may justifiably be treated as a human communication system.

Smith began her studies with the general hypothesis that communication of emotional meaning can be conveyed through touch in the absence of any other sensory cues. Put another way, she hypothesized that touch can function effectively as a separate communication system. To test this hypothesis her task was twofold. First, she had to devise some messages that might be communicated by touch. Second, she had to devise some practical method of human transmission of such messages by touch.

A pilot study convinced her that when one individual placed his hands on the hands of another individual (even when they are separated by a screen to eliminate the possibility of kinesic, proxemic, artifactual, or other cues) he was able to convey different emotions. Based on this early work she selected the five emotions which she believed were most commonly communicated by touch: detached, mothering, fearful, angry, and playful. A trained experimenter was then asked to attempt to communicate these five emotions to a number of different subjects. Taking the subjects one at a time, the experimenter joined hands with each one, and solely by different hand movements he attempted to convey the five different emotions (the experimenter was separated from the subject by a screen to make sure that the subject was receiving *only* tactile cues).

To determine the accuracy of perception Smith added an important step to her experimental investigation. She developed what is approximately known as the tactile communication index. In preliminary research she asked a group of subjects to apply their own adjectives to describe messages represented by such emotions as detached, mothering, and excited. The five adjectives most consistently chosen for each emotion were grouped together and weighted according to the number of times they were chosen. Thus, if caring was chosen twice as often as sympathy, to describe the qualities which the subjects associated with a mothering message, it was given a weight of 2 while sympathy was given a weight of 1.

Thus, when the subjects were holding hands with the experimenter and as the experimenter was trying to communicate a given emotion to each one, they were to look at the tactile communication index (see Figure 7-3) and choose those five words

afraid	detached	irritated	resentful
angry	distressed	joyful	sparkling
apathetic	enjoy	lively	sympathy
belonging	excited	loving	tender
calm	friendly	mad	thrilling
carefree	fun	needed	trusting
caring	gentle	neutral	understanding
comforting	important	peaceful	unfeeling
cruel	indifferent	playful	unfriendly
defensive	insecure	protective	warm

FIGURE 7-3 Tactile Communication Index. Reprinted with permission from A. I. Smith, "Non-Verbal Communication through Touch," Ph.D. Dissertation, Georgia State University, 1970.

which they felt best described the emotion being communicated to them. To determine how accurately each subject perceived the emotions being communicated to him by touch a special scoring system was used (see Figure 7-4).

Let us assume, for example, that in a given instance the experimenter is attempting to communicate the emotion of mothering to a subject by the different ways he touches the subject's hands. While being so touched, the subject is to select five words from the tactile communication index which best describe the message he thinks the experimenter is trying to communicate. If the subject chooses caring, comforting, protective, tender, and understanding as the five words, he gets a score of 10 (see Figure 7-4). As the reader can see, 10 is the maximum score that can be computed for the message of mothering and such a score indicates that the experimenter was able to communicate this particular message with complete clarity of meaning. On the other hand, if the subject had chosen none of the words grouped under mothering, the score would be 0; this would indicate that no part of the intended meaning was actually perceived by the subject. Hence, the tactile message would have been of the poorest possible quality or fidelity. Clearly, by determining a method of measuring accuracy of message perception, Smith has developed a useful and objective means of measuring the quality of tactile communication.[22]

FACTORS AFFECTING THE QUALITY OF TACTILE COMMUNICATION

Now that we know that messages can be both transmitted and received by tactile means, two important questions present themselves. First, what factors affect the qual-

MESSAGE	WORDS	SCORE
mothering	caring	2
	comforting	2
	gentle	1
	loving	1
	protective	2
	sympathy	1
	tender	2
	understanding	2
	warm	1
fearful	afraid	3
	defensive	2
	distressed	1
	gentle	1
	insecure	3
	playful	1
	unfriendly	1
detached	apathetic	2
	detached	2
	indifferent	2
	neutral	2
	unfeeling	2
	unfriendly	1
playful	carefree	2
	enjoy	1
	excited	1
	friendly	1
	fun	2
	joyful	2
	lively	2
	playful	2
	sparkling	1
angry	angry	2
	cruel	1
	defensive	1
	irritated	3
	mad	2
	resentful	2
	unfriendly	1

FIGURE 7-4   Scoring System for Tactile Communication Index. Reprinted with permission from A. I. Smith, "Non-Verbal Communication through Touch," Ph.D. Dissertation, Georgia State University, 1970.

ity of tactile communication? Second, what is the quality or fidelity of tactile communication?

Interestingly enough, two of the major factors which affect quality of tactile communication are quantity (how much touching takes place) and region of the body (where one is touched). Jourard is convinced that touching generally serves a therapeutic function and that the more touching that takes place the more open, honest, and trusting an individual will be in his interpersonal communication. He emphasizes that he has "found that some form of physical contact with patients expedites the arrival of this mutual openness and unreserve. So far, I have only held hands with a patient, put an arm around a shoulder, or given a hug—all in the context of an unfolding dialogue. I believe we are a nation of people who are starved for physical contact."[23]

Of course amount and location of touching are closely related since:

> the metaphor of "being turned on" describes the experience of physical contact. When part of your body is touched, you can't ignore that part of your body. It becomes "figure" in your perceptual field. One wonders about men or women who have never been touched or hugged, or have never been in intimate body contact with others. Could we say that their bodies have not come to life, that their bodies do not exist in the phenomenological sense? One wonders to what extent they feel that their bodies are alive. I even suspect that the transformation from virginity or even preorgasmic existence to the experience of having a sexual climax is so radical as to be equivalent to a kind of rebirth.[24]

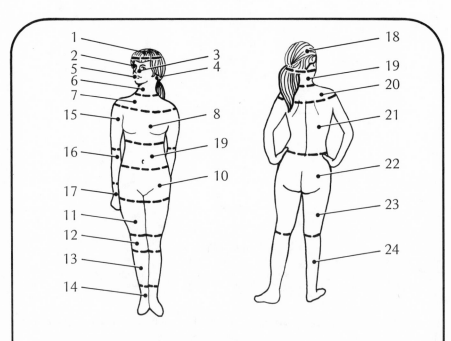

FIGURE 7-5 Diagram of the Front and Rear View of the Body as Demarcated for the Body-Accessibility Questionnaire. Reprinted with permission from S. M. Jourard, *Disclosing Man to Himself* (Princeton, N.J.: Van Nostrand Reinhold, 1968), p. 140.

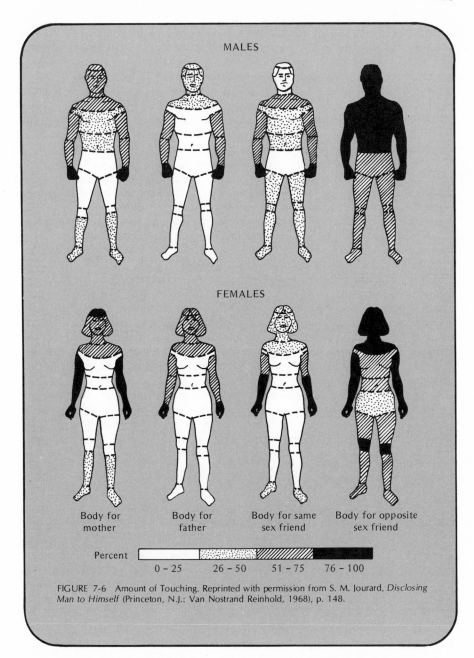

FIGURE 7-6   Amount of Touching. Reprinted with permission from S. M. Jourard, *Disclosing Man to Himself* (Princeton, N.J.: Van Nostrand Reinhold, 1968), p. 148.

Jourard has addressed the question of which body regions are most frequently touched and refers to this phenomenon as tactual accessibility. He divides the body up into 24 areas (see Figure 7-5) much like the butcher classifies meat from different parts of a beef carcass. Obviously, lovers who get into areas 8, 10, and/or 22 have established rather intimate tactile contact. What they do after reaching such body regions, however, may depend on their ingenuity as well as the touch taboos of their partner.

Figure 7-6 illustrates the amount of contact received by mothers, fathers, same sex friends, and opposite sex friends. It is obvious the bodies of the father and mother receive little intimate touching while the mother does a good deal more intimate touching of others. The most touching occurs between friends of the opposite sex with 76-100 percent of the females reporting that they have touched all parts of their male friend's body including area 10, while only 51-75 percent of the males report that they have touched their female friends in the genital area.[25]

The precise effects of amount and location of touching on the quality of tactile communication have not yet been precisely determined. The sexual implications of tactile communication are obvious. Anyone who has sustained body contact in area 10 for a substantial period of time will realize that such tactile stimulation has a rather good chance of gaining and maintaining the attention of a partner as well as inducing a good deal of mutual involvement in the proceedings. What is not so obvious is how the accuracy of reception of tactile messages is affected when the various non-erogenous regions of the body are touched separately.

To date we have limited knowledge as to the factors that affect the quality of tactile communication. We do know, however, that *individuals* differ markedly in their ability to transmit and to perceive accurately messages communicated by the skin. In addition certain *groups* of people, such as schizophrenics, exhibit significant differences in their ability to interpret touch messages accurately. Smith found that the decoding ability of schizophrenics was strikingly inferior to that of a group of normal subjects. On the other hand differences in age and sex seemed to have no effect on ability to determine the meaning of touch messages.[26]

We not only know that individuals differ significantly in their ability to communicate by tactile means, but that they can significantly improve the quality of their tactile communication. For example, one study examined the impact of sensitivity training on the ability of subjects to determine the meaning of touch messages. Ability to determine the meanings was measured by the tactile communication index (see Figure 7-3). The accuracy with which subjects assigned meanings to touch messages increased significantly after sensitivity training. Such a finding was anticipated because of the objectives of sensitivity training. Sensitivity trainers typically use exercises designed to clarify awareness and expression of emotion between the participants. Such exercises should increase sensitivity to touch messages. They did.[27]

We do not yet have sufficient normative data to provide the reader with a profile of the good tactile communicator. However, the reader can determine the quality of his or her own tactile communication—both as a transmitter and a receiver—by taking the following steps. First, try to communicate the following five emotions used by Smith: mothering, fearful, detached, playful, and angry. Try the following procedures on a number of your friends, but take one friend at a time: Sit with a screen separating you and your friend. Then join hands with your friend and through touch try to communicate each of the emotions listed above. Your friend should have a copy of the tactile communication index so that he can choose five words for each emotion which come closest to describing what you are trying to communicate to him. By using the scoring instructions described in connection with Figure 7-4 you can determine how successful you were in communicating to each of your friends by touch.

To determine how accurately you can *perceive* messages by touch, follow exactly the same procedure outlined above with one exception. Have your friends attempt to communicate messages *to* you by touch.

OLFACTORY COMMUNICATION

Olfaction is truly the forgotten sense. Few individuals make systematic use of pleasant odors to increase their personal appeal. In fact ours seems to be a society obsessed with stamping out body odors altogether. Ironically, while we struggle to overcome body odor, we often do little to control the noxious gases and pollutants which pour out of our major factories. Such gases and pollutants have the effect of deadening our sense of smell.

Undeniably "man today is surrounded by a physical environment that anesthetizes much of his sensory equipment."[28] We have

> formed the habit of either making the meal a hurried, mechanical refueling routine for the human machine or turning it into a gluttonous, wholesale assault on the tastebuds—so that the very range of complex flavors and tastes leads to a defensive masking of the sense of taste and smell. The closing or restricting of our senses to what is being communicated to us cripples our communication system: much that needs to be expressed and communicated never finds birth for our muffled senses keep it from being born.[29]

Ours has become an overdeodorized society. Every year another aerosol product is invented with the avowed purpose of stamping out another odor. We of course live in fear of bad breath, body odor, house odors, and genital odors even though sexual odors, for example, often have a highly beneficial effect on the behavior with which they are associated.[30]

Our obsession to rid ourselves of body odor has made olfaction the forgotten sense—forgotten because odors have rarely been used in a highly conscious and systematic manner to increase an individual's personal appeal as well as the sensory satisfaction he receives from pleasant odors. Such neglect of the positive uses of smell has had another unfortunate effect. It has made smell the "inarticulate sense," as well as the forgotten sense. Indeed "sense of smell is the Inarticulate Sense, . . . [because] it has little or no vocabulary."[31] As illustrated in earlier chapters, no parallel problem exists with vision or sound. Red, blue, and yellow bring to mind very definite colors, for example, and the sound attributes of a vocal cue can be described with considerable precision. In contrast, did you ever consider how much trouble you would probably have in describing the exact nature of the various odors, aromas, and fragrances which you experience in a single day? When you consider the question, you will probably agree that olfaction is the inarticulate sense.

The fact that smell is our forgotten and inarticulate sense is regrettable when we consider its importance. In particular, lack of words to describe smell

is all the more remarkable when we consider that the sense of smell is the most experienced of senses. Sight functions only in light; there are periods when the ear listens but hears nothing; the sluggard taste sleeps most of the time. But night or day there is no odorless place for the sensitive nose unless at great pains or expense it is made so artificially. Moreover, it is the most enduring of all the senses. It is the first dim twinkle breaking in upon the dark unconsciousness of birth, and, in old age, it is sometimes a tenacious flicker after the other lights have all gone out.[32]

THE NATURE OF SMELL

Smell is a very primitive sense. It is probably our most primitive sense.[33] One authority writes that the olfactory receptors of the nose are composed of sensory cells very similar to those that make up the earthworm. He emphasizes that olfactory receptors are only slightly modified, naked neuroepithelial cells. The nerve fibers of these olfactory receptors are unmyelinated and, therefore, permit only a low and crude form of neural conduction. The structural characteristics of these receptors "are typical of the most primitive sensory cells, and are at the other end of the evolutionary spectrum from the elegant specialization of the visual apparatus. Concomitantly, the function of the smell system is a most unrefined one."[34]

As a sense, smell is unique in two ways. First, perception of odors requires the incorporation of a particle of the external environment into the organism (while crude, smell is at the same time an extremely acute sense, as olfaction follows the exposure to as few as nine molecules of an odorant). Second, smell is the first distance receptor to have evolved in human phylogenesis. At a much earlier time in the evolution of man much of his brain was devoted to the function of smell. With the development of civilization the functional significance of smell decreased and so, predictably, did the size of the brain area devoted to smell. "As the smell brain grew relatively smaller in man's evolution, the overlying frontal lobes and association system were able to grow larger. This has altered both the shape and size of the brain and, therefore, the head which encloses it."[35]

Many highly technical theories have been offered to explain the nature of olfaction and its role in the maturational process.[36] While very valuable, such technical discussions are beyond the scope of this chapter. This chapter focuses especially on how odors are actually used in our society and *how they might more effectively be used.*

Historically, many rulers and other notable personages have used odor as an active agent either to give themselves pleasure or to make them more appealing to those with whom they interacted. For example Napoleon had an almost insatiable need for perfumes with a special fondness for the odor of aloes wood and eau de cologne. He used both in great quantities. Napoleon's fondness for eau de cologne is demonstrated by his quarterly perfume bill for the year 1806. It contains the following items:

162 bottles of eau de cologne	= 423 francs
20 superfine sponges	= 262 francs
26 ornamental pots of almond	= 366 francs
paste (paté d'amande)	

In 1810 Napoleon's perfume bill included a charge for 144 bottles of eau de cologne at 300 francs, and a large flask of extract of Spanish jasmine at 40 francs.[37] It is doubtful if Napoleon and other rulers of the time understood the psychology of smell. Almost certainly they did not understand why some odors were perceived as pleasant and others as unpleasant. They did recognize, however, that odors can function as a positive force in interpersonal relationships. In recent times many Americans have seemingly overlooked this fact in their haste to eliminate all odors.

Recently, our preoccupation with eliminating all body odors has almost precluded attempts to use products like perfume to enhance our own image. However, there is growing evidence that smell is now being used as a positive agent. Many Americans are increasingly concerned with the scents and aromas that they can use on their bodies to communicate an olfactory message. Men are making greater use of colognes and after-shave lotions derived from extremely complex formulas.

Once again in the last decade Americans have begun to use odors as a positive agent. The increased use of artificial scents by men, in particular, is significant. It reflects at least the subconscious realization that smell can be used to control behavior. Men use Old Spice, Jade East, and many other fragrances in the belief that the odor added to their bodies will make them more attractive to women. Most men probably expect fairly minimal changes in the behavior of those with whom they interact. Certainly, there is no known, universal aphrodisiac. However, one reputable scholar insists that the scent of the white jasmine can transform a woman into a nymphomaniac after the slightest inhalation.[38]

The psychology of smell and more specifically of fragrance is very complex. Until recently, it was little understood. Now, however, scholars like Moncrieff have done impressively detailed studies on the psychology of smell. He concludes that odors probably have a more direct impact on emotions, and, therefore, on certain behaviors, than any other sense. "Certainly odours affect the emotions; ylang-ylang will soothe anger born of frustration and wild rose will lift one out of a depression."[39]

Moncrieff focuses directly on the psychology of smell and attempts to answer the central question of why one odor is perceived as pleasant and another unpleasant. He maintains that five factors are involved in determining how odors are perceived: (1) reactions of the subject to odorants are usually spontaneous and involuntary, either of liking, or disliking or perhaps indifference; (2) analysis of the specific reasons for liking or disliking cannot usually be taken far since typically the liking or disliking seems to be without reason; (3) association of ideas with some former experience may occasionally play some small part in determining the reaction, whether of liking or not; (4) food smells may be colored with pleasantness or unpleasantness according to the needs of the body; (5) usually aesthetics is the factor that determines olfactory reactions—as we shall soon learn, people generally agree as to what violates their aesthetic sensibilities.[40]

ODOR AS A COMMUNICATION MEDIUM

ODORS AS CHEMICAL MESSENGERS: THE SUBCONSCIOUS LEVEL   Odor functions communicatively at both the subconscious and conscious levels. Thanks to recent research we not only know that odors do function communicatively, but *how* they function. In animals there can be little doubt that specific body odors serve as external chemical messengers with specific and often amazing effects on behavior. For example when 30 female rats are brought together each female's estrous cycle (analogous to the human menstrual cycle) becomes completely unpredictable. However, the arrival of one male near the group of female rats results in all estrous cycles promptly returning to the normal cycle: all of the cycles return simultaneously. The dramatic change in the female rats' behavior clearly results from the chemical messages they receive from the male rat in the form of body odor. Likewise, anyone who has observed a large ant hill must have been amazed that these seemingly primitive insects operate a complicated social structure, build artfully designed dwellings, divide their labors, attack others, and defend their own. The synchronized actions of the millions of ants in a colony is explained by their primitive sense of smell. Ants emit chemicals, pheromones, which act as external chemical messengers with the almost miraculous effect of completely organizing the ants' behavior.[41]

Based on his own creative research and reporting, Dr. Harry Wiener of the New York Medical College concludes that the same principle operates in human communication. Thus he formulates and supports the following, provocative hypothesis: Man emits and receives external chemical messages.[42]

The basic nature of external chemical messengers (body odors) has been summarized by Wiener in a series of propositions; for each proposition he provides an estimate of probability that the proposition is actually true. These estimates are based on detailed evaluation of available evidence. The most significant propositions which underlie the notion of external chemical messengers are listed in the table on p. 159.[43]

The implications of these propositions for human communication are immense. Many of these implications are obvious but some do need elaboration. The implications all relate directly to the realization that the external chemical messages discussed in this section operate at the subconscious level. Any messages conveyed without the conscious awareness of the communicator present him with a potential problem. First, the communicator, who conveys messages that he is unaware of transmitting, has little chance to control his environment in the positive sense. Second, he runs the very real risk of triggering negative responses to his subconscious chemical messages.

There is convincing evidence that subconscious messages are transmitted and received. Sweat represents probably the most significant form of an external chemical message (ECM) transmitted by man. We have known for at least four decades that sweat glands increase their output in response to emotional tension and that this increase can be measured quantitatively. Thus:

ESTIMATES OF PROBABILITY

STATEMENT	ESTIMATE
1. Man emits external chemical messengers.	0.90
2. Man's body odors are external chemical messengers.	0.90
3. Different external chemical messengers are emitted from different areas of the skin.	0.80
4. Man emits sex attractants.	0.95
5. Steroid sex hormones act as sex attractants.	0.80
6. Man possesses odor glands analogous in variety to those of other mammals.	0.95
7. The bulk of external chemical messengers are carried by sweat.	0.80
8. Man receives olfactory stimuli beyond those consciously noted by the sense of smell.	0.90
9. Man perceives sex odors.	0.95

there would appear to be good reason why in man the palmar sweat print and the galvanic skin response are used for the measurement of emotional states, and why the results obtained are so often confusing. If sweat is a major carrier of ECM, then the quantity and composition of sweat change from area to area and from minute to minute, depending not only on the overall emotional state, but also on the immediate interactions between subjects and experimenters.[44]

Many other examples support the notion that there is a close relationship between emotional states and olfactory communication. Thus, the colon displays marked hyperactivity when emotional subjects are discussed; such activity may result from the transmission of chemical messages to the intestinal mucosa. Similarly, we now know that a woman's capacity to receive chemical messages varies with particular phases of her menstrual cycle. These phases in turn are presumably directly related to the kinds and intensities of moods and emotions the woman experiences. For example, we know that exaltolide is a synthetic analog of mammalian sex attractants. Adult women easily detect exaltolide as a musk-like odor while prepuberal girls and men experience difficulty in detecting it in any form. Significantly, a woman's ability to perceive exaltolide reaches its peak during ovulation and nadir during the progestational phase.[45] During ovulation, then, the adult woman has a greatly expanded capacity to perceive accurately the meaning conveyed by the external chemical message represented by exaltolide. The effect on the adult woman's sexual behavior when she perceives such a message is well known.

Wiener has found that "the idea of chemical messages passing between me and thee, without either of us being aware of them, is a very hard one to swallow particularly for men concentrating on the basic sciences."[46] The reader should remember, however, that other improbable-sounding channels of man-to-man communication have recently been discovered or confirmed.[47]

Not all people have an equal capacity to accurately decode the meaning of external chemical messages, however. Individuals differ markedly in their sensitivity to chemical messages (body odors). Indeed, schizophrenics have a greatly heightened sensitivity to chemical messages. Ironically, since the schizophrenic is capable of perceiving many odors which the average individual cannot perceive, the schizophrenic often concludes that strange, outside forces are working on him. He comes to such a seemingly bizarre conclusion because of his hypersensitivity to external chemical messages. Such "hypersensitivity is conscious awareness of these complex patterns, symphonies of scent equivalent to Beethoven's symphonies of sound."[48]

Individual variation in ability to detect body odors is hardly confined to the mentally ill. It is most strikingly manifested in schizophrenics, however, and particularly in children. Wiener speaks directly to this amazing communicative phenomenon:

> Such children exist. They have unusual powers of many senses. They react to normally unfelt odors. Other sense impressions, too, have an extraordinary effect on these children—colors, lights, sounds, textures, tastes, and movements. At first, they seem to be budding geniuses; but on close look, they appear feebleminded or psychotic. These children suffer from schizophrenia.[49]

ODORS AS CHEMICAL MESSENGERS: THE CONSCIOUS LEVEL   While communication by odor at the subconscious level clearly takes place, communication at the conscious level may have more value. Unitl recently, we could say little on the subject, however. We knew neither which smells people perceived as pleasant and unpleasant nor what degree of agreement existed as to which odors were pleasant and unpleasant.

Thanks to the detailed investigation of Moncrieff we now know a good deal about how odors operate at the conscious level. To begin, Moncrieff recognized that most people would agree as to what odors were grossly pleasant or unpleasant. Thus "it was common knowledge that most people liked flower perfumes and fruity smells and that everybody disliked such revolting smells as bad eggs, bad fish, bad drains and so on. Badness and unpleasantness of odours went hand in hand. About the very good and the very bad smells it was plain that there would be very general agreement."[50]

Beyond such extreme odors as bad eggs and bad fish we knew little about people's olfactory preferences, however. To determine such olfactory preferences, Moncrieff made an intensive study of the odor preferences of twelve people. He began by collecting an exhaustive sample of 132 different smells; some were natural and others artificial. He then asked his subjects to arrange these 132 smells in order of preference. It was a monumental task to say the least. Table 7-1 reports a representative sample of his results. Those odors that ranked highest (1-17), middle (54-71), and lowest (118-32) are presented in the table.

Obviously, Moncrieff's subjects were perceiving these odors at the conscious rather than the subconscious level. Table 7-1 gives us real insight into the question of which odors are perceived as pleasant and unpleasant. Clearly, the odorant materials that are best liked are the flowers or fruits and the next dozen or more are primarily derived from natural products. Natural odors were much preferred to synthetics. People do not like rank, oily, fishy, pungent, sweetish, or burnt odors. In contrast they seem to perceive lemony, violet, and woody odors as neutral with respect to pleasantness or unpleasantness.[51] Beyond such generalizations, the reader is invited to study Table 7-1 and draw his own conclusions.

From a communicative standpoint, Table 7-1 tells us at least two things. First, the specific nature of smells perceived as pleasant or unpleasant is revealed, as well as the degree of pleasantness assigned to each smell. Second, the table demonstrates a high degree of consistency among people as to the odors they perceive. Certainly there is a high level of agreement among people of all kinds about really bad smells, and very good agreement about good smells. Not only are the judgments of the individuals composing the group of subjects highly consistent, but reproducibility of arrangement of a number of dissimilar odors in order of preference by the *same* subject is typically good. When two preference arrangements of ten dissimilar odorants are made by a group of people, about 40 percent of the placements will be the same in the two arrangements, about 30 percent will be only one place removed in the two arrangements, and the other 30 percent will be two or more places removed.[52]

Obviously, the reader is not going to collect 132 odorant materials to test his own olfactory sensitivity. However, the reader can very easily prepare his own olfactory meaning sensitivity test. Collect a sample of twenty different odors—including such things as different perfumes, colognes, stale beer, rancid butter, burned rubber—put a number on each odor-emitting source and have a friend mix up the sources randomly. Then rank order the twenty odors in order of preference. Have a group of your friends do the same things. By comparing results, you should come up with a reasonably precise and objective measure of your olfactory sensitivity.

The communicative implications of Moncrieff's and related studies are considerable. Since we know now which odors are perceived as unpleasant or pleasant it seems obvious that we can make systematic efforts to apply odorant materials to our bodies which others rate as highly pleasant. We do not yet have detailed evidence on the effects of such use of odors but it seems safe to conclude that prudent use of perfumes and colognes will have a very beneficial impact on one's image. Thus, the way one smells is probably related to one's chances for personal and social success.

In recent years Americans have begun to use manufactured odors in many ways. "We're living in an increasingly fragrance-oriented society. Some shampoos are sold more by fragrance than their ability to clean the hair. Used cars are sprayed so they'll smell 'new.' There have even been forays into scented toilet tissue."[53] By 1975, $900 million will be spent at retail stores for men's colognes. While the sales of after-shave lotions and related products have dropped, the sale of specific fragrances has increased dramatically. One major reason is that men are demanding a more noticeable impact from their fragrances.

In addition to perfumes and colognes odors are consciously used in many applied ways which have communicative relevance. First, adding oil lavender to draperies, curtains, cushions, scarves, underwear, and women's hose is becoming common. Significantly, the sales of such items—particularly the last three—have increased strikingly. Second, fabrics are often treated with a cyana purifying agent which inhibits sweat and the subsequent growth of bacteria; this in turn gives the individual the chance to get full positive impact from perfumes or colognes applied to the body. Third, furniture polishes are generally perfumed with the lavender scent.[54]

The attempt to increase one's personal appeal by consciously adding certain fragrances to one's body is not new. Often such attempts have been based on whim or guesswork, however. With the information presented in this chapter the reader can

TABLE 7-1 Odours Arranged in Order of Preference. Primary Records of Results of Tests with Many Odorants and Few Observers.

ODORANT	TYPE OF ODOUR	PLACING (1 IS MOST LIKED, 2 IS NEXT MOST LIKED AND 132 IS MOST DISLIKED) OF EACH ODORANT BY EACH OBSERVER																		AVERAGE	ODORANT IS RANKED
		RO	ELM	MH	RMM	RWM	RWM	WMM	SL	SL	ST	ST	ST	JET	EMT	ARL	WG	WG	WG		
Red rose, Ena Harkness, flower	Deep rose	—	6	—	1	2	3	6	8	5	4	2	—	3	4	17	—	—	—	5.1	1st
Fresh strawberries	Strawberries	—	—	—	6	3	1	1	3	2	16	24	—	2	1	2	4	6	—	5.5	2nd
Sweet peas, flowers	Floral	17	11	8	3	5	9	3	1	2	2	4	—	6	2	18	4	20	11	7.6	3rd
Rose, New Dawn, flower	Powerful wild rose type of odour	1	1	22	—	4	6	2	9	7	5	18	—	5	3	16	19	12	—	8.7	4th
Rose, Emily Gray, flower	Lighter than Red Rose	—	—	—	—	7	10	15	10	6	9	9	—	—	5	14	—	—	—	9.4	5th
Stock, double ten-week flower	Floral heavy	5	7	28	4	11	12	—	14	15	11	6	—	—	7	22	—	37	46	13.8	6th
Honeysuckle, flowers	Floral rich honey	—	2	55	2	1	2	12	2	3	1	8	—	1	6	24	—	57	—	14.8	7th
Wild rose (Dog rose), flower	Pure rose fresh, sweet	—	—	—	—	8	7	—	4	4	43	51	—	—	9	21	6	—	—	18.4	8th
Raspberry flavouring essence (ABR)	Fruity very true	10	10	12	32	49	43	28	19	31	46	10	49	11	22	1	6	3	—	20.8	9th
Sweet orange oil (RAN)	Orange light and very natural	49	20	3	8	9	11	14	18	13	27	49	—	38	28	87	1	18	—	24.6	10th
Lemon flavoring essence (BTS)	Lemon, slightly bitter	45	—	25	—	25	22	—	34	33	—	—	—	18	—	8	11	32	—	25.3	11th
Meadowsweet, flower	Rich floral, honey note	14	4	56	28	6	4	—	38	27	6	19	—	35	76	19	55	45	—	25.4	12th
P'permint flavouring essence (BTS)	Peppermint	15	14	1	11	19	29	47	57	28	29	33	—	42	24	13	10	7	—	26.9	13th
St'wberry flavouring essence 1512 (ABR)	Strawberry, very sweet	13	12	13	61	64	78	27	41	32	37	16	—	12	—	4	3	5	—	27.6	14th
Heliotrope, flower	Cherry pie	20	5	54	5	14	14	—	23	11	103	—	—	—	—	—	—	38	—	28.7	15th
Lemon flavouring essence (ABR)	Lemon, slightly sweet	50	16	17	7	24	21	17	35	34	79	61	—	27	33	3	9	—	—	28.9	16th
Banana flavouring essence (ABR)	Banana	11	38	11	54	56	77	18	44	59	26	15	—	20	23	5	5	8	—	29.4	17th
Onion, raw, cut	Onion	79	84	81	81	96	60	20	12	8	7	5	—	94	110	54	22	15	—	51.8	54th
Terpinolene (DIS)	Bitter, lemony, hint of hyacinth	60	88	42	59	29	35	38	46	79	62	59	—	77	43	37	56	20	—	51.9	55th

162

TABLE 7-1 Odours Arranged in Order of Preference. Primary Records of Results of Tests with Many Odorants and Few Observers. *(Continued)*

PLACING (1 IS MOST LIKED, 2 IS NEXT MOST LIKED AND 132 IS MOST DISLIKED) OF EACH ODORANT BY EACH OBSERVER

ODORANT	TYPE OF ODOUR	RO	ELM	MH	RMM	RWM	RWM	WMM	SL	SL	ST	ST	JET	EMT	ARL	WG	WG	AVERAGE	ODORANT IS RANKED
Tonka beans, tincture in benzyl alcohol (FLD)	Nutty, sweet, some coumarin	78	41	39	25	43	31	85	45	49	36	22	86	49	65	77	71	52.6	56th
Amyl acetate (M & B)	Pear drops	25	45	15	42	68	65	40	56	54	66	73	88	89	38	14	65	52.7	57th
Heliotropine cryst (piperonal) (GIV)	Floral, cherry pie	84	26	41	26	74	72	29	39	39	86	89	58	35	77	48	35	53.6	58th
Musk natural, 2 per cent tincture in alcohol (FLD)	Musk, sweet, heavy, slightly faecal	83	40	20	24	54	56	51	83	69	38	56	44	77	53	45	75	54.3	59th
Benzyl acetate (BDH)	Flowery, hyacinth note	18	53	57	43	65	83	—	92	104	25	74	39	74	56	16	21	54.7	60th
Ethyl alcohol 99/100 per cent, duty paid (BDH)	Sweet, spirituous	100	65	24	18	18	54	—	24	25	32	36	67	73	88	112	96	55.5	61st
Rose No. 2321, synthetic perfume concentrate (FLD)	Lemony rose	36	27	111	37	53	62	13	5	22	119	116	71	45	60	46	76	56.2	62nd
Alpine violet, perfume concentrate (FLD)	Strong fresh green odour, also violets	85	31	36	30	80	80	87	63	43	10	13	57	14	81	83	114	56.7	63rd
Oil of geranium, Bourbon (WHH)	Rich rose, bitter	32	—	96	94	42	58	98	68	75	57	12	14	16	69	70	69	58.0	64th
α-Ionone (P & S)	Violets lighter and sweeter than β-Ionone	47	56	30	48	81	57	44	47	82	97	43	73	18	42	107	72	59.0	65th
Camphor (CCC)	Camphor	94	68	101	13	38	45	42	80	57	91	71	114	42	52	31	29	60.5	66th
α-Ionone (ABR)	Violets light and sweet but not so light as 65th	48	74	46	49	40	41	73	85	86	90	63	62	13	31	109	60	60.6	67th
α-n-Methylionone (P & S)	Violets, slightly nutty. Softer and more flowery than α-Ionone	43	52	34	84	87	42	95	87	61	55	30	64	55	78	90	33	61.9	68th
β-Ionone (ABR)	Intense violets, slightly woody	55	35	103	72	46	49	56	75	65	89	82	59	20	55	108	28	62.3	69th
Oil of citronella, Ceylon (WHH)	Sweet, spicy, floral	37	55	98	92	60	93	23	65	62	88	55	55	17	67	43	113	63.9	70th
Patchouli, clear resin (FLD)	Bland Eastern odour. Rounder and milder than Patchouli oil (83rd)	71	79	40	44	28	51	84	81	74	49	32	60	54	106	104	86	65.2	71st

163

TABLE 7-1 Odours Arranged in Order of Preference. Primary Records of Results of Tests with Many Odorants and Few Observers. *(Continued)*

ODORANT	TYPE OF ODOUR	RO	ELM	MH	RMM	RWM	RWM	WMM	SL	SL	ST	ST	JET	EMT	ARL	WG	WG	AVERAGE	ODORANT IS RANKED
								PLACING (1 IS MOST LIKED, 2 IS NEXT MOST LIKED AND 132 IS MOST DISLIKED) OF EACH ODORANT BY EACH OBSERVER												
Pyridine (R & B)	Rank, gassy, repellent	98	82	118	68	131	125	115	105	108	95	106	96	100	114	102	85	103.0	118th
Hydrazine hydrate, 60 per cent in water (GEN)	Dull, ammoniacal	104	96	105	69	112	102	55	117	120	104	109	120	103	122	113	108	103.7	119th
Castor oil, medicinal	Oily, nauseating	73	114	104	99	120	118	110	120	100	117	117	97	101	105	89	82	104.1	120th
Herring oil (HBP)	Oily, fishy	—	105	121	119	104	107	76	121	111	106	121	115	97	112	88	81	105.6	121st
n-Butyric acid 50 per cent (TSH)	Sour perspiration	99	81	114	114	122	120	112	119	123	108	75	106	119	93	117	79	106.3	122nd
Chlorophyll, oil-soluble FCAS (SCB)	Rank, unpleasant	115	66	100	121	105	117	105	132	132	114	98	121	108	90	99	103	107.9	123rd
Formaldehyde 40 per cent (R & B)	Formalin, hospitals	108	108	117	66	116	122	74	116	121	98	100	119	114	123	115	111	108.0	124th
Phenyl acetylene (LLT)	Coal gas type	116	103	106	102	123	121	108	115	109	128	127	109	117	126	114	93	113.6	125th
Civet, Abyssinian (FLD)	Unpleasant sweet, faecal	101	113	75	122	132	132	118	112	128	126	130	123	124	127	98	102	116.4	126th
Ethyl mercaptan 0.5 per cent in water (LLT)	Foul, alliaceous	114	112	124	118	128	131	—	110	122	94	99	126	113	—	123	122	116.9	127th
Piperidine (BDH)	Sharp, pungent, ammoniacal	118	116	116	111	121	119	94	131	130	122	119	112	120	120	118	117	117.8	128th
Triethylamine (BDH)	Ammoniacal, organic, fishy	119	115	123	110	125	128	78	127	129	129	128	110	116	118	119	119	118.3	129th
p-Chlorothio-phenol (EVN)	Pungent, burnt, sweetish	120	117	108	120	124	126	116	126	118	125	126	124	106	125	122	120	120.2	130th
Carbon disulphide (G & T)	Spirituous, nauseating	103	110	120	109	127	130	114	128	126	130	129	122	123	119	120	116	120.4	131st
Thiomalic acid (EVN)	Pungent, rather like burnt rubber	117	118	122	112	126	127	106	130	131	124	122	125	122	117	121	121	121.3	132nd
Sex of observer		M	F	M	F	M	M	F	F	F	F	F	M	F	M	M	M		
Age of observer (years)		16	77	12	24	52	52	53	16	16	16	16	49	52	10	14	14		
Temperament of observer (introvert or extrovert)		I	E	E	E	I	I	I	E	E	E	E	E	E	E	E	E		
Number of odorants tested in run		121	118	125	122	132	132	118	132	132	130	130	126	124	127	123	122		

Notes: (1) In the table a dash instead of a number indicates that the odorant in question was not tested in that run; usually because it was unavailable at the time of test. When two runs were made by the same subject, e.g. RWM, SL, ST and WG, they were made on different days.
(2) The sources from which most of the chemicals were obtained are indicated in parentheses after the name of the chemical, e.g. Carbon disulphide (G & T) indicates that the material used for test was obtained from Griffin and Tatlock.

Reprinted with permission from R. W. Moncrieff, *Odour Preferences* (New York: Wiley, 1966), pp. 16, 19, and 23.

164

make conscious and intelligent use of such fragrances. He can be confident that he is matching fragrances coming from his body with the olfactory needs of the person with whom he is attempting to communicate.

CONCLUSION

Touch and olfaction are the forgotten as well as the inarticulate senses. We have forgotten them because they are mistakenly believed to be too primitive to have much communicative value. They are inarticulate because so little empirical research has been done on these two senses that we do not have adequate terminology to describe how they function.

In particular the skin is a sense organ of great value to interpersonal communication. Recent research demonstrates that the skin functions effectively both as a communication sender and receiver. By monitoring electrical impulses sent to the brain we know that the skin transmits much information as to kind and level of emotional arousal of the individual being monitored. Due to the work of Geldhard at Princeton's Cutaneous Communication Laboratory we also know that the skin has amazing receiving capacity. By transmitting electrical vibrations to nine vibrator cites on the body Geldhard has discovered the skin's capacity to decode complex messages. The messages are transmitted by an instrument known as the Optohapt which in turn uses an Optohapt alphabet. This alphabet is similar in principle to the Morse code.

The skin also functions well as a complete communication system. We now have a tested method of both transmitting and receiving tactile messages by human means. In addition we can measure how successfully a given tactile message has been communicated by application of the tactile communication index.

A number of factors probably affect the quality of tactile communication. At the moment, however, the amount of touching and the region of the body touched are seen as particularly important. The reader can easily determine the quality of his own tactile communication both as a sender and as a receiver. He should simply follow the instructions in this chapter for personal use of the tactile communication index.

Olfaction has been studied even less than touch. Our society seems to have an obsession with eliminating odors rather than using them in a positive way. Nonetheless, recent research on olfaction has demonstrated its communicative potential. This research has been accompanied by a growing recognition among men, in particular, that odors can be used in a systematic way to control the behavior of others and to increase one's own satisfaction.

We now know that odor is a very important communication medium which operates at two levels—subconscious and conscious. There is clear evidence that man both emits and receives odors in the form of external chemical messages; he is unaware of many of these. At the same time the intensive research of Moncrieff shows that man can consciously use odors with highly beneficial effects. By conscious use of known odor preferences man can match body fragrances with the olfactory needs of the individual with whom he is communicating.

NOTES

1. B. Scott, *How the Body Feels* (New York: Ballantine, 1973), p. 12.

2. Ibid., p. 10. A. Montagu [*Touching: The Human Significance of the Skin* (New York: Perennial Library, 1971), pp. 7-8] maintains that "as a sensory system the skin is much the most important organ system of the body. A human being can spend his life blind and deaf and completely lacking the senses of smell and taste, but he cannot survive at all without the functions performed by the skin. The experience of Helen Keller, who became deaf and blind in infancy, whose mind was literally created through the stimulation of her skin, shows us that when other senses fail, the skin can to an extraordinary degree compensate for their deficiencies."

3. Montagu, *Touching*, p. 1.

4. Ibid., p. 3. For highly technical discussions of the morphology, physiology, and psychology of the tactile system see *The Skin Senses*, ed. Dan R. Kenshalo (Springfield, Ill.: Charles C Thomas, 1968); F. A. Geldhard, *The Human Senses* (New York: Wiley, 1953); R. F. Rushmer, "The Skin," *Science*, 154 (1966), 343-48.

5. F. Davis, *Inside Intuition: What We Know about Nonverbal Communication* (New York: McGraw-Hill, 1973), p. 154.

6. M. G. Young, "The Human Touch: Who Needs It?, *Bridges Not Walls* (Reading, Mass.: Addison-Wesley, 1973), pp. 240-43.

7. B. F. Harlow, "The Nature of Love," *American Psychologist,* 13 (1958), 678-85 and B. F. Harlow, M. K. Harlow, R. O. Dodsworth, and G. L. Arling, "Maternal Behavior of Rhesus Monkeys Deprived of Mothering and Peer Associations in Infancy," *Proceedings of the American Philosophical Society,* 110 (1966), 58-66.

8. Montagu, *Touching,* p. 31.

9. M. H. Hollender, "The Need or Wish To Be Held," *Archives of General Psychiatry,* 22 (1970), 445-53. For an early, comprehensive treatment of this subject see A. C. Kinsey, *Sexual Behavior in the Human Female* (Philadelphia: W. B. Saunders, 1953), pp. 570-90.

10. M. H. Hollender, L. Luborsky, and T. J. Scaramella, "Body Contact and Sexual Enticement," *Archives of General Psychiatry,* 20 (1969), 188-91.

11. B. B. Brown, "Skin Talk: A Strange Mirror of the Mind," *Psychology Today,* 8 (1974), 52.

12. Ibid., 54.

13. Ibid., 55.

14. Ibid., 74.

15. Montagu, *Touching*, p. 1.

[16] F. A. Geldhard, "Some Neglected Possibilities of Communication," *Science,* 131 (1960), 1583-84. The author wishes to thank Dr. Geldhard for providing references to and copies of his comprehensive series of publications on tactile communication.

[17] Ibid., 1584-86.

[18] Ibid., 1585.

[19] Ibid., 1587.

[20] Ibid.

[21] F. A. Geldhard, "Body English," *Psychology Today,* 2 (1968), 45. For more detailed treatment of the same subject see F. A. Geldhard and C. E. Sherrick, "Multiple Cutaneous Stimulation: The Discrimination of Vibratory Patterns," *The Journal of Acoustical Society of America,* 37 (1965), 797-801; F. A. Geldhard, "Cutaneous Coding of Optical Signals: The Optohapt, *"Perception and Psychophysics,* 1 (1966), 377-81.

[22] A. I. Smith, "Non-Verbal Communication Through Touch," Ph.D. Dissertation, Georgia State University, 1970, pp. 1-45.

[23] S. M. Jourard, *Disclosing Man to Himself* (Princeton, N. J.: Van Nostrand Reinhold, 1968), p. 65.

[24] Ibid., p. 66.

[25] S. M. Jourard, "An Exploratory Study of Body-Accessibility," *British Journal of Social and Clinical Psychology,* 5 (1966), 221-31.

[26] Smith, "Non-Verbal Communication Through Touch," p. 45.

[27] Ibid., p. 46.

[28] H. A. Otto, "Sensory Awakening through Smell, Touch, and Taste," in *Ways of Growth: Approaches to Expanding Awareness,* ed. H. A. Otto and J. Mann (New York: Grossman, 1968), p. 49.

[29] Ibid., p. 50.

[30] Davis, *Inside Intuition,* p. 144.

[31] R. Bedichek, *The Sense of Smell* (Garden City, N. Y.: Doubleday, 1960), p. 20.

[32] Ibid., p. 21.

[33] C. Hix, "Smelling Swell," *Gentlemen's Quarterly,* 44 (1974), 82. In his thoughtful article Hix concludes that "of our five senses—touch, taste, smell, sight and hearing—smell is the most primitive. . . . As man evolved and learned to stand, then to use weapons, he relied more heavily on sight than smell for his existence, and his olfactory sense diminished. Smell has become our most primitive sense, and we know least about it. But we do know that our olfactory nerve is the only one of the cranial nerves to lead directly to the cerebrum enabling smell to arouse our emotions more than any other sense."

[34] W. Gorman, *Flavor, Taste and the Psychology of Smell* (Springfield, Ill.: Charles C Thomas, 1964), p. 25.

[35] Ibid., p. 24.

[36] A. Comfort, "Likelihood of Human Pheromones," *Nature,* 230 (1971), 432-33; A. E. Bourgeois and J. O. Bourgeois, "Theories of Olfaction: A Review," *Revista Interamericana de Psicologia,* 4 (1970), 19-31; B. Berglund, U. Berglund, T. Engen, and T. Lindvall, "The Effect of Adaptation on Odor Detection," *Perception and Psychophysics,* 5 (1971), 435-38; B. Berglund, U. Berglund, T. Engen, and G. Eckman, "Multidimensional Analysis of Twenty-One Odors," Reports from the Psychological Laboratories, University of Stockholm, 1972, No. 345; R. A. Schneider, "The Sense of Smell and Human Sexuality," *Medical Aspects of Human Sexuality,* 5 (1971), 156-68.

[37] C. J. S. Thompson, *The Mystery and Lure of Perfume* (London: The Bodley Head Limited, 1927), p. 165.

[38] Hix, "Smelling Swell," 84.

[39] R.W. Moncrieff, *Odour Preferences* (New York: Wiley, 1966), p. 184.

[40] Ibid., pp. 194-95.

[41] H. Wiener, "External Chemical Messengers: I. Emission and Reception in Man," *New York State Journal of Medicine*, 66 (1966), 3153.

[42] Ibid.

[43] Ibid., 3154.

[44] Ibid., 3157.

[45] Ibid., 3159.

[46] Ibid., 3160.

[47] Ibid. Wiener notes that "the speech of man carries cues far beyond the rational, verbal content. Electro-acoustic analysis of the voice shows that emotion creates changes not perceived consciously by speaker or listener. These changes correlate better with emotion than measures such as blood pressure or skin resistance. In psychotherapy, stances and movements characteristic of animal courtship gestures are found, and it is possible that changes in water retention occur. Movie excerpts of psychotherapeutic interviews were shown to psychotherapists and to professional dancers. On the basis of bodily and facial clues, they were able to evaluate the affective state of the patient. The professional dancers, most notably the dance therapists, did this much better than the psychiatrists. In the case of olfactory cues, I suspect that professional performers would do much better than psychiatrists in determining the affective state. But psychiatrists can do it, too, as witness the psychoanalyst who told Hall that he could distinguish the smell of anger in his patients at 6 feet or more."

[48] H. Wiener, "External Chemical Messengers: II. Natural History of Schizophrenia," *New York State Journal of Medicine,* 67 (1967), 1150.

[49] H. Wiener, "External Chemical Messengers: III. Mind and Body in Schizophrenia," *New York State Journal of Medicine,* 67 (1967), 1287.

[50] Moncrieff, *Odour Preferences,* p. 11.

[51] Ibid., pp. 15-29.

[52] Ibid., p. 143. In the intermediate range of odors, however, odor preferences are confused and there is much disagreement.

[53] Hix, "Smelling Swell," 82.

[54] Moncrieff, *Odour Preferences,* p. 309.

8

THE TELEPATHIC COMMUNICATION SYSTEM

Telepathic communication conveys meanings. "In 1967 telepathy pulsed in code from Moscow to Leningrad while sophisticated space-age equipment monitored the brain of the receiver. Soviet scientists say that with the help of the machines they were able to decode the message; they were able to transmit words telepathically from mind-to-mind across four hundred miles of space."[1] The idea of telepathic communication is very hard to accept. Indeed I was unable to give even qualified acceptance to the notion of telepathic communication until I had studied the subject carefully for over two years. Such sustained skepticism can be attributed to at least two factors. First, the idea of extrasensory communication seems to run counter to almost everything that we know. Second, many people associate extrasensory communication with the fanciful world of the medium or the allegedly fraudulent world of the psychic healer.

Since few people have had direct contact with the best laboratory experiments on psychic behavior, it is not surprising that they would have grandiose and errant notions as to what types of psychic behavior are currently receiving scientific attention. Not surprisingly, the uninformed person does not distinguish between the broad and loosely defined rubric of spontaneous extrasensory perception and the behavior that is studied under carefully controlled conditions in the laboratory. He does not realize that the psychic healer would be just as uncomfortable in such laboratories as Madelyne Murray at the annual convention of the National Council of Churches.

If serious laboratory research on psychic behavior has often been discredited because of unfair association with the fakes and the frauds, the true believer also presents a problem for the dedicated parapsychologist. Ironically, the disbelievers in psychic phenomena often disbelieve because they find the true believers so unbelievable. For example, not long ago I took a course on extrasensory perception (ESP) at a major university where I was a faculty member; the idea was to get direct exposure to the concepts and evidence which would then be assessed objectively in writing this chapter. Instead the course served primarily to emphasize the guilefulness of the instructor and the gullibility of the true believers who packed the large classroom.

The instructor of the course was a man we shall call Conan Bromley. Bromley began the class (members of the overflow turnout were forced to stand along the walls) with an interesting if highly speculative account of his theory of physics. Needless to say, Bromley's theory compelled him to conclude that ESP was not only possible but that he would demonstrate it time after time in his own classroom.

As evidence to support his contention that interpersonal communication does take place without the use of any of our known senses, Bromley cited the case of his son. Bromley's son would sit on one side of a stage with his back to Bromley and guess the symbol on cards which Bromley flipped over. Absolutely fantastic, said Bromley. Bromley claimed that on the first run his son got 25 correct out of 25. His accuracy dropped a bit on the next trial because there had been a heckler in the audience; Bromley assured class members that a percipient or receiver loses his concentration unless the audience members give him their cooperation and believe in him.

At this point, I became overwhelmed with the force of my own skepticism. Raising a hand I caught Bromley's attention and said: "Your son's performance was certainly impressive and I am also impressed with the psychic powers you say you have. I am sure you would be pleased to demonstrate them on the stage in front of us with your wife flipping cards and you attempting to identify them." There was a long pause; Bromley seemed to be a bit shaken. Finally, he turned and remarked "there is nothing I would rather do than give you a demonstration of my psychic powers. However, two years ago I was in an auto accident and my powers were severely impaired; last year I was in another accident and I lost more of my powers. Then, just last January, I was attacked in the parking lot at Pauley Pavilion and suffered another head injury. Since then, my powers have been very limited."[2]

Bromley coupled this implausible disclaimer with detailed stories about the great stimulation of going out in the desert and lying on his back to watch the space ships moving across the heavens, and the practical value of communicating with the dead; he had made me a strong disbeliever in psychic phenomena of any kind. Most of the members of the audience, however, seemed to be true believers with their capacity to think logically totally suspended or permanently missing.

To watch the true believer was to feel a twinge of sympathy. For many of these people the intensity of their belief in psychic phenomena served to remove the logical imperative of finding at least some empirical evidence to support extraordinary claims of communication that transcend the constraints of distance as well as our own mortality.

The true believer has a great need to reinforce his view of psychic phenomena and to become actively involved himself. Merchandisers have been quick to satisfy such a need. In 1967, for example, Ouija boards overtook Monopoly (the national favorite for many years) as America's favorite board game. Since 1967, approximately 10 million of these boards have been sold, making them a $50 million business; at least 20 million Americans have played with them. The reader should note that a Ouija board is so designed that the true believer can easily conclude that psychic forces are guiding him as he plays the game. "A Ouija board is a wooden square on which the alphabet, numbers, and words like 'yes' and 'no' are printed. On top of it rests a small pointer which can move across the surface. Two people sit close together, legs touching, the board resting on their knees. They place their fingers lightly on the pointer and wait. Within a few minutes the pointer begins to slide over the board indicating letters, numbers, words. The idea is to ask questions—preferably simple ones—and let the board answer."[3]

The Ouija board has been only the beginning. The $3 billion toy industry in the United States has moved quickly into the psychic market. Palm-reading and witchcraft games, ghost costumes, monster puppets, mechanical UFOs, plastic apparitions and skulls, walking zombies, magic wands, and assorted vampires are being marketed in large numbers. Indeed, some of America's most famous retailers are now devoting major sections of their stores to catering to the public's sustained need to explore psychic phenomena. In June 1970, Brentano's bookstores started a permanent boutique of the occult in their largest New York store. The department is devoted to mystic merchandise ranging from contemplation birthstones to zodiac stationery.[4]

Not surprisingly, the commercial appeals to the faithful do not seem to take the true believer seriously and probably do much to reinforce a state of disbelief among the skeptics. Examples are not lacking. In June 1970, Gail Kuhn opened the Witches' Cauldron, located in Manhattan. The Witches' Cauldron is basically a wholesaler of metaphysical products but adds a few touches to hold the attention of the buyer. For the debut of the Witches' Cauldron, selected groups of guests were taken to a separate room where a girl and boy witch, screened behind transparent gauze, went through an abbreviated "initiation ceremony"; both were very good looking and completely naked.[5]

The depth of the need to know about psychic behavior is perhaps best reflected in efforts of the publishing business to meet this need. Reputable publishing houses are now moving quickly into the occult business. Doubleday started the trend in 1956 with the publication of The Search for Bridey Murphy, which sold 157,000 copies, and followed with The Sleeping Prophet, a book on Edgar Cayce, the noted psychic healer, which sold over 123,000; over a quarter of a million sales in hardcover books is not bad. Similarly, Dell Publishing has been doing a flourishing business in paperbacks on psychics. Their paperback on Edgar Cayce, There Is a River, has gone through thirteen printings with over 1,050,000 copies sold, and Dell's horoscope magazines have sold over 8 million copies.[6]

The true believer's need to know is not reflected solely in the sale of merchandise. A number of individuals have become nationally famous by devoting their professional energies to the development and use of what they claim are psychic powers.

Those who make such an effort might be classified as prophets, astrologers, and mediums.

Among the more famous personalities who function as prophets in America are Jeanne Dixon, Maurice Woodruff, and Daniel Logan, "the reluctant prophet," who predicted on television the name of the Academy Award winners for 1966, 1967, and 1968. Their present fame is eclipsed by that of Edgar Cayce, "the sleeping prophet," however. Cayce is probably the most revered prophet in the history of psychic phenomena in America. A legendary figure among true believers, Cayce was a man of very limited education who discovered that, while asleep, he had the capacity to prescribe detailed medications for the seriously and terminally ill. Allegedly a great proportion of these patients made complete and miraculous recoveries. Testimonials from all over the United States serve as a type of documentation to Cayce's skills. Today, his son Hugh Lynn Cayce travels around the country promoting his father's legend. Exhibiting a meticulousness not characteristic of the prophet, Hugh Lynn has catalogued all his father's prescriptions as well as the testimonials to their effectiveness at the Association for Research and Enlightenment—Edgar Cayce Foundation. The foundation headed by Hugh Lynn Cayce is housed in the old Cayce hospital at Virginia Beach, Virginia.[7]

The astrologers are headed by personalities such as Bruce King, better known as "Zolar." Astrology has become so popular in the last few years that every reader should have at least a vague knowledge of what it involves. Consequently, astrology is no longer habitually confused with astronomy.

Finally, there are the mediums who are of two types: spiritual and physical mediums. The spiritual medium allegedly has among his powers the capacity to communicate with the dead. Partially because of the bizarre and seemingly impossible nature of the spiritual medium's task, his efforts have often been convincingly attacked as pure fraud. In contrast, the physical medium supposedly has the capacity to use some supernatural force to move objects. The alleged ability to make a table rise off the floor is one of the tricks of the physical medium most consistently exposed as fraudulent.

SPONTANEOUS EXTRASENSORY PERCEPTION

The work of prophets such as Edgar Cayce and the mediums are examples of *spontaneous* extrasensory perception. While hardly scientific in nature, the work of the prophet and the medium was at one time of interest to academicians who were studying psychic phenomena.

Perhaps such a seemingly naive interest was inevitable. We certainly do know that people have claimed an extrasensory or supernatural ability to communicate with both the living and the dead for centuries; such claims include the ability to communicate across great distances without the aid of any electronic equipment. While such reports have been coming in for centuries, no systematic and comprehensive effort was made to catalogue and record the sources of such reports until the latter part of the nineteenth century. In 1882 the Society for Psychical Research (SPR) was founded with Henry Sidgwick, a distinguished professor of Moral History at Cambridge, as its first president; the American Society for Psychical Research (ASPR) was founded in 1884.

It is perhaps worth noting that the first major organization dedicated to the study of psychic phenomena (the Society for Psychical Research) was founded in England, and to this day England remains a home for much of the best research on the subject—the home of some of the most distinguished proponents of telepathy in particular. Indeed "most of the leading British psychologists, for example, who have had anything to say on the matter of extrasensory perception including Sir Cyril Burt, Margaret Knight, Robert H. Thouless and H. J. Eysenck, leave no doubt that they regard its existence as proved."[8]

During the period from the founding of the SPR to the beginning of J. B. Rhine's experiments in the Parapsychology Laboratory at Duke (1882–1930) scholarly attention was focused on recording and examining every case of what became known as *spontaneous extrasensory perception.* The task of the SPR and its American counterpart, the ASPR, was extremely broad in scope and essentially descriptive in nature. To put it another way each report of a clairvoyant dream, or a seance with the dead, or any other psychic event was recorded and examined. However, no rigorous attempt was made to *prove* that such types of extrasensory perception were actually taking place.

The broad focus of the British and American societies can be comprehended by studying the early volumes of the journal for each organization; the journals began publication at about the time the societies were founded. The earlier issues of the journals in particular provide fascinating accounts of the types of subjects and claims that were the direct concern of the two societies. In the July 1884 issue of the *Journal of the Society for Psychical Research,* as in other quarterly issues, readers were provided with a supplementary library catalogue. The publications which made up that library presumably represented subjects of immediate and vital concern to the members of the society. The following titles and dates of publication are representative: *Surgical Operations in the Mesmeric State* (1843); *Sketches of the Philosophy of Apparitions* (1882); *Phantasmata, or Illusions and Fanaticisms of Protean Forms Productive of Great Evils,* 2 vols. (1857); *The Wonders of the Invisible World* (1862); *True and Perfect Account of an Apparition* (1672).[9]

The actual pages of the *Journal of the Society for Psychical Research* are filled with accounts of psychic phenomena such as apparitions and ghosts. Such accounts are accompanied by the firsthand report of one of the Royal Fellows of the Society and his evaluation of the person who had experienced the apparition, or who had been haunted. One G. A. Smith turned in the following report on November 22, 1884:

> In accordance with your instructions I have been to Norwich to gather all the available evidence in connection with the "hauntings" which you were informed occurred there. I called upon Mr. I. O. Howard Taylor (an Associate of the Society for Psychical Research), who first drew your attention to the matter, and ascertained from him the address of the person who was inhabiting the house at the time the disturbances were said to occur. He is a clerk, and we may call him Mr. X. He gave his evidence

clearly and *very* emphatically; he is an exceedingly intelligent witness, but I consider him to be of a somewhat nervous and excitable temperament, although, of course, his occasional highly-strung manner may have been due to the nature of the circumstances. His statements were to the following effect:—His wife was asleep; he could *not* sleep, but was lying quite still, and wide awake. Suddenly, on the first stroke of 12 from a clock in the city, there was an audible "swish," and the figure of a man stood before him, at the foot of the bed. The figure was that of a respectable old gentleman of about 60, with sharp, well-marked features. He was dressed in a black coat and waistcoat, and stood quite motionless, staring intently at him. Mr. X., without the ability to do otherwise, stared in return, until the last stroke of 12, when the apparition appeared to raise its arms and sink through the floor. This experience had a very marked effect upon his nerves. . . .[10]

Much like its British counterpart, the American Society for Psychical Research "was born during the heyday of mediumism and most of its early investigations dealt with allegedly psychic personalities who produced spirit knocks and levitations. Since then, however, both its aims and its methods have become vastly more sophisticated."[11] Gradually, both societies eliminated hauntings and apparitions from consideration. They now concentrate on the four types of psychic phenomena that are being explored under controlled conditions in experimental laboratories: telepathy, clairvoyance, psychokinesis, and precognition.

While the reports of hauntings and apparitions may strike the reader as slightly absurd, they are hardly confined to the nineteenth century. Reports of psychic events are being made at this very time which would blow the mind of the most stodgy academician if true. The most striking example of such reports comes in the form of the reported exploits of Uri Geller. In one sense they almost seem to make the apparition experienced by Mr. X. back in the 1880s appear a routine matter.

Uri Geller is a young (26 years old) and handsome Israeli who recently came to the United States to demonstrate his powers of telepathy and psychokinesis. The noted author Andrew Weil, a skeptic and a man who demands that claims be supported by empirical proof, was assigned to observe Geller and determine whether he could perform as claimed.

Geller claims that he can literally move objects and change their shape by concentrating his mental energy on them. Weil watched Geller perform before an audience. Geller asked if anyone in the audience had a watch which was not running. A woman volunteered; Geller placed his hands over hers and asked her to let him know if she felt any sudden heat or tingling. She did. As Weil opened her hands, he observed that the watch was running again. Next, Geller offered to drive a group of volunteers around Berkeley, California, while he was blindfolded. The volunteers reported that he made the drive successfully.[12]

Then Weil observed Geller at a private party. Geller began by noting that a number of high-placed American officials believed in him. The Defense Department expressed particular interest in his ability to erase magnetic tapes at a distance, Geller asserted. He also described how he blanked out an airport TV monitor in the presence of a United States senator. Geller laughed about an incident where he allegedly forced a movie projector on an airplane to spill tape all over the floor. He remarked that when he bent a nail or spoon simply by looking at them, people had weird explanations for his psychic powers—one man accused him of having a laser beam in his belt. Turning to Weil, Geller said, "I have these powers, and they just come through me. I want to show them to people. I want people to know that it's real, that there are no lasers in my belt and no chemicals. I just say to the key, 'Bend!' and I feel that it's going to bend, and it does." Weil: "I imagine that could be heavy for some people." Geller: "Sure, it's heavy for them."[13]

Uri had warmed up for this private session by asking different individuals at the party to draw any figure that came to mind on a piece of paper and place it in an opaque envelope. According to the skeptical Weil, Uri correctly identified the figures which were drawn by two individuals—one of a cross, the other of a Star of David. Then Uri turned to his specialty, psychokinesis; psychokinesis is the ability to bend and move objects solely by concentrating on them.

A lighting director who was attending the party handed Uri a heavy gold ring. Uri examined the gold ring carefully. Asking the lighting director to support the ring on its edge with his forefinger, Uri then held his hand over the man's hand but did not touch the ring. Weil was only a few inches away as this demonstration of psychokinesis was taking place. "Suddenly, the ring sagged into an oval shape. Uri exclaimed, 'There! Look at that. Did you feel anything?' 'I felt a strong tingling over the whole back of my hand, definitely some kind of energy,' was the reply. Uri held the ring for all to see. It was no longer circular, and would not fit back on its owner's finger. . . . There was little doubt in my mind that I had seen genuine psychokinesis—something I had always believed in but never witnessed. I left the apartment feeling absolutely elated."[14]

Weil needed one more demonstration to be sure, however. He had to see Geller bend something he owned to be convinced that the objects Geller used were real. Weil took off his large brass belt buckle and put it in his hand. Uri put his hand on one of Weil's and concentrated. Suddenly, Weil "felt a distinct throb inside [his] hands, like a small frog kicking. I told him so. 'You did?' he asked excitedly and opened my hands. I could see no change in the buckle. He pulled out a long steel key and cried out: 'It's bent, yes, it's bent! Do you see?' I did not at first. But then I noticed a slight bend. . . . Yes, it was definitely bent. . . . 'Let's see if we can bend it more,' he said. He touched the key to the other keys and stroked it again. After a few minutes the bend was about 25 degrees. Uri patted me on the back, making me feel that I had participated in the miracle. 'It's good you felt it jump, man,' he told me. 'Not many people can feel that.' "[15] Weil was elated and convinced that Uri Geller had demonstrated some extraordinary psychic powers which were impossible to deny.

Uri Geller, Israeli psychic, would appear to represent an unusually persuasive case history of spontaneous extrasensory perception which was demonstrated inches from the eyes of a highly respected skeptic and found to be entirely believable. Since Geller stresses that his powers can be exercised effectively only when conditions are right, the reader should note that Geller does not claim the ability to turn his psychic powers on and off like a computer; instead his powers are a very contemporary variety of *spontaneous* extrasensory perception.

Uri Geller's feats seem truly remarkable. Here is a man whose psychic behavior was described in detail by a respected writer in a respected magazine (*Psychology Today*). Weil and *Psychology Today* can hardly be considered as paid accomplices of Geller. And yet, what was Geller able to accomplish directly under the critical eye of an observing skeptic? He bent keys, rings, and silverware; he read the contents of hidden envelopes; he fixed long-broken wristwatches. He also told of driving a car blindfolded through the streets of Berkeley, of causing a rosebud to bloom, and of making an airliner's movie projector spew film across the floor.[16]

As the reader considers the remarkable case of Uri Geller, he may want to ask himself three questions: Is spontaneous extrasensory perception in the form of telepathy and psychokinesis, or in other forms, possible? Has the reader experienced, or might he experience, spontaneous extrasensory perception? Do we have scientific proof of the existence of spontaneous extrasensory perception?

The reader can provide his own answer to the first question. Certainly the pages of the journals of the Society for Psychical Research and the American Society for Psychical Research are replete with the apparently sincere reports of individuals who have had psychic experiences or who claim psychic powers. Those who publically acknowledge at least the possibility of spontaneous extrasensory perception are hardly limited to unlettered crackpots. Noted psychology professors such as William McDougall and Gardner Murphy, and individuals like Albert Einstein, Upton Sinclair, and the previously identified British academicians represent only a very small sample of respected public men who have risked at least some part of their reputations in firmly asserting the possibility of spontaneous extrasensory perception.[17]

The reader can also provide the best answer to the second question—has the reader experienced spontaneous extrasensory perception or might he? On the face of it this question might seem slightly ludicrous. But the reader is asked to think about it seriously. For many years I would have had a two-word answer for the question—no chance. A recent experience has at least weakened the strength of my disbelief, however. This summer while driving home from the University of Georgia after putting in a day at the office working on this book, I suddenly had a very strong and definite feeling of foreboding which was spelled out in the form of some amazingly specific imagery. I was suddenly aware of an image picturing my wife in some type of serious trouble. While the type of trouble was not clear, the image was so clear that I glanced at my watch to determine the exact time this very sharp image was experienced. It was 6 p.m.

After returning to the university for a nighttime session on this book, I arrived home well after 9 p.m. A few minutes after I walked in the door, the phone rang. My wife was on the other end of the line in Columbus, Georgia, talking in an agitated voice. She had driven her Toyota Corona to Columbus to do some consulting work in her professional capacity as an urban planner. At the end of the day she had inadvertently driven through a stop sign and had been broadsided by a large truck. She was badly bruised and shaken but sustained no serious or permanent injury. The force of the impact was so great, however, that the insurance company subsequently wrote the Toyota off as a total wreck. Recalling the sharp and focused sense of foreboding about my wife's welfare which I had experienced earlier in the evening, I asked her the obvious question. "What time did the wreck occur?" "Almost exactly at 6 p.m.," she replied.

Finally, a third question of major concern in considering spontaneous extrasensory perception is whether we have *scientific proof* for its existence. At this point the answer is no. That is not to say that we do not have evidence. At minimum, to establish the existence of a particular type of behavior by scientific means, certain conditions must be met: (1) the relevant factors and conditions must be kept under control; (2) the phenomenon under study must be repeatable; (3) the behavior being studied must be consistently and predictably related to other types of behavior.

The countless cases of *spontaneous* extrasensory perception—beginning with the least believable, such as experiencing ghosts and apparitions, to the most believable, such as some form of telepathy—do not meet these standards of scientific proof. Spontaneous cases of extrasensory perception by definition are not subject to control because we do not know when they will occur or under what conditions. Thus, such cases often take place with no one else present. The individual who experiences spontaneous extrasensory perception is thus forced to rely on the accuracy of his own recall. Those receiving the report are forced to rely on the uncorroborated testimony of the person experiencing the psychic phenomenon. Scientists are unwilling to rely on uncorroborated testimony as scientific proof.

Second, most spontaneous extrasensory experiences are not repeatable at least without a change in the conditions under which they allegedly occurred. Many scientists consider repeatability of behavior to be an essential factor in application of the scientific method. Thus, birth control pills were not approved as effective after only one woman took the pill. The pill-taking had to be repeated over and over before medical authorities could be assured of the effects with which it was associated. Since most extrasensory experiences cannot be repeated, many scientists are unwilling to accept such experiences as scientific proof for the existence of ESP.

Finally, students of psychic experiences have not been able to relate them on a predictive basis to other types of behavior. The scientist is able to predictably relate one behavior such as cigarette-smoking to lung cancer because he has a sufficiently large sample of occurrences so that he can explore the relationship via correlation. But since a person may have only one or a handful of psychic experiences it is virtually impossible to determine, for example, if we can predict whether the behavior of a person pictured in a clairvoyant dream will exhibit certain, specific anti-social qualities.

At this point the reader may be puzzled. He may understand how I could discount my own clairvoyant experience as a mere coincidence or the work of selective recall. But how, the reader may ask, can I discount the amazing and seemingly verified feats of Uri Geller recounted above? Appropriately, we now return to Uri Geller and take a second, more critical look at his alleged powers of extrasensory perception.

As the reader will recall, the Israeli psychic Uri Geller has apparently demonstrated amazing powers of spontaneous extrasensory perception. He is able to determine the nature of the contents of sealed envelopes, he makes wristwatches begin running by simply looking at them and he bends keys, silverware, and a ring inches from the eyes of a skeptical observer. But let us take a closer look at Uri Geller. Is he really a great psychic or a great magician?

The same question occurred to Andrew Weil, the author who had observed Uri Geller's feats firsthand. Consequently, Weil went to see James (the Amazing) Randi. Randi is a professional magician who is convinced that Geller is a psychic fraud although he concedes that Geller is an outstanding magician; Randi openly professes a desire to expose Geller.

Randi began his demonstration for Weil by duplicating one of Geller's favorite performances. He gave Weil 10 film canisters and asked Weil to stuff one of them full of nuts and bolts with enough padding around them so that they would not rattle. Randi went out of the room while Weil stuffed one canister full of nuts and bolts, and mixed up the ten canisters. Randi then returned and without touching the empty film canisters he eliminated them one by one until he had only one canister remaining. He indicated that the remaining canister was the one filled with nuts and bolts. It was. Weil was amazed. How had the Amazing Randi pulled off this trick? Easy, said Randi.

There was a very subtle but easily perceptible difference between the full and the empty canister.

Randi then turned on a videotape machine which showed Geller failing to identify the film canister with nuts and bolts in it when he appeared on the Johnny Carson television show. Strangely, Uri Geller had successfully completed the canister feat many times under different conditions. Why did Geller fail on the Carson show, asked Weil? Randi claimed that he and Carson, an amateur magician, had used canisters with non-malleable sides so that Geller was unable to perceive the subtle difference in shape in the filled canister.[18] Randi then proceeded to show how he could bend a nail (it is an optical illusion with Randi palming the straight nail while supplying a bent one), how he could determine the nature of the contents of a sealed envelope (again an optical illusion), and how to bend a key (divert the audience's attention for an instant while jamming the key against a leg of a chair).[19]

Certainly the magic tricks of Randi the Amazing provide ammunition for the sniping skeptic, but do they really expose Uri Geller as a fraud with no powers of spontaneous extrasensory perception? One might think so, but the available evidence does not lend itself to a clearcut answer. In the first place, the magician, Randi the Amazing, was unable to duplicate some of Geller's most impressive feats such as making the gold ring droop. Second, Geller was apparently able to convince a group of renowned physicists at the Stanford University that his psychic powers are genuine. Psychology professor Ray Hyman of the University of Oregon may give the most balanced reaction to Geller's apparent demonstration of his powers of spontaneous extrasensory perception. Hyman states, "I can't say with certainty that Uri Geller doesn't have the powers he claims. I have an intuitive conviction that such powers exist. I also have a strong feeling that Uri is, among other things, a brilliantly artistic stage magician, whose ability to create belief is great. But I am not sure that stage magic can explain completely everything I saw him do."[20]

THE SCIENTIFIC STUDY OF TELEPATHIC COMMUNICATION

The study of *spontaneous* extrasensory perception has produced some fascinating case histories. Many have more than a surface plausibility. Evidence supporting the existence of spontaneous extrasensory perception does not, however, meet the criteria that would make it acceptable as scientific proof.

The period from 1882 to 1930 focused on recording, and assessing the plausibility of, reported cases of extrasensory perception. All reported cases took place in the field rather than the laboratory. The period of 1930 to 1950 marked the advent of a significant new era in the study of psychic phenomena, however. In those two decades the four primary forms of psychic behavior were studied in the laboratory under controlled conditions.[21] Moreover, these laboratory studies yielded evidence supporting the existence of telepathic communication which hostile scientists have still not successfully refuted as this chapter is being written.

The laboratory studies begun in the 1930s focused on the four primary kinds of psychic behavior: (1) *telepathy*—the ability of a receiver to perceive the thoughts of the sender without using any of the known sensory channels; (2) *clairvoyance*—the ability to acquire knowledge of an object or an event that is occurring without using any of the known sensory channels; (3) *psychokinesis*—the ability to move a physical object or influence an event by thinking about it; (4) *precognition*—the ability to acquire knowledge of another person's future thoughts (*precognitive telepathy*), or of future events (*precognitive clairvoyance*).[22]

The reader will note that the author's sense of foreboding as his wife had the auto accident apparently was an example of clairvoyance while Uri Geller's successful efforts to bend nails, silverware, and rings are clearly examples of psychokinesis. On the basis of present evidence, the four types of psychic behavior might be placed on a credibility continuum with telepathy viewed as most believable and precognition as least believable. In fact a good portion of psychic research done in the past few years focuses on the least believable types of psychic behavior—psychokinesis and precognition—or on rather esoteric methodological questions that have nothing to do with the basic question of whether psychic communication really takes place.[23]

While all four major forms of psychic behavior have been studied in the laboratory during the last four decades, only telepathy will be examined in detail in this chapter as a type of psychic communication. The main reasons for focusing exclusively on telepathic communication here are: (1) telepathic communication, unlike clairvoyance, psychokinesis, and precognition, focuses on communicative *interaction* between at least two human beings; (2) telepathic communication has a much greater body of laboratory evidence and qualified authorities (particularly among the British experts) to support its existence than the other three types of psychic behavior;[24] (3) psychokinesis and precognition suggest a surface implausibility that current evidence does little to refute while clairvoyance has nothing to do with *interpersonal* communication per se.

TELEPATHIC COMMUNICATION IN J. B. RHINE'S LABORATORY AT DUKE   While much laboratory research has now been done on telepathic communication, two sets of experiments seem to provide the best evidence for its existence. The first is a set of pioneering experiments conducted by J. B. Rhine in the Parapsychology Laboratory at Duke University. The second is a set of experiments, which are in progress at this time, conducted in the Dream Laboratory of the Maimonides Medical Institute in Brooklyn.

Rhine's experiments were conducted during the 1930-50 period and have had a pervasive impact on virtually all subsequent research conducted on psychic behavior. The fascinating history of all the Duke experiments is covered by Rhine and others.[25] While Rhine did many experiments on clairvoyance and related psychic behavior, this section of this chapter is devoted exclusively to a description of his experiments on telepathic communication and the evidence which he adduced therefrom.

The basic parts of the procedure which Rhine used for his tests in pure telepathy have become the norm among parapsychological researchers today. First, Rhine developed a set of five cards, each card with a different symbol on it. These cards were used to form an ESP deck which contained twenty-five cards with one of the five basic symbols on each of the twenty-five cards (see Figure 8-1). A deck of ESP cards can

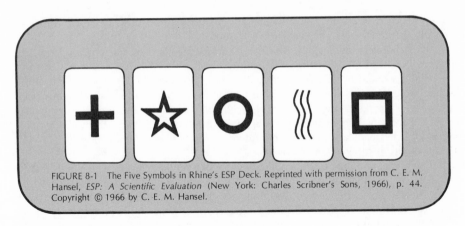

FIGURE 8-1   The Five Symbols in Rhine's ESP Deck. Reprinted with permission from C. E. M. Hansel, *ESP: A Scientific Evaluation* (New York: Charles Scribner's Sons, 1966), p. 44. Copyright © 1966 by C. E. M. Hansel.

now be obtained at most major retail outlets. Second, Rhine calculated the mathematical probability that a given number of "hits" or correct choices of cards by the percipient could have been due to chance. For example, one correct choice out of the five could be due to chance—anything greater than 1 correct choice out of five exceeds chance. Since 5 choices obviously is too small a sample of choices, the sender is often asked to make 200 choices. If he makes 40 correct choices out of 200 he is operating at the chance level; in a 200-choice sample, anything over 40 correct choices might be taken as evidence for the existence of extrasensory perception. Third, Rhine keeps records on the number of correct choices to determine if they are at the chance level, above it, or below it.

In *New Frontiers of the Mind* Rhine gives a fascinating, firsthand account of his telepathic experiments. He begins by noting that the general public thought many of his earlier experiments dealt exclusively with telepathy, but clairvoyance may also have been involved. For example, in the early experiments at Duke, the typical design was to have a receiver (percipient) attempt to guess the symbol on a card that a sender was turning over; the percipient and sender were separated physically so that Rhine was convinced that the sender could not use subtle physical cues to transmit information about a given card to the sender. When the percipient correctly guessed the symbol on a card the sender was concentrating on, the correct guess was usually taken as a sign of telepathic communication. As J. B. Rhine perceptively notes, "such results in the part were called evidence for telepathy. . . . The early experimenters did not realize how much of an assumption they were making, for they were not alive to the possibility of clairvoyance in such cases. As we understand the matter now, such undifferentiated tests as these—which we now call general ESP tests—are useful mainly for exploratory purposes. Perhaps a subject may be able to score better if he is exposed to both clairvoyant and the telepathic influence at the same time."[26]

Rhine had to devise some method to make sure that the guesses of the percipient were due to telepathic influence and not to clairvoyance. To do so he had his sender or agent memorize the order in which he would arrange the five symbols (on five separate cards), but he did not actually arrange the cards until after the percipient had made his choices. Since the sender did not know what choices the percipient was making, there was no way to arrange the cards fraudulently to coincide with the percipient's choices. With this method the receiver was forced to rely exclusively on his ability to read the thoughts of the sender in order to correctly identify the symbol on a given card. Hence, the percipient's "hits" or correct choices had to be attributed solely to telepathic communication, not to clairvoyance.

Rhine describes a number of experiments he conducted to determine whether telepathic communication actually occurs. Perhaps his most noted telepathy experiment was the Ownbey-Zirkle experiment (Ownbey, a female, was the sender or agent and Zirkle, a male, was the receiver or percipient). Rhine observes that "throughout the duration of the test the electric fan was going and Zirkle sat with his back to the experimenter. His eyes were closed and his mind adjusted to the greatest degree of abstraction of which he was capable in the normal waking state. The ready signal, or notice that the sender was concentrating on a new card, was given by means of a telegraphic sounder. The receiver called his choice aloud; the experimenter recorded it, and if correct, checked it."[27] Zirkle averaged 13.6 hits in each run of 25 trials which greatly exceeds the chance expectations identified above.

In one of a group of follow-up studies Ownbey again served as the telepathic sender and Turner (a female) as the receiver. The unique thing about this experiment was that Turner was separated from Ownbey—who was in the Duke laboratory—by two hundred and fifty miles. A comparison of the symbols Ownbey tried to send on the first day against the calls which Turner actually made shows 19 hits out of 25 choices; 16 hits out of 25 on the second day; 16 hits out of 25 on the third day.[28] In evaluating these and similar experiments on pure telepathy Rhine observes "if the work is correct, we have for the first time in the history of the subject experimentally separated telepathy and clairvoyance. Further, we have shown that there is a process of telepathy and that it works."[29]

Rhine's studies in the Parapsychology Laboratory at Duke precipitated a national wave of interest which was reflected in uncritical adulation for Rhine by his devotees on the one hand and bitter denunciation of his work by critics on the other. From the perspective of the parapsychologist Rhine must be viewed as a giant whose basic methodology is still being used over forty years since he initiated his experiments at Duke; while Rhine continues to write and speak widely, his serious experiments at Duke were conducted during the 1930-50 period.[30]

To his most caustic critics Rhine was a well-meaning man who trusted his subjects and, as a result of such trust and the less than meticulous design of his experiments, left himself open to at least the possibility of being charged with fraud. Since the results of Rhine's studies run directly counter to the very values so central to many an academician's basic philosophy, many professors could not bring themselves to accept his results and indeed were led to the unscientific act of dismissing Rhine without carefully studying his work. Indeed:

> It is difficult for a layman to appreciate the significance of this in scientific terms, but when Rhine published the results of tests in 1934 he caused one of the greatest furors in academic history. There were professors who wouldn't—couldn't—bring themselves to believe in the validity of Rhine's findings, which shook the very basis of their rationalist philosophy. After R. A. Fisher, the country's leading specialist in probability calculus, found Rhine's statistics accurate, attacks were launched against his system of precautions. Additional safeguards were implemented, but still the test results continued high above chance levels.[31]

In his old age Rhine still finds himself buffeted by two forces. He is a revered figure among those who accept psychic behavior as real and typically appears as the honored speaker at annual conventions of organizations such as the American Society for Psychical Research and the Parapsychological Association. On the other hand, while his critics have dwindled in number, the intensity of their criticism has lost none of its sting.

Professor C. E. M. Hansel has written what is widely regarded as the most comprehensive, current critique of parapsychology in general and J. B. Rhine's experiments in particular. It is a monument to Hansel's meticulous approach that he recently visited Duke University and went over the very rooms where Rhine's experiments were conducted with a fine-tooth comb. Hansel notes that he interviewed one of Rhine's most famous subjects, J. G. Pratt, and that during the interview Pratt "mentioned that since 1934 structural alterations had been made to both rooms. We first visited Pratt's old room 314, in the social sciences building. I located the position of the table. . . . Pratt then pointed out that the wall beside the table had been further back in 1933. After its original position had been located, it was apparent that the room in its original state contained a large clear-glass window that would have permitted anyone in the corridor to see into the room at the time of the experiment."[32]

The Parapsychology Laboratory at Duke is now closed and only an occasional intrepid investigator comes to check out the rooms where the internationally famous experiments in telepathic communication were conducted; Rhine and his wife, Louisa, have established a private institution with less specific aims—the Foundation for Research on the Nature of Man. Reasonable men may still argue over the evidential weight of the Duke experiments, but it seems safe to conclude that "regardless of what emerges from the later venture, his [Rhine's] old testing ground in Durham, North Carolina, will remain a pioneering monument akin to Freud's modest consulting office in Vienna's Berggasse."[33]

TELEPATHIC COMMUNICATION IN THE SOVIET UNION Just as research on telepathic communication in the 1930-50 period was not confined to J. B. Rhine's laboratory at Duke, research in the modern period (1950 to the present) is not confined to a single laboratory. In fact some of the most exciting research being reported currently comes from laboratories in Russia. This chapter began with a quotation describing the abilities of two Russians to communicate telepathically from Moscow to Leningrad. Astounding reports have been coming from the Soviet Union for some time. They receive hyperbolic treatment in a new, best-selling book entitled *Psychic Discoveries behind the Iron Curtain* by Ostrander and Schroeder. The Russian feats reported in this book represent work which extends upon the pioneering efforts of L. L. Vasiliev—the most famous academic figure in Russia to study psychic behavior in the laboratory. Vasiliev had impressive credentials. He graduated from Petersburg University in 1914 as a teacher of the biological sciences. He was head of the Physiology Department, Bekhterev Brain Institute, Leningrad from 1921 to 1938 and, reappearing after the Stalin purges, he was Professor of Physiology at Leningrad University from 1943 until his recent death.

In his fascinating book, *Mysterious Phenomena of the Human Psyche,* Vasiliev reveals a propensity for the sensational that has drawn many people to the Russian research on psychic behavior and turned off others. He emphasizes that telepathic communication far from being implausible or impossible is a very natural phenomenon. "Telepathy resembles communication which is effected by wireless or radio;

telesthesia—television; telekinesis—telechanics: that is, the control of various apparatus and processes at a distance by means of electronic equipment."[34]

To this point Vasiliev seems restrained in his assertions. Telepathic communication is accomplished, he claims, by the transmission of electrical impulses from the brain of the sender to the brain of the receiver. However, in his attempt to explain the nature of telepathic communication, Vasiliev quickly moves to a mind-boggling example. To support his contention Vasiliev casually mentions that the Russians have recently developed a human hand that performs admirably by receiving electrical impulses (without the benefit of any connecting wires) from the brain of the user of the hand. Writes Vasiliev:

> Recently members of the Moscow Prosthetic and Orthopedic Institute made ingenious use of bioelectrical currents in constructing a remarkable model of a functioning human hand. The hand is made of metal with mobile fingers. Its mechanism is connected by wires to a circular current-detector, worn as a bracelet on the arm of any subject. The mechanical hand executes the same movements which the subject thinks of at the given moment. For instance: the moment he thinks of making a fist, the artificial hand will do the same thing. This technical 'miracle' comes about in the following way: at the thought of the movement to be made, the brain sends impulses of excitation to the appropriate muscles of the hand, that is, bioelectric currents which cause contraction of these muscles. The manual bioelectric currents which are picked up by the current-detector are transmitted to an amplifier which includes special equipment for putting into motion the fingers of the artificial hand. Thus, man's ideomotor activity can direct a machine—today by means of wires: tomorrow, conceivably without wires, through utilization of electromagnetic transmission.[35]

At the date this chapter is being written, leading Russian authorities continue to support the brain-wave theory of telepathic communication. Two well-known scientists—Dr. Lutsia Pavlova, an electrophysiologist at the Physiology Laboratory at the University of Leningrad, and Dr. Genady Sergeyev, mathematician at the A. A. Uktomskii Laboratory run for the Soviet military—claim that Kamensky (the sender in Moscow) communicated telepathically with Nikolaiev (the receiver in Leningrad) by the use of brain-wave transmission.[36]

In March 1967, a team of scientists boarded the Red Arrow Express for Leningrad with Nikolaiev. Once there, their goal was to determine if Nikolaiev could pick up Kamensky's telepathic signals from Moscow.

> Nikolaiev sat in a soundproof isolated room bound up and wired to a lab full of monitoring machines. Outside in another section of the laboratory Dr. Pavlova with Sergeyev and Naumov watched the graphs steadily recording Nikolaiev's respiration, heartbeat, eye movement, muscle activity, and most importantly, his brain waves. . . . During the first hour Nikolaiev's brain beamed a steady alpha rhythm, the pattern of rest. The graphs hummed, the computer waited, the scientists waited. Isolated in a chamber in Moscow, Kamensky began his telepathic transmission. Abruptly, three seconds later, in a faraway room in Leningrad, Nikolaiev's brain waves changed drastically. The Soviets had caught the moment when telepathy lights up in the brain.[37]

Surrealistic as they may sound, the reports of Russian research on telepathic communication deserve serious mention; a number of independent sources have come up with very similar reports on the Russian research. On the other hand, the author is not willing to accept accounts of the Russian research as verified at this point and, consequently, the Russian research can certainly not be taken as *scientific evidence* for the existence of telepathic communication.

The reader should note that the description of the Russian experiment above is taken largely from *Psychic Discoveries behind the Iron Curtain*. A check of the footnotes in that volume for the section which described the telepathic research by the Russians revealed the following: one footnote cited the April 9, 1967, issue of *Pravda*, another footnote cited papers with extremely abstract titles which were presented in Moscow on August 4, 1967, and a final footnote cited an article in *Sputnik* with no page numbers given. Such sources are not likely to be accepted on the international level as models of probity and objectivity.

TELEPATHIC COMMUNICATION IN THE DREAM LABORATORY AT MAIMONIDES MEDICAL CENTER   In addition to the Russian research some recent laboratory experiments on telepathic communication in America show promise.[38] However, for ingenuity in design, internal coherence over a number of studies, and data which are fairly easy to interpret, the most praiseworthy laboratory studies on telepathic communication are currently being conducted in the Dream Laboratory of the Maimonides Medical Center in Brooklyn.

Beginning in 1964, the Maimonides experiments provide striking evidence which suggests that the telepathic receiver (who in this case is having a dream) can determine with a fairly high degree of precision the meanings being transmitted by the sender.

At this point the basic methodology of the Maimonides laboratory studies began to evolve: (1) A subject sleeps in a sound-isolated room while his EEG tracings are monitored. Observers monitoring the readings of the electroencephalograph wait until the subject gets into a rapid eye movement (REM) phase of his sleep cycle. The REM phase has been established as that period during which the sleeping individual is dreaming. (2) An agent or sender in a separate room randomly selects an art print from a group of twelve by closing his eyes and pointing to a random-number table, then counting down the envelopes until he reaches that number. The sender waits until notified that the receiver is in the REM phase of his sleep cycle. The sender or agent then concentrates on a given art print and tries to communicate the content of that print to the sleeping subject. The agent renews his efforts throughout the night whenever the experimenter signals him that the subject has begun a REM period as indicated by the EEG. As the REM period concludes, the experimenter wakes the subject, gets his dream report, and lets him go back to sleep until the next REM period. (3) Transcripts are made of the subject's description of his dreams and sent along with the target pool of twelve prints to three independent judges. The judges then rank the transcripts for correspondence against all of the twelve targets from 1 for most correspondence down to 12 for least correspondence. The subjects also ranked the targets against their dreams. Ideally, the words of the receiver (which make up the transcript) should provide an accurate description of the art print which the sender or agent was attempting to transmit. In those cases where there is a high degree of correspondence between the description of the dream in the transcript and the art print, the judges would rate the effort of the receiver a ''hit.''[39] ''This initial experimental study of dream telepathy suggested that telepathy could be a powerful force in influencing dream content, even more powerful than post-hypnotic suggestion.''[40]

FIGURE 8-2 *Both Members of This Club* by George Bellows, used as a target picture (*National Gallery of Art, Washington, D.C.* Gift of Chester Dale, 1944).

To increase the sender's sense of involvement with the art picture he was trying to transmit, the sender was asked to draw a picture of the person or behavior in the art picture, or act out the behavior symbolized by the picture.[41]

In one of the most striking experiments at the Maimonides Laboratory, Erwin served as the dreaming subject while Feldstein served as the sender. On the first night of the experiment, Feldstein randomly selected the print of *The Barrel Organ* by Daumier. It features a group of French men and women singing hymns around a portable organ. Erwin's dreams did not focus on hymn singing. Music was prominently featured, however. In his second dream, a "little girl was banging on the planking, in some way playing. . . . I don't know where the guitar came in. That might have been what the little girl had—a guitar. . . . Someone was playing a guitar."[42] On the fourth night the target was *Both Members of This Club* (Figure 8-2) by Bellows, which shows a crowd watching two boxers fighting. Erwin reviewed the associations which stood out in his dream: "There were a number of people . . . It would be . . . competition. . . . Ships were being pounded and driven into the beach. . . . The water would pound in a great distance . . . It picked up a car and slammed into another car . . . The waves were pounding us in and we were being pushed toward another car . . . Maybe I enjoyed the violence in the dream . . . The violence . . . was exciting. . . ."[43] The judges gave Erwin's perceived meanings in his dream a rating of 78.7, or a first rank. This suggests a very strong similarity in the meaning(s) in the painting in Figure 8-2, which the sender was trying to transmit to the dreaming receiver, and the actual meanings perceived by the dreaming subject. The laboratory study "produced extraordinary results: six nights out of eight were 'direct hits' by ranking and the remaining two nights were very high 'hits.' . . . A statistical analysis of the ratings demonstrated that dream telepathy was indeed occurring—again as in Erwin's first study—with odds on the order of one thousand to one against chance."[44]

The researchers at the Maimonides Dream Laboratory continue to perfect their technique for determining degree of correspondence between the telepathic impression which the sender attempts to transmit and the association which the dreaming subject picks up. Clearly, much work remains to be done. Unless the researchers are successfully charged with fraud, however, even the skeptic must be impressed with the results as very real evidence supporting the existence of telepathic communication.

THE SCIENTIFIC EVALUATION OF LABORATORY RESEARCH ON EXTRASENSORY COMMUNICATION

What we have just described is hard to accept. Communication which does not rely on the known senses seems as improbable as space missions did just a few decades ago. The parapsychologists realize that theirs is a sizable burden of proof. For this reason they become upset when an observer confuses their serious research with the exploitation of the occult revival by everything from fortune-tellers to witch doctors. Professor John Beloff, speaking as president of the Parapsychological Association, emphasizes that "public interest in the paranormal has in the past mainly been of a practical kind, so that mediums, fortune-tellers, water-diviners, witch-doctors and other assorted magicians have always been able to count on plying a lucrative trade. . . . [In contrast] parapsychology has always stood for the scientific approach to the paranormal and it would be unfortunate, perhaps even in the long run disastrous if, out of a temptation to cash in on this new trend, we were to lend respectability to what, in effect, is rank superstition."[45]

The task of the parapsychologist is not an easy one. As Rhine has recently written, the nature of psychic communication is such that it runs directly counter to what we have long believed in. In contrast to psychic communication "all other modes of communication are recognizably physical; but one of the ways in which spontaneous psi manifestations challenged natural law was that they appeared to take place, as a rule, under circumstances in which no conceivable physical explanation could be supposed. Thus they gave the appearance of magic or miracle."[46]

Beloff of the University of Edinburgh recognizes that our conditioning is such that it is much easier to reject than accept extrasensory perception as fact. In his presidential address to the Parapsychological Association he noted even-handedly that "before you dismiss the skeptic as willfully obtuse, consider how it looks from his point of view. If we did not have evidence that ESP exists, nothing in all of science would have suggested it. Is it therefore *so* unreasonable if the skeptic prefers to think that there must be some flaw in your evidence even if he cannot spot it, some factor X which you have forgotten to control for which would allow for a normal explanation of your findings?"[47]

Clearly the parapsychologist is concerned with evaluation of his research from the scientific perspective. At this point, therefore, we will attempt to look at laboratory research on telepathic communication specifically and extrasensory research in general from the perspective of scientists currently looking at such research.

Since Rhine began his pioneering laboratory experiments at Duke in the 1930s the scientific community has been providing critiques of parapsychological research. It is difficult to make safe generalizations about such critiques but certain conclusions seem justified: (1) a large part of the scientific community has been openly hostile to parapsychology and many scientists remain so; (2) while many scientists do not believe that we currently have *conclusive* proof for the existence of psychic behavior, well over a majority of those recently polled considered the investigation of ESP a legitimate scientific undertaking;[48] (3) the careful efforts of people like Rhine, and Ullman and Krippner in the Dream Laboratory at Maimonides are leading to increased scientific acceptance of parapsychology—the Parapsychological Association was accepted as an affiliate member of the American Association for the Advancement of Science in December 1969.

Scientific reaction to and debate over the merits of research on psychic behavior has focused on at least four major issues: (1) nonrepeatability; (2) fraud; (3) improper mathematical methods; (4) improper interpretation of evidence. Lawyer Champe Ransom has recently done an extremely insightful and balanced job of examining current dialogue on these issues.[49]

The position of the parapsychologist is perhaps weakest on the first issue of nonrepeatability. Traditional scientists point out that any experiment which cannot be repeated cannot be accepted as scientific. Parapsychologists reply that often subjects cannot repeat their scores on a given test of telepathic communication, for example, because of distractions, hostility of the examiner, or simply because psi phenomena are highly variable and a percipient will score very high on one occasion and relatively low on another. Obviously, such a position could provide the parapsychologist with a rationalization for even the poorest performance by his subjects.

On issues 2, 3, and 4, however, the parapsychologist seems to be in a strong position and the critic in a rather weak one. Critics like Hansel do not offer the charge that there is fraud in laboratory experiments on psychic behavior, but argue "simply that if fraud (or anything else, for that matter) is a *possible* alternative explanation for the result, then that experiment cannot be offered as *conclusive* proof of ESP."[50] This seems a curiously flawed argument on the part of the critic. Critics like Hansel maintain that the possibility of fraud is enough for them to suspend judgment even though they were unable to detect fraud despite the most meticulous efforts to do so.

The question of whether parapsychologists are using proper statistical methods seems more of an academic than actual issue when closely inspected. In 1937 the Institute of Mathematical Statistics approved in general the validity of statistical analysis of ESP research and nothing done since then suggests that parapsychologists are any more subject to the use of improper statistical methods than psychologists, sociologists, or any other social scientists. The fact that some scientists dismiss probability statistics altogether says little about the appropriateness of statistical techniques employed by parapsychologists.

Critics are probably on weakest ground when they attempt to dismiss parapsychological research on a priori grounds—they argue that ESP is incompatible with current scientific theory and, consequently, no matter what the nature of the experiments or results they must be rejected. Assuming for the moment that scientists could agree on the basic postulates of scientific theory, what serious scientist would be willing to maintain the eternal and unvarying truth of his theory? Rhine notes, ironically, that "whereas in western science there is vigorous resistance to parapsychology as not conforming to the mechanistic philosophy of nature, in the USSR the new findings are being hailed as the effective scientific answer to the 'superstitious supernaturalism' of authoritarian religion, leaving to the indefinite future the ultimate explanation as to just how the accommodation with physics will be made."[51]

In short, there is now something approaching consensus among scientists who have taken a careful look at psychic research in general and laboratory studies of telepathic communication specifically. While many scientists will argue that *conclusive* evidence still must be found for the existence of ESP, critics such as Hansel will agree there is indisputable evidence that telepathic subjects are able to make decisions in identifying symbols that clearly exceed chance. Such results can be taken as evidence of psychic communication or evidence of fraud.[52] Since no one has been able to establish that the major experiments discussed in this chapter involved fraud, the reader can draw his own conclusions.

In perspective, of course, the reader *must* draw his own conclusions about telepathic communication. While not the ultimate test, perhaps the most convincing test of telepathic powers is to test your own. Consequently the reader is urged to take the telepathic communication test first as percipient or receiver, and then as agent or sender. When you function as receiver get yourself a pack of ESP cards such as those in Figure 8-1.

Have an objective friend who believes in the possibility of extrasensory perception serve as the sender. He should thoroughly mix the deck of ESP cards and draw out five of them. Then your friend should decide how he will arrange the five cards without actually doing so. He should concentrate on the order of the cards and the symbols on each card. At this point you should attempt to guess the identity of each card. Your guesses are known as "calls" and should be recorded under call in column 1 in the telepathic communication test form in Figure 8-3. After your first five calls have been recorded, the actual "cards" your friend had in mind should also be recorded in column 1 without him seeing your calls. Each time your call was the same as the card your friend had in mind, put a circle around the common symbols in each column. Figure 8-3 provides you room for recording the results of ten trials with twenty-five calls per trial—hence you can record 250 calls on a form similar to that in Figure 8-3. To provide a thorough test of your telepathic abilities, you should make at least 500 calls. When you want to test your ability to communicate telepathically as a sender rather than a receiver simply reverse the procedure described above.

Scoring of the telepathic communication test is simple. As you can see from Figure 8-3 telepathic subject D. Gordon Lather got 8 correct choices for trial 1, 6 correct choices for trial 2, etc. Lather got a total of 80 correct choices out of 250 which far exceeds chance expectation—50 correct choices would equal chance expectation.

In retrospect the reader should keep at least two facts in mind. First, individuals vary dramatically in their capacity to exchange meanings by telepathic communication. Second, practice with an instrument such as the telepathic communication test can lead to impressive development of that capacity.

The obvious question at this point is how can I improve my capacity to use telepathic communication? Many concrete steps can be taken but one is prerequisite to all the rest. While attempting to communicate telepathically you must suspend any

Telepathic Receiver _____

Telepathic Sender _____

Date _____

Time _____

No. of Test _____

1		2		3		4		5		6		7		8		9		10	
Call	Card	Call	Card	Call	Card	Call	Card	Call	Card	Call	Card	Call	Card	Call	Card	Call	Card	Call	Card
≈	+	•	■																
+	■	≈	★																
★	★	≈	+																
■	•	■	•																
•	•	★	≈																
•	+	+	•																
★	≈	≈	■																
•	★	★	★																
+	+	■	•																
≈	■	+	★																
■	•	•	•																
★	+	■	+																
•	★	★	★																
+	■	+	■																
■	•	+	≈																
★	★	■	+																
≈	■	★	★																
■	■	≈	+																
★	+	•	■																
+	•	■	≈																
≈	≈	★	★																
+	≈	•	■																
■	•	•	≈																
•	+	≈	+																
•	•	+	★																
7		5		9		13		8		6		11		6		6		9	

Please note that in this illustrative form of the TELEPATHIC COMMUNICATION TEST the calls of the telepathic receiver, D.Gordon Lather, are itemized only for the first two columns to show how the test is scored. When the calls of the receiver and the cards turned over by the sender are the same they are circled (see columns 1 and 2 above). The seven circles in column 1 indicate that the receiver made the correct choice seven times out of twenty-five. Hence, the number 7 is recorded at the bottom of column 1. The other totals at the bottom of the columns are simply to indicate how D.Gordon Lather did on this test which includes 250 choices.

FIGURE 8-3 Telepathic Communication Test. [This is a modified form of an ESP recording form published in and reprinted with permission of Parapsychology Today, ed. J. B. Rhine and R. Brier (Secaucus, N.J.: Citadel Press, 1968), p. 50.]

tendency to be skeptical that telepathic communication will work; indeed the confirmed disbeliever should not even make the attempt. Above everything else, telepathic communication requires the ability to exclude all competing stimuli from one's thought processes.

Since telepathic communication clearly requires the use of complicated mental processes, we must concentrate a maximum amount of our mental energy on such an undertaking. Anything which detracts from a higher order of concentration is undesirable. Therefore, the reader should take the following precautionary steps before taking the telepathic communication test a second time: (1) make sure that you are completely relaxed and concentrating totally on your objective of exchanging meaning(s) telepathically—a warm bath or an hour in front of your stereo may help you attain this goal; (2) make sure that no individual who disbelieves in telepathy is in your presence; (3) ask yourself if you have achieved the type of concentration necessary to deal effectively with a complicated intellectual task; (4) try to eliminate any other factors which might detract from intense concentration. Once these conditions have been met, take the telepathic communication test again. Repeat this test or similar tests over a period of weeks. Past experience suggests that such a procedure will significantly increase your ability to use telepathic communication.

A final question occurs at this point. Even if I can increase my telepathic capacity, does it have any practical value for me? This question is difficult to answer. Research on the subject is in its very early stages. Limited research suggests, however, that telepathy can have significant practical value for the airline pilot who has lost contact with ground control, the patient who cannot reach his doctor by traditional means, or even the undercover agent who is apprehensive about transmitting his messages even in coded form by electronic means. If these limited examples strike the reader as surrealistic he should consider recent reports that telepathy has been used by such hard-headed, scientifically oriented individuals as the commanders of nuclear submarines, and astronauts.

In your own case the practical potential of telepathy may depend on your motivation and the situations in which you attempt to communicate. Whatever your motivation or situation, however, you should recognize that telepathic communication gives you the potential (1) to avoid the complicated use of known sensory channels (such as movement, sound, or touch) or fallible electronic mechanisms (such as the telephone or television), and (2) to avoid the time-bound nature of the traditional types of communication—experiments by the Russians and others suggest that, even when separated by hundreds of miles, there is no measurable time interval between the sender's attempt to transmit meaning and the receiver's perception of that same meaning.

CONCLUSION

The field of extrasensory perception and extrasensory communication has often been attacked because of the gullibility of the true believer and the promotional hyperbole of merchandisers who are exploiting a sustained national interest in psychic phenomena. For many skeptics the efforts of the professional prophets, astrologers, and mediums have given psychic phenomena a surrealistic or even fraudulent flavor.

The systematic study of extrasensory communication began in the latter part of the nineteenth century. In 1882 the Society for Psychical Research was founded in England with the American Society for Psychical Research founded in 1884. At first both societies functioned as central repositories for filing reports of psychic events ranging from apparitions to clairvoyant dreams. Over the decades since they were founded, both societies have tightened up their procedures for reporting and evaluating such events, and both now sponsor an increasing number of studies which are conducted in their own ultra-modern laboratories.

Reports of spontaneous extrasensory perception are hardly limited to the nineteenth century. Uri Geller, the Israeli psychic, has consistently demonstrated the capacity to bend nails, steel keys, etc.; Geller identifies such feats as forms of psychokinesis. While some skeptics maintain that Geller is simply an outstanding magician, a number of leading scientists have found his feats to be convincing demonstrations of psychic powers. In spite of the efforts of Geller and countless cases of spontaneous extrasensory perception reported to the SPR and the ASPR, we do not have scientific proof for its existence. Existing reports on spontaneous extrasensory perception do not constitute scientific proof because (1) the events were not observed under controlled conditions, (2) the phenomena are not consistently repeatable, and (3) spontaneous extrasensory behavior has not been consistently and predictably related to other types of behavior.

The laboratory studies of psychic behavior were begun in the 1930s and have concentrated on four primary kinds of behavior: (1) telepathy; (2) clairvoyance; (3) psychokinesis; (4) precognition. This chapter concentrates exclusively on telepathic communication because only telepathic communication focuses on communicative *interaction* and because telepathic communication has the greatest body of laboratory research supporting its existence.

The two most comprehensive and convincing sets of laboratory experiments have been conducted by Rhine at the Parapsychology Laboratory at Duke and by Ullman and Krippner at the Maimonides Dream Laboratory in Brooklyn. Rhine's experiments were conducted during the 1930-50 period and he developed the basic methodology used by most parapsychologists: (1) the deck of ESP cards; (2) the calculation of the mathematical probability that the choices of a given telepathic receiver could be due to chance; (3) recording forms to keep scores of telepathic subjects.

In his old age Rhine remains a revered scholar to those who accept his work and a naive experimenter to those who attack it. In perspective, no truly convincing attack on his classic experiments has been made. Even his most persistent critic, Hansel, is forced to the limited claim that Rhine has not provided *conclusive* evidence for the existence of psychic communication because the possibility of fraud exists.

The most exciting laboratory research on telepathic communication done recently continues to take place at the Dream Laboratory at the Maimonides Medical Center. Ullman and Krippner have devised a highly innovative method of measuring the success a sender has in telepathically communicating the meaning(s) of an art print to a dreaming receiver. Their data provide credible evidence supporting the existence of telepathic communication.

The scientific evaluation of laboratory experiments on extrasensory communication has focused on the issues of nonrepeatability, fraud, improper mathematical methods, and improper interpretation of evidence. Parapsychologists seem to be on shaky ground on the first issue, but provide convincing rebuttals on the last three. In the final analysis the reader has to reach his own conclusions as to the validity of telepathic communication. To test his own telepathic powers the reader should use the telepathic communication test.

NOTES

[1] S. Ostrander and L. Schroeder, *Psychic Discoveries behind the Iron Curtain* (New York: Bantam, 1971), xviii.

[2] "Extrasensory Perception," course offered by UCLA extension, 1972. While Bromley was lecturing, the author was making rather unflattering notes about his credibility in the margins of his notebook. At one point, the author was called from the classroom to take a telephone call. He returned with some trepidation when he noticed that the imposing elderly lady seated next to him had been studying the critical comments in the margins. To his surprise she smiled and said: "That's all right. I agree that Bromley isn't very good, but have you heard of the psychic in Beverly Hills? He has great command. I go to his course and we have been communicating with my dead husband for some time." Bromley's credibility was not helped when, later in the course, he claimed to communicate with the dead to determine who was the author's "keeper." Apparently, "keepers" are individuals who have been dead for a few decades or a few centuries. They choose a living individual to whom they give spiritual guidance and with whom they communicate. The reader who detects a certain archaic quality in the author's writing style will probably not be surprised to learn that the author's keeper is an Indian maiden who lived back in the 1500s.

[3] J. Godwin, *Occult America* (Garden City, N.Y.: Doubleday, 1972), pp. 271-72.

[4] Ibid., p. 274.

[5] Ibid., pp. 274-75.

[6] Ibid., pp. 279-80.

[7] Interview with Hugh Lynn Cayce by Elliot Mintz, KABC radio, Los Angeles, California, 11-12 midnight, January 19, 1973. See also J. Furst, *Edgar Cayce's Story of Attitudes and Emotions* (New York: Berkley, 1972).

[8] C. E. M. Hansel, *ESP: A Scientific Evaluation* (New York: Charles Scribner's Sons, 1966), p. 4.

[9] *Journal of the Society for Psychical Research,* 1 (1884), 88.

[10] Ibid., 313.

[11] Godwin, *Occult America,* p. 255.

[12] A. Weil, "Uri Geller and Parapsychology," *Psychology Today,* 8 (1974), 46.

[13] Ibid., 48.

[14] Ibid., 49.

[15] Ibid., 50.

[16] A. Weil, "Parapsychology: Andrew Weil's Search for the True Geller—Part II: The Letdown," *Psychology Today,* 8 (1974), 75.

[17] For absorbing, early accounts of spontaneous extrasensory perception see U. Sinclair, *Mental Radio* (Pasadena, Calif.: Upton Sinclair, 1930), and R. Fischner, *Telepathy and Clairvoyance* (New York: Harcourt, Brace, 1925). Albert Einstein prepared brief, introductory remarks for the Upton Sinclair volume in which he suggested that interesting evidence supporting the existence of telepathy was in Sinclair's book and that it should be seriously considered.

[18] Weil, "Parapsychology: Andrew Weil's Search for the True Geller—Part II," 76.

[19] Ibid., 76-77.

[20] Ibid., 78.

[21] Two of the most useful reviews of the history of psychic research are L. E. Rhine, "The Establishment of Basic Concepts and Terminology in Parapsychology," *Journal of Parapsychology,* 35 (1971), 34-56, and M. Ryzl, *Parapsychology: A Scientific Approach* (New York: Hawthorn Books, 1970), pp. 22-157. Rhine breaks research in parapsychology down into three periods: (1) the pre-experimental period before 1930, (2) the early experimental period from 1930 to 1950, and (3) the modern experimental period from 1950 to the present.

[22] Hansel, *ESP*, pp. 1-2. These definitions represent a modification of those presented by Hansel.

[23] Ostrander and Schroeder, *Psychic Discoveries behind the Iron Curtain*, pp. 68-69. Russian housewife Nelya Mikhailova is allegedly the most successful practitioner of psychokinesis in the world today. Ostrander and Schroeder claim to have watched a famous Russian film in which Mikhailova moves a number of objects simply by concentrating on them. Ostrander and Schroeder write, "It sometimes takes Mikhailova two to four hours to rev up her supernormal powers. . . . The strain etched the dimples deep in her cheeks. Twenty minutes passed. Her pulse raced to 250 beats a minute. She moved her head from side to side gazing intently at the compass needle. Her hands moved as though she were conducting some unseen orchestra. And then, as if the atoms in the compass needle were tuned in to her, the needle shivered. Slowly it began to spin counterclockwise, turning like the second hand of a clock. Then the entire compass, plastic case, leather strap, and all, began to whirl."

The following articles are representative of a trend in contemporary psychic research to concentrate on method rather than substance: J. Ehrenwald, "A Neurophysiological Model of Psi Phenomena," *Journal of Nervous and Mental Disease*, 154 (1972), 406-18; M. E. Turner and O. Karlis, "A Probability Model for Symbol-Calling Experiments," *Journal of the American Society for Psychical Research*, 64 (1970), 303-12; M. Ware and M. A. Butler, "Chance: An Adequate Control for Clairvoyant Research?" *Psychology*, 8 (1971), 44-52; J. Palmer, "Scoring in ESP Tests as a Function of Belief in ESP: The Sheep-Goat Effect," *Journal of American Society for Psychical Research*, 65 (1971), 373-408.

[24] S. G. Soal and F. Bateman, *Modern Experiments in Telepathy* (London: Faber & Faber Ltd., 1954).

[25] J. B. Rhine, *Extra-Sensory Perception* (Boston: Bruce Humphries, 1935), Hansel, *ESP*, and Ryzl, *Parapsychology*.

[26] J. B. Rhine, *New Frontiers of the Mind: The Story of the Duke Experiments* (New York: Farrar and Rinehart, 1937), pp. 159-60.

[27] Ibid., pp. 164-65.

[28] Ibid., pp. 168-69.

[29] Ibid., p. 171.

[30] J. B. Rhine, ed., *Progress in Parapsychology* (Durham, N.C.: Parapsychology Press, 1971), pp. 236-57 and 262-92.

[31] Godwin, Occult America, p. 259.

[32] Hansel, ESP, p. 76.

[33] Godwin, Occult America, p. 259. For an interesting comparison of the merits of Rhine's work vs. the arguments of his chief detractor see J. B. Rhine and J. G. Pratt, "A Reply to the Hansel Critique of the Pearce-Pratt Series," Journal of Parapsychology, 25 (1961) and Hansel, ESP.

[34] L. L. Vasiliev, Mysterious Phenomena of the Human Psyche, trans. Sonia Volochova, with an introduction by Felix Morrow (New York: University Books, 1965), p. 144.

[35] Ibid., pp. 109-10. Vasiliev includes a diagram of the hand and its mechanism. The publisher includes the following comment with the diagram: "Competent medical authority describes the diagram as neither clear nor convincing."

[36] The brain-wave theory has been dismissed by J. B. Rhine and many leading authorities in America. However, the recent research on the bodily aura with Kirlian photography (the idea that the body gives off electrical impulses which can be photographed) by Professer Thelma Moss of UCLA and others has again served to popularize the brain-wave theory. For recent research on the bodily aura see T. Moss and K. Johnson, Harper's (1973), 9.

[37] The author wishes to thank Professor Thelma Moss of UCLA for the prepublication release of a number of her papers which deal with her trip to Russia and interviews with many of the leading figures in extrasensory research in the Soviet Union including the sender (Kamensky) and receiver (Nikolaiev) described above. See T. Moss, "Psychical Research in the Soviet Union," in Psychic Research: A Challenge to Science, ed. John W. White (in press). Moss, after meeting both men, writes that "Kamensky proved to be a young, intense biophysicist, not only immersed in microwave physics, but also in Eastern meditative techniques; and Nikolaiev was a dynamic character actor with red-blond hair, a deep baritone voice, and a booming infectious laugh. Both men had had much practice in hatha yoga, particularly the breathing exercises, which they use in their telepathic experiments in an effort to synchronize their 'vibrations.' "

[38] T. Moss, A. Change, and M. Leavitt, "Long Distance ESP: A Controlled Experiment," Journal of Abnormal Psychology, 76 (1970), 288-94.

[39] M. Ullman, S. Krippner, and A. Vaughan, Dream Telepathy: Experiments in Nocturnal ESP (New York: Macmillan, 1973), pp. 97-98.

[40] Ibid., p. 106.

[41] Ibid., p. 118.

[42] Ibid., p. 118-19. The authors note that when trying to communicate the message contained in the target print Downpour at Shono "Feldstein hopped into the shower adjoining his agent's room several times that night, glad that there was no one around to see him with his toy umbrella."

[43] Ibid., p. 121.

[44] Ibid., p. 125.

[45] Research in Parapsychology 1972, Abstracts and Papers from the Fifteenth Annual Convention of the Parapsychological Association, 1972, ed. W. G. Roll, R. L. Morris, and J. D. Morris (Metuchen, N.J.: Scarecrow Press, 1973), p. 116.

[46] J. B. Rhine and associates, Parapsychology from Duke to FRNM (Durham, N. C.: Parapsychology Press, 1965), p. 44.

[47] Research in Parapsychology 1972, p. 191.

[48] L. Warner, "What the Younger Psychologists Think about ESP," Journal of Parapsychology, 19 (1955), 228-35.

[49] C. Ransom, "Recent Criticism of Parapsychology: A Review," *Journal of the American Society for Psychical Research,* 65 (1971), 289-307.

[50] Ibid., 293.

[51] J. B. Rhine and R. Brier, *Parapsychology Today* (New York: Citadel Press, 1968), p. 210.

[52] Hansel, *ESP*.

9

OBSERVING, CLASSIFYING, AND MEASURING THE QUALITY OF NONVERBAL COMMUNICATION

Chapters 2 through 7 shared a common purpose and focus. Each was designed to illustrate the basic nature and functions of a major system or type of nonverbal communication. Thus, chapter 2 examined communication through movement (kinesics), chapters 3 and 4 demonstrated how we communicate through use of space in, respectively, interpersonal relationships and the urban scene (proxemics), and chapter 5 explored how we use major means such as clothing and cosmetics (artifacts) to communicate. Thus, each of these chapters focused on a separate system of nonverbal communication. Taken collectively, the kinesic, proxemic, and artifactual systems of nonverbal communication share at least one important attribute. The meanings communicated within each system are decoded by sight. Hence, these four types of nonverbal communication are really part of a larger system. This system was identified in chapter 1 as the visual communication system.

Chapter 6 defined and illustrated the functions of vocalic communication. Since vocalic communication is so distinctive and important, it can legitimately be viewed as a separate and major system of nonverbal communication in its own right. Vocalic messages are decoded through hearing. Consequently, this system will be identified as the auditory communication system.

Chapters 7 and 8 describe and analyze three different types of nonverbal communication which share an important defining attribute—the means by which messages are transmitted and received are invisible. Thus, chapter 7 emphasizes that both tactile and olfactory messages are invisible just as chapter 8 on telepathic communication stresses the invisible nature of telepathic messages. Because they share the vital attribute of invisibility, tactile, olfactory, and telepathic communication are seen as part of the large invisible communication system.

The major nonverbal communication systems—visual, auditory, and invisible—serve to dramatize a very important fact. Nonverbal communication is an extremely complex type of behavior which is not easily analyzed and evaluated. This book deals directly with such complexity while trying to make the various types of nonverbal communication more understandable through the use of photographs and illustrations. Such photographs and illustrations are designed to be illuminating, but they probably have led the reader to an inescapable conclusion: To fully understand the great variety of meanings communicated by nonverbal means requires repeated observation.

OBSERVATION

How does a person arrange for repeated observations? That is the question. Most students of nonverbal communication will see a given facial expression, or gesture, or posture and not be quite sure what meaning it communicates. They want to prolong their period of observation. Unfortunately, few human beings can be expected to repeat a movement for the benefit of the observer.

DISTINCTIVE OBSERVATIONAL PROBLEMS   Experts do not agree on the best methods for observing nonverbal communication. They debate three issues. First, they differ on whether such observation should take place in the laboratory or in naturalistic settings. Second, there is dispute over whether observers should concentrate on the specific movements of a single individual or on *interaction* between individuals. Third, there is disagreement over whether the observer should use electronic aids such as slow-motion projection to observe micromomentary expressions that would be invisible to the unaided eye.[1]

For reasons that will be made clear later in this chapter, the author believes that observation can be undertaken most effectively in the laboratory, the observer should focus on communicative *interaction,* and the observer should study only those be-haviors which can also be seen by the interactants as they attempt to communicate with one another.

Whatever the reader's position on the three issues of observation described above, it is clear that nonverbal communication "requires (ideally) repeated re-viewings . . . before it can be understood and extracted."[2] The consensus is that vid-eotape is a very valuable technique for attaining this goal; videotape will make a permanent record of the relevant nonverbal communication and all or parts of that record can be replayed until the investigative curiosity of the observer is satisfied.

VIDEOTAPED OBSERVATION IN THE LABORATORY Videotaping of nonverbal communication in the laboratory rather than the field is most useful for the observer at this point. Of course communication that takes place in a laboratory is subject to the charge that it is unnatural or artificial. Careful design of experiments to make them realistic can overcome such objections, however. Clearly, an observer has much more control over conditions which make for optimal observation in the laboratory. Lighting can be controlled, exact camera angles checked since the individuals to be videotaped remain stationary or nearly so, and extraneous noises and people moving in front of the videotape camera are no problem in the laboratory.

In contrast, videotaping in the field is apt to present many problems. For example, the author recently had a group of graduate students who wanted to study the nonver-bal communication characteristic of leave-taking and farewells. Consequently, they decided to take their camera to Atlanta International Airport and film people getting on and off airplanes. Their plan of action was meticulously laid out. Nevertheless, prob-lems soon arose. First, the airport manager withdrew a promise of cooperation. Sec-ond, it was difficult to get close-ups of airplane passengers without disrupting their normal behavior. Finally, the group of students discovered, when reviewing the film, that their hand-held camera had moved just enough to blur most of their moving pictures so that they were useless. Such an experience does not establish that vid-eotaping in the field is impossible or even negate its great potential value, but it does suggest that an observer has much greater control over observational conditions in the laboratory.

Indeed field observation of different types of nonverbal communication has much potential as a learning vehicle. Field observation allows the student to choose the type of nonverbal communication and situation which are of particular interest.

The author makes extensive use of field observation in his own classes, with par-ticular emphasis on proxemic and artifactual communication. Students are required to go into a community and violate the proxemic expectations of shoppers in a super-market, diners in a restaurant, people waiting in a doctor's office. The students care-fully observe the reaction to the violation of proxemic expectations, write a brief paper on it, and lead a discussion in class—an example of violating proxemic expectations was the student who kept elbowing her way into check-out lines in supermarkets.

In the case of artifactual communication, students are required to visit a series of public places, alter their appearance in some distinctive way, return to the public places, and see if their altered appearance affects the way people communicate with them. Among the more drastic, if not plausible, alterations in appearance were the following. One student frequented a local McDonald's restaurant, making sure that he had contact with the same waitress and was dressed the same way each time.

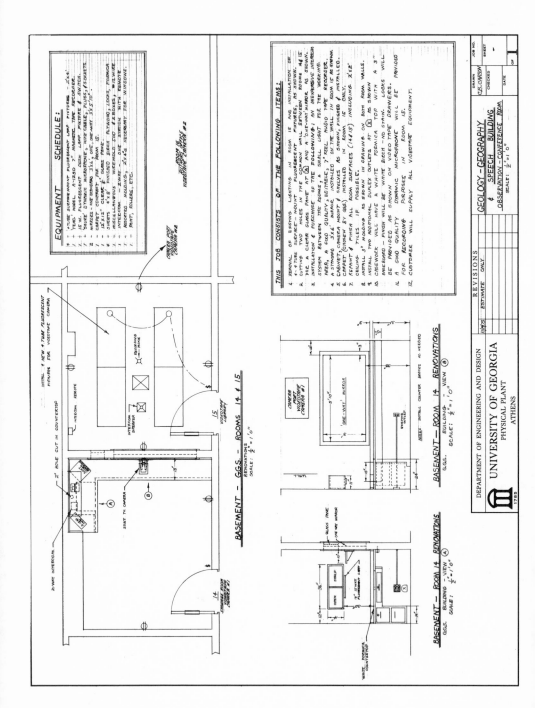

However, one morning at 10 a.m. he came walking in with a tuxedo on and ordered a hamburger. His description of the effects of this change in appearance had class members fascinated. Another enterprising student worked during off hours as an elevator operator; hence he kept encountering and communicating with the same people. One night he assumed his position dressed like Groucho Marx with appropriate mustache, glasses, and cigar. At each floor he would get out of the elevator and flick the ashes off his cigar while rolling his eyes at those entering the elevator. The verbal and nonverbal reactions were interesting to say the least.

While such field observation serves to get the student intensely involved in the study of nonverbal communication, it can serve another important purpose. The students can use such observation to generate hypotheses. Such hypotheses typically spell out predicted relationships (an example would be that high status individuals have less eye contact with their addressees than low status individuals) that should be subjected to empirical test. Field observation is a particularly rich source for such hypotheses. The hypotheses can then be tested in the laboratory.

The cost of equipping and converting an ordinary room to an observation room for videotaping is modest. Since one of the aims of this book is to encourage as many students as possible to study nonverbal communication, the reader is provided with actual blueprints used by the author to develop an observation room or laboratory for videotaping. The laboratory described is currently being used by the author to conduct follow-up studies on nonverbal communication to those which will be described in chapter 10.

The requirements for a videotaping laboratory are fairly minimal. A small room is a prerequisite; those individuals who have an abundance of unused space can use a bigger room and give themselves the potential of studying nonverbal communication in public speaking. In addition to the observation room (the room in which nonverbal interaction between your subjects will take place) you will need access to the immediately adjoining rooms on each side of your observation room—in our example room 15 is the observation room; room 14, a room of about the same size, will house one of the two videotape cameras. Room 16 in this case is the author's office and it too will house a videotape camera.[3]

Figure 9-1 indicates the changes which have actually been made in the videotape laboratory (room 15). The reader will note that a camera port was cut in two walls of room 15. These camera ports extend nearly to the ceiling because of the need to get the videotape cameras high enough to shoot over the heads of subjects with their backs to a camera while still focusing on the individuals facing a given camera. As the reader can see, one videotape camera is mounted in room 14 and records the nonverbal behavior of the three people seated at the table in room 15 who are facing the camera. Similarly, the second camera is mounted in room 16 and records the behavior of the three subjects facing it.

The holes in the wall, a discussion table and chairs, and videotaping equipment are all that is absolutely essential for a videotape laboratory. In Figure 9-1 the reader will note, however, that a number of other changes are laid out in the blueprints for this laboratory. These include a one-way mirror in the wall between rooms 14 and 15 to allow direct, visual observation of the participants, cabinets to store videotape, new

FIGURE 9-1   Blueprint for Speech Communication Laboratory. (Courtesy Christopher B. Carson, Engineering Department, Physical Plant, The University of Georgia)

carpeting to deaden sound, additional electrical outlets, and, most importantly, the installation of new 4 x 4 foot surface-mounted fluorescent fixtures in the ceiling.

Once the holes in the wall are cut, the observer will need at minimum two complete videotaping ensembles which include camera and videotape replay (VTR) unit. In addition, the observer will need a special effects generator which will give him the capacity of synthesizing the input from the two cameras in such a way that he has split screen capacity. If the observer was starting from scratch, he would need the following equipment for his laboratory:

ITEM NO.	QUANTITY OF UNIT	DESCRIPTION AND SPECIFICATIONS
1	2 each	Sony VCL-08 lens-fl/5/8.5uu
2	1 each	Sony ECM-19 B microphone
3	2 each	Sony AVE-3210 DX camera ensemble
4	1 each	Sony CVM-1920 monitor
5	2 each	Sony AV 3650 VTR
6	1 each	Sony SEG-special effects generator

With such a videotape laboratory the observer will have the capacity to take close-up shots of *both* the communication sender and receiver *simultaneously*. He can play back the communication of both parties simultaneously via split-screen tv monitors, use the stop-action capability of the Sony 3600 VTR unit during replay, and observe the recorded nonverbal communication as many times as necessary via replay to determine every nuance of meaning that was communicated by kinesic, proxemic, artifactual, and other channels.

The observer would have this capacity for a very modest cost. Since many observers already have access to a single videotaping unit, such an individual would merely have to add one complete videotaping ensemble and a special effects generator to give him split-screen capacity.

Directly below the camera ports in rooms 14 and 16 the observer would have to build a simple shelf to hold his camera or have the cameras sit on top of portable dollies which would make the lens on each camera sit at approximately the 9' or 8' level. This way the cameras could be focused through the ports to pick up people seated around a table or on a sofa in room 15.

For individuals who cannot continuously monitor an event or who want to compare very specific nonverbal communicative behaviors, Ekman has developed the visual information display and retrieval system (VID-R). VID-R allows observers to view videotaped events at actual, slowed, or fast speed, to code and recall any frame or sequence of frames almost instantaneously through the use of a computer, and to assemble similar events or events which are hard to code while retaining the original videotaped record. Finally, VID-R stores an observer's notations so that the nonverbal communication behavior to which they refer can be automatically retrieved.[4] VID-R clearly represents a technique of great potential value for the observer of kinesic behavior even if the capability of speeding up or slowing down behavior is of questionable value.[5]

While this section emphasizes the importance, indeed the necessity, of videotape for the thorough observation and study of nonverbal communication, the reader may be left with at least one unanswered question. Is videotape as effective a means of observation as direct visual observation? The author's own experience and very recent research on the question combine to provide an affirmative answer. Eisler, Hersen, and Agras note that "the facility of modern videotape equipment to record and store massive amounts of complex behavioral information with the capability for an indefinite number of relatively instantaneous replays would appear to make it an invaluable research tool in the study of human interactive behavior.[6] More pertinently their study of direct observation vs. videotaped observation revealed that "overall it appeared that reliabilities from observation of the video interaction were equally as high as observation from viewing couples live, with variation between observer pairs about equal to variations between the modes of observation."[7]

CLASSIFICATION

In chapter 2 we described the two fundamental approaches to nonverbal meaning: denotative and connotative. While these approaches were examined as they apply specifically to facial communication, proponents of each approach have applied them to all types of visual communication. Those who adopt the denotative approach to visual communication maintain that at any given instant we communicate a single, dominant meaning. This is true no matter whether we communicate by movement, by use of space, or by such artifactual means as clothing. In contrast, those who accept the connotative approach to meaning take a different position. They maintain that any single facial expression, gesture, or posture, for example, conveys a number of "dimensions" of meaning. Advocates of the denotative approach typically use categories to classify nonverbal behavior unit by unit. Consequently, they distinguish one type of meaning from another on the basis of the category in which a given unit of behavior is placed. Those who use the connotative approach typically use scales to determine the degree to which certain types of meanings or qualities are conveyed by given types of nonverbal behavior.

Most classification systems deal exclusively with the visual communication system. That is they focus on nonverbal communication behavior which is decoded by sight. As the reader will recall, kinesic, proxemic, and artifactual behaviors make up the major nonverbal communication subsystems which require sight for decoding of messages.

Birdwhistell has probably made the most famous and comprehensive attempt to classify the different types of kinesic behavior. He has developed a notational system that includes a symbol for every isolable movement. His system is based on the following assumptions:

1. Like other events in nature, no body movement or expression is without meaning in the context in which it appears;

2. Like other aspects of human behavior, body posture, movement, and facial expression are patterned and, thus, subject to systematic analysis;

3. While the possible limitations imposed by particular biological substrata are recognized, until otherwise demonstrated, the systematic body motion of the members of a community is considered a function of the social system to which the group belongs;

4. Visible body activity, like audible acoustic activity, systematically influences the behavior of other members of any particular group;

5. Until otherwise demonstrated such behavior will be considered to have an investigable communicational function;

6. The meanings derived therefrom are functions both of the behavior and of the operations by which it is investigated;

7. The particular biological system and the special life experience of any individual will contribute idiosyncratic elements to his kinesic system, but the individual or symptomatic quality of these elements can only be assessed following the analysis of the larger system of which he is a part.[8]

Birdwhistell's kinesic macrorecording key includes a detailed set of symbols to identify movements associated with the head and face, the shoulders and trunk, and the legs and feet. When studying this notational system the reader must be impressed with the scholarship and self-discipline which went into it; Birdwhistell first began developing the system over twenty years ago at the University of Louisville.

The substantial merits of Birdwhistell's classification scheme are apparent. On the other hand, the system provides some problems for the student of nonverbal communication. First, the system is so detailed that even the youngest user runs the risk of winding up in a geriatrics ward before memorizing all the symbols. Second, the proliferation of symbols makes Birdwhistell's "macrorecording" unwieldy and difficult to use. Third, while Birdwhistell correctly asserts that rather specific movements may carry specific meanings, the symbols he attaches to the specific movements really give the user no idea what meaning the movement may be communicating.

Any individual who attempts to classify nonverbal communication must deal with the question of what unit he will classify;[9] the problems of defining a recording unit can be easily illustrated. Let us assume that two people (A and B) are conversing and that we want to make a record of the nonverbal communication of person B. Do we record every facial and bodily movement which person B makes? Do we record every change in the distance separating the two individuals? Do we describe in minute detail the personal appearance of person B? Do we record only those movements which seem to be particularly important? Do we record only those movements where person B seems to be responding to A, or only those where B is not responding to A?

If we record every identifiable movement, we are using the kine as our recording unit. If we use only B's direct response to A's effort to communicate to B we are using the feedback response as the recording unit (thus all movement which took place during feedback is part of that unit). In some highly illuminating research, Condon and Ogston maintain that we should use the "process unit" rather than the "discrete unit" which is characteristic of Birdwhistell's notational system.[10]

Condon and Ogston maintain that the meaningful units of communication are not an endless number of small, discrete units such as the word or even the sentence in verbal communication, or the kine or kinemorph in nonverbal communication. The observer who focuses his attention on such particulars is much like the old miner who pans for fools gold while his associates mine a large vein of real gold with the latest technology. Neither the observer nor the old miner is likely to attain his larger objective because his attention is much too narrowly focused.

The principle is the same whether we are classifying verbal or nonverbal communication. We should separate one behavior from another *only* when we can clearly associate a separate meaning with each behavior. For example, observers who classify verbal behavior often use the sentence or even the word as their recording unit. Their observational focus tends to be too narrow. This is true because a communicator may require many words and often many sentences to communicate a single meaning; in this context the classification of every single word is not only inefficient but misleading. Similarly, to communicate a meaning nonverbally an individual may use many movements rather than a single movement. Observers who tend to use the smallest identifiable behavior as their recording units are dealing in "discrete units." Those who group movements together on the basis of the number of movements necessary to communicate a central meaning are using "process units."[11]

A number of recent studies deal with this important question of recording unit, provide fresh insights as to which kinds of nonverbal behavior should be classified, and provide a different nomenclature for the specific behaviors.[12] Since many of these efforts fall outside the conceptual framework of this book or seem of less practical value to the reader, a number of original and illuminating classification efforts must be left for the reader to examine on his own.

Many of the classification systems for kinesic behavior have received very little use because of their narrow frame of reference and a narrowly defined recording unit which makes it difficult for the observer to distinguish the meaningless movement from the meaningful. In contrast Hall has developed a classification system for proxemic behavior that has been widely used.

Hall's system is described in detail in chapter 3 although the emphasis in that chapter was on describing the nature and functions of proxemic behavior rather than on classifying such behavior. As the reader should recall, Hall makes use of all our senses to (1) determine the distance which actually separates people and (2) determine whether that distance is appropriate given the socially conditioned expectations of two or more people who are trying to communicate. The sensory inputs which help determine distance and its appropriateness are: (1) postural—sex identifiers; (2) sociofugal-sociopetal orientation (SFP axis); (3) kinesthetic factors; (4) touch code; (5) retinal combinations; (6) thermal code; (7) olfaction code; (8) voice loudness scale.

The reader can study Hall's system for classifying distance by referring back to Figure 3-1 in chapter 3. Each sensory input in effect gives the communicator some basis for determining the distance which separates him from the person with whom he is trying to communicate, and for determining whether that distance is socially acceptable. For example, by our sense of smell we can determine whether another person is communicating with us at an intimate distance or a personal distance. We should be able to detect the fragrance of the washed skin and hair at the intimate distance (1½ feet separation or less) but not at the personal distance (1½ to 4 feet). Similarly, if we are using vision to determine distance we will note that at the intimate distance the ear, eye, and mouth area of the face of the person we are communicating with is apt to be distorted. When the communicator's facial features are no longer distorted we will conclude that he has moved out to at least the personal distance.[13]

The methods of classification we have discussed so far have all had demonstrable merits. Generally, however, they have emphasized very detailed classification systems; Birdwhistell's macrorecording system goes so far as to classify every movement which takes place. These classification systems have also concentrated on recording *amounts* of communication associated with a particular part of the body without regard to the functions of the communication involved.

Ekman and Friesen started a new trend in the classification of nonverbal communication behavior. They placed such behavior into general categories which were distinguished from each other by the *dominant function of the class of communication.* They contend that nonverbal communication functions in five different ways and can, therefore, be classified into one of five categories: (1) *emblems;* (2) *illustrators;* (3) *affect displays;* (4) *regulators;* (5) *adaptors.*[14]

Emblems are nonverbal acts that have a verbal equivalent which can be expressed in a word or two. Much like highly denotative words, emblems express commonly accepted meanings. For example, the middle finger raised in the air, the index finger and middle finger raised in the form of a V, and the thumb and index finger forming a circle each communicate a specific meaning. *Illustrators,* as the name implies, function simultaneously with speech and tend to clarify and illustrate the central meaning the communicator intends to communicate by words. *Affect displays* are associated most closely with different facial expressions which convey emotions or affective states. *Regulators* are those acts which tend to control and regulate communication between individuals. The section in chapter 2 on the use of eye contact with the away gaze described in detail how regulators work. For example, when A wants to continue what he is saying he simply looks away from B; when he wants B to respond he looks at B. Likewise, if B smiles while A is talking, B can assume that this positive reinforcement will regulate A's behavior in the sense that it will prolong it. Similarly if B frowns during A's discourse, the negative reinforcement may bring A to a rather abrupt halt.

Finally, *adaptors* are types of nonverbal behavior which show how the communicator has adapted or adjusted to previous conditions or environments in his life. For example, the author's closest friend as an undergraduate in college was an intense pre-law student who was constantly kidded about being overweight. He adapted to this condition by constantly jabbing at his waist with his fingers to determine whether his waist was shrinking as a result of his diet. Recently, the author visited his friend and family. The friend, now an attorney, is very trim but he was still jabbing at the midriff. His nonverbal adaptor persisted.[15]

Recently, Wiener, Devoe, Rubinow, and Geller have made a stimulating attempt to extend and refine at least part of Ekman and Friesen's classification scheme. Wiener et al. maintain that there are four major classes of behavior which have communicative significance: search, correction, regulators, and message modulations. Search typically occurs when a speaker pauses noticeably while looking away and searching for the word and/or gestures which will convey the exact meaning he has in mind. Correction is usually associated with a retraction and change in the verbal content (e.g. "I meant to say 'irrelevant' not 'irrevelant' ") with the concomitant use of hand and other gestures to indicate to the addressee that the speaker is attempting to change the meaning he had conveyed. While search and correction are important functions of both verbal and nonverbal communication, Wiener et al. speculate that "the infrequent occurrences of search and correction for nonverbal forms is a function of the relatively small number of components in these nonverbal codes."[16]

In contrast, regulators and message modulations serve very important functions in nonverbal communication. Regulators are behaviors which are taken by addressees and emitters as signs that encoding or decoding is occurring, although Wiener et al. do not consider regulators to be part of the code itself. The basic types of regulators are addressor (sender) regulators and addressee (receiver) regulators. The authors maintain, much like Ekman and Friesen, that addressors regulate the behavior of addressees by eye movements and vocal variation in the form of inflection and pauses. Thus, to regulate behavior, the addressor typically looks at the addressee at the end of completed thoughts; if the addressee makes eye contact and/or nods the addressor assumes the addressee is decoding and continues speaking. Similarly upward inflections are taken as questions which need an answer. In combination "however, a pause and extended eye movement to the side or eyes rolled up, even with inflection changes, seem to be taken by the addressee as an indication that the emitter is thinking or searching and will continue to speak; no response is required by the addressee."[17]

In contrast to addressor regulators, addressee regulators are behaviors emitted by the addressee which seem to be taken by addressors as cues that decoding, understanding, agreement, or disagreement is occurring. Wiener et al. identify four specific subtypes of addressee regulators associated with eye contact; each seems to communicate different meanings: (1) the addressee moves his eyes upward without speaking (meaning = the addressee is thinking and the addressor should wait); (2) the addressee maintains a blank look without speaking (meaning = addressee is confused and the addressor should attempt clarification); (3) the addressee maintains eye contact with a slow rhythmic head nod (meaning = the addressee understands and the addressor may continue speaking); (4) the addressee maintains eye contact and smiles (meaning = the addressee understands but has nothing to add).[18]

The authors do not indicate precisely how they derived their categories and subcategories of regulators (content analysis procedures, for example, would be useful). They do suggest, however, that the types of regulators identified above occur repeatedly and the nature of the regulator and the frequency with which it is used will lead to predictable variations in the content of subsequent nonverbal communication.

At the same time, Wiener et al. maintain that the functions of search, correction, and regulation (regulators) are not part of the communication code. To be part of the nonverbal code, communication behaviors must meet four standards:

1. The behaviors must be emitted by the particular communication group studied—that is they must be socially shared rather than idiosyncratic behaviors;
2. The behaviors must occur in several different contexts;
3. The behaviors must be more likely to occur in verbal contexts than in any or all other contexts—thus scratching can occur in any context with or without anyone else present and as such has little to do with communication;
4. The behaviors as code components should encompass a relatively short time duration—this criterion serves to focus on ongoing experience rather than on socially prescribed patterns of behavior or on behavior related to personality styles.[19]

Wiener et al. have developed a set of categories which spell out the type of gestural (hand and arm) communication which meets the four criteria outlined above. Their category system, presented in Figure 9-2, emphasizes the significance (meaning) and functions of the various gestures. While the terminology used in this gestural classification system deviates a bit from the language of this book, the focus is the same—the categories are designed to identify explicitly the meaning(s) conveyed by a given gesture.

By studying Figure 9-2 the reader will be able to understand the categories and subcategories which comprise this system. The reader will note that the major classes

A. PANTOMIMIC GESTURES.

1. *Formal pantomimic gestures* are stylized movements of the arms and hands for which there is a culturally prescribed consensual meaning. Typically, such gestures have an object or event significance and function as nouns do in the verbal channel. Formal pantomimic gestures are almost invariant in meaning despite variations in the context, situation, time, or addressee; this relative invariance in meaning is similar to the relative invariance in meaning of words in the verbal channel. Formal pantomimic gestures can take the place of words; when they co-occur with words, the function of the gesture is that of emphasizing by adding redundancy to the verbal communication. Examples of formal pantomimic gestures are waving goodby, depicting two wavy lines in the air to designate a well-proportioned female, "the finger," and forming a circle with the index finger and thumb, remaining fingers extended to signify "okay" or "perfect."

The number of gestures which have a culturally prescribed meaning is typically limited within the general population, although some subgroups within a culture may make more extensive use of gestural substitutes for words than other subgroups, and may even develop their own formal pantomimic gestures. For example, in nineteenth-century Russia, the sophisticated balletomane knew that a gesture in which the thumb touched the left, middle, and right side of the forehead meant "king," while a gesture in which the hand encircled the face meant "beautiful girl." Revivals of nineteenth-century ballets still include long portions of pantomime, in which stylized gestures are used to tell the story of the ballet. Other examples are evident in special groups such as an army unit, or pilots, or other groups who communicate over long distances. In games such as charades, gestures which are consensually defined would be classified as formal pantomimic gestures, while other gestures used in charades, which are not consensually defined, fall into the category of improvisational pantomimic gestures.

2. *Improvisational pantomimic gestures.* Although we have no reason to believe that these forms have as much prescribed meaning as do formal pantomimic gestures, meaning seems to accrue in a particular context as a function of *some perceptual attribute* of an object, of an action performed on or with an object, or of the reaction to an object or event. The improvisational pantomimic gestures also have a noun or event quality, but since the meaning ascribed to the gesture is dependent on the situation, context, or content, these particular gestures occur most frequently in a context which has co-occurring verbal communication. For the most part, improvisational pantomimic gestures seem to serve the function of emphasizing, concretizing, or focusing on a particular aspect of the communication occurring verbally. Examples of gestures within this category of communicative movements are drawing a number of circles in the air around one point to depict the concept concentric and swinging an imaginary bat. There is a special set of circumstances in which improvisational pantomimes seem most prominent; that is, when more typical communicative patterns are blocked—for example, when speaking to a foreigner.

B. SEMANTIC MODIFYING AND RELATIONAL GESTURES.

These gestures usually accompany speech and are hypothesized to (a) serve the function of modification and specification of the communication, the same function served by adjectives and adverbs in the verbal channel; (b) specify the speaker's relationship to the addressee and to his communication; or (c) specify the relationship of one aspect of the communication to another aspect of the communication. The occurrence of these nonpantomimic gestures seems to be dependent on the communicative content co-occurring in other channels, but the forms of the gestures, when they do occur, seem to be relatively invariant and appear to have independent meaning. In general, the dimensions of these nonpantomimic gestures, along which variations seem to indicate differences in communicative significance, are (a) pointing and its direction, (b) orientation of palms, (c) semantic forms, and (d) location and size of gestures.

1. *Deictic movements* are pointing movements which can be done with the index finger, two or more fingers, or all fingers. Deictic movements are hypothesized to serve the function of specifying or reducing the ambiguity of the verbal referent. For example, the pronoun "you" can mean a specific person or a generalized other. When accompanied by a pointing to the addressee the meaning of "you" is the addressee; if pointed somewhere else than at the addressee it means "other than you, but not present" or "not I." Pointing gestures are also used to specify the relative positions of objects in space or events in time—"not here, not now" instances.

2. *Orientation of palms*—The position of the palms in a gesture indicates the speaker's relationship to the addressee—for example, mutual versus nonmutual—and/or about the speaker's attitude toward his communication—certain versus uncertain. Palms up is equivalent to uncertainty or to "I think" or "I believe" or "It seems to me" in a verbal statement, and adds for the addressee the message that the issue need not be pursued since noncertainty is indicated. Palms down indicates an assertion with the speaker again communicating that the subject matter is not open to question—equivalent verbal statements are "clearly," "absolutely," "without doubt," etc. Palms out (i.e., facing toward the addressee) is a statement of assertion and is equivalent to the statement, "I shall say it" or "Don't interrupt." These last gestures also seem to function as regulators of the communication interaction.

3. *Semantic forms*—Five gestures or gestural pat-

FIGURE 9-2   Reprinted from M. Wiener, S. Devoe, S. Rubinow, and J. Geller, "Nonverbal Behavior and Nonverbal Communication," *Psychological Review,* 79 (1972), 210-11. Copyright 1972 by the American Psychological Association. Reprinted by permission.

terns have been isolated: (a) circling gestures, (b) oscillation gestures, (c) arhythmic "chopping" gestures, (d) rhythmic "chopping" gestures, and (e) expansion-contraction gestures. Each of these will be described briefly and its hypothesized, communicative significance posited.

a. Circling gestures—a slow, continuous series of circular movements of any part of the hand including the arm which is hypothesized to indicate nonspecificity, globality, or generality of the verbal components in the communication. In words, this gesture is posited as indicating "I mean more than the specific words I have used," or "The specific referent term is only one general attribute of the event I'm describing."

b. Oscillation gestures—a series of slow to moderate, semicircular, back and forth movements of the hand which seem to indicate "either or" or "one or the other" of two components, or "on one hand versus on the other hand."

c. Arhythmic chopping gestures—linear, staccatolike movements of the arm and hand, usually performed in a limited series of one or two in which the same plane is maintained throughout the movement. The chopping gestures seem to be associated with the speaker's experience of discreteness of the elements or contents of his verbal communication. For example, a verbal statement in the form of "We have to consider A and B and C" is likely to be accompanied by a series of three "chops"—one for each component. The verbal statement in the form, "We have to consider John and his behavior" with a single chop at the end is interpreted to mean only his behavior—discreteness indicator—versus two chops where John in general

is to be considered and his behavior is to be considered separately.

d. Rhythmic chopping gestures—also linear, staccato movements, usually more than one or two, which have a rhythm independent of the rhythm of the co-occurring verbal content. In this form, the staccato chop is interpreted to mean emphasis rather than discreteness.

e. Expansion-contraction gestures—a slow expansion and contraction of the arm in which the addressor looks as if he were playing a concertina. Typically these movements indicate a size or extent dimension of the referent carried in the verbal channel.

In sum, the semantic forms seem to serve the function of specification and modification served by adjectives and adverbs in the verbal channel of communication; the palms seem to indicate the speaker's relationship to his communication, the addressee, or the relationship of one part of his communication to another part of his communication. However, much of the information communicated through the gestural channel appears to be redundant with that communicated through other channels. For example, tonal changes are effective indicators of the emphasis a speaker wishes to place on any portion of his verbal communication; facial expressions can communicate doubt or uncertainty as easily as gestures. The chief communicative functions of the gestural channel appear to be to specify the referent of an ambiguous verbal statement, to specify the addressor's relationship to his verbal communication, and to indicate intensity or emphasis by introducing redundancy into the message.

FIGURE 9-2   Continued.

of gesture are pantomimic gestures, and semantic modifying and relational gestures. Furthermore, the major subclasses of pantomimic gestures are formal pantomimic gestures and improvisational pantomimic gestures. The formal pantomimic gesture has a culturally prescribed consensual meaning which cuts across contexts while the improvisational pantomimic gesture has a rather constant meaning within a given context.

In contrast to pantomimic gestures, semantic modifying and relational gestures do not depend on context for meaning, but solely on content of the gesture. These types of gestures appear to "serve the same type of function of specification and modification" which is served by adjectives and adverbs in verbal communication. Taken collectively, the major communicative functions of gestures are to "specify the referent of an ambiguous verbal statement, to specify the addressor's relationship to his verbal communication, and to indicate intensity or emphasis by introducing redundancy into the message."[20]

Finally, Wiener et al. point out honestly that their classification system draws on many previous category systems such as those by Efron, and Ekman and Friesen, for example. Nonetheless, this category system should be particularly useful for the observer who wants to classify communicative gestures. It not only classifies gestures by the meaning to which they refer, but it presents a limited number of categories which should be easily used by the observer who wishes to distinguish one nonverbal behavior from another on the basis of the communicative function it serves.

The classification system developed by Wiener et al. emphasizes that the meaning communicated by movement may be determined by cultural context in some instances. In other cases the content of the communication and not the context is the crucial factor. Many category systems make no attempt to allow for the effects of context. Consequently they are of more limited value. Scheflen has recognized this problem in classification and to deal with it has devised what he appropriately identifies as *context analysis.*

Scheflen notes that observers often become so absorbed with content that they pay no attention to context. Indeed "this tradition has produced, in the name of science, a plethora of counts and correlations of isolated variables such as words per minute, noun-verb ratios, foot tape, therapists' interpretations, and so on. It is not surprising that such data and their analyses have tended to divide the psychiatric clinician and the psychiatric researcher. Such scores and statistical categories seem unfamiliar and unsatisfying to the clinician who has experienced the unity and flow of the psychotherapeutic session. This world of bits and pieces does not represent the richness of his experience. Concepts like rapport or empathy are destroyed rather than captured or sharpened by such dissection."[21]

Clearly, the observer can easily find himself impaled on the horns of a dilemma. On the one hand, he may feel that he must be highly microscopic in his attempts to classify behavior. With this attitude he may classify every movement as Birdwhistell does but become so overwhelmed with detail that he cannot see the larger behavioral patterns which are characteristic of certain types of nonverbal communication. On the other hand, the observer may feel that he must take a highly macroscopic approach to observation. Such an approach may conjure up images of the highly contemplative pipe-smoker who misses all the subtle nuances in meaning because his thoughts are lost in the smokey residue of his global ruminations.

Scheflen maintains that we can and should avoid the horns of such an observational dilemma. To do so, he advocates that we use context analysis. Context analysis includes four steps: (1) recording and transcribing; (2) ascertaining the structural units; (3) synthesizing the larger picture to determine the meaning or function; and (4) setting up the natural history experiment.[22] To follow these steps Scheflen suggests that sound motion picture recording be used (presumably, videotaping could be substituted) and transcripts be made from film. With particular ingenuity he notes that to determine the meaning communicated we have to be aware of *three different contexts* which may apply to such communication: immediate, mediate, and remote contexts. The immediate context is the particular situation where the communication takes place while the mediate context often refers to the social group or institution involved. Finally, remote context refers to such general factors as cultural ideals and middle-class values.[23] Not surprisingly, then, Scheflen defines meaning operationally as the relation of a specific unit of communication and its context or contexts.[24]

The concept of context analysis, like much of Scheflen's other research, exhibits much creativity and potential value for the observer of nonverbal communication. As a classification system, it might be faulted on one ground, however. Context analysis is somewhat abstract in theory and in application it still seems to lack specificity.

MEASUREMENT

Observers who classify nonverbal communication behavior use category systems. While some category systems incorporate some form of scaling technique, most do not. The failure to use scales is a severe limitation. As we shall see, exclusive reliance on the classification of nonverbal communication behaviors into categories limits the observer to making *quantitative* judgments about the nature of communication; he can make no definitive judgments about *the quality of communication*. The observer may learn, for example, that deictic movements were used seventy-five times in one discussion, but he will be unable to determine whether the deictic movements raised or lowered the quality of subsequent nonverbal communication.

With the exception of Hall's category system for proxemic behavior (which incorporates scales with the categories), category systems for describing nonverbal communication have been of fairly limited use. Thus, Mehrabian writes that "notation and category systems generally have failed to relate meaningfully to communicator states, feelings, emotion, communicator characteristics, relations among communicators, or other communication behaviors. Therefore, the systems are seldom used by other investigators. In contrast, the categories that have been elaborated with a view to their significance in the communication process (as exemplified by the proxemic categories of Hall, 1963) have been far more productive in generating research and empirical findings for the communication process."[25]

Measurement requires scales. When you go to your doctor and he takes your temperature, he is measuring your temperature not classifying it. He must *measure* your temperature in degrees (in this case with a Fahrenheit thermometer) and each degree your temperature exceeds the normal 98.6 is a direct measure of how sick you are. Let us assume that the range within which your temperature may fall is 98.6-106 degrees; anything higher than 106 and you are apt to be dead. Any temperature falling near the lower end of this range or scale would be considered desirable; likewise anything near the top end of the scale would be considered undesirable.

The same principle applies in attempting to measure the degree to which desirable or undesirable qualities are present in the nonverbal communication you are studying. If you assume, for example, that an individual will exhibit varying degrees of attentiveness through his gestures, you will want to measure the degree of attentiveness by using a scale which has attentive on one end and unattentive on the other. As soon as you take this step, you are adopting the connotative approach to the communication of meaning by nonverbal means.

The connotative approach to nonverbal communication is grounded in the empirical finding that there are certain dominant "dimensions" of meaning which best describe that behavior. Furthermore, each dimension of meaning may be represented by one or more scales which have a desirable property on one end and an undesirable property on the other end. The connotative approach to facial meaning is described in detail in chapter 2 and appendix A; the reader is asked to study these sections carefully. The assumptions made in applying the connotative approach to the face are the same as in applying it to the behaviors which comprise all of nonverbal communication; the notion most central to the connotative approach is the concept of semantic space.

Schlosberg began the attempt to study and measure nonverbal communication within a connotative framework. The major follow-up research was done by Osgood, and has been explained and elaborated on by Mehrabian and others.[26] In his admirable job of elaborating on Osgood's research, Mehrabian typically talks about a set of scales which can be applied to kinesic behavior in general, although one must emphasize that Osgood initially focused solely on the dimensions of meaning which are conveyed by facial expressions.

Mehrabian has certainly been a leader in recognizing that "the need for a reasonably general description of the referents of nonverbal communication can be seen by considering the difficulty one might encounter if he were to proceed without such a conceptualization. What nonverbal behaviors should one select to study as a part of nonverbal communication?"[27] He emphasizes that Osgood found the following dimensions to be primary referents of facial expressions: (1) pleasantness; (2) control; (3) activation. Mehrabian's own research has confirmed that the meanings conveyed through nonverbal communication can be adequately described by these three major dimensions of meaning. Using his own terminology Mehrabian labels these dimensions of meaning (1) positiveness, (2) potency or status, and (3) responsiveness.[28]

MEASURING QUALITY OF COMMUNICATION IN THE INDIVIDUAL NONVERBAL SYSTEMS The quality of nonverbal communication may be measured in at least two ways. The quality of communication associated with each of the subsystems of nonverbal communication—such as the kinesic, proxemic, and artifactual systems, for example—may be measured separately. The second means of measuring the quality of nonverbal communication is to consider all nonverbal communication subsystems as they function together and assess the overall quality of that communication. Clearly, up to this point, this book has been designed to provide new and practical means for measuring the quality of communication for each of the nonverbal systems. Thus, the facial meaning sensitivity test in chapter 2 may be used to determine how accurately meanings can be *conveyed* by nonverbal means and how accurately *perceived*. Only chapters 3 and 4 on proxemic behavior do not provide original instruments for measuring quality of communication associated with one of the nonverbal systems. Since Hall's combination of categories and scales has proved so useful for measuring proxemic behavior, no attempt was made to provide a new instrument for measuring the distances which separate people and the appropriateness of such distances.

Chapter 5 deals with the nature and function of the artifactual communication system. Once again a new measuring instrument, the body image test, is presented. Since body image was found to be integrally related to the quality of one's communication, the reader can use the body image test to compare the body image he is *trying to communicate* to others with the body image he is *actually conveying*. The vocalic meaning sensitivity test provides him with one measure of the quality of one's vocalic communication. Since the meanings to be conveyed in the vocal meaning sensitivity test and the facial meaning sensitivity test are identical, the reader can make a direct comparison of the quality of his facial and vocal communication.

Chapter 7 and chapter 8 deal, respectively, with the tactile and olfactory, and the telepathic communication systems. By using the tactile communication index the reader can directly measure the quality of his own tactile communication whether he is functioning as a sender or receiver. Similarly, the reader can use the olfactory meaning sensitivity test to determine his ability to perceive accurately the various odors which are detectable as he interacts with others. Finally, by using the ESP deck of cards with five symbols and by taking the telepathic communication test, the quality of one's telepathic communication, either as a sender or a receiver, can be determined.

Ideally, the reader should measure the quality of his communication within each of the nonverbal systems. By computing scores for each system the reader will have a profile of his own communicative effectiveness which is extremely detailed. He will also have an objective basis for determining whether he must work harder to improve the quality of communication.

The author believes that these tests are uniquely useful instruments for measuring the quality of communication. At the same time, it is only fair to present what appear to be some particularly useful scaling techniques developed recently. They can be used in conjunction with or substituted for the measuring instruments already presented in this book.

For measurement of the quality of kinesic communication Mehrabian provides a set of semantic-differential type scales. Eighteen scales are provided to measure each of three dimensions of meaning (six for each dimension): pleasantness, responsiveness, and dominance. While the scales are deduced for research dealing directly with facial expressions, Mehrabian concludes without explanation that they can be used to rate any subset of nonverbal behaviors including vocal expressions.[29]

Aside from the body image test presented in this book, scales designed to measure the quality of artifactual communication are conspicuous by their absence. Work has been done in a field closely related to artifactual communication, however: aesthetics. Artifactual communication is directly concerned with the constituents of beauty; the study of aesthetics shares a very similar focus. More specifically, the experimental aesthetician has recently concerned himself with determining the factors which comprise an aesthetic decision. In layman's terms, when we look at a painting what factors make us judge it to be appealing or ugly? Berlyne writes that the experimental aesthetician must be directly concerned with "the behaviour of the appreciate. What goes on inside him after confrontation with a work of art or other stimulus pattern is what generally receives most attention. But we must take care not to neglect the behaviour that precedes, and leads up to, this confrontation, and it has been inexcusably neglected in the past."[30]

After reviewing studies which attempt to determine which factors make up an aesthetic judgment, Berlyne discusses his own research which was designed to answer that question. He concludes that the aesthetic judgment is made up of the following factors: (1) *complexity-uncertainty* (can be measured by a simple/complex scale, for example); (2) *hedonic value* (can be measured by the displeasing/pleasing scale); (3) *cortical arousal* (can be measured by the weak/powerful scale).[31] Clearly the reader can take a person or a work of art and apply the scales above to measure precisely what meanings are communicated to him and from an aesthetic standpoint whether the quality of that communication is high or low.

Also working within the aesthetic framework, Breskin has developed a unique instrument to measure nonverbal behavior. He worked on the assumption that the rigid person will find closed figures such as the complete circle aesthetically pleasing because such a figure will satisfy his need for closure. In contrast people who exhibit nonrigid behavior will be more inclined to choose figures such as the open circle. When taking the Breskin rigidity test, an individual is asked to choose between fifteen pairs of symbols. If well over half the individual's choices suggest a need for closure, he is by definition a rigid person. Breskin and other researchers have reason to believe that nonverbal rigidity is related to a number of socially undesirable behaviors. The reader interested in measuring the degree of his own rigidity is referred to the Breskin test.[32]

Finally, a thorough review of the measuring instruments developed recently reveals two new instruments which might be used in measuring the quality of vocalic communication: The sonograph and TENVAD. The sonograph is an instrument much like the spectograph which literally traces changes in such vocal attributes as frequency, amplitude, and duration. By applying it to a recording of his own voice and by using the material presented in chapter 6 the reader could determine whether he is employing the proper frequency, amplitude, and duration to convey the *intended* meaning(s).[33]

TENVAD (which stands for Test of Nonverbal Auditory Discrimination) is a more comprehensive and probably more useful means of measuring the quality of vocalic communication. Developed by Peabody, TENVAD is strictly a test of *auditory perception* as opposed to a test of one's ability to transmit meanings by vocal means. It is comprised of tape with ten sounds for each of five vocal variables: pitch, loudness, rhythm, duration, and timbre. A paper and pencil test is used to determine how accurately an individual can differentiate between the 50 tones on the tape.[34]

MEASURING OVERALL QUALITY OF COMMUNICATION   Measuring the quality of communication within each of the nonverbal subsystems has great merit as just demonstrated. However, we rarely communicate solely by facial expression or gesture, or posture, or by our use of space or clothing, or by vocal means. All of the subsystems of nonverbal communication *function together* in a high proportion of instances. When they do function together we need some means of measuring the meanings communicated. We need to know the degree to which we were successful in communicating our *intended meanings*.

A given communicator must have some measure of how well he is doing as a communicator and what the quality of his communication really is. In the parlance of the systems analyst the communicator's best source of information as to the quality of his attempts to communicate is the quality of feedback he receives. "If no information is transferred calling for a correction, the feedback is termed positive. Negative feedback occurs when there is information which calls for a change; it shows that the system can act in its own defense."[35]

The systems approach to measuring the quality of communication is based on a mechanical analogy. The central heating system in your home, for example, has a built-in feedback loop connected to the thermostat. If you have set your temperature for 72° the thermostat will immediately detect any significant deviation from that setting and feed back to the central heating (or cooling) unit the electrical command to begin functioning. If the feedback loop in your heating system fails, your home will probably become oppressively hot or cold.

The same principle applies to human communication. The effective communicator carefully monitors the feedback he receives and takes the necessary corrective actions in subsequent efforts to communicate. Since we have found nonverbal cues to be a much more accurate reflection of an individual's true feelings than verbal cues, the informed communicator will rely on nonverbal rather than verbal feedback to give him a detailed reading as to the success of his efforts to communicate.

Unfortunately, most communicators probably do not know how to make use of the nonverbal feedback they receive. They may not even be sure whether that feed-back is positive or negative (feedback which signals the communicator that he must change the nature of his communicative efforts). This is so because no systematic attempt has been made until recently to determine what meanings make up the non-verbal feedback response or to measure the degree to which the qualities of the non-verbal feedback response are signaling the communicator that he must make a change.

We now have an instrument which was developed expressly for the purpose of measuring the dominant meanings contained in the nonverbal portion of any feedback response. This instrument provides the user with detailed information about the feed-back to his own communication that suggests (1) *whether* any corrective action should be taken and (2) *what types of corrective actions* should be taken.

The Leathers nonverbal feedback rating instrument is the result of over two years of testing and development. Phase I in the development of this instrument is described in appendix A. In phase I the nonverbal portions of feedback responses of individuals in problem-solving discussions were selected from videotapes of a number of labora-tory discussions already filmed. These responses were placed on a master videotape and studied to determine what types of behavior were consistently present which would be useful in signaling a communicator that the addressee was not perceiving his intended meanings and that, consequently, the communicator must modify his mes-sage. For example, if confusion was consistently conveyed in the nonverbal portion of the feedback response, this would signal the communicator that an attempt at clarifica-tion was necessary. In fact the author discovered that over twenty-five types of be-havior (some were very similar) were consistently present in the nonverbal portion of the feedback response.

Each of these twenty-five behaviors was represented by semantic-differential scales. A group of feedback responses was randomly selected and over 125 subjects were asked to apply the scales to the feedback responses. These ratings were factor analyzed. The objective of this factor analysis was to determine how many classes of behavior were part of the nonverbal portion of the feedback response. As Figure A-2 in appendix A indicates, the nonverbal portion of the feedback response is composed of the following four classes of behavior: involvement, feeling, analysis, and control.

From these, data scales were selected for development of the Leathers nonverbal feedback rating instrument. Each scale selected had to meet three criteria.[36] In its final form the scales of the LNFRI are listed in random order. The reader should note, however, that factor 1 (involvement) is represented by the involved/withdrawn, attentive/unattentive, responsive/unresponsive, and interest/disinterest scales; factor 2 (feeling) is represented by the pleased/displeased and friendly/hostile scales; factor 3 (analysis) is represented by the deliberative/spontaneous and analytical/impulsive scales; factor 4 (control) is represented by the confident/uncertain and clear/confused scales.

The Leathers nonverbal feedback rating instrument is presented in Figure 9-3. Ordinarily the behavior represented by each end of the scales will not be illustrated with photographs. To make sure that the LNFRI can be used with ease by every reader, however, the series of posed photographs was made with one of the author's trusted assistants. The reader should assume that the man seated at the table in the photo-graphs is reponding to an individual on the other side of the table—even though that person cannot be seen. The photographs actually represent nonverbal behaviors which are typically present in the nonverbal portion of the feedback response.

To use the LNFRI the reader would simply have a videotape made of a situation

FIGURE 9-3 Leathers Nonverbal Feedback Rating Instrument.

CONFIDENT 7 : 6 : 5 : 4 : 3 : 2 : 1 UNCERTAIN

INVOLVED 7 : 6 : 5 : 4 : 3 : 2 : 1 WITHDRAWN

ATTENTIVE 7 : 6 : 5 : 4 : 3 : 2 : 1 UNATTENTIVE

PLEASED   7   :   6   :   5   :   4   :   3   :   2   :   1   DISPLEASED

DELIBERATIVE   7   :   6   :   5   :   4   :   3   :   2   :   1   SPONTANEOUS

RESPONSIVE   7   :   6   :   5   :   4   :   3   :   2   :   1   UNRESPONSIVE

Continued on next page.

FIGURE 9-3 *Continued.*

CLEAR 7 : 6 : 5 : 4 : 3 : 2 : 1 CONFUSED

FRIENDLY 7 : 6 : 5 : 4 : 3 : 2 : 1 HOSTILE

where he is attempting to communicate with one other individual. Each time an individual responds directly to the reader's attempt to communicate we have a feedback response. Each feedback response should be rated on the scales of the LNFRI. If you look at an individual responding to you on videotape and you decide by studying his nonverbal behavior that it is very uncertain and withdrawn, neither attentive nor pleased, moderately deliberative and responsive, and very confused, hostile, impulsive, and disinterested you would put a check mark over number 1 for scales 1 and 2, a check mark over number 4 for scales 3 and 4, a check mark over number 5 *or* number 6 for scales 5 and 6, and a check mark over number 1 for scales 7, 8, 9, and 10.

In extensive testing in the experimental laboratory, in the classroom, and with a great variety of executives and engineers LNFRI has proved to be an extremely practical and useful instrument for measuring the quality of one's own communication. Generally speaking, the author would consider the behaviors represented by the right side of the scales to be negative feedback and a sign to the communicator that there is

FIGURE 9-3 *Continued.*

ANALYTICAL   7   :   6   :   5   :   4   :   3   :   2   :   1   IMPULSIVE

INTEREST   7   :   6   :   5   :   4   :   3   :   2   :   1   DISINTEREST

a gap between the addressee's *perceived meaning* and the communicator's *intended meaning.* For example if a communicator receives feedback which is characteristically withdrawn, unattentive, and confused, he has reason to be concerned. There is probably something about the nature of his message (which of course includes all of the nonverbal factors discussed in this book) that is making the respondent withdraw and be unattentive and confused. Involvement and attentiveness are defining features of high quality communicative interaction. Similarly, nonverbal feedback which is consistently confused suggests that something about a message is resulting in a perceived distortion of the intended meaning by the respondent. In each case the communicator has rather concrete signals to indicate that his actions are lowering the quality of his communication, and that he should take corrective action immediately.[37]

The Leathers nonverbal feedback rating instrument can be used in many ways.[38] The ingenuity of the reader will probably lead to many unexplored uses. Above everything else, it should increase the reader's sensitivity in perceiving and accurately interpreting the corrective signals which are an integral part of nonverbal feedback in interpersonal communication. The next time the reader is exposed to a feedback response which exhibits uncertainty, withdrawal, unattentiveness, and displeasure, for example, he should take immediate, corrective action. In contrast, when the nonverbal feedback signals that the addressee is confident, involved, attentive, and pleased the reader can take momentary pleasure in the realization that the quality of his own communication is high.

CONCLUSION

Careful and repeated observation is necessary to fully understand nonverbal communication. Observers are faced with at least three issues. They must decide whether observation will take place in the laboratory or the field, whether they will concentrate on a single individual or on communication interaction between at least two people, and whether they will use slow-motion projection. Whatever the observer's stand on these issues, observation requires videotaping—a videotaping laboratory is illustrated in this chapter.

Classification of nonverbal behaviors is based on the denotative approach to meaning. Birdwhistell's kinesic macrorecording system is probably the most comprehensive classification system for kinesic behavior. Many existing classification systems fail to specify the *function* of a given kind of nonverbal behavior, however. Ekman and Friesen have recognized this deficiency. They have devised five categories which include the major functions of nonverbal communication: (1) emblems; (2) illustrators; (3) affect displays; (4) regulators; (5) adaptors. Wiener, Devoe, Rubinow, and Geller have recently made a stimulating extension of Ekman and Friesen's classification system.

Many classification systems make no provision for the impact of communication context. To alleviate this problem, Scheflen has devised a system which he calls context analysis. Scheflen emphasizes that nonverbal communication may take place in the immediate, mediate, or remote context.

Attempts to classify nonverbal behaviors as to kind or type have at least one major limitation: They allow the observer to make *quantitative* judgments about the nature of the communication, but he can make no definitive judgments about the *quality of communication*.

Quality of communication may be measured in at least two ways. First, the quality of communication within each of the nonverbal communication systems may be measured. Second, the overall quality of communication of the systems functioning together may be measured. The first type of measurement is perhaps best accomplished by applying tests such as the facial meaning sensitivity test and the body image test, which are presented in this book.

Measuring the overall quality of communication is best accomplished by a careful reading of the feedback the communicator is receiving. When the communicator receives negative feedback, he must modify his messages. When he receives positive feedback, it is a sign to him that the addressee's perceived meaning is the same as the communicator's intended meaning.

The Leathers nonverbal feedback rating instrument is provided as an objective means for determining whether any corrective action should be taken by the communicator and, if so, what type of corrective action should be taken. Negative and positive behaviors as measured by the LNFRI are illustrated by a set of photographs.

NOTES

[1] M. L. Knapp and R. P. Harrison, "Observing and Recording Nonverbal Data in Human Transactions," paper presented at the annual convention of the Speech Communication Association, Chicago, Ill., December 1972.

[2] R. Renneker, "Kinesic Research and Therapeutic Processes: Further Discussion," in *Expressions of the Emotions in Man*, ed. P. H. Knapp (New York: International Universities Press, 1963), p. 150.

[3] In this instance room 14 serves in addition as a storeroom for the videotape equipment and tapes.

[4] P. Ekman, W. V. Friesen, and T. J. Taussig, "VID-R and SCAN: Tools and Methods in the Analysis of Facial Expression and Body Movement," in *Content Analysis*, ed. G. Gerbner, O. Holst, K. Krippendorff, W. Paisley, and P. Stone (New York: Wiley, 1969).

[5] M. Wiener, S. Devoe, S. Rubinow, and J. Geller, "Nonverbal Behavior and Nonverbal Communication," *Psychological Review*, 79 (1972), 185-214. The authors maintain that videotape replay should be at the same speed as recorded. To speed up or slow down replay may be interesting but simply serves to emphasize behaviors which were not consciously perceived by the interactants.

[6] R. M. Eisler, M. Hersen, and S. Agras, "A Method for the Controlled Observation of Nonverbal Interpersonal Behavior," *Behavior Therapy*, 4 (1973), 420.

[7] Ibid., 423.

[8] R. L. Birdwhistell, *Kinesics and Context: Essays on Body Motion Communication* (Philadelphia: University of Pennsylvania Press, 1970), pp. 183-84 and pp. 257-304. Birdwhistell recognizes Hutchinson's notational system for the movements in dancing as the most comprehensive in existence. For a detailed look at this classification system see A. Hutchinson, *Labanotation: The System for Recording Movement* (New York: Theatre Arts Books, 1970).

[9] B. Berelson, *Content Analysis in Communication Research* (Glencoe, Ill.: Free Press, 1952) and R. W. Budd, R. K. Thorp, and L. Donchew, *Content Analysis of Communication* (New York: Macmillan, 1967) treat the matter of the recording unit and related issues in classification in detail.

[10] W. S. Condon and W. D. Ogston, "Sound Film Analysis of Normal and Pathological Behavior Patterns," *Journal of Nervous and Mental Disease*, 143 (1966), 338. The reader's attention is directed back to Birdwhistell's sixth assumption on page 204: the meanings derived therefrom are functions both of the behavior and of the

operations by which it is investigated. The way an observer defines his recording unit will affect the number and kinds of meanings he sees communicated in a given situation.

[11] Ibid., 340-44.

[12] B. M. Brant, "A Method for Analyzing the Nonverbal Behavior (Physical Motions) of Teachers of Elementary School Language Arts," *Dissertation Abstracts International*, 31 (Columbia University, 1970), 4A; C. M. Galloway, "The Challenge of Nonverbal Research," *Theory into Practice*, 1 (1971), 310-14; M. Server, "Teaching the Nonverbal Components of Assertive Training," *Journal of Behavior Therapy and Experimental Psychiatry*, 3 (1972), 179-83; A. E. Scheflen, *How Behavior Means* (New York: Interface, 1973); A. T. Dittmann, *Interpersonal Messages of Emotion* (New York: Springer, 1973).

[13] For an extension of Hall's classification system for proxemic behavior see O. M. Watson, "Conflicts and Directions in Proxemic Research," *Journal of Communication*, 22 (1972), 443-59 and S. E. Jones, "A Comparative Proxemics Analysis of Dyadic Interaction in Selected Subcultures of New York City," *Journal of Social Psychology*, 84 (1971), 35-44.

[14] P. Ekman and W. V. Friesen, "The Repertoire of Nonverbal Behavior: Categories, Origins, Usage, and Coding," *Semiotica*, 1 (1969), 49-98.

[15] P. Ekman and W. V. Friesen, "Hand Movements," *Journal of Communication*, 22 (1972), 353-74. One of Ekman and Friesen's latest attempts to refine their functional approach to nonverbal category systems focuses on hand movement. This research was treated in detail in chapter 2.

[16] Wiener et al., "Nonverbal Behavior and Nonverbal Communication," 207.

[17] Ibid.

[18] Ibid., 208.

[19] Ibid., 209.

[20] Ibid., 211.

[21] A. E. Scheflen, "Natural History Method in Psychotherapy: Communicational Research," in *Methods of Research in Psychotherapy*, ed. L. A. Gottschalk and A. H. Auerbach (New York: Appleton-Century-Crofts, 1966), p. 265.

[22] Ibid., p. 270. See also A. E. Scheflen, *Communicational Structure: Analysis of a Psychotherapy Transaction* (Bloomington, Ind.: Indiana University Press, 1972), pp. 311-39, for Scheflen's most recent elaboration on the method of context analysis.

[23] Ibid., pp. 279-82.

[24] Ibid.

[25] A. Mehrabian, *Nonverbal Communication* (Chicago: Aldine-Atherton, 1972), p. 6.

[26] C. E. Osgood, "Dimensionality of the Semantic Space for Communication via Facial Expressions," *Scandinavian Journal of Psychology*, 7 (1966), 1-30; A. Mehrabian, "A Semantic Space for Nonverbal Behavior," *Journal of Consulting and Clinical Psychology*, 35 (1970), 248-57. Recent attempts to study nonverbal communication by using scaling techniques include D. Mostofsky, V. Bossche, S. Sheinkopf, and M. Noyes, "Novel Ways to Study Aphasia," *Rehabilitation Literature*, 32 (1971), 291-94; J. G. Teresa, "The Measurement of Meaning as Interpreted by Teachers and Students in Visuo-Gestural Channel Expressions Through Nine Emotional Expressions," *Dissertation Abstracts International* 32 (University of Michigan, 1972), 7A; G. C. Cupchick, "Expression and Impression: The Decoding of Nonverbal Affect," *Dissertation Abstracts International* 33 (University of Wisconsin, 1973), 11B.

[27] Mehrabian, *Nonverbal Communication,* p. 195.

[28] Ibid.

[29] Ibid.

[30] D. E. Berlyne, "Ends and Means of Experimental Aesthetics," *Canadian Journal of Psychology,* 16 (1972), 303-25.

[31] Ibid., 319.

[32] S. Breskin, "Measurement of Rigidity, A Non-Verbal Test," *Perceptual and Motor Skills,* 27 (1968), 1203-6. L. H. Primavera and M. Higgins, "Nonverbal Rigidity and Its Relationship to Dogmatism and Machiavellianism," *Perceptual and Motor Skills,* 36 (1972), 356-58, is a study illustrative of recent efforts to relate nonverbal rigidity to other types of socially significant behaviors.

[33] L. Rubenstein and D. E. Cameron, "Electronic Analysis of Nonverbal Communication," *Comprehensive Psychiatry,* 9 (1968), 202.

[34] N. A. Buktenica, "Auditory Discrimination: A New Assessment Procedure; Test of Non-Verbal Auditory Discrimination," *Exceptional Children,* 38 (1971), 237-40.

[35] D. Pedersen and L. M. Shears, "A Review of Personal Space Research in the Framework of a General System Theory," *Psychological Bulletin,* 80 (1973), 367.

[36] (1) Loading of a scale on a factor had to exceed .70; (2) The scales chosen had the highest reliability figures as measured by analysis of variance; (3) The number of scales chosen to represent each factor was based on the amount of variance which each factor accounted for. Since factor 1 (involvement) accounts for over .40 of the total variance it is represented by four of the ten scales which comprise the final forms of the Leathers nonverbal feedback rating instrument. Two scales represent each of the other three factors.

[37] The reader should note that the scales of the LNFRI are applied only to nonverbal behavior. In that sense the LNFRI represents a measurement of the quality of nonverbal communication in the form of the nonverbal portion of the feedback response. Perhaps more importantly, however, the LNFRI provides the communicator with a measure of the overall quality of his communication—when he receives nonverbal feedback which is measurably negative he knows that there are qualitative deficiencies in the messages he is transmitting. Finally, the reader should note that whether the feedback quality on the right side of the scale is really negative often depends on the situation or objectives of the communicator. Thus, a communicator in a t-group would consider spontaneous feedback to be highly desirable while he might place a negative value on spontaneity in a problem-solving group.

[38] For details on how a similar instrument can be used see Dale G. Leathers, "The Feedback Rating Instrument: A New Means of Evaluating Discussion," *Central States Speech Journal,* 22 (1970), 33-42; the rationale underlying the Leathers feedback rating instrument can be found in Dale G. Leathers, "Process Disruption and Measurement in Small Group Communication, *Quarterly Journal of Speech,* 54 (1969), 287-300.

10

COMMUNICATION SYSTEMS

Communication systems may be used to exchange meanings. Properly used such systems facilitate the accurate and efficient exchange of such meanings. Improperly used they may have very deleterious effects on the quality of interpersonal communication. To this point the functional capacity of the individual nonverbal communication systems has been examined separately. Such systems do not operate in a vacuum, however. They typically interact with each other and with the verbal communication system.

This chapter is designed to illuminate the nature of such interaction. As with earlier chapters, the express purpose is to expand the communicative potential of the reader and, consequently, his ability to achieve his communicative objectives. With this overriding purpose in mind, the chapter (1) describes and contrasts the functional components of the communication systems, and rates the functional capacity of the individual nonverbal communication systems, (2) examines the impact on interpersonal communication when the systems are interacting congruently and incongruently, and (3) discusses the implications of the possible types of interaction between and among the communication systems.

To begin we must take a careful look at the components of a human communication system.

The components of a communication system can be identified rather readily; the number of components identified of course depends upon the breadth or narrowness of the analysis being undertaken. The primary components with which we shall deal in this chapter are *dimensions of meaning, functions of the system, channels of communication, feedback, boundaries,* and *environments.*

The concept of *dimensions of meaning* has already been discussed in detail in this book. Osgood originated the idea that human beings communicate in a "semantic space." When the communication is verbal, the three major dimensions of meaning which are communicated are evaluation (good/bad), potency (strong/weak), and activity (active/passive). Osgood maintains that the same three basic dimensions of meaning are communicated by facial expression.[1] Significantly, the dimensions of meaning which can be communicated and the effectiveness with which they can be communicated vary from one type of nonverbal system (or subsystem) to another. While the dominant dimensions of meaning communicated by the face are evaluation, interest, intensity, and control, we communicate the dimensions of domination, approval, extroversion, and self-confidence by our use of space.

The reader should recognize that in any given situation either the positive or negative quality of a dimension may be perceivable. For example, as I move closer to you I am apt to be perceived as more dominant, approving, extroverted, and confident, but as I move away I will be seen as *less* dominant and approving, *or* even more submissive, unapproving, introverted, and uncertain. Researchers have typically used scales to measure the degree to which a positive or negative quality of a dimension of meaning is perceptible in a given situation.

The dominant *communicative functions* of nonverbal systems and subsystems also vary. The face functions primarily as an affect display system to transmit information about the type of emotion a communicator is experiencing, while we use space to signal degree of involvement in a situation, or withdrawal. In contrast we use different clothing styles, or glasses, or cosmetics (all integral parts of artifactual communication) to establish or reshape our social identity.

The third major component of human communication systems is *channel.* Dittmann in his extremely insightful book *Interpersonal Messages of Emotion* sees a channel as any set of communicative behaviors which is perceived by the interactants and which can be studied independently of other co-occurring behaviors.[2] Interestingly, Dittmann classifies channels into audible and visible channels. Audible channels are composed of (1) short-term spoken language (messages on this channel are brief and describe the emotional state of the communicator—examples are "I am angry," and "Oh, s_____!"; (2) long-term spoken language (long passages of speech which may have subliminal meanings); (3) vocalization ("tone of voice" and nonfluencies). Visible channels are composed of (1) facial expression; (2) body movement; and (3) psychophysiological responses. The psychophysiological channel is particularly interesting because it suggests a channel not commonly examined. Some examples of messages carried by this channel are "blushing, very heavy or rapid breathing, profuse sweating that is visible or makes the person wipe his hands frequently, and a strong pulse that produces resultant movement such as a slightly swinging foot when the legs are crossed."[3]

Even if the notion of psychophysiological responses does not increase the reader's understanding of nonverbal communication, it should expand his or her conversational options. The next time you sense that your date is responding well to your amorous advances you can turn and say "I am really relieved to see that your psychophysiological responses are in order."

The reader will recognize that each of the communication systems and subsystems discussed in this book has its own channel. While Dittmann's interesting classification of channels does describe the psychophysiological channel, it does not cover the proxemic, artifactual, tactile, olfactory, or telepathic channels examined in detail in this book.

Channel capacity of the communication systems varies significantly. In particular the nonverbal channels vary as to ability to separate their own signals from those being transmitted through other channels, nature of the information they convey, speed with which they transmit information, visibility of the message, and in a number of other ways.[4]

The fourth component of a communication system, *feedback,* has already received considerable attention in this book. Communication systems have both negative feedback processes (*morphostasis*) and positive feedback processes (*morphogenesis*). Negative feedback in human communication works much like the thermostat in the home or the governor on an automobile. Negative feedback works as a self-correcting mechanism for the central system. Just as the thermostat signals the central heating system that more or less heat is needed, the communication receiver may signal the sender that he must clarify his message since the receiver is confused.

As Ruben points out, "the thermostat and other cybernetic self-regulating, self-steering, or control systems as they are variously termed, operate by detecting gaps, differences, *errors* and *deviations*. Systems which look for deviation, error, or difference which are designed to counteract, eliminate, or equalize are traditionally termed *negative feedback systems.*"[5] In a communication system which is working well negative feedback should serve to correct deviations from the norm or disruptive forces which are impairing communicative effectiveness. In contrast a system dominated by positive feedback tends to increase both the frequency of and the magnitude of disruptive communicative behavior.

Boundaries are also important components of human communication systems. Boundaries determine the physical, psychological, social, and even chemical limits beyond which a system cannot operate or beyond which the operation is inefficient or counterproductive. Just as cells have walls, our eyes have physical limits beyond which they cannot see or at least see clearly, and our ears have limits beyond which they cannot assimilate sounds or at least assimilate them in such a way that the receiver perceives the communicator's intended meaning. From the communicator's perspective there are psychological boundaries (intimate distance is proper only for intimate associates) and social boundaries (an individual's attire is often dictated by his role or profession) which are violated only at the cost of great communicative disruption. Similarly, from the receiver's perspective the boundaries of each communication system serve as filters which admit desirable or particularly strong communicative stimuli and exclude others.[6]

Finally, systems operate within or are part of a given set of physical, spatial, or temporal conditions which are called *environments*. To the extent that a given system interacts with its environment it is said to be *open*. Conversely, a system with little interaction with its environment is said to be *closed*. The ultimate state of a closed system is predictable and its ultimate fate is deterioration. The state of an open system at any point in time is less predictable but within the human frame of reference the open system is more apt to survive and prosper. One example of a closed communication system detached from its most relevant environment was the Nixon administration particularly during the Watergate scandal. In contrast President Andrew Jackson emphasized an open communication system—the manure from visiting farmers' boots which was left on White House carpets provided pungent support for this point.[7]

NONVERBAL COMMUNICATION SYSTEMS

We now know that in the aggregate nonverbal communication systems are an extremely important part of interpersonal communication. We know relatively little, however, about the comparative communicative potential of the individual systems and subsystems which compose nonverbal communication. Part of the reason for our lack of knowledge may be the fact that students of nonverbal communication often do not use a common frame of reference and, even when they do, the terminology used to describe nonverbal communication systems and behaviors is frequently so varied that assimilation of current knowledge is difficult. Perhaps most importantly, there is no existing conceptual framework which is really suitable for comparing the communicative potential of the various nonverbal communication systems.

The practical value for the reader in making such an attempt outweighs the difficulties which are inherent in it, however. Table 10-1 has been designed to allow the reader to compare the communicative potential of the nonverbal systems. In studying the operating components of the individual communication systems the reader should recognize that our fund of knowledge is much larger for facial, gestural, and vocalic communication, for example, than it is for tactile, olfactory, or telepathic communication. Therefore, while everything in the table in Table 10-1 is based directly on existing studies or on inferences from existing knowledge, the latter three nonverbal communication systems are necessarily treated more inferentially than the other three.

The value of the table will probably be directly related to the study and thought which the reader gives it. Because of its detailed nature, no attempt will be made to interpret all information contained in the table or even all the judgments made by the author. However, an attempt will be made to describe and illustrate the components of the individual systems which are set out in the table.

The terms *dimensions of meaning, functions, channel, feedback, boundaries,* and *environment* are emphasized because they are essential components of any communication system. The nature of these components varies widely from one nonverbal communication system (and subsystem) to another, however. Furthermore, in some cases the functional capacity of given components can be assessed in such a way that a direct comparison can be made between the same components in different systems—this is particularly true for the system components of channel and feedback.

Illustrating the essential nature of the components of each of the systems which make up nonverbal communication and rating the communicative capacity of the channels and feedback of the respective systems should help put the communicative potential of the nonverbal systems in perspective for the reader.

In Table 10-1 *dimensions of meaning* refers to the numbers and kinds of meaning that are communicated within a given system. For example, by facial expression the communicator can communicate varying degrees of evaluation, interest, control and intensity. By contrast the communicator who uses clothing to modify appearance—one important part of artifactual communication—will communicate varying degrees of fashionability, socialization, and formality.

The term *functions* of communication, while very important, should be self-explanatory. As Ekman has observed, the face (and head) carries primarily information about what affects or emotions are being experienced by the communicator, while body cues communicate information primarily about *level of arousal* or intensity of feeling.[8] In contrast we use the artifactual communication system to communicate our social identity.

Each of the communication systems has its own channel which in turn has at least five attributes. Channels differ with regard to (1) the *speed* with which they can *transmit signals,* (2) the ability of the *channel to separate its own signals* from those of other *channels,* (3) how *accurately meanings* are *communicated* through the channel, (4) the *effectiveness* with which the *channels communicate emotional information,* (5) the *effectiveness* with which the *channel communicates factual information.*

The channel capacities of the nonverbal communication systems (and subsystems) differ substantially with regard to the five important attributes identified above. To attempt to highlight these differences the author has rated channel capacity for each system using a five-point scale where 5 = very good, 4 = good, 3 = average, 2 = poor, and 1 = very poor.[9]

Because of the complex musculature of the face a communicator can and frequently does change from one facial expression or signal to another almost instantaneously (hence the rating of 5 on speed of transmission). The face is also highly visible so that the meaning transmitted facially should not be confused with a meaning communicated by touch, for example (hence the rating of 5 on channel separation). We know from use of the facial meaning sensitivity test that the face is a rather accurate instrument for communicating meanings (hence the rating of 4 on accuracy). The face handles emotional information very effectively (rating of 5) but factual information rather ineffectively (rating of 2).

To fully explore the implications of the rated capacity of the different channels the reader can make many comparisons. He will note for example that the speed with which a communicator may change the meanings communicated by his body odor is very limited (olfactory rating on speed of 1); the channel separation for olfactory messages (rated 4) is very good since the signal is a chemical one and will not be easily confused with body movement, increased distance between communicators, etc. Similarly the reader will note the speed of transmission for telepathic communication is rated a 5 because the receiver picks up the image transmitted by the sender almost instantaneously according to the laboratory research discussed in chapter 8.

TABLE 10-1 Operating Components of Individual Nonverbal Communication Systems (and Subsystems).

COMMUNI-CATION SYSTEM	DIMENSIONS OF MEANING	FUNCTIONS	CHANNEL (CAPACITY)	FEEDBACK (CORRECTIVE POTENTIAL)	BOUNDARIES	TESTS OF COMMUNICATIVE BEHAVIOR WITHIN SYSTEMS
Facial	Evaluation Interest Intensity Control	Displays emotions	Speed=5 Channel Separation=5 Accuracy=4 Emot. Information=5 Fact. Information=2	4.	Physical: flexibility of facial and bodily musculature; acuity of eyesight at different distances, etc.	Facial Meaning Sensitivity Test
Gestural	Activation Evaluation Dynamism Control	Controls Interaction; signals intensity of emotion	Speed=5 Channel Separation=3 Accuracy=4 Emot. Information=4 Fact. Information=3	5.		Leathers Nonverbal Feedback Rating Instrument
Postural	Responsiveness Immediacy Agreement Power or Status	Some control of interaction; signals role expectations	Speed=2 Channel Separation=2 Accuracy=2 Emot. Information=3 Fact. Information=1	3.		
Proxemic (Interpersonal)	Domination Approval Extroversion Self-Confidence	Signals degree of involvement	Speed=3 Channel Separation=2 Accuracy=3 Emot. Information=4 Fact. Information=1	4.	Psychological: intimate, personal, social and public distance; turns, sheaths, personal space, and possession territory	
Proxemic (Urban)		Determines perceptual distance; affects interaction	Speed=1 Channel Separations=5 Accuracy=3 Emot. Information=4 Fact. Information=2		Psychological and Physical: paths, edges, districts, etc.	

TABLE 10-1 Operating Components of Individual Nonverbal Communication Systems (and Subsystems). *(Continued)*

COMMUNI-CATION SYSTEM	DIMENSIONS OF MEANING	FUNCTIONS	CHANNEL (CAPACITY)	FEEDBACK (CORRECTIVE POTENTIAL)	BOUNDARIES	TESTS OF COMMUNICATIVE BEHAVIOR WITHIN SYSTEMS
Artifactual	Body Types: lazy, talkative, warm, mature, self-reliant, suspicious, etc. Clothing: fashionability, socialization, and formality	Shapes reflective image and social identity	Speed=1 Channel Separation=4 Accuracy=4 Emot. Information=4 Fact. Information=3	2.	Social: roles dictate clothing and acceptable types of social interaction	Body Image Test
Vocalic	Aggressiveness Potency Introversion Passionate	Shapes perceived; personality characteristics; signals emotions	Speed=5 Channel Separation=2 Accuracy=3 Emot. Information=4 Fact. Information=1	5.	Physical: producibility and audibility of attributes of sound	Vocalic Meaning Sensitivity Test
Tactile	Mothering Fearful Detached Playful Angry	Warning and alert signals for primitive emotions	Speed=1 Channel Separation=2 Accuracy=3 Emot. Information=4 Fact. Information=1	1.	Physical: must be close enough to touch or be touched	Tactile Communication Index
Olfactory		Modification of reflective image; conveys emotions	Speed=1 Channel Separation=5 Accuracy=3 Emot. Information=4 Fact. Information=1	1.	Chemical: natural and artificial odors are difficult to control and manipulate	Olfactory Meaning Sensitivity Test
Telepathic		Transmission and reception of Imagery	Speed=5 Channel Separation=1 Accuracy=1 Emot. Information=2 Fact. Information=1	Not Known	Extrasensory: energy source for signals is unknown	Telepathic Communication Test

The feedback capacity of the individual systems is also rated in terms of the corrective potential of the feedback within each system. If a communicator is transmitting a confused message, can the receiver most effectively reflect his confusion in the form of a facial expression, a modification of his vocal cues, by touching the communicator, or by using the other nonverbal channels available to him? The type of nonverbal feedback which provides the communicator with the most and most useful information—as to what is wrong with his attempt to communicate—has the greatest corrective potential.

Some types of *nonverbal feedback* clearly have more corrective potential than others. Tactile feedback has limited utility, for example, because interactants are often not close enough to touch each other or may not consider it appropriate or comfortable to do so. Furthermore, the meanings communicated by tactile feedback are not apt to be either very broad in scope or precise in nature (hence, tactile feedback is rated only 1). In contrast a great variety of meanings can be conveyed with considerable precision via facial feedback (hence, the rating of 4).

The *boundaries* of the nonverbal systems differ both in substance and in the type of impact they are apt to have on communicative interaction. Spatial boundaries are primarily psychological. There is no physical barrier preventing us from communicating with a stranger at an intimate distance. The barrier is psychological since we know that at minimum we will make a person very uncomfortable by violating his proxemic expectations. At maximum we may expect a sharp rebuff. In contrast our choice of clothing often has the effect of establishing social barriers. Anyone who has shopped in department stores knows that the difficulty encountered in cashing a check is often directly related to how far out your clothing is.

Perhaps the best way to determine how effectively meanings can be communicated within the various nonverbal systems is to measure that effectiveness. Instruments such as the facial meaning sensitivity test and the body image test are designed for this express purpose. For example, classroom application of the tests described in this book suggests that individuals can communicate and perceive meanings much more accurately by facial than vocal means. By using all of the tests identified in Table 10-1 the reader should have a better idea of his own ability to use a given communication system as well as a much more precise idea of the communicative potential of each of the nonverbal systems.

RELATIONSHIPS BETWEEN THE NONVERBAL AND VERBAL COMMUNICATION SYSTEMS

As stated previously in this chapter, the nonverbal communication systems may function at least in the short term as independent systems; the last section of this chapter is designed to contrast the communicative potential of these systems when functioning independently. More often nonverbal communication systems interact with each other and/or with the verbal communication system in one of two ways—congruently or incongruently. Whether the systems interact in a congruent or incongruent manner, the interrelationships are typically very complex.

NONVERBAL AND VERBAL COMMUNICATION SYSTEMS IN THE CONGRUENT STATE When the nonverbal and verbal communication systems are communicating essentially the same meaning, we can say the systems are in a congruent state. Figure 10-1 is designed to illustrate how the systems may interact in a congruent state. The dark gray color in the middle of the diagram suggests the systems are interacting congruently. If the color were light gray it would suggest that the nonverbal systems were communicating meanings that conflicted either with each other or with the meanings being communicated verbally. The fact that each system is colored one-third light gray in the diagram suggests that the potential for incongruent interaction between and among the systems is considerable.

Our need to know how communication systems interact in the congruent state is great. Our current understanding of such relationships is limited.

Duncan puts the problem in perspective when he concludes that our knowledge of how the nonverbal systems of communication interact with the verbal is very modest. Indeed "at this stage of our understanding of face-to-face interaction . . . it is not known a priori which behaviors in the stream of communication are the important cues for any given communication function."[10] Significantly in his study of the mechanism of turn taking in conversations Duncan found that "the cues comprising this signal were found in every communication modality examined: content, syntax, intonation, paralanguage, and body motion."[11]

While our current knowledge of the relationships between verbal and nonverbal communication is limited, the need to know is apparent. Scheflen has been among the pioneers in recognizing the need for a comprehensive communication theory and in recognizing that "such a comprehensive theory will have to deal with face-to-face communication, with some model of multichanneled behavioral coding."[12]

In this brief section it would be presumptuous to try and give a definitive or detailed description of the essential nature of verbal communication. Certainly we recognize that verbal communication has its syntactic, semantic, and pragmatic dimensions that are affected by a great variety of variables. We recognize that meaning in verbal communication is strongly associated with such structural units as the paragraph, sentence, word, and phrase. We also recognize that verbal communication in the form of speech is used to inform, persuade, and often control others as well as enhance one's own image and to shape interaction with others. The structural and content factors which determine one's success in using speech to achieve these objectives (and not so incidentally determine the quality of verbal communication) are numerous and would require another volume to treat.

Here the emphasis is on *relationships* between verbal and nonverbal communication. Verbal communication depends on nonverbal in many ways:

1. Each interactor must signal continuously his attentiveness and responsiveness to others;
2. There must be continuous regulation of speaking and listening;

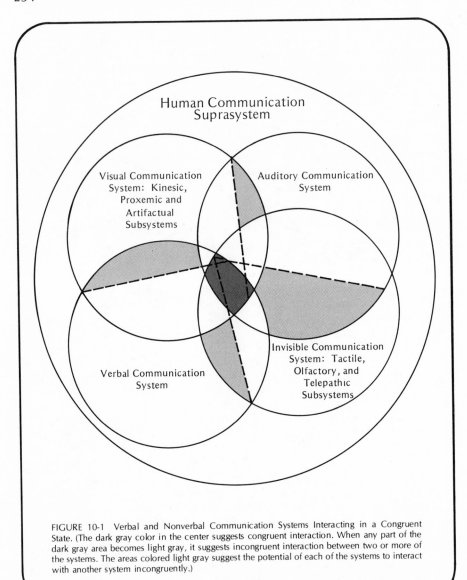

FIGURE 10-1 Verbal and Nonverbal Communication Systems Interacting in a Congruent State. (The dark gray color in the center suggests congruent interaction. When any part of the dark gray area becomes light gray, it suggests incongruent interaction between two or more of the systems. The areas colored light gray suggest the potential of each of the systems to interact with another system incongruently.)

3. Interactors must signal their attitudes and intentions toward others;
4. Gestures accompany speech to illustrate it in various ways;
5. Speakers need continuous feedback about how their utterances are being received.[13]

When the meanings communicated verbally and nonverbally are congruent there can be little doubt that speech and body movements are related to each other in very definite patterns. In his superb essay, "Some Relationships Between Body Motion and Speech," Kendon concludes that each unit of speech (such as a sentence) seems to have its equivalent in body motion; the larger the speech unit the more body parts involved; prior to each speech unit there is a change in position of one or more body parts; the larger the speech unit the earlier and more extensive the preparatory movements.[14]

Dittmann and Llewellyn have established that there is a highly significant relationship between speech rhythm and body movement. The reader might think of this relationship as one of which the communicator is not likely to be conscious. For the most part this is probably true; in many cases the movement seems to be an habitual and unthinking accompaniment of speech—as when one looks at someone as he finishes talking. On the other hand, communicators often take advantage of pauses in the speech stream to introduce movements which have additional meanings. Thus "if a person wishes to convey the idea that what he is expressing is important or difficult to conceptualize or exciting, he will introduce movements along with his speech to get this extra information across. The timing of these movements will tend to follow the pattern of timing he is familiar with, that is, early in encoding units or following hesitations in speech."[15]

Clearly we have no adequate theory to explain the relationships between verbal and nonverbal communication at this point. Much more work must be done to subject propositions which would make up such a theory to empirical test. However, previous research and the author's own work suggest that a compensatory or balance theory has the most promise for explaining such relationships.

Originally the compensation theory was applied only to the interaction of nonverbal systems. Argyle and Dean helped pioneer his theory. They write that:

> nonverbal "intimacy" between interacting persons is a function of interpersonal distance, eye contact, body orientation, smiling, and other related variables. Because intimacy is multi-determined, any one or more of these behaviors can be altered to effect a change in total intimacy. Typically, once a comfortable level of intimacy has been reached, any change in one of the components requires a reciprocal change in another to maintain equilibrium.[16]

Patterson finds striking support for this theory in his thorough review of research on nonverbal immediacy behaviors. He observes that reviewed studies generally support a "compensatory relationship between various immediacy behaviors. . . . The clearest support for compensation appears to be in the relationships between eye contact and distance and between distance and orientation. In these cases the closer approaches typically result in less directly confronting orientations and decreases in the level of eye contact."[17]

In effect this amounts to a balance theory of human communication. It suggests that a number of communication systems are capable of transmitting meaning and when one is not working effectively another takes over or compensates for the deficiency of the other system(s). The theory seems to apply with particular force to the relationships between verbal and nonverbal communication. Individuals with very little facial expression often seem to use emotive language while people with a great deal of facial expression may speak in a near monotone. Significantly, when people use great variation in both facial expression and the emotional content of their verbal message they are often perceived as overdoing it—their communication systems are out of balance. Generally, however, the nonverbal and verbal communication systems seem to interact in a homeostatic fashion. The man who speaks very fluently often uses very few gestures while the nonfluent individual may use many gestures. How often have you found yourself in a situation where you were speaking fluently and using few gestures only to find yourself beginning to pause and grope for words? If you are honest, you will probably also recall that at such moments of crisis you may have leaned forward (proxemic channel), touched the person with whom you were attempting to communicate (tactile channel), and begun gesturing (kinesic channel) in a very explicit way in order to regain your communicative effectiveness. When in need, the other communication systems often seem to become more dominant in a compensatory way that results in a balanced communicative effort.

Specific studies which would test such a tentative theory are still limited in number. However, a number of experiments have been conducted very recently which focus explicitly on the interrelationships between the verbal and nonverbal communication systems. The relationships identified below have been confirmed by empirical test and are particularly relevant to the discussion above:

1. The most accurate communication occurs when both verbal and nonverbal symbols are consistent.[18]
2. The visual communication system conveys substantially more affective information but less overall information—less factual information, and less information about personal traits other than emotional or interpersonal ones—than verbal or vocal communication.[19]
3. When different communication systems interact in the congruent state, nonverbal communication systems represent the dominant source of meaning.[20]
4. The facial-vocal combination of conveying emotional messages is more accurate than the vocal, gestural, or gestural-vocal modes.[21]
5. The nonverbal systems of communication seem to be far more effective than the verbal in building empathy, respect, and a sense that the communicator is genuine.
6. When communication cues are transmitted simultaneously the different channels acting together have a compensatory and additive effect.[22]

The hypotheses above hint at the complexity of interaction between the verbal and nonverbal communication systems. Birdwhistell explicitly emphasizes this complexity and affirms the interlocking nature of the systems when he writes that communication units are

> always multi-functional; they have distinguishable contrast meaning on one level and a cross-referencing function (meaning) on others. . . . The exciting thing about such an assembled, multilevel description of the communicational process is that it becomes immediately clear that it is just as easy (and unrewarding) to describe the lexical material as modifiers of the remainder of the behavior as it is to define the remainder of the communicational behavior as modifying the lexical.[23]

NONVERBAL AND VERBAL COMMUNICATION SYSTEMS IN THE INCONGRUENT STATE   When communication systems are functioning in the congruent state (communicating essentially the same or supplemental meanings), communication is apt to be of high quality. It is when the systems begin to function incongruently that trouble begins. Communication systems in incongruent states are grist for the analyst's mill. Few phenomena have greater diagnostic significance for the communication consultant than verbal and nonverbal communication systems functioning in an incongruent state.

Double-bind Communication.   The study of incongruent communication is based to a large extent on the double-bind theory of interpersonal communication. Not surprisingly, this theory evolved from a study of schizophrenic patients. Frequently, such patients communicate incongruent messages. Indeed "where double-binding has become the predominant pattern of communication, and where the diagnostic attention is limited to the *overtly* most disturbed individual, the behavior of this individual will be found to satisfy the diagnostic criteria of schizophrenia."[24]

A double bind is a situation where (1) two or more ego-involved individuals are attempting to communicate on matters of substantial physical or psychological value for them (parent-child, husband-wife interactions are examples); (2) a message is transmitted which (a) asserts something, (b) asserts something about its own assertion, and (c) these two assertions are mutually exclusive (the meaning of the messages appears to be undecidable in the traditional sense); (3) the recipient is often so tied to his own frame of reference that he is unwilling to seek or incapable of obtaining clarification as to the *intended meaning of the message*. Therefore, even though the message may be mildly contradictory at best or logically meaningless at worst, it is communicational reality. The communicator

> cannot *not* react to it, but neither can he react to it appropriately (non-paradoxically), for the message itself is paradoxical. This situation is frequently compounded by the more or less overt prohibition to show any awareness of the contradiction or the real issue involved. A person in a double bind situation is likely to find himself punished (or at least made to feel guilty) for correct perceptions, and defined as "bad" or "mad" for even insinuating that there be a discrepancy between what he does see and what he "should" see.[25]

Like the author, every reader has probably encountered a situation in which he or she would be considered to be in a bit of a "bind." I vividly recall a situation when a girl I had been dating called me and asked me to deny a rumor she had picked up which made her furious. She had heard that I was throwing a Halloween party to be attended by fellow graduate students and faculty members in my department, *and* that the hostess was going to be a girl other than herself. I could tell immediately from the piercing and strident nature of her vocal cues that I was in a bit of a bind, but I was not in a double bind. I had never transmitted a message to her which included mutually exclusive assertions (you are number one in my heart, but number two on my dating and hostess list). Being in a bind, as above, is uncomfortable. Being in a double bind, as we shall see, can be excruciatingly painful.

The nonverbal subsystems of communication are probably the most frequent and troublesome source of double binding. When the meanings conveyed by these subsystems are incongruent with each other or the verbal system, the individual communicator is faced with a very real problem. Undeniably, double binding occurs frequently in interpersonal communication.

Mehrabian is perhaps the foremost student of incongruent communication. He recognizes that "the basic issue behind the study of multichannel communications is the meaning or functions of inconsistent versus consistent (redundant) messages."[26] The meaning or functions of congruent, and thus redundant interaction of the communication systems was covered in the previous section. This section examines the functions and effects of the systems interacting incongruently.

For our purposes communication is defined as incongruent if the meaning transmitted through one channel is inconsistent with the meaning transmitted through one or more of the other channels. Mehrabian distinguishes between two types of inconsistent or incongruent communication—*positive and negative inconsistency*. A communication is positively inconsistent when the nonverbal channels carry meanings with a positive connotation (a girl smiles at her lover or coos at him) while the verbal channel carries a negative connotation ("I don't like you very much"); a communication is negatively inconsistent when the meanings conveyed nonverbally have a negative connotation (irritated facial expression) while the verbal channel carries a positive connotation ("Oh that's beautiful! Just great!").[27]

Mehrabian has conducted a series of studies which feature inconsistent positive communications (the vocal component indicated a positive and the verbal component a negative attitude) and inconsistent negative communications (a negative vocal and a positive verbal component). While Mehrabian's experiments are often rather complex and difficult to interpret, they provide very valuable insights as to the impact of incongruent messages on the processes which make up interpersonal communication. In particular the following conclusions seem to have particular diagnostic value for the communication analyst: (1) When there is inconsistency in meaning associated with the systems and subsystems which comprise the suprasystem of interpersonal communication, the communicator typically relies on the nonverbal systems rather than the verbal for the source of meaning. (2) Congruent communication is preferred over incongruent, and negatively inconsistent messages are preferred over positively inconsistent ones. (3) The facial subsystem of nonverbal communication is the most important source of meaning.[28] In fact "inconsistent communications of attitude frequently relied on facial expressions. For instance, when some subjects were instructed to say something negative with positive vocal expression, they actually spoke with a neutral vocal expression but assumed a positive facial expression, so that audio recordings of their statements did not reflect substantial inconsistency."[29] (4) Communicators found incongruent messages more offensive in formal than informal settings. (5) The verbal portion of inconsistent messages conveyed attitudes toward the actions of the addressees, whereas the nonverbal portion conveyed attitudes toward the addressee himself.[30]

THE IMPACT OF INCONGRUENT MESSAGES ON VERBAL AND NONVERBAL SYSTEMS   Instructive as many of the experiments on incongruent communication may be, they typically have not focused on communicative interaction. Recently, the author undertook a study with this specific focus. Twenty problem-solving groups were formed. Half the groups were exposed to messages where the verbal and nonverbal meanings conveyed were congruent with each other while half were exposed to messages where the same meanings were incongruent.

Drawing on his own research and experience in teaching courses in discussion and small group communication, the author devised eight messages which were negatively incongruent. These eight messages were chosen because review of videotapes of previous discussion groups suggested that these particular messages occurred frequently and were realistic. Two carefully trained "plants" introduced the eight incongruent messages into discussion groups at planned intervals. The eight incongruent messages are listed below.

MESSAGE NO.	VERBAL CHANNEL (MEANING)	VISUAL CHANNEL (MEANING)
1	"That's good. Really good."	Disgust
2	"I realize that."	Surprise
3	"You know, that thought is fascinating. Just fascinating."	Disinterest
4	"Yes, that seems entirely clear to me."	Confusion
5	"That was a very perceptive statement."	Condescension
6	"That's been my view all along."	Disappointment
7	"I have no fixed views on that. Whatever you say is all right with me."	Stubbornness
8	"I'm relieved to see that the group is reaching consensus on the question."	Anxiety

Let us assume that the reader is in one of the ten groups receiving the incongruent messages. The reader has just made a statement. At this point another discussant (in reality a plant) turns to the reader and says, "That's good. Really good," while getting a very disgusted look on his face. How would you be apt to respond to this incongruent message?

The results in Table 10-2 indicate the average response of discussants who responded to the incongruent messages, and the table contrasts their responses with those of discussants in the other groups who responded to the same lines but without the conflicting facial expressions—the messages were congruent in those groups.[31]

The impact of the incongruent messages was measured by applying the Leathers feedback rating instrument to the verbal part of the feedback response and the Leathers nonverbal feedback rating instrument to the nonverbal part. To understand the results the reader should study the terms which make up the scale for each instrument.[32]

The reader can easily understand and interpret the results in Table 10-2 if he keeps the following facts in mind: a minus figure means that the feedback to the incongruent messages was rated on the right-hand side of the scales and reflects the communication quality listed on that side of the scale; a plus figure means feedback was rated on the left-hand side of the scale. For example, the reader should look at how nonverbal feedback was rated for message 2 on scale 1.

The mean rating (mean difference) of −4.6 means that feedback to incongruent message 2 ("I realize that" accompanied by a facial expression of surprise) was rated on the average 4.6 points closer to the uncertain end of scale 1 than feedback to the same line when the facial expression was congruent.[33] Similarly, nonverbal feedback to message 2 was rated much more hostile (scale 4) and confused (scale 7) but also more involved, attentive, responsive, and interested—see the plus figures in the table.

The same principle should be applied in reading the other results in Table 10-2.

TABLE 10-2 Nonverbal Feedback: Mean Differences in Rated Feedback to Congruent vs. Incongruent Messages.

MESSAGE	FEEDBACK DIMENSION (SCALE)									
	Confident	Involved	Attentive	Pleasing	Deliberative	Responsive	Clear	Friendly	Analytical	Interest
1	-4.6		+3.5						+2.4	+3.1
2	-4.4	+3.8	+4.9	-2.8	+2.9	+3.1	-4.3			+3.7
3							-4.9	-2.4		+2.8
4		+2.8	+4.6		-2.5					+4.4
5	-3.2					-2.1	-5.2	-2.0		
6	-4.6		+2.8				-3.5			+2.7
7	-3.8						-4.5			
8	-5.5	-3.3		-3.8		-2.6	-4.7	-2.9		

Verbal Feedback: Mean Differences in Rated Feedback to Congruent vs. Incongruent Messages.

MESSAGE NO.	FEEDBACK DIMENSION (SCALE)								
	Deliberateness	Relevancy	Atomization	Fidelity	Tension	Ideation	Flexibility	Digression	Involvement
1				-3.9	-2.9	-2.3		-2.9	
2	+2.5			-4.1	-4.1	-3.6		+4.9	-3.4
3			-3.6	-4.1	-3.1	-2.5		+3.4	-3.9
4				-5.3	-2.2				
5		-2.9							
6								-3.0	
7		-2.8	+3.9			-3.6		+4.6	-5.1
8	-2.1	-2.6	-4.7					-4.0	

The reader should note that the figures in Table 10-2 represent mean differences in the rating of feedback responses to incongruent messages. Thus, we note that discussants who were responding to message 2 exhibited much less confidence (uncertainty), were much less pleased, and were much less clear (confused) in their response. At the same time, however, their nonverbal feedback also suggested that they were more involved, attentive, responsive, and interest(ed). By using this example the reader should have no difficulty in reading and interpreting the other results reported in the table.

240

As a rule of thumb, the reader should consider any mean difference of over 2.0 to be highly significant.

This is probably the first time that a direct comparison has been made of the effects on verbal *and* nonverbal feedback of multichannel messages which are incongruent. The results are subject to many interesting interpretations. However, the following conclusions seem to be both warranted and useful.

By studying Table 10-2 the reader can see that the impact of incongruent messages on subsequent nonverbal feedback is complex. Part of the impact is strikingly negative. For example, not only does the nonverbal feedback of the discussants become much more *uncertain* and *confused,* but the degree of increase in uncertainty is really almost startling as the reader can see. In addition the feedback to messages 3, 5, and 8 is decidedly more *hostile.* The impact of the incongruent messages was not entirely negative, however. The nonverbal feedback response reflected greater *attentiveness* and *interest* on the part of the responding discussant with greater *involvement* when the response was to messages 2 and 4.

To fully appreciate the disruptive impact of incongruent messages on nonverbal feedback the reader would have to view the videotapes which were made of this experiment. The next best option is to study still photos which were made from the videotape monitor. While the quality of these photos is necessarily lower than desired, the rather striking spontaneous reactions of live subjects is worth the closer scrutiny these photos require.

In Figure 10-2 (photo 1) the girl on the right, who is a plant trained by the author, has just introduced message 3 (by saying, "You know, that thought is fascinating. Just fascinating" while showing disinterest by turning away from the girl on the left in the picture).

Figure 10-2 (photo 2) captures the nonverbal feedback response of the girl seated to the plant's right. A close examination of the eyes and mouth of the girl on the left suggests more than a little *hostility.*

In the sequence of photos in Figure 10-2 (photos 3-6) the plant begins by introducing message 5 (she has just said, "That was a very perceptive statement" to the male in the white shirt and she is completing a facial expression designed to convey condescension—note the angle of her face as she looks down her nose at the subject in the white shirt). In photo 3 the respondent's eyes are downcast and almost closed as he seems to be slightly unresponsive. In photo 4 the respondent is studying the face of the plant as if he is confused. Photo 5 is a bit more ambiguous but may suggest some displeasure. Finally, photo 6 rather clearly seems to suggest that the respondent is uncertain. Interestingly, a check of the results for nonverbal feedback shows that the nonverbal feedback to message 5 was characteristically rated uncertain, unresponsive, confused, and hostile. Photos 3-6 in Figure 10-2 represent a sequence with the entire feedback response lasting a matter of seconds.

The verbal portion of the feedback response to the incongruent messages in the experiment was also complex. On the negative side we see that the verbal feedback to incongruent messages was characteristically much more *confused, tense, personal* (the person conveying the incongruent message was directly criticized), *withdrawn,* and *irrelevant.* The incongruent messages had few beneficial effects on the verbal feedback. Interestingly, the verbal feedback to incongruent messages 3, 4, and 7 was more *concise* but the feedback to messages 2, 6, and 8 was more *digressive.* How can this seemingly contradictory finding be explained? Not easily. However, previous laboratory experiments by the author confirm the conclusion that feedback becomes much

1

2

3

FIGURE 10-2

4

5

6

FIGURE 10-2 *Continued*.

more concise in the face of negative reinforcement. Since the incongruent messages did provide a type of negative reinforcement, one would expect the feedback to be more concise. On the other hand discussants find it very difficult to respond logically to the incongruent messages. They may have concluded, therefore, that when in doubt as to the proper type of response the safest thing to do is digress.

Both the nonverbal and verbal portion of the response reflected confusion and a seemingly closely related quality, uncertainty, in the nonverbal feedback. In addition nonverbal hostility and verbal personal attack were also dominant in the feedback responses to incongruent messages. While somewhat different, both of these feedback qualities reflect something of the visceral tone of the feedback response.

The nonverbal and verbal feedback also reflected some very different qualities. While the nonverbal feedback revealed consistent and significant increases in attentiveness and interest, the verbal feedback reflected a significant increase in withdrawal. How can this be? Answers are not easy to find since we have virtually no previous data or precedents to use in making a comparison of the dominant qualities in feedback responses to multichannel messages. However, we may infer that the discussants became more attentive and interested nonverbally because they felt such increased concentration might reveal additional cues which would allow them to decode the incongruent messages to their satisfaction—the reader will remember that this is one way of responding to double-bind communication. The verbal feedback may have reflected withdrawal, or an attempt to change the subject either because the discussant was stalling for time or because he felt he would be unsuccessful in determining the meaning of such messages. The fact that the verbal feedback also exhibited a good deal of irrelevance is consistent with the notion the discussants find it difficult, if not unpalatable, to come directly to grips with the subject at hand in the face of incongruent messages.

In broadest perspective the reader can see that incongruent messages have an extremely disruptive impact on interpersonal communication when measured either in terms of the number of negative qualities reflected in the feedback or the *degree of shift* toward such seemingly undesirable communication qualities as uncertainty or confusion. A reader who encountered a communicator who was *uncertain, confused, hostile, tense, personal* (abusive), and *disgressive* would undoubtedly think that this was a caricature of the ineffectual communicator. Interestingly, such communication qualities are not the work of the cartoonist or the comedian. They are the qualities which have been demonstrated by empirical study to be strongly associated with incongruent communication.

Incongruent messages can have great diagnostic significance in the study of interpersonal communication. We now know that such messages not only produce highly disruptive communication but that the degree of disruption which results is often extreme. On a theoretical level Watzlawick, Beavin, and Jackson have predicted that individuals will react to double binding or incongruent messages in one of three ways. Each reaction in itself is disruptive and provides a good basis for predicting what type of communication is apt to follow the incongruent messages: (1) "Faced with the untenable absurdity of his situation, a person is likely to conclude that he must be overlooking vital clues either inherent in the situation or offered him by significant others." (2) "On the other hand he may choose what recruits quickly find to be the best possible reaction to the bewildering logic, or lack of it, in army life: to comply with any and all injunctions with complete literalness and to abstain overtly from any independent thinking. Thus rather than engaging in an interminable search for hidden meanings, he will discard a priori the possibility that there is any other than the most literal, superficial aspect to human relationships or, furthermore, that one message should have any more meaning than another." (3) "The third possible reaction would be to withdraw from human involvement. This can be achieved by physically isolating oneself as much as possible and, moreover, by blocking input channels of communication where isolation alone is not possible to the desired extent."[34]

Deception and Leakage Cues in Incongruent Communication.   There are of course many kinds of incongruent communication. The type with the most practical implications for the professional and personal life of the reader, however, is deception. Deceptive communication comes both in intentional and unintentional forms. In layman's language intentional deception often takes the form of lying.

The best way to protect oneself against deceptive communication is to increase one's sensitivity to the subtle cues which are part of multichannel communication. We have a good deal of conscious control over the meanings we communicate verbally or facially but much less over our use of gestures or what have been identified in this chapter as psychophysiological responses (blushing, sighing, etc.).

The communicative cues over which we have little control provide the receiver with the most information as to our true intentions. Most often these cues are nonverbal and when such cues reveal information about a communicator which he is trying to conceal they are called "leakage" cues. Our best protection against deceptive communication is our ability to read leakage cues accurately.

Conversely, our effectiveness as a communicator is directly related to our ability to communicate in a congruent way while controlling leakage cues if we really do have anything to hide. Certainly the image we project—which is so closely related to how competent, trustworthy, and honest we are perceived to be by others—is controlled to a large extent by our ability to communicate congruently.

Many observers believe that John Kennedy won the Kennedy-Nixon debates because he projected a more positive image. Often they cannot pinpoint what factors shaped that image, however. Those factors are undoubtedly multiple and complex. Existing theory and research would suggest one very important factor, however: John Kennedy's image was perceived to be much more positive than Richard Nixon's image in large part because Kennedy's multichannel communication was more congruent.

This conclusion can be concretely illustrated. When Nixon asserted in the debates that he was absolutely confident of the correctness of his position on foreign policy (while beads of perspiration were clearly visible on his upper lip) what conclusion would you draw? Similarly, when Nixon contrasted his alleged ability to be cool and poised in moments of extreme crisis with Kennedy's youthful impulsiveness (as Nixon became increasingly nonfluent during the tension of the debate) what conclusion would you draw?

Communication which is incongruent is often a very subtle thing. Only trained and sensitive observers are able to detect a slight change in the facial expression or gesture, for example, which conveys a meaning inconsistent with the manifest verbal content. Telltale cues are not easy to detect but they are perceptible. These cues are perceptible because a given communicator, much like Nixon in the Kennedy-Nixon debates, is subconsciously allowing "nonverbal leakage" to become part of his message. Often the communicator is attempting to deceive the communicatee in some way in order to project an image which is inconsistent with the facts. For example:

Most deceptive situations not only dictate the need to conceal one item of information but also require the substitution of a false message. It is not sufficient, for example, for the job applicant to inhibit signs of nervousness or inexperience, or for the hospitalized depressive patient to inhibit signs of melancholia; the goal of the deception requires that to gain employment the applicant simulate cool confidence, that to gain release from the hospital the patient simulate feelings of optimism, well-being and insight. The extent of simulating is thus related to how extensive the lie may be. . . . [35]

Double binding is hardly limited to the image-molding efforts of politicians or the attempts of an accused felon to lie convincingly before a jury. The most basic institution in our society is the scene of much double-binding and, as our divorce rates suggest, the nonverbal cues of the interactants in the family scene often reveal hidden information about the parties that is unpalatable to one or both of the interactants. Even that hallowed model of truthfulness and high moral principle, the university professor, has been known to communicate incongruently in such a way that he is assured of success in the current experiment he is conducting.

In their suggestively titled article, "The Paralanguage of Experimenter Bias," Duncan, Rosenberg, and Finkelstein make clear that vocal cues which contradict the verbal meaning an experimenter is transmitting to subjects can function as an effective channel for transmitting bias. In fact "in experimental situations where face-to-face interaction between experimenter and subject is deemed necessary or desirable, it now appears important for the careful researcher to evaluate the experimenter's messages to the subject for nonverbal directional cues."[36]

Ironically, the communication systems with the greatest sending capacity seem to be the poorest source of leakage cues. For example, facial communication is potentially more effective than any other type of nonverbal communication, but facial expression is also easiest for the lying communicator to control in such a way that his facial expression is congruent with, and thus reinforces, the lies which are part of a communicator's verbal messages.

It is important to note that "the face is the best sender, the feet/legs the worst."[37] Indeed "the face has the shortest potential transmission time; . . . The facial musculature allows for a great number of discriminable stimuli patterns, far more than are provided by legs/feet. The face has the greatest visibility."[38] Significantly, "the availability of leakage and deception clues reverses the pattern described for differences in sending capacity, internal feedback, and external feedback. The worst sender, the legs/feet, is also the least responded to and the least within ego's awareness, and thus a good source for leakage and deception clues."[39]

CONCLUSION

This chapter examines the communicative capacity of the individual nonverbal communication systems when they are operating as independent systems, when they are interacting with each other, and when they are interacting with the verbal communication system. Particular emphasis is given to the primary components of communication systems: dimensions of meaning, functions of the system, channels, feedback, boundaries, and environments.

The operating components and functional capacity of each communication system are very important. The reader should pay particular attention to the channel capacity and the corrective potential of the feedback associated with each system. Channel capacity is determined by rating speed of transmission, ability of a channel to separate its own signals from those of other channels, accuracy of communication, and the effectiveness with which a channel communicates emotional and factual information. Similarly, the feedback capacity of each system is rated in terms of the corrective potential of the feedback.

This chapter examines the interaction between and among the nonverbal and verbal communication systems in detail. When such interaction is congruent, the individual systems seem to function in a compensatory manner. If one system is not working effectively, another one often takes over or supplements the other system in such a way that it compensates for the deficiency of the other system.

The double-bind theory of communication provides the best current explanation of incongruent interaction between the nonverbal and verbal communication systems. Often the meaning communicated by one system is inconsistent with the meaning communicated by another system. The incongruent messages which result have a highly disruptive impact on subsequent communicative interaction. Nonverbal feedback to incongruent messages characteristically becomes more uncertain, confused, and hostile while also reflecting increased attentiveness, interest, and involvement on the part of the discussants. By comparison, verbal feedback to incongruent messages is typically confused, tense, withdrawn, and irrelevant.

Individuals frequently communicate incongruently. When they do so, they may be lying. The best protection against lying and other forms of deceptive communication is to increase one's sensitivity to the subtle cues which are part of multichannel communication. With sufficient sensitivity one is able to detect the subtle cues to a communicator's true intentions which are often perceptible in the form of nonverbal leakage (nonverbal cues which the communicator tries unsuccessfully to suppress). To detect such nonverbal leakage we should concentrate on those parts of the body which are rarely under the conscious control of the communicator.

NOTES

[1] C. E. Osgood, "Dimensionality of the Semantic Space for Communication via Facial Expressions," *Scandinavian Journal of Psychology,* 7 (1966), 1-30.

[2] A. T. Dittmann, *Interpersonal Messages of Emotion* (New York: Springer, 1972), p. 121.

[3] Ibid., p. 115.

[4] Ibid., pp. 120-133.

[5] B. D. Ruben, "General System Theory: An Approach to Human Communication," in R. W. Budd and B. D. Ruben, *Approaches to Human Communication* (New York: Spartan Books, 1972), p. 132.

[6] Ibid., pp. 125-26.

[7] Ibid., p. 129.

[8] P. Ekman, "Differential Communication of Affect by Head and Body Cues," *Journal of Personality and Social Psychology*, 2 (1965), 726.

[9] While these ratings have been calculated with considerable care, they are not intended as absolute or final judgments. Some of the evidence used to make the ratings is not entirely consistent, and a rater's conceptual perspective may also be a biasing factor.

[10] S. Duncan, "Some Signals and Rules for Taking Turns in Conversations," *Journal of Personality and Social Psychology*, 23 (1972), 291.

[11] Ibid.

[12] A. E. Scheflen, "Human Communication: Behavioral Programs and Their Integration in Interaction," *Behavioral Science*, 13 (1968), 52.

[13] M. Argyle, *Social Interaction* (Chicago: Aldine, 1969), p. 119.

[14] A. Kendon, "Some Relationships Between Body Motion and Speech: An Analysis of an Example," in *Studies in Dyadic Communication*, ed. A. W. Siegman and B. Pope (New York: Pergamon, 1972), pp. 204-5.

[15] A. T. Dittmann and L. G. Llewellyn, "Body Movement and Speech Rhythm in Social Conversation," *Journal of Personality and Social Psychology*, 11 (1969), 104.

[16] M. Argyle and J. Dean, "Eye Contact, Distance, and Affiliation," *Sociometry*, 28 (1965), 288.

[17] M. L. Patterson, "Compensation in Nonverbal Immediacy Behaviors: A Review," *Sociometry*, 36 (1973), 245.

[18] E. K. Fujimoto, "The Comparative Communicative Power of Verbal and Nonverbal Symbols," *Dissertation Abstracts International*, 32 (Ohio State University, 1972), 7A.

[19] J. E. Gartner, "A Study of Verbal, Vocal and Visual Communication," *Dissertation Abstracts International*, 33 (Columbia University, 1972), 5B.

[20] A. Mehrabian, *Nonverbal Communication* (Chicago: Aldine-Atherton, 1972), p. 182.

[21] C. A. Deets, "Nonverbal Communication of Emotions," *Dissertation Abstracts International*, 32 (Indiana University, 1972), 11A.

[22] D. T. Tepper, "The Communication of Counselor Empathy, Respect, and Genuineness Through Verbal and Nonverbal Channels," *Dissertation Abstracts International*, 33 (University of Massachusetts, 1973), 9A.

[23] R. L. Birdwhistell, *Kinesics and Context* (Philadelphia: University of Pennsylvania Press, 1970), p. 88.

[24] P. Watzlawick, J. H. Beavin, and D. D. Jackson, *Pragmatics of Human Communication* (New York: W. W. Norton, 1967), pp. 214-15.

[25] Ibid., pp. 212-13.

[26] Mehrabian, *Nonverbal Communication*, p. 104.

[27] Ibid., p. 110.

[28] Ibid., p. 121.

[29] Ibid.

[30] Ibid., p. 131.

[31] Dale G. Leathers, "Meta-Incongruent Communication in the Small Group," an experiment in the UCLA series, winter 1972.

[32] The Leathers feedback rating instrument is designed to measure the impact of messages on the verbal portion of the feedback response. The nine scales of the LFRI are listed below with the positive quality for each scale on the left side within the parentheses and the negative quality on the right side: (1) deliberateness (symbol/signal), (2) relevancy (relevant/irrelevant), (3) atomization (unified/atomized), (4) fidelity (clear/confused), (5) tension (relaxed/tense), (6) ideation (ideational/personal), (7) flexibility (flexible/inflexible), (8) digression (concise/digressive), (9) involvement (involved/withdrawn). Most of the feedback qualities are self-explanatory with the possible exceptions of signal and atomized. Signal feedback is immediate, unthinking, and visceral while atomized feedback features disjointed expressions, thought fragments, and a number of people talking at the same time. The Leathers nonverbal feedback rating instrument is described in chapter 9.

[33] Since two judges applied the LFRI and the LNFRI the mean scores in Table 10-2 should be divided by two to convert to numbers which are within the seven-point range of the feedback scales.

[34] Watzlawick, Beavin, and Jackson, *Pragmatics of Human Communication,* pp. 217-18.

[35] P. Ekman and W. V. Friesen, "Nonverbal Leakage and Clues to Deception," *Psychiatry,* 32 (1969), 90.

[36] S. D. Duncan, M. J. Rosenberg, and J. Finkelstein, "The Paralanguage of Experimenter Bias," *Sociometry,* 32 (1969), 217.

[37] Ekman and Friesen, "Nonverbal Leakage and Clues to Deception," 93.

[38] Ibid., 93-94.

[39] Ibid., 99.

APPENDIX A

THE KINESIC COMMUNICATION SYSTEM

To fully understand the connotative approach to communication by movement, the reader must be familiar with a rather complex conceptual model developed by Osgood.[1] This conceptual model is grounded in the theory that human beings communicate within a "semantic space." Semantic space is defined as:

> a region of some unknown dimensionality and Euclidian in character. Each semantic scale, defined by a pair of polar (opposite-in-meaning) adjectives, is assumed to represent a straight line function that passes through the origin of this space and a sample of such scales then represents a multidimensional space. The larger or more representative the sample, the better defined is the space as a whole. . . . To define the semantic space with a maximum efficiency we would need to determine that minimum number of orthogonal *dimensions* or axes (again assuming the space to be Euclidian) which exhausts the dimensionality of the space.[2]

Since semantic space is a three-dimensional concept, it is not easy to illustrate. Let us start with the assumption that the meaning of any person (or concept) at any point in time can be determined by rating the person on three seven-point scales (−3 represents the term on the left-hand side of the scale and +3 the term on the right-hand side). These three scales represent the three major dimensions of meaning which Osgood et al. have found to pass through and comprise semantic space—respectively, these scales represent the dimensions of meaning which are labeled evaluation, potency, and activity. The three scales are good/bad, strong/weak, and active/passive. Using these three scales you are asked to determine the connotative meaning of (1) Richard Nixon (as perceived after Watergate), (2) Joe Namath, and (3) Billy Graham.

Figure A-1 represents the three-dimensional semantic space that is necessary to define what a given individual or concept means to a given person. The separate dots for Nixon, Namath, and Graham specify rather precisely what each man "means." Osgood identifies and emphasizes the real importance of those dots or points in semantic space. They represent "the point in space which serves us as an operational definition of meaning (and) has two essential properties . . . . We may identify these properties with the *quality* and *intensity* of meaning, respectively."[3]

Note, for example, the dot in semantic space which defines the meaning of Richard Nixon. The dot specifies not only whether he is seen as weak or strong (quality of meaning), but how weak or strong (intensity of meaning) he is seen to be. Nixon's meaning is defined by showing the *relationships* between and among the three major dimensions of meaning: (1) evaluative dimension (good/bad scale); (2) potency dimen-

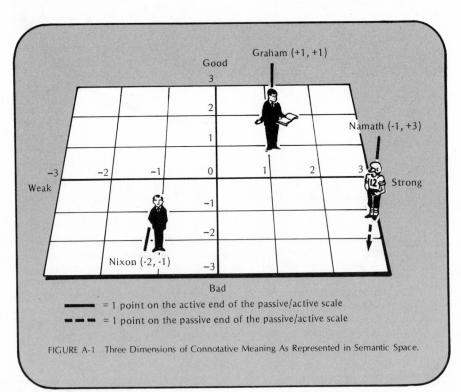

FIGURE A-1   Three Dimensions of Connotative Meaning As Represented in Semantic Space.

sion (strong/weak scale); (3) activity dimension (active/passive scale). If you visualize the lines representing the activity dimension as running through the grid, you will note that the graph gives the illusion of three-dimensional space.

You will note, furthermore, that Nixon's point in semantic space defines him as a rather bad and slightly weak man (-2 rating on the good/bad scale and a -1 rating on the strong/weak scale) of slight activity ($+1$ rating on the active/passive scale). In contrast Joe Namath is defined as slightly bad (-1) but as extremely strong ($+3$) and very active ($+2$). Finally, as you might expect, the Reverend Billy Graham was rated as slightly good ($+1$) as well as slightly strong ($+1$) and very active ($+2$).

The connotative meaning of individuals and concepts may change over time. While Richard Nixon was probably defined as bad and weak largely because of his alleged participation in the Watergate coverup, this image may change as we gain historical perspective. Similarly the rather positive images of Joe Namath and Billy Graham could deteriorate because of real or imagined changes in their behavior.

Osgood has applied his concept of semantic space to facial expression. Facial, gestural, and postural communication were treated as separate communication systems in chapter 2. We did not attempt to examine in detail the dimensions of meaning which may be communicated when the face, gestures, and posture act together, however.

When these three sources of nonverbal meaning interact, the nature of the interaction is complex and difficult to describe. This is probably a major reason why researchers tend to focus on facial communication *or* gestural communication *or* postural communication.

As we have noted, numerous studies have now been done on facial, gestural, and postural communication. Valuable as these studies have been, they typically concentrate on some specific kind of facial or gestural or postural communication. They rarely focus on all of these types of kinesic behavior in such a way that kinesic communication, or the transmission of meaning by movement, is viewed as a system.

The author recently conducted a study which did treat kinesic communication as a system.[4] Even though facial, gestural, and postural communication are obviously different in ways which have already been discussed, they also function together to transmit meanings. The primary objective of the recent study, therefore, was to determine how many and what kinds of meanings are transmitted by movement when the impact of all types of movement was considered as a single communicative unit.

The communicative unit in this case was the feedback response. The specific aim was to determine what general classes and specific kinds of meanings were communicated in the nonverbal portion of feedback responses in 20 groups at UCLA which were discussing the subject of women's liberation. Over 160 feedback responses were selected from these groups and studied in detail by means of a master videotape on which all sound was blocked out.

Since the details of the research are reported in chapter 10, it should be sufficient to note that the data were subjected to both content analysis and factor analysis. The results are reported in Table A-1. While the feedback response is only one major unit of communication in interpersonal exchanges and the small group, the classes and kinds of nonverbal behavior that are characteristically part of the response should tell us much about the various meanings that are conveyed by human movement. Because of the design of this experiment, the movements which are part of facial, gestural, and postural communication were viewed as inextricably interrelated communicative behaviors.

TABLE A-1

KINDS OF NONVERBAL COMMUNICATION COMPRISING EACH CLASS	ROTATED FACTOR LOADINGS				
	INVOLVE-MENT	FEELING	ANALYSIS	CONTROL	FLEXI-BILITY
Participating/Detached	.86	.25	.12	.20	.01
Interest/Disinterest	.83	.25	.09	.14	.06
Attentive/Unattentive	.80	.23	.04	.10	.09
Agreeable/Disagreeable	.24	.82	.07	.18	.06
Gracious/Surly	.31	.82	.07	.18	.04
Respect/Disdain	.26	.81	.17	.07	.09
Analytical/Impulsive	.13	.12	.85	.03	.08
Deliberative/Spontaneous	.23	.03	.83	.03	.01
Reflective/Emotional	.18	.12	.80	.03	.01
Confident/Uncertain	.33	.02	.04	.85	.01
Clear/Confused	.31	.10	.02	.82	.00
Self-Assured/Self-Doubt	.40	.02	.02	.80	.09
Flexible/Inflexible	.10	.60	.05	.11	.66
Yielding/Unyielding	.04	.59	.07	.16	.68

As Table A-1 suggests, when functioning together as part of the larger kinesic system of communication, facial, gestural, and postural movements combine to communicate five general classes of meaning. We identify these classes of meaning as (1) involvement, (2) feeling, (3) analysis, (4) control, and (5) flexibility. Each class of nonverbal meaning is in turn composed of specific types of meanings that are closely related to each other but basically dissimilar from the types in another class. For example, individuals who appear to be participating, interested, and attentive are communicating three types of closely related meaning that are part of the larger class of meaning labeled involvement. On the other hand an individual who appears to be detached, disinterested, and unattentive is also communicating three similar types of meaning which are also part of the larger class of nonverbal communication identified as involvement, but these three meanings obviously reflect minimal involvement while an individual who is participating, interested, and attentive is communicating maximum involvement. The same principle applies to all the other classes and specific kinds of nonverbal communication identified in Table A-1.

As the results from factor analysis indicate, the different classes of nonverbal communication are very distinct from one another. Only feeling and flexibility seem to include some of the same kinds of nonverbal communication.

In addition to the results reported in Table A-1 the factor analysis indicated that class 1 (involvement) is also composed of the following specific kinds of nonverbal communication: involved/withdrawn, outward/inward, animated/inactive, expressive/unexpressive, responsive/unresponsive, approaches/avoids, and talkative/silent. Class 2 (feeling) also includes adaptable/stubborn, pleased/displeased, and friendly/hostile. Class 3 (analysis) also includes thoughtful/instinctive and symbol/signal. Class 4 (control) also includes comfortable/uncomfortable and relaxed/tense.

Throughout this book the reader may have been impressed with the apparent fact that many movements are highly facilitative in interpersonal communication and greatly help to clarify the intended meaning of the communicator while other movements are highly disruptive and tend to obscure or confuse the intended meaning. Immediately, this knowledge raises the significant question as to which types of movements are facilitative and which disruptive. More specifically, given the data in Table A-1, are movements which communicate participation, interest, and attentiveness facilitative while movements which communicate detachment, disinterest, and unattentiveness disruptive? The content of this book should suggest that the answer to that complex question depends on many factors.

NOTES

[1] C. E. Osgood, G. J. Suci, and P. H. Tannenbaum, *The Measurement of Meaning* (Urbana, Ill.: University of Illinois Press, 1957), pp. 1-75.

[2] Ibid., p. 25.

[3] Ibid., p. 26.

[4] D. G. Leathers, "Meta-Incongruent Communication in the Small Group," an experiment in the UCLA series, winter 1972.

APPENDIX B

THE VOCALIC COMMUNICATION SYSTEM

Communication by sound is a complex subject. The study of the subject has perhaps raised more questions than it has answered. Certainly there are many important questions about vocalic communication which were beyond the scope of chapter 6. Appendix B focuses on two of the more important of these questions: (1) What types of sounds should be of primary interest to the student of human communication? (2) What physiological factors interact to produce sound?

The acoustician is primarily concerned with those physical features of sound that are readily identifiable by the human ear. Thus Ostwald in his fascinating book, *Soundmaking: The Acoustic Communication of Emotion,* maintains that sound has seven qualitative dimensions. Each of the qualitative dimensions can be illustrated with polar terms on the ends of seven-point scales. He identifies these qualitative dimensions as:

1. rhythmicity (regular vs. irregular)
2. intensity (loud vs. soft)
3. pitch (high vs. low)
4. tone (tonal vs. noisy)
5. speed (fast vs. slow)
6. shape (impulsive vs. reverberant)
7. orderliness (compact vs. expanded)[1]

Ostwald clearly believes that the sound qualities on the left-hand side with the parentheses are more conducive to high quality communication than those on the right-hand side and he gives examples to support this viewpoint. Rhythmicity he identifies with the steady ticking of a clock while sound of suitable intensity is below 120 decibels. Sound at or above that intensity level produces pain in the ears. Acceptable pitch is produced by vibrations of the vocal cords which vary from 20 to 20,000 cycles per second although this very broad range of pitch includes many sounds that are relatively unacceptable. Tonal as opposed to noisy sound is represented by the difference between pure tone versus overlapping vibratory frequencies of the type you may hear on a poorly tuned car radio. Speed of sound refers to the number of sounds that are emitted over a given period of time such as a second. "At fast speeds, successive acoustic impulses merge together, producing the sensation of a steady sound. . . . At the slow end of the gradient there is a lapse of consciousness after about 0.8 second, so that when impulses fall below the rate of one sound per second the listener needs additional cues—say a melody or meaningful context to sustain his attention to the sound."[2] While the effects of sounds delivered at a very slow rate can be highly disruptive to interpersonal communication, fast rate can also be highly disruptive. For example, triple tonguing flutists and clarinetists may approach the fast limits of sound which causes "sound blurring."

The shape of a sound depends on whether it is impulsive or reverberant. The impulsive sound is perceived as clear and direct while the reverberant sound is much like the echoes of the Swiss yodler or water running into an empty rain barrel. Finally, a sound has the quality of compactness if its single units are combined in an orderly recognizable pattern such as the chiming of Big Ben or the Morse code.[3] Expanded sounds, in contrast, may be properly identified with the dissonant cacophony sometimes associated with the electrically amplified repetitive sounds produced by instruments of a hard rock group.

In contrast to the acoustician, a number of researchers study the production and reception of sounds as a prosodic system. In his scholarly work *Prosodic Systems and Intonation in English,* Crystal defines a prosodic system as a "set of mutually defining phonological features which have an essentially variable relationship to the words selected, as opposed to those features [for example, the segmental phonemes, the lexical meaning] which have a direct and identifying relationship to such words."[4] In effect Crystal seems to be saying that he is not dealing with the word meanings which are necessarily transmitted by sound, but with a certain limited number of features of the sounds which have a psychological impact on those hearing the sounds. Thus, the primary sound features, or "prosodic parameters," which are of concern to the prosodist are pitch, loudness, and duration. While tone and speed of sound are among the physical characteristics on which we rely to identify the sounds made by one human being as opposed to another, the prosodist believes that *pitch, loudness, and duration are the "psychological attributes" which are primarily responsible for the effects of given sounds on other human beings.*[5]

Although the prosodist has a much more specific frame of reference than the acoustician, there can be little doubt that both are studying vocalic communication because of their concentration on sound. The frame of reference of the paralinguist is not quite so clear, however. The paralinguist is a little like the paratrooper. While it may be difficult to determine whether the paratrooper's operational domain is in the air or on land, it would also be difficult to determine whether the paralinguist's primary concern is language or sound variables.

Crystal in his definitive treatment of sound strongly supports the view that the paralinguist concentrates mainly on the vocal rather than the linguistic features of interpersonal communication.[6] He emphasizes that vocal effects which are primarily the result of physiological workings of the pharyngeal, oral, or nasal cavities are referred to as "paralinguistic features." Coughing, belching, and yawning, for example, have typically been referred to as paralinguistic phenomena. One belch or yawn is distinguished from another by variation in such vocal variables as pitch, loudness, and duration. Belching and yawning, as we know, often represent interruptions in the communicator's attempt to express himself through the use of language. In that sense such variables might be viewed within a linguistic framework. Since factors like belching and yawning are essentially distinct vocal phenomena and since they are not governed by the rules of language usage, they may be thought of as paravocal rather than paralinguistic in nature.

Even Traeger's famous typology of paralanguage suggests that paravocal is a more appropriate term than paralinguistic to describe the factors involved. Traeger includes voice qualities in his definition and classification of paralanguage but he concentrates on vocal factors which are not typically identified as the defining sound attributes of vocal cues: (1) vocal characteristics like laughing and crying; (2) vocal qualifiers which include vocal intensity and duration; (3) vocal segregates which include noises such as *uh, ununh, sh, tsk.*[7]

The nature of the production of human sound is a complex phenomenon. However, the reader must have an understanding of the rudiments of sound production if he is to fully appreciate the effects of sounds in interpersonal communication.

The larynx is composed of two vocal folds which are made up of muscle tissue covered by mucous membrane. The length of these vocal folds in conjunction with the speed with which they vibrate determines the basic or modal pitch of a given voice, although obviously pitch can be varied by using the muscles which make up the vocal tract in different ways. When the vocal cords are vibrating, individuals produce voiced sounds (such as vowels). When they are not, we produce one of two types of voiceless sounds—fricative sounds like *sh* and *th,* and plosive sounds like *p, t,* and *k.*

Both voiced and voiceless sounds are produced by our control of the airstream which we expel. With mouth open the air coming from the lungs through the vocal tract causes the vocal cords to vibrate and the speed of vibration determines pitch at that moment. When the tongue, lips, and teeth and mouth, respectively, are used to impede the stream of air being expelled we produce fricative and plosive sounds. If you have any doubt, try saying first *th* and then *p.* As Fisher so accurately points out "a vocal tone is produced by the operation of two opposing forces. The first is a column of air moving upward in the trachea. The second is the pair of vocal folds which are pulled together to interrupt the air flow. The essence of efficiency in phonation is the delicate balance between these two forces. The synchronization necessary to regulate voice quality and intensity requires a skillful control of function in opposing musculatures."[8]

The length and mass of the vocal cords in conjunction with the frequency with which the vocal cords are vibrating determines pitch at a given instant, while our control of the airstream with muscles of the vocal tract, tongue and mouth, and lips determines the type of sound. The loudness of the sound is a function of the force with which the air is expelled and, consequently, how far the vocal folds vibrate back and forth (amplitude). These are not the only factors which have a defining impact on the nature of human sound, however.

Resonance affects both loudness and vocal quality. The tone or sound produced within the vocal tract itself is usually not loud enough to be heard very far away. Obviously, human sounds are heard at long distances so they must be amplified. The amplification of human sound is called resonance.

The nature of resonance can perhaps best be illustrated by describing how sound is amplified by musical instruments. The reed tone of a clarinet, the string tone of a violin, or even the string tone of a piano would be relatively weak if the reed and strings were not attached to their respective instruments. The sounding board of a piano to which the strings are attached, for example, resonates or vibrates when one or more strings are set in motion by the hammers attached to the piano keys. Such vibration of the piano board greatly increases the loudness of the sounds emitted from the piano. Obviously, a grand piano amplifies the sound more than a spinet because of the size of the sounding board.

If you have ever been in the Carlsbad Caverns, or similar underground caves, you know that cavities serve as resonators. Generally speaking we know (1) the greater the cavity volume, the lower the frequency it will resonate, (2) the smaller the opening into the cavity, the lower the frequency it will resonate, (3) the longer the neck of the opening into the cavity, the lower the frequency it will resonate, and (4) the more elastic and dense cavity walls, the higher the frequency it will resonate.[9] Those of you who have tried to make sounds with Coke and other types of bottles will confirm the validity of these principles of resonation.

The resonating capacity of the human vocal system is basically determined by three different cavities: the oral, the pharyngeal, and the nasal. The oral cavity, or mouth, can obviously be changed in size and dimension by using the tongue, cheeks, and muscles which surround the cavity. The most variable of the three resonating cavities of the body, the oral cavity can have a major impact on both the quality and loudness of sound.

The pharyngeal cavity is simply the tube which extends from the tongue to the larynx. The width and length of this cavity can be controlled by using the muscles attached to and surrounding the cavity. The effect of pharyngeal resonation is due largely to the amount of tension in the pharyngeal muscles. This has the effect of amplifying the higher tones being emitted.

Finally, the nasal cavity is used infrequently and is least subject to conscious control by the communicator. Anyone who has had a cold or read the most basic textbook on physiology has a rather good idea of what the nasal cavity is. The nasal cavity typically has a dampening effect on sound waves because it tends to cause deflection and reflection of the sound waves. While the nasal cavity tends to produce the infamous nasal vocal quality, it also tends to decrease rather than increase the loudness of sound as it resonates.[10]

Obviously, resonance affects the quality as well as the loudness of the sound. If this were not the case, musicians would not search the world for specific Stradivarius violins or pay astronomical sums for pianos made by certain companies in certain years.

After reading this Appendix the reader may want to return to chapter 6. This necessarily brief description of the rudiments of the physiological production of sound should help illuminate the potential of vocalic communication as an important medium for the exchange of meanings.

NOTES

[1] P. F. Ostwald, *Soundmaking: The Acoustic Communication of Emotion* (Springfield, Ill.: Charles C Thomas, 1963), p. 25.

[2] Ibid., pp. 25-28.

[3] Ibid., pp. 27-28.

[4] D. Crystal, *Prosodic Systems and Intonation in English* (Cambridge: Cambridge University Press, 1969), p. 5.

[5] Ibid., pp. 5-6.

[6] Ibid.

[7] G. L. Traeger, "The Typology of Paralanguage," *Anthropological Linguistics,* 2 (1969), 18.

[8] H. B. Fisher, *Improving Voice and Articulation,* ed. 2 (Boston: Houghton Mifflin, 1975), p. 37.

[9] Ibid., p. 90.

[10] Ibid., pp. 91-102. Fisher notes that the sinuses and chest may also serve as resonators, but any attempt to control them by the communicator is not likely to succeed.

BIBLIOGRAPHY

Amidon, P. *Nonverbal Interaction Analysis.* Minneapolis, Minn.: P. S. Amidon and Associates, 1971.

Anderson, J. A. "Single-channel and Multi-channel Messages: A Comparison of Connotative Meaning." *A. V. Communication Record,* 17 (1969), 428-34.

Argyle, M. *Social Interaction.* Chicago: Aldine, 1969.

Barker, L., and Collins, N. B. "Nonverbal and Kinesic Research." In *Methods of Research in Communication,* ed. P. Emmet and W. D. Brooks. Boston: Houghton Mifflin, 1970.

Beck, R. "Spatial Meaning and Properties of the Environment." In *Environmental Perception and Behavior,* ed. D. Lowenthal. Chicago: University of Chicago, Department of Geography, Research Paper No. 109, 1967.

Bercheid, E.; Walster, W.; and Bohrnstedt, G. "The Happy American Body, A Survey Report." *Psychology Today,* 7 (1973), 123.

Birdwhistell, R. L. *Kinesics and Context.* Philadelphia: University of Pennsylvania Press, 1970.

Bosmajian, H., ed. *The Rhetoric of Nonverbal Communication.* Glenview, Ill.: Scott, Foresman, 1971.

Buttimer, A. "Social Space and Planning of Residential Areas." *Environment and Behavior,* 4 (1972), 279-318.

Craik, K. H. "Environmental Psychology." In *New Directions in Psychology,* ed. K. H. Craik, B. Kleinmunta, R. L. Rosnow, R. Rosenthal, J. A. Cheyne, and R. H. Walters. New York: Holt, Rinehart, and Winston, 1970.

Crystal, D. *Prosodic Systems and Intonation in English.* Cambridge: Cambridge University Press, 1969.

Davis, F. *Inside Intuition: What We Should Know About Nonverbal Communication.* New York: McGraw-Hill, 1973.

Davitz, J. R. *The Communication of Emotional Meaning.* New York: McGraw-Hill, 1964.

Dittmann, A. T. *Interpersonal Messages of Emotion.* New York: Springer, 1972.

Downs, R. M. "Geographic Space Perception: Past Approaches and Future Prospects." *Progress in Geography,* 2 (1970), 84-85.

Duncan, S. O., Jr. "Nonverbal Communication." *Psychological Bulletin,* 72 (2), (1969), 118-37.

Duncan, S. O.; Rosenberg, M. J.; and Finkelstein, J. "The Paralanguage of Experimenter Bias." *Sociometry,* 32 (1969), 207-17.

Dunphy, D. C. *The Primary Group: A Handbook for Analysis and Field Research.* New York: Appleton-Century-Crofts, 1972.

Efron, D. *Gesture and Environment.* New York: Kings Crown Press, 1942.

Ekman, P., ed. *Darwin and Facial Expression.* New York: Academic Press, 1972.

Ekman, P. "Differential Communication of Affect by Head and Body Cues." *Journal of Personality and Social Psychology,* 2 (1965), 725-35.

Ekman, P.; Friesen, W. V.; and Ellsworth, P. *Emotion in the Human Face: Guidelines for Research and an Integration of Findings.* New York: Pergamon, 1972.

Ekman, P.; Friesen, W. V.; and Tomkins, S. S. "Facial Affect Scoring Technique: A First Validity Study." *Semiotica,* 3 (1971), 37-58.

Ekman, P., and Friesen, W. V. "Hand Movements." *Journal of Communication,* 22 (1972), 353-58.

————. "Head and Body Cues in the Judgement of Emotion: A Reformation." *Perceptual and Motor Skills,* 24 (1967), 713-16.

————. "The Repertoire of Nonverbal Behavior—Categories, Usage, and Coding." *Semiotica,* 1 (1969), 49-98.

————. *Unmasking the Face.* Englewood Cliffs, N.J.: Prentice-Hall, 1975.

Goffman, E. *Interaction Ritual.* Garden City, N.Y.:Doubleday Anchor, 1967.

————. *Relations in Public.* New York: Harper Colophon, 1971.

————. *Strategic Interaction.* Philadelphia: University of Pennsylvania Press, 1969.

Haggard, E. A., and Isaacs, K. S. "Micromomentary Facial Expressions as Indicators of Ego Mechanisms in Psychotherapy." In *Methods of Research in Psychotherapy,* ed. L. A. Gottschalk and A. H. Auerbach. New York: Appleton-Century-Crofts, 1966.

Hall, E. T. *The Hidden Dimension.* New York: Doubleday, 1969.

Hansel, C. E. M. *ESP: A Scientific Evaluation.* New York: Charles Scribner's Sons, 1966.

Harrison, H., and Howard, W. A. "Role of Meaning in Urban Images." *Environment and Behavior,* 4 (1972), 39.

Harrison, R. P. *Beyond Words: An Introduction to Nonverbal Communication.* Englewood Cliffs, N.J.: Prentice-Hall, 1974.

Hindy, R. A., ed. *Nonverbal Communication.* Cambridge: Cambridge University Press, 1972.

Jones, S. E. "A Comparative Proxemics Analysis of Dyadic Interaction in Selected Subcultures of New York City." *Journal of Social Psychology,* 84 (1971), 35-44.

Jourard, S. M. *Disclosing Man to Himself.* Princeton, N.J.: Van Nostrand Reinhold, 1968.

Kefgen, M., and Touchie-Specht, P. *Individuality in Clothing Selection and Personal Appearance: A Guide for the Consumer.* New York: Macmillan, 1971.

Knapp, M. L. *Nonverbal Communication in Human Interaction.* New York: Holt, Rinehart, and Winston, 1972.

Knorr, N. J.; Edgerton, M. T.; and Hoopes, J. E. "The Insatiable Cosmetic Surgery Patient." *Plastic and Reconstructive Surgery,* 40 (1967) 285-89.

Knorr, N. J., and Edgerton, M. T. "Motivational Patterns of Patients Seeking Cosmetic (Esthetic) Surgery." *Plastic and Reconstructive Surgery,* 48 (1971), 553-54.

Laszlo, E., ed. *The Relevance of General Systems Theory.* New York: George Braziller, 1972.

Leathers, D. G. "Process Disruption and Measurement in Small Group Communication." *Quarterly Journal of Speech,* 54 (1969), 287-300.

————. "The Process Effects of Trust-Destroying Behavior in the Small Group." *Speech Monographs,* 37 (1970), 180-87.

————. "Quality of Group Communication as a Determinant of Group Product." *Speech Monographs,* 39 (1972), 166-73.

———. "Testing for Determinant Interaction in the Small Group Communication." *Speech Monographs*, 38 (1971), 182-89.

Lidenfeld, J. "Verbal and Non-Verbal Elements in Discourse." *Semiotica*, 3 (1971), 223-33.

Lyman, S. M., and Scott, M. B. "Territoriality: A Neglected Sociological Dimension." *Social Problems*, 15 (1967), 237-41.

McCrosky, J. C.; Larsen, C. E.; and Knapp, M. L. *Introduction to Interpersonal Communication*. Englewood Cliffs, N.J.: Prentice-Hall, 1971.

Mehrabian, A. "Nonverbal Betrayal of Feeling." *Journal of Experimental Research in Personality*, 5 (1971), 64-73.

———. *Nonverbal Communication*. Chicago: Aldine-Atherton, 1972.

———. "Orientation Behaviors and Nonverbal Attitude Communication." *Journal of Communication*, 17 (1967), 324-32.

———. *Silent Messages*. Belmont, Calif.: Wadsworth, 1971.

Moncrieff, R. W. *Odour Preferences*. New York: Wiley, 1966.

Montagu, A. *Touching: The Human Significance of the Skin*. New York: Perennial Library, 1971.

Osgood, C. E. "Dimensionality of the Semantic Space for Communication via Facial Expression." *Scandinavian Journal of Psychology*, 7 (1966), 1-30.

Osgood, C. E.; Suci, G. J.; and Tannenbaum, P. H. *The Measurement of Meaning*. Urbana, Ill.: University of Illinois Press, 1957.

Patterson, M. L. "Compensation in Nonverbal Immediacy Behavior: A Review." *Sociometry*, 36 (1973), 243-52.

Patterson, M. L.; Mullens, S.; and Romano, J. "Compensatory Reactions to Spatial Intrusion." *Sociometry*, 34 (1971), 116-20.

Pearce, W. B., and Conklin, F. "Nonverbal Vocalic Communication and Perception of a Speaker." *Speech Monographs*, 38 (1971), 235-41.

Pedersen, D., and Shears, L. M. "A Review of Personal Space Research in Framework of a General System Theory." *Psychological Bulletin*, 80 (1973), 367-88.

Rhine, J. B. *New Frontiers of the Mind: The Story of the Duke Experiments*. New York: Farrar and Rhinehart, 1937.

Roach, M. E., and Eicher, J. B. *The Visible Self: Perspectives on Dress*. Englewood Cliffs, N.J.: Prentice-Hall, 1973.

Rosenthal, P. I. "Concept of the Paramessage in Persuasive Communication." *Quarterly Journal of Speech*, 58 (1972), 15-30.

Rosenthal, R. *Experimenter Effects in Behavioral Research*. New York: Appleton-Century-Crofts, 1966.

Ruben, B. D. "General System Theory: An Approach to Human Communication." In R. W. Budd and B. D. Ruben, *Approaches to Human Communication*. New York: Spartan Books, 1972.

Ryan, M. S. *Clothing: A Study in Human Behavior*. New York: Holt, Rinehart and Winston, 1966.

Scheflen, A. E. *Body Language and the Social Order*. Englewood Cliffs, N.J.: Prentice-Hall, 1972.

———. *Communicational Structure: Analysis of a Psychotherapy Transaction*. Bloomington, Ind.: University of Indiana Press, 1972.

———. "Natural History Method in Psychotherapy: Communicational Research." In

Methods of Research in Psychotherapy, ed. L. A. Gottschalk and A. H. Auerbach. New York: Appleton-Century-Crofts, 1966.

Scott, B. *How the Body Feels.* New York: Ballantine Books, 1973.

Sommer, R. "Man's Proximate Environment." *Journal of Social Sciences,* 22 (1966), 59-70.

————. "Sociofugal Space." *American Journal of Sociology,* 72 (1967), 654-60.

————. *Tight Spaces: Hard Architecture and How to Humanize It.* Englewood Cliffs, N.J.: Prentice-Hall, 1974.

Sutherland, J. W. *A General Systems Philosophy for the Social and Behavioral Sciences.* New York: George Braziller, 1973.

Thayer, L. *Communication and Communication Systems.* Homewood, Ill.: Richard D. Irwin, 1968.

Ullman, M.; Krippner, S.; and Vaughn, A. *Dream Telepathy: Experiments in Nocturnal ESP.* New York: Macmillan, 1973.

Warner, L. "What the Younger Psychologists Think About ESP." *Journal of Parapsychology,* 19 (1955), 228-35.

Watson, O. M. "Conflicts and Directions in Proxemic Research." *Journal of Communication,* 22 (1972), 443-59.

Wiener, M.; Devoe, S.; Rubinow, S.; and Geller, J. "Nonverbal Behavior and Nonverbal Communication." *Psychological Review,* 79 (1972), 185-214.

AUTHOR INDEX

SUBJECT INDEX